IN THE MIRROR
OF THE
THIRD WORLD

CAPITALIST DEVELOPMENT
IN MODERN EUROPE

SANDRA HALPERIN

CORNELL UNIVERSITY PRESS

ITHACA AND LONDON

First published 1997 by Cornell University Press.

Printed in the United States of America.

TCF This book is printed on Lyons Falls Turin Book,
a paper that is totally chlorine-free and acid-free.

Library of Congress Cataloging-in-Publication Data

Halperin, Sandra.
    In the mirror of the third world : capitalist development in modern Europe / Sandra
Halperin.
        p. cm.
    Includes bibliographical references and index.
    ISBN 0-8014-3195-6 (alk. paper). — ISBN 0-8014-8290-9 (pbk. : alk. paper)
    1. Europe—History. 2. Capitalism—Europe—History.
3. Dependency. 4. Developing countries. 5. Economic development.
I. Title.
HC240.H3135   1996
338.94'0903—dc20   96-38826

Cloth printing   10 9 8 7 6 5 4 3 2 1

Contents

Contents

Preface

For years scholars have been proclaiming that the field of development studies is in crisis.[1] They have generally assumed that this crisis is the result of weaknesses in, and conflicts between, the two dominant sets of approaches to the study of development. Liberal/neoclassical/ modernization approaches are criticized for parochialism and lack of historical perspective, and for failure to pay sufficient attention to international structures of power and to consider seriously the utility of class and modes of production as analytical categories. Dependency approaches have been faulted for their failure to recognize and account for the ability of capitalism to generate development in the periphery.

Recent attempts to resolve these problems have led to important refinements in both approaches. Liberal/modernization approaches have become more concerned with differing historical contexts, the relationship between international and domestic realms, and the interrelationship of political and economic factors.[2] Neo-Marxist and dependency writings have delineated possible alternative paths to capitalist development in the periphery.[3] With these refinements as a basis, a body of studies has grown up that integrates key elements of both approaches. This literature, which

1. See, e.g., Seers 1979; Caporaso 1980; Hirschman 1981; Livingstone 1981; Sen 1983; Lal 1983; Streeten 1983; Lewis 1984; Booth 1985; Arndt 1987; Toye 1987; Leeson 1988; Mouzelis 1988; Ranis and Schultz 1988; Leys 1996.
2. See, e.g., Katzenstein 1984; Skocpol 1979. See also the contributions in Diamond et al. 1990; Evans et al. 1985; Grew 1978b; Tilly 1975b.
3. These include the semiperipheral, dependent, associated-dependent, and unequal paths. See, e.g., P. Evans 1979; Wallerstein 1974a; Cardoso and Faletto 1979; Amin 1976; Cardoso 1973. Theories of peripheral development continue to be refined. See, e.g., Hettne 1990; Kay 1989; Larrain 1989; Becker et al. 1987.

Peter Evans and John Stephens call "the new comparative historical political economy," represents a significant step toward genuine synthesis: it is much more sensitive to international factors but rejects the idea that they determine the dynamics of domestic development; it treats economic and political development as interrelated; it recognizes the possibility of diverse, historically contingent developmental outcomes; and it focuses on patterns of interaction among global changes, states, and classes.[4] Yet though this literature is an important advance in the evolution of development studies, the sense of crisis continues to pervade the field.[5] Despite a decade of refinement and synthesis, we seem as far as ever from constructing an adequate theory of development and underdevelopment. In this book I argue that four key errors have prevented our construction of such a theory: (1) we have accepted a seriously distorted account of European historical development; (2) on the basis of this account, we define distinctions between European historical and contemporary Third World development which, in fact, do not exist; (3) in order to explain why Europe and the Third World followed different paths, we exaggerate differences between the world historical structures and international contexts of the past and present; and (4) we treat international and state structures both as sociologically neutral and as key agents of social change, thus obscuring the social roots of economic and political development.

Underlying these errors are two basic assumptions. The first is that in nature and pattern contemporary Third World development differs significantly from European development in the nineteenth and early twentieth centuries. But, as this book shows, that assumption is based on a substantially erroneous account of European historical development, one accepted by both liberal/modernization theories and theories of dependent development. The second assumption is that external relations should be the starting point for analyzing dependent development. This assumption, too, needs to be challenged.

My aim in this book is to show (1) that the "European model," which has served implicitly or explicitly as a point of departure and basis of comparison for the study of contemporary Third World development, is more fiction than fact; (2) that actual social, economic, and political development in Europe followed a path similar to the one now being followed by Third World countries; and (3) that the path to prosperity and democracy was in the past and is today fundamentally shaped by internal class configurations and alignments.

4. See Evans and Stephens 1988 for a review of this literature.
5. The sense of crisis is prevalent in development sociology (Booth 1985; Vandergeest and Buttel 1988; Sklair 1988; Corbridge 1990), and is becoming more evident across the various arenas of development theory (Slater 1992; Pieterse 1991; Manzo 1991).

My intention here is not merely to show that attributes of dependent development were to be found in parts of Europe in the course of that region's industrialization. Many scholars agree that European industrial development exhibited such features of dependency as dualism, monoculture dependence, inequality, and subordination to international capital. They also agree that democracy was achieved later and with a great deal more volatility and loss of life than has been generally assumed. But in this book I demonstrate something more: that the pattern displayed in contemporary Third World dependent development is analogous to the pattern of development in pre-1945 Europe, and that the categories and concepts needed to describe and classify dependent development are applicable to European development as well. External dependence, dualism, inequality, political instability, authoritarianism, and other well-documented aspects of the contemporary Third World should not be treated as constituting a pattern unique to that world. We should not continue to use frameworks and theories that define contemporary Third World development as sharply different from the European experience.[6]

Some might wish to argue that though attributes of dependency were common to European historical development, they are more extreme in the contemporary Third World. But neither the magnitude, the causes, nor the consequences of these conditions in Europe differed in any substantial way from those in the Third World today. Dependency theory claims to identify a definite mechanism that generates the set of socioeconomic and political outcomes which constitute dependent development. One task of this book, therefore, is to spell out the mechanism that generated such outcomes in nineteenth-century Europe.

In *The Shape of European History* (1974), William McNeill observes that after World War I historians ceased to speak of European history as a chronicle of progress in the advance of reason and freedom, an idea embraced in the last decades of the nineteenth century. Thereafter, the whole notion swiftly sank from consciousness. He notes, however, that though the central ideas of traditional European historiography ceased to be convincing, yet "the stately structure raised at the close of the nineteenth century to accommodate European history still stands. The roof may be leaky and the plumbing deplorable, but in the absence of any alternative housing . . . the Victorian edifice continues to give shape to what . . . graduate students learn and what their teachers choose to emphasize amidst all the buzzing . . . confusion of the accessible European past" (McNeill 1974: 3–4).

6. I locate my arguments with respect to theories of development in Chapter 8. However, it is necessary to repeat at this point that the arguments to be presented are not based on the assumptions of liberal modernization and development theories.

Twenty-plus years later the Victorian edifice of conventional European historiography, though tottering, still stands; for while its roof may leak, the foundation has proved impervious to the corrosive impact of the disconfirming data that already exist in abundance and continue to accumulate. Further evidence of inadequacy will probably not help to clear the ground for a sturdier structure. What this book proposes to do, instead, is to show how recent research on European historical development readily produces a "gestalt shift." More specifically, it sets aside the traditional structure of assumptions about the European past and, by stressing elements different from those which are usually emphasized, causes its parts to form a different pattern, and so produce a different picture, from the one we are accustomed to see.

What the term "gestalt shift" implies can be illustrated by the famous face-goblet sketch devised by Edgar Rubin to demonstrate figure-ground reversibility. With a switch of attention, figure and ground reverse, and the figure can be seen either as a pair of facial profiles or as a goblet. No new lines are added to produce the alternative view: both pictures emerge from the same data.

By re-viewing the historical record in light of the contemporary one, I attempt here to produce a similar gestalt shift. The data used are available for anyone to see. But a preexisting pattern of expectations has caused us to filter out certain facts as irrelevances, so that the facts that support the standard interpretation are those most clearly in view. When we start with a different set of expectations, those we have with respect to developing regions of the contemporary world, a very different picture of European history emerges.

Let us assume that Europe on the eve of World War I looked a lot like Latin America does now (an assumption, in fact, made in this book). With this assumption as a starting point, we expect to find, and in fact do find, enclave economies oriented to foreign markets; weak middle classes; alliances between the state, traditional landowning elites, and new industrial classes; unstable and partial democracy; sharp inequalities; and increasing poverty. We expect to find, and in fact find in abundance, all the features characteristic of Third World dependent development, for these features were as characteristic of European society on the eve of World War I as they are of the Third World today.

Most studies of European historical development focus on dynamic (but actually limited and scattered) focal points of growth found across the European social landscape of the nineteenth century. As a result, they emphasize urbanization, industrialization, liberalization, urban working-class movements, and democratization. But when we use the experience of the contemporary Third World as an analytical starting point, other features of nineteenth-century Europe come into view: colonial institutions; the still-dominant agricultural sector and its still-dominant traditional landowning class; and the persistence of rural, preindustrial, feudal, and autocratic structures of power and authority. We notice that Europe is urbanizing but not urban; industrializing but not industrial; liberalizing but neither liberal nor bourgeois. We find that, in fact, the bulk of Europe's population lived and worked in rural Europe and that, in nearly every country, the seat of national political power and the dominant social ethos were to be found there. By using the experience of the Third World today, we not only bring into clearer focus these features of European development, we recall to view aspects of European history that seem to have disappeared down the memory hole altogether—for instance, the revival of a militant, literal religion in Europe and the critical role this played in the class struggles that emerged as the nineteenth century progressed.

By pointing out these neglected but crucial aspects of industrial capitalist development in Europe, I seek to alter the conventional picture of European historical development, and thus finally to topple the Victorian edifice of conventional European historiography. The picture I present is not really new, nor does it emerge as the result simply of a different set of assumptions; it grows from a way of looking at the evidence which has been explicitly discussed by authors cited throughout the book but has not been coherently pulled together.

A key conclusion of this study is that European economic and political history diverged decisively from that of the rest of the world only after 1945, and that the pivotal event in the development both of industrial capitalism and liberal democracy in Europe was the two-phased regional war in the first half of the twentieth century (1914–45). Generations of social scientists and historians have asserted that the critical turning point in these developments was the French Revolution. For them, the Revolution marked the end both of the subordinate status of the rising industrial and commercial class and of the values and policies of a decayed feudal order. In this view, the Revolution represents not only "the first experience of democracy" (Furet 1978: 109), but a revolutionary break with the past which set the spread of liberty and equality in motion. An enormous scholarly investment has gone into creating and sustaining this foundation myth of the modern world. Thus, the argument that the Revolution did not actually inaugurate far-reaching change can be expected to raise hackles.

This book is a work of comparison and synthesis that presents a mixture of historical insights, comparative contrasts, and statistical data (though not statistical testing). It is based not on new discoveries but on a reading of the available works of modern historians and on scholarly evidence that is widely accessible and, in other contexts, widely used. It fleshes out themes that emerge repeatedly in the works of modern scholars but are given insufficient emphasis there. It draws on available statistical data but reads them through different lenses. Thus, it shows how these same data may suggest new conclusions. My major focus, however, is on less quantifiable aspects of dependent industrial capitalist development, such as the nature of the social structure, class interests and class formations, and the general sociopolitical legacies of colonialism. I begin with the conviction that economic and political development cannot fruitfully be examined in isolation one from the other,[7] and so I draw from and seek to synthesize recent research both on economic development and on democracy.

I do *not* argue that capitalist development is a unitary process or that no differences exist between the experience of industrial capitalist development in Europe and in the Third World. I contend, rather, that the differences between European historical and contemporary Third World development have been greatly exaggerated and that, in the pursuit of detail and difference, the overall picture has become muddled. My aim is not to interpret, in terms of a reinterpreted European past, the experience of the contemporary developing world, but to reinterpret both past and present in terms of the other.

Getting this history right is important. Misconceptions concerning development in the West have limited the capacity of scholars to understand the socioeconomic and political problems of contemporary developing regions. European historiography has been powerfully influenced by the revolutionary rhetoric of 1789 and by the ideology of European superiority that emerged during the age of imperialism. Having accepted the oversimplified view of European progress that this historiography presents, we naturally concluded that the Third World was not replicating the European experience. But when we recognize that the Third World experience is not significantly dissimilar from the European experience, our focus of concern shifts from the question of why the Third World is underdeveloped to the question of what changed in Europe and why. We are forced to ask again how parts of Europe achieved prosperity and democracy and why Latin America, for instance, did not, and to come up with better and more useful answers.

7. Nor can the two aspects of development be examined in a short time frame, as does some of the literature focusing on "transitions to democracy." See, e.g., Baloyra 1987; Drake and Silva 1986; O'Donnell et al. 1986; Diamond, Linz, and Lipset 1980; Linz and Stepan 1978. As Daniel Levine points out: "A focus on transition alone is unlikely to get to the heart of the matter. Complete understanding requires that transitions be set in the larger context of democracy's social, economic, cultural, and institutional bases. Only then can the relation between transitions and the possibilities for subsequent democratic politics be elaborated in full and convincing fashion" (Levine 1988: 393).

Note that I have frequently used current country names to refer to the territory that countries now include, sometimes eliding details of changing boundaries and national affiliations. Complete information about such changes and affiliations is given in the Political Appendix.

Also, missing in this account of European development is the story of more than a century of conflicts which culminated in two world wars. Between 1789 and 1945 Europe was continually torn by civil wars, revolution, counterrevolution, and antirevolutionary violence. Waves of revolution swept through Europe in the 1820s, the 1830s, in 1848, and between 1917 and 1922. After each one, the property-owning classes joined forces to prevent new social upheavals. In the 1800s, this coalition consisted of dynasties, aristocracies, and churches. By the twentieth century, it also included heavy industries and parties affiliated with them.

In a forthcoming book, I explore the interrelationship of social forces, industrial development, and conflict in Europe between 1789 and 1945. During this period, wars in Europe involved a recurrent set of issues, actors, and alliances, and were continually replayed, or were fought continuously but intermittently over long periods of time. The forthcoming book describes three dimensions of industrial development, the types of conflicts to which each led, and the domestic and international wars that match each type. It presents, as well, an exposition of what changed in Europe in the course of the two world wars and why. It explores how and how much the historical processes of European development that culminated in two world wars can be diverted in the Third World today.

David Wilkinson made detailed and provocative comments on an early draft and offered helpful advice on a late one, Maurice Zeitlin challenged and inspired me through his teaching and scholarship, James Caporaso and Ellis Goldberg offered invaluable suggestions, and William Gray contributed many productive insights and provided steadfast encouragement and support.

SANDRA HALPERIN

Pittsburgh, Pennsylvania

IN THE MIRROR OF
THE THIRD WORLD

The Development of Industrial Capitalism and Democracy in Europe and in the Contemporary Third World

The division between the advanced industrial world and the Third World has become a convention for social science.[1] It is generally assumed that these two exclusive categories are a further evolution of processes that defined the separation of Europe from the non-European world.[2] During the "long sixteenth century" (Braudel 1981, 1972; Wallerstein 1974a), Europe experienced enormous growth. By the start of the Industrial Revolution, it is often assumed, western Europe had become rich compared to other parts of the world (see, e.g., Landes 1969: 12–13). But in the seventeenth century European growth had halted and, in some areas, reversed. Thus, on the eve of the Industrial Revolution the level of GNP per capita in

1. The phrase "Third World" was first used, as far as I can tell, by Alfred Sauvy in 1952. In an article in *L'Observateur* (14 August 1952), Sauvy, first director of the French Institut National d'Études Démographiques, wrote: "For this Third World, ignored, exploited and despised, exactly as the Third Estate was before the Revolution, would also like to become something." Georges Balandier used the phrase, citing Sauvy, at a conference of twenty-nine African and Asian nations in Bandung in 1955, referring to the peoples of these countries as constituting a Third World between the two blocs. The phrase seems to have had the meaning both of a "third force" nonaligned with the communist or western blocs, and of a world that was "undeveloped," "backward," or "underdeveloped" compared to the West.

2. Historians, of course, offer a variety of dates for the rise of Europe as a hegemonic power within the world system. It is generally thought that the trends of change that led to Europe's rise were set in motion in the Middle Ages with the creation of the institutions of western European feudalism. Sometime in the sixteenth century, and following a long transition, capitalism emerged from feudalism, making Europe a center of wealth, power, and influence from that point forward.

Europe was, in fact, about even with that of the non-European world.[3]

Scholars have argued for over a century that the very concept of an Industrial Revolution is misleading. With the publication in 1884 of Arnold Toynbee's *Lectures on the "Industrial Revolution,"* the expression was adopted by the purveyors of European triumphalism and, despite objections, incorporated into historical terminology.[4] Recent research confirms that the period we call the Industrial Revolution was not the radical break with the past that the term suggests (North 1981: 162; Cameron 1981, 1985; Fores 1981). During the classic Industrial Revolution, Britain actually experienced only gradual industrialization (Crafts 1983; Harley 1982).

Europeans in the late nineteenth century, however, impressed by the technological advances of the time, accepted the idea that Europe's level of economic well-being and its rate of progress were incomparably superior to anything that had gone before.[5] This was decidedly not the case. Colin Clark calculates that the level of income in Britain by the middle of the nineteenth century and in Germany or France in 1870 was comparable to that of classical Greece (Clark 1957: 677; see also Rostovtzeff 1957: 1:3). According to Clark the real earnings of a typical British factory worker in 1850, and those of an Italian worker in 1929, were approximately equivalent to those of a free artisan in Rome in the first century A.D. (1957: 652, 654). Europe's rate of growth, though faster than it had been, was not spectacular in the nineteenth century; compared to European rates after

---

3. Bairoch estimates the level of GNP per capita of future developed countries around 1750 at $182 (in 1960 U.S. dollars and prices). For the future Third World he estimates the figure to be $188, a level of income some 3 to 4 percent above that of the future developed countries. Thus, he concludes that the differential in level of income was 1 to 1.02, or parity (Bairoch 1981: 7–9). More recently, Maddison has taken up the question in a series of papers (1983, 1989, 1990). Using Maddison's most recent data for 1913, 1870, and 1830, Bairoch (1993) calculates the weighted average GNP per capita income for the Third World in 1750 as $170 to $190, similar to his own 1981 estimate. Maddison's figures for the future developed world can lead to a level expressed in 1980 dollars of $550 to $600 for Europe (including Russia) around 1750, which in 1960 dollars and prices translates to $180 to $215. Therefore, Bairoch can claim, according to Maddison's most recent effort, a differential in 1750 between future developed countries and the future underdeveloped countries on the order of 1 to 1.3, compared to his own 1981 estimate of 1 to 1.1 (Bairoch 1993: 105–6). Bairoch reviews other attempts to measure the difference (e.g., Zimmerman 1962; Kuznets 1966, 1971; Landes 1969; Crafts 1984). See Bairoch 1993: 102–10.

4. Cameron (1985) provides a brief survey of the scholarly objections voiced at the time. Tocqueville used the phrase as early as 1850–51 (1978: 113–14). Others had used the phrase earlier, as well. Anna Bezanson shows that, following the French Revolution, the term "revolution" was much in vogue and was applied, rather indiscriminately, to changes in arts, manufactures, social institutions, religion, consumption, politics, morals (1921–22: 347).

5. Clark 1957: 652. Such beliefs, perhaps because they helped to shape the identity of Europe in relation to areas of the world being exploited by European governments and peoples and because they were used as a rationale for that exploitation, became deeply embedded in the historical consciousness of that and subsequent generations.

World War II (4.5 percent), its annual growth during the nineteenth century (0.9 to 1.0 percent) was slow.[6] Nor was Europe's growth spectacular relative to that of the rest of the globe (see Statistical Appendix, Tables 10 and 11). Between 1870 and 1913, per capita national income in Britain and France and in much of central and southeast Europe was growing more slowly than in Colombia, Brazil, and Mexico (Lewis 1978a: 216; Furtado 1963: 162–65). At the end of World War I, Europe as a whole had achieved a level of economic well-being about equal with that of Latin America (see Statistical Appendix, Tables 1 and 2) and was still "pre-eminently pre-industrial" (Mayer 1981: 187, 301). In all of Europe except England, agriculture was still the single largest and weightiest economic sector. Even after World War I, France still drew its wealth principally from agriculture, and approximately half of the population was engaged in agricultural pursuits (Ogg 1930: 185). Central Europe had not yet begun its industrial takeoff; eastern and southern Europe had neither developed industrially nor moved significantly into agricultural exports; in fact, as World War I began, exports of primary products were lower from these areas of Europe than they were from Latin America (Lewis 1978a: 166). In 1910, most of Europe was still rural (see Statistical Appendix, Table 4), and most of rural Europe had not changed substantially since the Middle Ages.

Other regions did not stand still as Europe was inching forward; nor was their industrial development retarded or distorted by European growth, as various schools of thought on development have argued. In fact, before the world wars, the character and nature of European and non-European growth was essentially the same. What disparities existed in 1914 resulted from the earlier start on industrialization made by some European countries and from differences in natural resource endowments. It was the world wars that divided the fortunes of Europe and what today we call the Third World. Had those cataclysmic wars not radically altered Europe's traditional class structure, Europe and Latin America today would not look significantly dissimilar.

The European Model

Karl Marx warned Germany in 1867 that its path to industrial capitalist development would be no smoother than the path which England was traversing at the time. The conditions of German workers, he predicted, would someday be as miserable as those of English industrial and agricultural laborers. He believed, in fact, that the experience of industrial

6. The figure for the nineteenth century comes from Bairoch 1976: 309. The preceding figure is an average for the period 1950–70 and comes from Bairoch 1993: 142.

development would be the same for all countries: "The country that is more developed industrially shows to the less developed the image of its own future."[7] Today, Marxist and non-Marxist scholars reject this view.[8] They assume not that the Third World has escaped the miseries of European industrial development, but that Europe escaped the miseries of contemporary Third World development. This notion conflicts not only with the writings of Marx but with those of countless nineteenth-century social scientists and reformers (from William Cobbett to Matthew Arnold, Max Weber to Beatrice Webb); with the speeches, official documents and reports, and other writings of European statesmen (from Sir Robert Peel and Lord Shaftesbury to Benjamin Disraeli and Lloyd George); and with the works of the nineteenth-century's greatest literary figures (e.g., Balzac, Dickens, and Zola). Writers of all views and parties—conservatives and liberals, capitalists and socialists—invariably referred to social conditions in the emerging industrial capitalist order of Europe as a veritable abyss of human degradation.[9]

The story of European industrial growth which these writers tell differs sharply from the one constructed by late nineteenth- and twentieth-century social scientists and historians. In this radically revisionist ac-

7. Marx 1909: 1:xvii. Some of Marx's journalistic writings on India, Poland, and Ireland are more pessimistic about the prospects for capitalist development on the periphery. But from Marx's point of view, had capitalism taken firmer hold in these countries they would have looked more like the Europe he describes. For a discussion of Marx's position see Avineri 1968.
8. Until fairly recently, both liberals and Marxists assumed that the Third World would replicate the path followed by Europe (e.g., Black 1966; Eisenstadt 1966; Levy 1966; Apter 1965; Rostow 1960; Shils 1960; Almond and Coleman 1960; Lerner 1958). Eventually, however, they took the view that the Third World was not following that path. In the late 1960s and early 1970s critics began to attack the literature on Third World development for its teleology, unidirectionality, and evolutionary determinism (e.g., Shiner 1975; Schwartz 1975; Tipps 1973; Huntington 1968; Frank 1967; Whitaker 1967; Gusfield 1967; Eisenstadt 1964). Today there is a general consensus that the Third World is following a path to industrial capitalism wholly dissimilar from that followed by Europe. Scholars remain divided as to whether the two trajectories are related. Liberal and neoclassical theorists treat the two as unrelated, while neo-Marxist, dependency, and world systems theorists see them as integral parts of a single historical process, the global expansion of capitalism. Among Marxists, Marx's view survives as a minority opinion. See, for instance, Warren 1980.
9. The pervasive concern with misery and with poverty in the nineteenth century was a result, not of some greater measure of social consciousness at the time, as is sometimes supposed, but rather of its unprecedented scope and magnitude. Some nineteenth-century writers wrote memorably about the horrifying conditions in Europe's overseas colonies, for instance, Joseph Conrad. Centrally concerned with a critique of imperialism and the consequences of imperialist penetration, Conrad describes the backwaters of the globe (Patusan, Costaguana) but does not compare them enough with the imperial powers to allow us to say that he believed that capitalist development in the periphery was distinct from capitalist development in Europe. A greater concern with capitalist development rather than with imperialism might have alerted him to the similarities. In fact, in *The Secret Agent* (1907) he provides a dark portrait of the squalor and misery of the lives of the poor in London.

count, all the characteristic aspects of European industrial development with which nineteenth-century social scientists were principally concerned—domination, exploitation, uneven development, inequality, political instability, authoritarianism—recede into the background.[10] The foreground is occupied by the marvels resulting from mechanical power and machinery, increased productivity, and the accumulation of wealth. The revised account portrays industrial capitalist development in Europe as gradual and evolutionary. Set in motion by endogenous cultural and institutional transformations,[11] a new urban bourgeoisie rose to power, historic or ethnic national communities evolved into nation-states, and a more or less even and internally focused development led to the gradual expansion and integration of the domestic market.[12] The European model of development, used by many theorists as a starting point and basis of comparison for analyzing contemporary Third World development, is based on this account.

Clearly, this picture of western historical development does not show to the less developed the image of its own future. In fact, it presents a picture of development so sharply different from that of the Third World as to persuade most scholars that the processes through which Europe developed are not repeatable. For development in the Third World is hampered by its ethnically heterogeneous and artificially constructed states and by populations that lack a shared history and sense of nationhood, a strong indigenous urban bourgeoisie, and a capacity to sustain liberal institutions. There, development is exogenously stimulated, and at the same time retarded by colonial and traditional structures and forces: dualism, monopoly, a lack of internal structural integration, and dependency on outside capital, labor, and markets.[13] These are indeed all well-

10. For some notable exceptions, see Lis 1989, 1979; and Goldstein 1983.

11. Despite their emphasis on trade as an engine of growth, neoclassical writers maintain that endogenous institutional transformations made possible the expansion of trade. The major types of endogenous institutional change include: changes in the law defining property rights and their enforcement (governments gradually strengthened exclusive ownership rights and property relations, transforming conditional land ownership into absolute private property); elimination of legal and political barriers to trade among regions, making it cheaper to exploit new economic opportunities; enlargements in industrial and commercial private enterprises as well as public transportation services to make it possible to capture returns from economies of scale; an increase in the preponderance of capitalist enterprises using wage labor and family enterprises producing for profit; creation of new organizations or transformation of existing ones by particular socioeconomic groups to protect themselves from unfavorable consequences of economic and technological change (i.e., falling prices and wages, competition from new technologies, or underselling by foreign competitors).

12. For examples of this revised account, see Benson 1989; Chenery 1986; Kedourie 1984; Gray 1981; Rubinstein 1981; Weiner 1981; North 1981; Joyce 1980; Murdoch 1980; Chirot 1977; Binder et al. 1971; North and Thomas 1973, 1970; Huntington 1968; Rostow 1960.

13. See, e.g., Roxborough 1979; Cardoso 1973; Dos Santos 1970; Frank 1967; Baran 1957.

documented features of Third World development. What contemporary studies have generally failed to recognize, however, is that these features were characteristic of European development as well.

A sense of crisis began to pervade the field of development studies in the 1970s. It began with the recognition that existing models of dependent development, though accurate at the level of description, failed to provide an accurate understanding of processes of change in the Third World. In the mid-1970s, scholars began to reexamine European development, looking for models they could use to analyze change in developing regions.[14] In an influential volume edited by Charles Tilly (1975b), several scholars showed that national integration and state-building in Europe were not as smooth or as successful as had been assumed. Other scholars drew attention to similar patterns of uneven development and peripheralization in eastern Europe and in the contemporary Third World (e.g., Wallerstein 1974a, 1980; Berend and Ránki 1982; Turcan 1969; Spulber 1963). Applying a variety of models to European development in the nineteenth and early twentieth centuries, Morris and Adelman (1988) concluded that the neoclassical model of growth applied fully only to Great Britain, France, Belgium, and Switzerland. I shall argue, however, that not only in eastern Europe, but in western Europe as well, structural features and processes of industrial capitalist development were essentially similar to those we see in the Third World today. These structures and processes produced similar patterns of development in Europe and the Third World, for the historical and international contexts within which European and Third World development took place were largely similar as well.

Development in Europe in the
Nineteenth and Early Twentieth Centuries

According to dependency theory, what distinguishes the Third World from Europe is its colonial history. This story of Third World development begins, in fact, with the colonial and imperial policies of European powers, either direct forms of imperial control and colonial subjugation or new forms of imperialism, which in the postcolonial era ensure continuing dependence. On this view, colonialism created interrelated structural "distortions" within Third World societies, including dual economies, in which a modern and dynamic sector exists within a traditional and stagnant economy,[15] and dependence on a narrow range of export goods and a

14. See Migdal 1983 for a review of some relevant studies.
15. See Sunkel 1993. Not all dependency theorists accept the notion of dualism. Much of the

small number of trading partners. These distortions tie growth patterns to the ebb and flow of the international market and lead to a high degree of foreign input into decisions affecting the national economy. The technology used in the export sector is taken in a more or less unadapted form from developed states, is in various ways inappropriate to the production and consumption needs of the importing countries, and helps to perpetuate structures of dependency.[16]

Among the most important structural distortions of dependent development is the emergence of a local bourgeoisie, crippled by the domination exerted by international capital and too weak and dependent to act as an effective agent of national development (for this view, see Portes 1985; Cardoso and Faletto 1979; Coatsworth 1993). As a result, local leadership in the process of industrialization passes into the hands of the state and, in some places, of a "state bourgeoisie" which has achieved a separate base of power (Cardoso 1977: 16; Cardoso 1979: 53). Development in the contemporary Third World is thought to be inegalitarian relative to that which Europe experienced and less democratic.[17] The mass of the population in most contemporary Third World countries is excluded from the political life of the nation. Where democratic forms of government are found, they tend to be partial and highly unstable.

Colonial domination and exploitation were, in fact, as much a part of the experience of European countries in the nineteenth century as they are of the Third World today. In the nineteenth century, Norway, Finland, Italy, Czechoslovakia, Hungary, Poland, Ireland, Belgium, Greece, the Baltic states, Romania, Bulgaria, Yugoslavia, and Albania experienced domination by an outside imperial power. During the century, protectorates and other indirect forms of colonialism were established in parts of eastern, southern, and southeastern Europe identical in form and consequence to those established in areas of the Third World. Moreover, the process of nation-building in nearly all of Europe was, in its essence, origins, and methods similar to colonialism and had a similar impact on large populations.

Most European economies in the nineteenth and early twentieth centuries were dualistic. Great Britain, France, Italy, Germany, Spain, Portugal, the Austro-Hungarian Empire, Russia, Belgium, and much of the Bal-

---

literature on Asia and southern Africa, for instance, emphasizes the effects of labor migration and changes in land tenure rules on production in the modern sector but deemphasizes the idea of dualism.

16. See, e.g., Amin 1977; S. Amin 1974; Alavi 1975, 1964; Stewart 1974; Cardoso 1972.

17. For inegalitarian Third World development, see Coatsworth 1993: 24, 26–27; Evans and Stephens 1988: 755. For development in the Third World as less democratic see O'Donnell 1979; Schmitter 1971; Chalmers 1969; King 1968; Cardoso and Faletto 1969.

kans had a dynamic, foreign-oriented economic sector that failed to transform the rest of society. Many countries in Europe, both in the east and in the west, were unable to diversify their exports or trading partners until well into the twentieth century. In 1900, 60 percent of Denmark's exports went to Britain (Jörberg 1973: 395). In 1910, 66 percent of Austria-Hungary's trade was carried out with four countries and 62 percent of Belgium's trade was carried on with five (Mitchell 1975: 569, 573).

Most European countries adopted from abroad an already developed technology while retaining their "traditional" social structure, and all were dependent on foreign capital to finance growth: British capital in France and Belgium; British and French capital in Germany; French and German capital in Austria; German capital in Sweden and other Scandinavian countries. Nowhere in nineteenth-century Europe was a strong, independent industrial capitalist bourgeoisie to be found. In most of Europe, the bourgeoisie was either a foreign class or politically and economically weak, regionally confined, and dependent on the state or the landholding aristocracy. Development was financed not by an independent indigenous capitalist bourgeoisie but by the state, by banks, and by foreign investment. Business and landed interests forged an alliance for purposes similar to those for which such an alliance has been forged in the Third World, and with similar consequences for class structure and national development. In fact, these alliances were so successful in preserving and reinforcing preindustrial civil society that, on the eve of World War I, Europe was still largely "agrarian, nobilitarian, and monarchic" (Mayer 1981: 129).

The distribution of income in Europe throughout the nineteenth century was comparable to that prevailing today in Latin America (see Statistical Appendix, Table 3, for a comparison of pre-World War I Europe and post-World War II Latin America). In 1900, the gulf between rich and poor in Europe was greater than in any previous or subsequent period of European history (Romein 1978: chap. 13). "Britain in 1901 was the equivalent of an underdeveloped country in such a critical condition that nowadays the relief agencies of the world would be mounting huge campaigns to work there" (Warner 1979: 17). In 1914, England consisted of small islands of luxury and ostentation surrounded by a sea of mass poverty and misery (Joad 1951: 558). Widespread poverty, squalor, and poor health were characteristic features everywhere in Europe.

In 1914, Norway was the only country in Europe with universal and equal suffrage. Everywhere else, democracy was partial and unstable. Constitutions and democratic civil liberties were continually thwarted by extralegal patronage systems and by corruption. Only after World War II did universal, equal, direct, and secret suffrage become the norm throughout western Europe.

Different analysts emphasize different elements within the set of features associated with dependent development. All, however, share a conviction that socioeconomic and political structures and patterns of change in Third World countries are significantly conditioned by external relations. This idea was one of the key innovations of dependency theory, and is now accepted by most other approaches to the study of development. James Caporaso (1978) has drawn a useful distinction between the external reliance of well-integrated nation-states on one another ("dependence") and the integration of less-developed and less-homogeneous societies into the global division of labor ("dependency"). Interactions among well-integrated nation-states, he argues, have consequences different from those between well-integrated nation-states and the less-developed states of the Third World. Under this definition, every European country was, at one time or another, also in a position of dependency and was also less developed and not yet fully integrated within the world capitalist system (see Chapters 2 and 3). England, for example, was a follower when commercial capitalism was triumphing in Holland in the seventeenth century. Immigrants from Flanders built England's woolen industry; foreign manufacturers established its first papermaking factory and helped build its first cannon foundries (Clough 1952: 174, 178–79, 185). After 1815, this former follower became an advanced country, and countries like Holland, Spain, and Sweden, which had once been advanced in military technology, or in agricultural or industrial production, in turn became followers of England. British experts, laborers, investment capital, steam engines, and cotton machinery flooded Europe (Bendix 1977: 412–13; Nef 1967: 1; Hobsbawm 1962: 51).

The same structural features and processes characterize industrial capitalist development in the past and in the present, and external relations exercised as much influence on national development then as they do now. It might be objected, however, that their impact was not the same because development today takes place within different historical and international contexts. Let us explore this claim.

The Incommensurability Thesis

The vast majority of scholars in development studies assume that Third World countries are not following in the path of the advanced industrial countries. As a result, their focus of concern has been to develop an explanatory framework to account for these divergent paths. The most influential explanations converge on the conviction that European and contemporary Third World development were crucially shaped by contexts that are incommensurable.[18] Factors thought to differentiate these contexts include qualitative changes in the world capitalist system, the colonial experience of the contemporary Third World, late and state-led development; international political constellations and events, and international learning.[19] I have already discussed some of these factors; let us now examine the others, in each case looking first at how European and Third World situations are claimed to be different, and then at whether the difference is supported in recent research.

It is often claimed that changes in the world capitalist system have shaped development differently in different periods. Cardoso and Faletto (1979), for instance, claim that the various phases of the development of international capitalism (mercantile, industrial, commercial, corporate) had important structural consequences for the internal configuration of Latin American states. According to their argument, as commercial and then industrial capitalism expanded, the nonindustrial economies that were linked to the world market went on to occupy different positions and perform different functions within the international system: some produced industrial goods (today's advanced industrial countries), others produced raw materials (today's less-developed countries). Cardoso and Faletto maintain that the nature of dependence in Latin America differed according to which country was acting as center. Thus, Great Britain's economic expansion "required some measure of development in the peripheral economies, since it relied on them to supply raw materials." On the other hand, the United States had its own raw materials and in some cases even competed in raw materials markets, and so exercised a different kind of influence on Latin American development (Cardoso and Faletto 1979: 16–21, 23–24).

But European and other western states—Denmark, Sweden, Finland, Poland, Russia, the United States, Canada, and Australia—were them-

---

18. For instance, Moore (1966) has argued that although there have been certain common problems in the construction of industrial societies, the task remains a continually changing one because the methods of modernization chosen in one country change the dimensions of the problem for the next countries that take the step. Morris and Adelman have offered similar arguments (1989: 1420). Cardoso and Faletto assert that the developing countries are not repeating the history of the developed countries because "historical conditions are different. . . . Not only the historical moment but also the structural conditions of development and society are different" (Cardoso and Faletto 1979: 24, 172).

19. For changes in the world capitalist system, see Cardoso and Faletto 1979, 1969; Frank 1969. For the colonial experience of the contemporary Third World, see Murdoch 1980; Amin 1979; Emmanuel 1972; Frank 1970; Baran 1957. For late development, see Morris and Adelman 1989, 1988; Bendix 1977; Moore 1966; Gerschenkron 1962. For state-led development, see O'Donnell 1979; Collier 1979b. For international political constellations and events, see Cardoso and Faletto 1979; O'Donnell 1979; Jackson et al. 1978; Chirot 1977. For international learning, see Rueschemeyer et al. 1992; Luebbert 1991; Marks 1989; Morse 1976.

selves integrated into the world economy as raw materials exporters. Moreover, the development of European countries was also crucially affected by the economic structures of other countries. Before 1815, German agriculturalists in East Prussia concentrated on producing grain for English markets. When English landlords succeeded in imposing tariffs on foreign grain, the Prussian landowners shifted to production of wool for the expanding English textile industry. When the Corn Laws were suspended in 1846, they turned once again to produce grains for export.

More general arguments claim that economic development varied with the timing of industrialization. But Friedrich List made this argument more than a century and a half ago. In *The National System of Political Economy* (1841), he argued that the success of Britain altered the conditions encountered by later developing countries. Alexander Gerschenkron (1962) shows that the experience of late development is as common to Europe as to the Third World. In fact, as Raymond Grew rightly points out "most European nations thought of themselves as late developers; many felt that they had too long been a cultural or economic colony of others (Italy, Germany, Poland); nearly all experienced the contradictions between efficiency and equality, change and stability" (Grew 1978a: 35). Dieter Senghaas, in an overview of industrialization in the "core" as well as in cross-regional comparisons (e.g., of Denmark and Uruguay), shows that the dynamics of peripheralization for late developers in Europe and in the Third World were more similar than is commonly assumed (1985: 105–12, 127–30, 138–44).

Analyses of political development claim that the European route to democracy was rooted in historical conditions and processes not likely to be repeated (O'Donnell 1979; Moore 1966; de Schweinitz 1964; Baran 1957). Paul Baran (1957) claims that democratic development in Europe was the outcome of class alliances that were tied to specific and historically bounded conditions. Because of the Russian Revolution of 1917 and the threat of socialist revolution in other major countries, middle classes in the contemporary Third World formed an alliance with the traditional aristocracy and foreign interests to guarantee their own safety, rather than developing democratic support from the poorer masses. But the revolutions of 1848 and the rising tide of socialism in Europe had the same consequences for class alliances and for the development of democracy in Europe (see Chapter 7). In Germany, middle-class fear of social-democratic agitation at the end of the nineteenth century made it possible for the Junkers to forge an alliance with the middle class by persuading them that none of their privileges would survive a social-democratic revolution. Barrington Moore ties his three routes to democracy to specific conditions characteristic of successive phases of world history: "The route that ended up in capitalist democracy was itself a part of history that almost certainly will not be repeated" (1966: 5). Like Baran, Moore bases his analysis on different patterns of class alliance. However, the alliances described by Moore and Baran, as subsequent chapters will show, are not tied to successive phases of history, but in fact tend to recur under similar circumstances, and with substantially similar results.[20]

Some scholars assert that conditions for development have been altered by international learning—the ongoing change in human consciousness as a result of developmental processes in social life. On this view, democratization is different today because liberal democracy has come to be regarded universally as a clearly definable goal (e.g., Marks 1989: chap. 3). Recent studies suggest, however, that the causes and conditions of democratic development today are not substantially different from those of yesterday. They suggest, too, that democratic development is shaped not by ideas but by local distributions of socioeconomic power.[21] The notion of international learning implies that change in human consciousness is continual, unilinear, collective, and cumulative. But in spite of new ideas, technological developments, and changes in modes of production, human behavior and social processes tend to recur. Capitalism comes and goes, though in forms that vary in conjunction with the development of productive forces. Democracy also recurs, though it changes as the development of productive forces mobilizes and radicalizes new social groups and movements. On balance, processes of development and of democratization have varied far less over time than the incommensurability thesis suggests.

Were different international structures of power responsible for producing different development outcomes in Europe and the Third World? Marxist analyses of colonialism,[22] as well as world systems theories, have

20. Rueschemeyer and his coauthors (1992) recently noted important problems in the role Moore attributes to different classes (1993: 25, 141–42). These will be discussed in Chapter 7. The point here is that similar processes of class formation and alliance have recurred throughout history, a theme to be elaborated in Chapter 8.
21. See, e.g., Rueschemeyer et al. 1992: 41, 291; Olson 1993: 573; Vanhanen 1990: 48–51; Diamond 1990: 18–19; Dahl 1971.
22. At the end of the nineteenth century, a debate emerged among Marxist theorists over whether colonialism was necessary for industrial capitalist development. In *Capital,* Marx describes capitalism as self-expanding value, because the circuit of capital (exchange, production, and realization) reproduces capitalist society. However, a number of theorists have disputed this. Luxemburg (1951) sought to show that capital accumulation cannot take place in a closed capitalist system. Capitalism, she argued, can expand only in a noncapitalist environment which provides the effective demand for the capitalists' surplus value and thus enables them to accumulate. Lenin (1948) and others (e.g., Baran and Sweezy 1966) have argued that surplus capital generated in advanced capitalist states caused them to seek outlets in less developed regions. Critics of these views have challenged the notion that there is an a priori impossibility of capital accumulation in a closed capitalist system, or that there is a rising economic surplus which must be absorbed. Even if there were, they argue, the non-

tried to establish that direct political control of noncapitalist societies was in some way a result of the reproductive requirements of European capitalist development in the nineteenth century. Immanuel Wallerstein argues that the world system needed both "strong" and "weak" states: strong, national states in the core areas of the world economy to protect the capitalist classes who dominated those societies; weak states to allow imperialist exploitation by core states (Wallerstein 1974a: 51, 93–95, 237, 269, 349).

Colonialism was not necessary, however, for the development of today's advanced industrial countries. Nineteenth-century Europe was, except in cotton,[23] "self-sufficient and not dependent on the supply of foodstuffs and agricultural and raw materials from the Third World" (Senghaas 1985: 67). The minerals of the Industrial Revolution (iron ore and coal) were found in abundance in the core countries. These countries were almost totally self-sufficient in raw materials and, in fact, exported energy to the Third World (Bairoch 1993: 172). Coal, the main energy source, as well as iron ore and nonferrous metals, were produced in sufficient quantities in Europe itself during the nineteenth century. "Only towards the end of the nineteenth century did imports of fats and oils, leather and wood, raw rubber and a limited number of minerals from the Third World increase" (Senghaas 1985: 68). The minerals prominent in tropical trade today did not come to the fore until the end of the nineteenth century.[24] Colonialism in the Third World was therefore not a necessity for industrial growth in the core (see, also Strikwerda 1993b: 1139). Rather, it was an expression of "competitive exclusion" (Carneiro 1978: 209), though *not* prompted by conditions of scarcity. Dominant groups within European countries were reluctant to expand domestic markets and so competed for resources and markets abroad. Colonialism was, first and foremost, a form of protection for dominant groups seeking to avoid the development of the domestic market, and thus to preserve their monopoly position at home. At the national level, inasmuch as colonialism led to the neglect of domestic investment and the development of domestic markets, it helped to create the conditions that eventually caused social polarization and economic stagnation in the core (see Chapter 8).

---

capitalist environment would not (nor did it) offer a remedy. For a discussion of these views and critiques see Porter and Holland 1988; Brewer 1980; Bleaney 1976; Cohen 1973; Owen and Sutcliffe 1972.

23. The cotton came from the United States, which many scholars believe was never part of the Third World.

24. Lewis 1978a: 201. Minerals amounted to only 13 percent of tropical exports in 1913, compared with 29 percent in 1965. In 1913, minerals were prominent in the exports only of Peru and Mexico.

The gains made from colonialism accrued not to nations but to individuals, regions, or sectors. Paul Bairoch argues that, in fact, at the national level, there is a negative correlation between colonialism and economic growth and industrialization:

> If one compares the rate of growth during the nineteenth century it appears that non-colonial countries had, as a rule, a more rapid economic development than colonial ones. There is an almost perfect correlation. Thus colonial countries like Britain, France, the Netherlands, Portugal, and Spain have been characterized by a slower rate of economic growth and industrialization than Belgium, Germany, Sweden, Switzerland and the United States. The "rule" is, to a certain extent, also valid for the twentieth century. Thus Belgium, by joining the colonial "club" in the first years of the twentieth century, also became a member of the group characterized by slow growth. The loss of the Netherlands' colonial Empire after World War II coincided with a rapid acceleration in its economic development. (Bairoch 1993: 77)

Bairoch suggests that one of the reasons Britain was relatively underrepresented in the "new" industries at the end of the nineteenth century was that Britain's "ability to sell easily non-sophisticated manufactured goods to its colonies forestalled the need for modernization" (Bairoch 1993: 167).

But whether or not international structures of power benefited the now advanced countries, the assumption of much of the literature is that these structures imposed intrinsic limitations on the development of the Third World, particularly with respect to terms of trade for Third World exports[25] and investment strategies.[26] Bairoch has argued, however, that terms of trade improved for the less-developed countries during the nineteenth century and the first decades of the twentieth.[27] It was only after World War II (in the 1950s, and again in the 1980s) that terms of trade in primary goods deteriorated (Bairoch 1993: 113–14). Moreover, poor terms of trade in developing countries are primarily related not to international structures but to the low productivity of food farmers, which in turn stems from the predatory activity of landowners and from their power to block land reform (see, e.g., Lewis 1978a: 71, 74, 224, 243). Focusing on international structures of power as the primary issue cuts too late into the chain of causation.

25. See, for example, the analyses of leading economists of the Economic Commission for Latin America (ECLA) beginning in the 1940s (e.g., Prebisch 1950a, 1950b; Singer 1950; ECLA 1950). Good discussions of ECLA's first contributions in the late 1940s and early 1950s are Rodríguez 1980 and Love 1980.
26. For reviews of this literature see Bornschier and Chase-Dunn 1985; Evans 1981.
27. The exception, and it is an important one for Latin America, is the terms of trade for sugar, which deteriorated by 25 to 35 percent between 1830 and 1910 relative to manufactured goods.

Some observers claim that in contrast to investment strategies pursued by the now developed countries, in the Third World investment strategies have been subverted by the interests of international capital. For instance, Cardoso and Faletto (1979: 22) argue that

> at the beginning of the development process in the central countries, market forces generally act[ed] as arbiter in the conflict of interests between the dominant groups. Thus, economic rationality . . . was made a norm of society; and consumption and investment were limited by the growth of the economic system. Expansion of the system was due to a dynamic group that controlled investment decisions and imposed upon the entire society an orientation based on its own interests. The rising economic class possessed efficiency and consensus in capitalistic terms.

But this was *not* the case in Europe. Before 1945, foreign investment was pursued in many European countries at the expense of domestic investment and to the detriment of domestic growth. In Britain and France, the two largest foreign investors during the nineteenth century, domestic industry clearly suffered because investors failed to exploit opportunities at home.[28] In Britain, though domestic industries—railroads, shipping, steel, and cotton after 1868—along with banks and insurance companies, could get access to the London new-issues market, financial institutions were more highly organized to provide capital to foreign investors than to domestic industry. "For the most part . . . the flow of savings was aimed abroad and not to domestic industries" (Kindleberger 1964: 62). Britain was the world's largest foreign investor, at a time when its own industries, particularly textiles, coal, iron, steel, and shipbuilding, were falling behind international competitors. French investments helped to industrialize considerable parts of Europe (e.g., Germany, Spain, Italy, Russia, and the Balkans) even though France was technologically backward and clearly needed much larger home investment. By 1914, its total industrial potential was less than half of Germany's. These countries and others in Europe experienced real conflicts between the interests of international capital and of national development.

Other arguments concerning the effects of different international structures of power assert that early industrializers succeeded because "they consolidated their economies at a time when there were no *superior* countries to interfere" (Cardoso and Faletto 1979: 23). Third World countries have been handicapped, in contrast, because the bipolar superpower rivalry after World War II increased the power that stronger states exercised

28. Trebilcock 1981; Lewis 1972: 27–58; Cameron 1961: 123, 152; Cairncross 1953: 225; Lévy 1951–52: 228; Sée 1942: 360.

on the national development of weaker states (e.g., O'Donnell 1979; Jackson et al. 1978; Chirot 1977). But in the nineteenth and early twentieth centuries many European countries occupied an international position similar to that of contemporary Third World countries. Many were caught up in Great Power rivalries. The evolution and outcome of class alliances and conflicts in Europe were profoundly affected by Great Power efforts to shape political outcomes in other European countries with arms, money, intelligence, and occasionally direct military intervention. Great Powers set up new states in Europe to serve their strategic and economic interests, and within the Balkan countries, Belgium, Italy, Scandinavia, and the countries of eastern and central Europe, changes in political structures were linked to the Great Power balance in Europe. As in the Third World today, nondemocratic governments in nineteenth-century Europe were maintained at times with the economic, political, and military support of more powerful states. Support from and military intervention by Great Powers in European domestic affairs helped to preserve the essential contours of local class structures until 1945.

Some people claim that today's world is an exceptionally "internationalized" one in which "flows and influences that cross national boundaries have become increasingly important relative to those that move within them. . . . [As a result] the necessity of taking international influences into account when analyzing the development of domestic institutions has increased correspondingly" (Evans and Stephens 1988: 756). Such arguments suggest that international factors had less of an impact on the earlier development of domestic institutions in Europe than they do in the Third World now. This is decidedly not true. When Europe industrialized, no country in the region could develop or organize its industry effectively without support from others. The development of industry in each country in Europe "was vitally affected by its place in the general advance, by those ahead of it as well as those trailing behind it" (Pollard 1973: 637). Every country in Europe depended on more advanced countries for the development of modern capitalist conditions. As time went on, economic development took place within, and was crucially shaped by, an increasingly interdependent industrial system. Advanced sectors within European economies were more closely tied to advanced sectors within the economies of other European countries than to the more backward sectors within their own. Since interdependent parts must grow in some sort of balance if profitability is to be maintained, European countries had an interest in supporting and maintaining the growth of advanced sectors in other countries. This contributed to the maintenance of the uneven and dual patterns of development that are characteristic of industrial capitalism both in nineteenth-century Europe and in developing regions today.

Some theorists claim that in contrast to Europe's development, a key feature of Third World development is the internationalization of the domestic market. Central to this development is the formation of an "internationalized bourgeoisie" dominated by a "transnational kernel" (Sunkel 1973: 146)—"a complex of activities, social groups and regions in different countries . . . closely linked transnationally through many concrete interests as well as by similar styles, ways and levels of living and cultural affinities" (Cardoso and Faletto 1970: 135).

European development, however, was also shaped and directed by an elite that was closely tied by culture and concrete interests to an international class. In fact, until World War II, elites in Europe generally were more closely tied to an international elite than to the classes below them in their own countries.[29] States in Europe were built up within a common social structure dominated by a pan-regional elite. This structure continued to overlap and intersect local class structures during centuries of state-building and throughout the course of industrial capitalist development. Organized agencies linked together the various bases of Europe's transnational elite through feudal and church hierarchies and later through international commerce and finance.

Thus far it has been argued that (1) socioeconomic and political structures and patterns of change in the Third World are not significantly different from those characteristic of European development before the world wars; and that (2) the historical and international context within which Third World development is taking place today is not radically different from that which existed at the time that Europe industrialized. It will be the task of subsequent chapters to present the evidence for these assertions. After the world wars, European and Third World development began to diverge rapidly, and today the political, economic, and social structures of European and Third World societies differ, in many cases quite sharply. A consideration of what factors or agents were responsible for this change is the task of the next section.

The Analysis of Development and Underdevelopment

The most recent writing on development and underdevelopment focuses attention on how patterns of interaction among global changes, states, and classes shape developmental outcomes in different periods and different

29. See Arendt 1958: 163–64, and the works cited there.

regions of the world.[30] While much of this literature is concerned with a variety of structures and forces, international or state structures are usually the starting point for the analysis and receive the greatest emphasis overall. Consequently, this section will consider arguments that assign those structures a primary role in development and underdevelopment.

The World System

The central claim of both world systems theories and dependency theories is that the fortunes of different regions of the world are linked to the international division of labor in the world capitalist system. World systems theory, and particularly the work of Wallerstein, has provided the most systematic and detailed exposition of how this system has shaped developmental outcomes in the western European core. Dependency approaches focus instead on the periphery of the world capitalist system and on the structural distortions arising from its place within the international economy.

Wallerstein has argued that the development of the core can be traced through a process beginning with the expansion of trade and the incorporation of greater human and natural material resources needed to sustain it. In response to the market, there grew up different systems of production, and with them, specialized labor control systems, which led to more effective modes of ruling-class surplus extraction in different regions of the system. In the western European core, the development of strong state structures made possible the transfer of surplus from the periphery and led to the buildup of wealth there (Wallerstein 1974a: 38).

In an influential critique of this approach, Robert Brenner takes issue with it on a number of counts, many of which center on Wallerstein's definition of capitalism. Brenner (1977) claims that neither the expansion of trade, nor regional specialization, nor the transfer of surplus from peripheral regions can account for sustained capitalist development, which entails, on his view, "the development of the forces of production through a process of accumulation by means of innovation." Production for profit in a market does not necessarily lead to innovation. Brenner argues that in order to understand the mainsprings of capitalist development, it is necessary to take as an analytical starting point processes that revolutionize

30. See Evans and Stephens (1988) for a review of what they call "the new comparative historical political economy"; see also Hettne 1990; Diamond et al. 1990; Kay 1989; Larrain 1989; Becker et al. 1987; Wallerstein 1986, 1980; Evans et al. 1985; P. Evans 1979; Cardoso and Faletto 1979.

social relations of production at the local level and lead to innovation in the production process.[31]

The evidence and data summarized in subsequent chapters suggest that Wallerstein and Brenner are both correct. Wallerstein is right to describe capitalist expansion in Europe before 1945 as having been generated by processes of incorporation, specialization, and transfer of surplus. He fails to recognize, however, that these processes did not succeed in generating a dynamic process of capitalist growth, but in fact led, even in the dynamic focal points of growth through which capitalist growth had largely proceeded, to stagnation and crisis. Thus Brenner is also right to argue that such processes cannot have generated sustained capitalist growth. In fact, they did not: processes of growth generated by incorporation, specialization, and the transfer of surplus culminated in a devastating two-phased world war. It was only after the wars, and the consequent alteration of European social structures, that Europe, in both the east and west, experienced dynamic and sustained growth. This growth was the result, not of the exogenously driven processes that had generated capitalist expansion previously, but of a far-reaching process of internal restructuring made possible by a new balance of class power, and consequently of new relations of production, at the local level.[32] Different processes and patterns of growth characterized European development before and after the world wars. The shift from one to the other was not generated by alterations in the world system, but by changes in class relations that culminated and were completed in the two world wars.

Dependency and world systems theories both attribute underdevelopment in the periphery to its incorporation into the world economy as an area for the production of raw materials (e.g., Wallerstein 1974b: 392; Cardoso and Faletto 1979: 16–21, 23–24). But the export of primary products is not a route to underdevelopment and peripheral status in the world system. Many countries that followed this route ended up in the advanced capitalist core (e.g., Denmark, Sweden, the United States, Canada, Australia). Latin American countries had as much opportunity to industrialize with the revenues from staple exports as did the United States, Canada,

31. Brenner 1977: 31. Brenner precipitated a debate between adherents of the classical Marxist view, which takes as its analytical starting point relations of production at the local level, and the Wallersteinian/world systems/neo-Marxist or "neo-Smithian" Marxist view, which takes as its starting point a world capitalist system. On the Brenner-Wallerstein debate see also the useful discussions by Denemark and Thomas (1988); Bergesen (1984). See also Stern 1988 and Wallerstein 1988.

32. This argument is developed in my forthcoming book on war and social change in Europe in the nineteenth and early twentieth centuries. It is not an "end of history" argument: Europe's post–World War II boom ended in the 1970s. The reasons for both the upswing and its inflection point will be addressed.

Denmark, and others. In fact, those Latin American countries that participated in the world economy through the export of primary products experienced a rapid internal accumulation of capital and the growth of the
productive forces and of capitalist relations of production. The question,
then, is why did raw material production and export and the internal
accumulation of capital not "spur the growth of domestic industry"?
(Zeitlin 1984: 17; see also, e.g., Lewis 1978a).

World systems and dependency theories cannot explain why some raw
materials exporters joined the core and others fell into the periphery, but
the study of local class relations can. Success in exporting motivates entrenched groups and classes dependent on the export trade not to industrialize but to monopolize resources and to block reforms that favor the
emergence of new classes. Where the balance of class forces will enable
these groups and classes to retain their power, the export of raw materials
will reinforce a narrow distribution of resources and income, and thus a
partial and uneven pattern of growth. The difference between European
and Latin American growth was ultimately determined by the change of
the balance of class forces in Europe. This change was brought about not
by the operation of the world system after the sixteenth century, but by the
two world wars of the twentieth century.

The State

Approaches that focus on the role of the state as an autonomous and
central actor in shaping and driving economic and political development
have achieved considerable influence in recent years.

The degree to which states are autonomous from social forces is historically variable. Different degrees of embeddedness and autonomy have
existed at various times and places. The autonomy or embeddedness of
state institutions is itself an outcome of social forces and derives from
historically specific patterns of class struggles. These cannot be understood, nor can differences in states' capabilities in various periods and
places, if the problem is already defined away by assuming the state to be
an autonomous entity.

Theda Skocpol, a key figure in focusing attention on the role of the state
in social change, has defined autonomy as the ability of states "to imple-
ment official goals, especially over the actual or potential opposition of
powerful social groups or in the face of recalcitrant socio-economic circumstances" (1985: 9). In an influential work, Skocpol (1979) placed autonomous states at the center of an analysis of social revolutions in France,
Russia, and China. Skocpol's analysis of these revolutions failed, however,
to sustain her assumptions regarding state autonomy.

According to Skocpol the absolutist state, especially as it developed in France, was a quasi-bureaucratic apparatus that opposed the dominant feudal class and realized goals fundamentally counter to the interests of the feudal class by directly attacking its material base. Yet her own analysis suggests that state institutions played a clearly partisan role in the class struggles that triggered social revolutions. She argues that absolutist states were constrained by "agrarian class structures and political institutions" and that, as a result of these constraints, ancien régimes were unable to respond to external military threats and hence broke down. She states that "the property and privileges of dominant classes" became vulnerable to attack when this occurred. Thus according to her own analysis it would appear that such régimes, prior to their breakdown, protected the property and privileges of dominant classes, and that it was only the régimes' protection that prevented "revolts from below" from threatening the interests of those classes.[33] If the notion of state autonomy is difficult to support on empirical grounds, its logic is suspect as well. It has been argued that, in the course of the development of the nation-state, state elites eventually became a separate stratum with an identifiably separate identity and with interests and goals distinct from and even in conflict with those of the ruling class. For instance, some theorists maintain that technocrats and public managers have gained control of both overall allocation and individual markets through direct production. These officials are relatively free from private-sector influence and allocate resources in a way that expands their own power and wealth. According to this thesis, state elites comprise a separate and cohesive stratum, a new class with identifiable interests, ideas, and policies opposed to those of the dominant groups within society, and with the capacity to pursue their own interests and projects independently and, if necessary, over the opposition of other social interests.

While state officials may tend to constitute self-conscious groups, this does not prove that they identify themselves in distinction from or in conflict with the ruling class. Even if state entrepreneurs and bureaucrats occupy positions of widespread power, their basic interests as a group are not necessarily different from those of the dominant class (Baer et al. 1976: 84–85). As Leroy-Beaulieu stresses, "The state is not society's brain; it has no qualification, no aptitude, no mission to lead society or to blaze its trails" (1911: 520). A bureaucracy has a high organizational capacity but

---

33. Quotation from Skocpol 1979: 285. Skocpol's account of the French Revolution ends with the breakdown of state institutions and the flight of the scions of the ancien régime. This leaves a crucial part of the story untold: the successful effort undertaken by international forces working in concert to bring about the *restoration* of the ancien régime following the French Revolution.

cannot set its own goals. Rationalized systems of social organization do not create values, but only function as a means to the furtherance of existing values (Weber 1978: 2: 1402).

While "the state can create new classes . . . it is not necessarily able to give them political strength" (Leca 1990: 183). Thus, even if state functionaries do eventually form a distinct stratum and discover interests different from or in conflict with those of the dominant class, they would not find themselves capable on a long-term basis of imposing policies that threatened the interests of that class.

Some theorists have posited that state officials can bring about a "revolution from above" to transform society and create the socioeconomic conditions for modern economic development, against the interests of the old dominant classes (e.g., Trimberger 1978). But such a revolution by a faction of the state apparatus (e.g., the military) cannot bring about a transformation of economic and political structures. As Moore notes, a revolution from above implies modernization carried out under the leadership of the aristocracy without any change in the social structure (1966: 442).

The transformation of social-property relations is usually beyond the ambition and means of any group of politicians and state officials. Even if they develop the ambition, politicians and bureaucrats cannot "change the fundamental rules and overturn the distribution of power" within society "without the backing of a formidable social movement" (Mann 1984: 6). Short of a total overthrow of the old regime, reforms must be carried out in the context of existing institutional structures.

The dominant class can continue to exercise political control under new relations of production or employ the services of a governing class (e.g., Woodburn 1980; Anderson 1979). Domination rests on power, whether based on military or economic strength, on ideological authority, or on unequal information (Knorr 1975: 240). The property-owning class dominates because its monopoly of resources provides it with a continuing political and economic base. More generally, possession of wealth in all forms confers political power, as William Reddy points out: "It is not necessary to put the wealth to use, through bribes, contributions, or other influence peddling, to get political power—though this is usually possible. Wealth is a form of political power already" (Reddy 1987: 112). While dominant classes may not determine the actual decisions regimes make, their possession of resources limits the options available to state elites and thus the capacity of the state to impose collective goals distinct from the private goals of the dominant classes.

By 1913, most Latin American countries had been politically independent for a century. They were free to formulate their own fiscal, monetary, banking, tariff, exchange-rate, and commodity-stabilization policies. During the 1950s, 1960s, and 1970s, several Latin American governments attempted to foster redistributive processes and improve living conditions through a variety of mechanisms (agrarian reform, nationalization of industry, measures to alter labor and capital incomes, various fiscal policies). Some of those governments, such as the Christian Democrats in Chile, tried to achieve this through reforms based on some sort of social consensus. Others attempted more radical processes of asset redistribution and socialization, as was the case in Chile during Salvador Allende's government. Still others tried to achieve the goals by a sort of state populism, as in Peru by Velasco and Garcia and in Mexico by Echeverria and Lopez-Portillo. Economic and political obstacles have stood in the way of their effectiveness (see Lustig 1993; Dornbusch and Edwards 1989; Sachs 1989; Ascher 1984).

Adelman and Robinson (1978) have found that government tax and financial policies on average improve income distribution only where they are part of a market socialist package or a strategy for simultaneously providing the poor with access to technology, knowledge, and credit. This is a strategy seldom carried out. In fact, when redistributive policies are part of a socialist platform, external mistrust and pressures are added to the internal pressures exerted by the property classes. This was as much a part of the European experience as it is of the Third World today. As Chapter 3 will show, until the world wars class power stood in the way of state autonomy in Europe. These wars, by bringing about the collapse of Europe's traditional social structure, allowed states in Europe to gain greater autonomy. In fact, states in Europe were able to gain sufficient autonomy to pursue policies of redistribution that put economies on a fundamentally different footing. It was this that produced sustained growth and unprecedented prosperity in Europe after World War II.

Approaches that focus on state or international structures to understand processes of change begin too far along the causal sequence underlying change to tap the constellation of forces, structure of choices, and system of social relations within which these changes arise. Any system is set up to advance the interests of its dominant groups. In Europe, a landowning elite survived from the days of feudalism through the ages of absolutism and nationalism and into the twentieth century. Though it underwent profound metamorphosis in the centuries after the Middle Ages, "from the beginning to the end of the history of absolutism" the feudal aristocracy "was never dislodged from its command of political and economic power."[34] The nation-state system which succeeded absolutist states and

34. Anderson 1979: 18; Mattingly 1955; Duby 1980; Mayer 1981; Strayer 1970.

empires in Europe was set up to serve the interests of what at that time was still the dominant group within European society: the land-owning aristocracy.

Despite the sizable literature chronicling the survival of the European aristocracy throughout the nineteenth and early twentieth centuries,[35] most scholars of European historical development, as historian Arno Mayer has observed, give insufficient attention to the persistence of traditional structures (1981: 5). Moore (1966, chap. 1), for instance, ends his survey of Britain with the early nineteenth century, implying that industrial democracy had been achieved in Britain with the passage of the 1832 Reform Act and the Factory Acts, and with the end of the corn laws.[36]

In the nineteenth century, landed and industrial elites forged an alliance to maintain legal, social, and land institutions that effectively excluded the majority of the population from political and economic participation. The elites worked together to pass protective tariffs and block suffrage as well as educational and social reforms that threatened to erode the traditional political order. The dualism characteristic of European economies emerged when processes of development designed to preserve the economic bases of these elites restricted growth to within the constraints posed by the concentration of capital and land ownership. States were unable to undertake more than a largely bureaucratic and military modernization which promoted conservative objectives and produced the minimum development functionally necessary for the survival of the political elites themselves.

Industrial development in Europe became increasingly characterized by monopoly, poor use of resources, maldistribution of income, and inequitable tax systems. By 1914 stagnation, social polarization and conflict were evident throughout Europe. These tensions culminated in the world wars and the complete destruction of the structures of traditional European society. While previous regional conflagrations had been followed by restorations (e.g., the Napoleonic Wars, the revolutions of 1830 and 1848, and World War I), the destruction of the traditional order in Europe during World War II made restoration impossible. Instead, a thoroughgoing reconstruction took place on the basis of redistributive policies that, before the world wars, had been effectively blocked. It was this that made possi-

35. See, e.g., Lieven 1992; Gibson and Blinkhorn 1991; Cannadine 1990, 1980; Rubinstein 1987; Higgs 1987; Beckett 1986; Schissler 1986; Lambert 1984; Blum 1978; Anderson 1979; Trimberger 1978; Spring 1977; Weiss 1977; Stanworld and Giddens 1974; Berdahl 1972; Bateman 1971; Montagu 1970; Guttsman 1969; Dahrendorf 1967; Thompson 1963; Veblen 1915.

36. My areas of agreement with Moore are great. In my view, he correctly affirms the necessity (at least as evidenced by history) of a revolutionary break with the past. He is wrong, however, about when representative democracy emerged in Britain and France and about the dominance of the middle classes in that process.

ble the widespread prosperity and stable democratic politics of post-World War II western Europe.

Thus, it was not until after 1945 that Europe's society, economy and polity conformed to the European model upon which so much of contemporary development theory is based. And Europe achieved prosperous, stable democratic societies not through a process of gradual, smooth development in the course of the nineteenth and early twentieth centuries, but as a result of the massive human and material destruction wrought by the world wars.

Organization of the Book

This work uses the contemporary Third World experience as a starting point and basis of comparison for reexamining European history, in order to bring into focus aspects of European industrial capitalist development that have been lost to view. Analyses of political and economic development in the Third World often begin with a consideration of the legacies of colonial domination and, in particular, of the consequences for development of the "artificial" states which western colonialism and imperialism constructed in the Third World. Europe also had a colonial past. In Chapter 2 I show that large populations, in both western and eastern Europe, were subjected to various forms of colonial and imperial domination in the nineteenth century, and suffered similar consequences. Moreover, European states were also artificial. The older states in Europe were formed through a process of territorial expansion from political centers or cores, and by the absorption of areas with distinctly different traditions and political institutions, a process that bore all the political, economic, cultural, and military features of imperialism and colonialism. The newer states were created by the Great Powers to serve their strategic and economic interests.

It is often assumed that the establishment of nation-states in Europe represented the coming to power of a new, liberal, industrial capitalist bourgeoisie, and the emergence of rationalized, autonomous state institutions which operated to advance national interests. But the emergence of nation-states did not represent the victory of a new rising capitalist bourgeoisie in Europe. In fact, as I contend in Chapter 3, nationalism in Europe was a reaction by traditional elites to the growing autonomy of absolutist states and to monarchical attempts to rationalize and liberalize state structures. The eradication of state autonomy was the central concern of nationalism. By ensuring that civil servants would be drawn from local privileged groups, eliminating extrasocietal sources of military power and depriving foreigners and minorities of their economic power and position, nationalism allowed traditional classes to maintain or gain control of the state and of capitalist development.

Many people assume that dependent development in the Third World prevented the indigenous bourgeoisie from acquiring either political or economic hegemony, but that in Europe a strong, independent capitalist bourgeoisie emerged in the nineteenth century and played an important role in the development of both industrial capitalism and democracy there. In Chapter 4 I demonstrate that (1) no strong, independent capitalist bourgeoisie emerged in the course of industrial development in Europe; (2) rising bourgeois elements fused with landed and other traditional elites to form a single dominant class; and (3) within this dominant class, the landed and traditional element remained hegemonic into the twentieth century.

Studies have documented that, in many areas of the Third World, development is dualistic, monopolistic, and dependent on outside capital, labor, and markets. This dependent development is frequently contrasted to a more benign and independent European development. But after delineating the key features of what, according to the literature, dependent and independent development should look like, I show in Chapter 5 that European development before 1945 conformed more closely to the dependent model than to the independent one.

Studies have also demonstrated that, in the Third World, capitalist penetration accelerated some of the preconditions for capitalist expansion while at the same time fostering a political and social coalition dedicated to the defense of existing feudal structures. But capitalist penetration in Europe produced the same outcome. In Chapter 6 I show that industrial development took place within a vast restrictive system that enabled elites to preserve the traditional bases of their political and economic power, to monopolize gains from economic development, and to exclude other classes and groups from political and economic life. In eastern Europe as a whole, the agrarian system remained, until World War I, a "peculiar mixture of feudalism and capitalism" which gave the landlords all the benefits of both systems and the peasants all the disadvantages (Volgyes 1980: 99). In western Europe, capitalist development was shaped not by a liberal, competitive ethos, but by monopoly and by rural, preindustrial, feudal, and autocratic structures of power and authority.

In contrast to the political evolution of societies in the contemporary Third World, it is often claimed that, in Europe, democratization began relatively early and proceeded relatively smoothly, steadily, and peacefully until it engulfed the whole of Europe (before it was reversed in the east by communism after 1945). However, a review of political development in

Europe indicates that democracy and political stability are not old and enduring characteristics of the European experience, but are very recent acquisitions. In fact, I demonstrate in Chapter 7 that before 1945, what has uncritically been accepted as democracy in Europe was a severely limited form of representative government that excluded the great majority of adults from participation. Until then, Europe, in common with parts of the contemporary Third World, experienced partial democratization and reversals of democratic rule. Where liberal electoral politics were introduced, governments had difficulty in maintaining them for sustained periods of time.

Development in Europe during the nineteenth and early twentieth centuries was similar to Third World dependent development. Throughout that period, Europe's most effective elites were traditional and aristocratic, landowning and rent-receiving, and oligarchic. No new elite emerged in Europe in the industrial revolution or in the course of the nineteenth century. In fact, throughout the century industrial development worked to strengthen the power of traditional landowners. Industry was penetrated by feudal forms of organization and characterized by monopolism, protectionism, cartelization, and corporatism, forming small industrialized islands within impoverished, backward agrarian economies. Political institutions excluded the great majority of adults from political participation. In sum, on the eve of the world wars, the dominant social, economic, and political system of Europe paralleled that which existed at the time in other regions, and which still exists in many areas of the Third World today.

Europe's Colonial Past and "Artificially" Constructed States

It is often claimed that political and economic development in the Third World has been uniquely shaped by a prior history of colonial domination. In Third World regions, "the colonial powers left behind nations whose economic, political, and social structures have been so fundamentally distorted that they tend to be incapable of recovering from their history of exploitation."[1] It is therefore claimed that, for instance, "much of the history of the Middle East in the twentieth century can be viewed as an unraveling of the consequences of nineteenth-century domination" (Anderson et al. 1993: 68).

The most important of the colonial legacies are the new states created by western colonialism and imperialism in the Third World. These "artificial" constructions are often contrasted with states in Europe which, it is supposed, developed "naturally" and gradually from preexisting national communities. In contrast to Europe, where the nation supposedly preceded the state, in the Third World the state preceded the nation.[2]

But Europe too had a colonial past. The experience of a previous history of domination by an outside power is one that is shared by Norway, Finland, Italy, Hungary, Poland, Ireland, Greece, the Baltic states, Romania, Bulgaria, Albania, Spain, and the Hapsburg territories which after World War I became the states of Czechoslovakia and Yugoslavia. These

---

1. Murdoch 1980: 232. See also Brown 1984; Amin 1982, 1979; Williams 1978; Caldwell 1977; Cardoso 1972; Rodney 1972; Emmanuel 1972; Stein and Stein 1970; Furtado 1970.
2. For this view see Jackson 1990: 21; Esman 1988: 272–74; Smith 1986: 241–48, 252–54; Ben-Dor 1983: 230–31; Seton-Watson 1977: 8–9.

countries, as well as large areas within France and Great Britain, were subjected to various forms of colonial and imperial domination.

Moreover, states in Europe did not evolve gradually from preexisting communities. They were not based on cultural uniformity, and they did not correspond to historic or ethnic divisions. As numerous scholars have pointed out, European states, like those in the Third World, were also deliberately constructed entities. They came into existence and defined their boundaries by violent and protracted struggles.[3] In fact, states in Europe, like those in the Third World, were also the product of various forms of colonialism and imperialism. The older European states were created by the expansion of political centers or cores into areas with distinctly different traditions and political institutions. The states that came into being in Europe in the nineteenth and twentieth centuries were created to suit the economic and strategic interests of the Great Powers and their allies. In most European states the process of nation-building was, in its essence, origins, and methods, similar to colonialism and imperialism. Moreover, the impact of these forms of colonialism on large populations within Europe and on European economic and social development was similar to the impact of colonialism on the peoples and societies of the Third World.

Colonialism and Imperialism within Europe

Europe was the product of major processes of conquest and colonization (Bartlett 1993). From its bases in France, western Germany, and north-central Italy, Latin Christendom expanded into the European periphery as Germans emigrated to Slavic eastern Europe, French merchants and crusaders penetrated the eastern Mediterranean, and Englishmen colonized the remnants of the Celtic world. In eastern Europe, waves of conquest by Slavs, Bulgars, Magyars, Germans, Swedes, Turks, and Poles subjugated the Czechs, Slovaks, Slovenes, Vlachs, Ruthenes, White Russians, Finns, Lithuanians, and the Balkan races. Later German, Jewish, Greek, Polish, and Italian colonists settled in parts of central and eastern Europe. Until the late nineteenth, and in some places the early twentieth century, many towns in Slav, Magyar, or Romanian areas of central and eastern Europe were German, Jewish, Italian, or Greek. The towns in Poland, Bohemia,

---

3. For the constructed nature of European states see, e.g., Duby 1980; Poggi 1978; Anderson 1979; Strayer 1970; Mattingly 1955. For the struggles involved, see Howard 1976; Tilly 1975d. Tilly cites the prevalence of tax rebellions, food riots, movements against conscription, and related forms of protest during the great periods of state-making as indications of the amount of coercion it took to bring people under the state's effective control. See, in the same volume, Tilly 1975a; Braun 1975; Bayley 1975.

Moravia, and southeastern Austria were, for many centuries, exclusively German. All the larger towns of Hungary, including Pest, were dominated by Germans well into the nineteenth century. In the Slovene districts of Austria, and in Bohemia, Moravia, Latvia, and Estonia, the landed and industrial wealth was in German hands. In Lithuania, Romania, and parts of Poland, Jews constituted the main urban class; Vilna and Kishinev, for instance, were predominantly Jewish towns. Bucharest was a Greek town in the early nineteenth century. Lemberg, the center of Ruthene East Galicia, was largely Polish. In the Slavic-populated lands of Istria, Gorizia, and Dalmatia, the towns were Italian (Macartney 1934: 142; Kedourie 1960: 119).

At the end of the eighteenth century, vast areas of Europe came under the direct colonial and imperialist control of France as Napoleon's armies swept through Europe. By 1810, the French directly governed, as part of France, Belgium, the Netherlands, areas of northern Germany, the territories on the left bank of the Rhine; Savoy, Piedmont, Liguria, and Italy west of the Apennines down to the borders of Naples; and the Illyrian provinces from Carinthia down to and including Dalmatia. Northern Italy (the Kingdom of Italy) was transformed entirely into an economic dependency of France. French family or satellite kingdoms and duchies ruled Spain, the rest of Italy, the rest of Rhineland-Westphalia, and a large part of Poland (Heckscher 1964: 297). Napoleon attempted to seal the Kingdom of Italy off from the industrial products of all other countries, while keeping it as a market for French goods and a source of raw materials for the French silk industry. It was also used as a barrier to prevent goods from France's competitors from penetrating into Naples, Sardinia, and southern Europe in general. Naples, to use the expression of the French envoy there, was to be "France's richest colony" (in Heckscher 1964: 277)—a source of cotton for French cotton goods industries, which had expanded enormously after a prohibition was placed on British imports in 1806, and which were plagued by a shortage of raw materials due to the blockaded sea routes. Holland and the Hanseatic States were forced to serve as a market for French goods, but their goods were treated as foreign when they were conveyed to France.

Following the Napoleonic Wars, many areas of Europe were subordinated to the Great Powers through direct rule; other areas were administered, occupied, annexed by or otherwise incorporated into larger European powers. Poland was divided up among Russia, Prussia, and Austria. A rebellion in 1863 in the Russian-controlled territories was followed by a program of total Russification: the Polish language was banned in the schools, administration, and public life, and the use of the Latin script was forbidden. A policy of wholesale Germanization was pursued in the Prussian territories, and in 1886, the German government set up a Colonization Commission to facilitate the settlement of Germans in Polish territories (Macartney 1934: 84, 112, 128–29, 130–32). Norway, in the seventeenth and eighteenth centuries, was a unit in a state structure dominated, both politically and culturally, by the Danes. In 1814, it became a subordinate unit in a personal union with Sweden after suffering a military attack launched by Swedish Crown Prince Bernadotte (later to be known as King Charles XIV). The Czech people lived under the domination of a foreign ruling class after the mid-seventeenth century. Belgium was a victim of French imperialism during the Napoleonic Wars. It was dominated by the Dutch until 1830 and occupied by the Germans between 1914 and 1918.[4] Finland was made a subordinate territory within the Russian Empire following the Napoleonic Wars and remained so until 1917. Ireland was subjugated by force to English rule and was dominated by a favored minority of ex-conquerors throughout the nineteenth century. Poland, Norway, Czechoslovakia, Finland, and Ireland, as well as Albania, remained dependent territories until the twentieth century. Table 1 lists territories within Europe which were subjected to direct colonial and imperial rule.[5]

In addition to those countries that were directly subordinated to other powers, many areas in Europe were subject to forms of indirect colonial and imperial control. After the Napoleonic Wars, France and other European powers imposed extensive economic concessions on their weaker neighbors, including highly uneven trade agreements, particularly in the Balkans and in southern Europe. In Spain, for instance, foreign capital was granted concessions through a system of exemptions to the regulations for limited companies; these exemptions granted foreigners almost complete liberty to found every type of company. The railways, the first to take advantage of the regulations, were built to facilitate export of mining products. The system paid little attention to the convenience of internal traffic, and instead of constituting a network, it radiated from Madrid, with terminal points at the seaports. Before 1914, the railways thus had little if any impact on the development of other sectors of the economy (Nadal 1973: 552–53; Carr 1966). Several Balkan countries obtained foreign

---

4. During its occupation of Belgium, Germany deported Belgian workers from October 1916 to February 1917. Workers were arbitrarily rounded up in Belgium and brought to Germany under the harshest conditions and housed in concentration camps pending their assignment to munitions factories. In October and November, 20,000 men were deported each week; in December, the number was reduced to 2,000 a week. Germany also confiscated Belgian gold reserves and anything else of use to its war effort. See Armeson 1964; Passelecq 1928.

5. What follows is not a complete list. Missing are the southern Slav lands which became Yugoslavia after World War I, the Russian expansion into the Baltics (and into Asia), and Austrian rule in various parts of the Italian peninsula. The Russian and southern Slav experience is discussed in later sections of this chapter.

Table 1. Colonialism and imperialism in Europe, 1795–1945

Colonized/ imperialized	Colonizer/imperialist	Method	Dates
Albania	Turkish Empire	Direct rule	–1913
Albania	Italy, Germany	Occupation	1938–1945
Austria	Germany	Incorporation	1939–1945
Belgium	France	Incorporation	1795–1830
Belgium	Netherlands	Incorporation	1815–1830
Bulgaria	Turkish Empire	Direct rule	–1878
Czechoslovakia	Germany	Occupation	1938–1945
North Schleswig	Prussia/Germany	Incorporation	1864–1920
Finland	Russia	Administration	1809–1918
Alsace-Lorraine	Germany	Annexation	1871–1918
			1940–1944
Saarland	France	Administration	1920–1935
Greece	Turkish Empire	Direct rule	–1829
Ionian Islands	Britain	Administration	–1964
Southern Ireland	Britain	Direct rule	1801–1921
Northern Ireland	Britain	Direct rule	1801–Date
South Tyrol	Italy	Direct rule	1919–1945
Fiume	Italy	Incorporation	1922–1945
Norway	Sweden	Direct rule	1814–1905
Romania	Turkish Empire	Direct rule	–1878
Poland	Prussia, Russia, Austria	Direct rule	1795–1918
	Germany	Incorporation	1939–1944
	USSR	Occupation	1939–1944
Lombardy	Austria	Direct rule	–1859
Venetia	Austria	Direct rule	–1866
Hungary	Austria	Incorporation	
Bosnia-Herzegovina	Austria	Occupation	1878–1908
		Annexation	1908–1918
Serbia	Turkish Empire	Direct rule	–1878

loans for development at high rates and went bankrupt attempting to pay off the interest. Greece went bankrupt toward the end of the nineteenth century, and for decades a committee of the representatives of foreign bondholders played a very important role in the public finances of the state (Levandis 1944). After Serbia went bankrupt in 1895, a committee of Serbian, German, and French delegates, set up to insure the repayment of German and French loans to Serbia, came to play a prominent role in Serbian politics through its control of the public revenue and regulation of policy concerning state monopolies. At the beginning of the twentieth century, Bulgaria had its state revenues placed under the control of France and, later, of Austria, Great Britain, and Holland (Berend and Ránki 1974: chap. 6). Foreign loans to and investments in the Balkans, and in eastern and southern Europe, did little to transform the economies there. These areas remained suppliers of agrarian products to the more industrialized countries of Europe throughout the century.

European powers intervened militarily during the nineteenth century to suppress revolutionary activity in regional states and to insure the continuity of arrangements and conditions that advanced their own interests. The French Revolution provoked international efforts to restore the aristocratic order in France. After the Napoleonic Wars and throughout the nineteenth century, the Great Powers worked to repress new revolutionary risings. In 1815, an alliance was concluded by Great Britain, Russia, Austria, and Prussia "to facilitate major power cooperation in keeping order."[6] The Congress of Troppau in 1820 established the principle of intervention by this alliance in any state where a revolution had broken out. Four main waves of revolution swept through the region during the subsequent one hundred years.[7] In each, the military intervention of powerful states helped to defeat liberal middle-class and working-class elements and restore the authority of reactionary or autocratic regimes. Table 2 lists civil conflicts in Europe between 1820 and 1946 in which European powers directly intervened in domestic struggles.

The most widespread forms of imperialism and colonialism in Europe were those related to state formation and nation-building. States in Europe were formed through a process of territorial expansion from political centers or cores. This involved the absorption of areas with distinctly different traditions and political institutions, and it bore all the political, economic, cultural, and military features of imperialism and colonialism. Although the term "imperialism" came to be used exclusively to mean the direct or indirect domination of overseas colonial territories by modern industrial states,[8] the process of building states in Europe and empires abroad was essentially identical. State-building in Europe, like empire-building abroad, involved military conquest and subjugation by a dominant core over subordinate territories.

Typically the relationship of the conquered areas to the center was one of economic dependence, reinforced through juridical, political, and military measures imposed by the core. State policies made peripheral regions backward in relation to the centers or kept them so (e.g., Flanders in

6. France joined three years later. English translation is in Hertslet 1891: 1:375, art. 6.
7. The first wave occurred in 1820–24 with Spain (1820), Naples (1820), and Greece (1821) as its epicenters. The second wave came in 1829–34 and affected all Europe west of Russia. The third wave began in 1848, when revolutions broke out almost simultaneously in France, all of Italy, the German states, most of the Hapsburg Empire, and Switzerland. The unrest also affected Spain, Denmark, Romania, Ireland, Greece, and Britain. A fourth wave of revolutions swept through Europe following the Bolshevik Revolution in 1917 and lasted until 1920.
8. "Imperialism" originally referred to the personal sovereignty of a powerful ruler over numerous territories, either in Europe or overseas. See Koebner and Schmidt 1965.

Table 2. Intervention by regional actors in European domestic conflicts beginning 1820–1945

Conflict	Intervention by	Date
Naples	Austria	1820
Spain	France	1820
Sardinia	Austria	1821
Greece	France, Britain Russia, Venice	1821
Spain	France	1822
Spain	France	1823
Portugal	Spain, Britain, France	1826–1833
Belgium	Britain, France	1831
German States	Austria, France	1831
Italian States	Austria, France	1831
Spain	Britain, Portugal	1833–1840
Naples	Austria	1848
Milan	Austria	1848
Rome	France	1848
Bavaria	Prussia	1848
Sardinia	Austria	1848–1849
Hungary	Russia	1849
Rome	France	1849
Italy	Austria	1859
Sicily	France	1860–1861
Austria	France	1866
Herzegovina	Austria, Russia	1862
Crete	France, Britain, Greece	1866–1869
Russia	Czechoslovakia, France, Germany, Britain, Italy	1918–1921
Finland	Germany, USSR	1918
Hungary	Romania	1919
Spain	Germany, Italy, USSR, Britain, France	1936–1939
Greece	Britain, Yugoslavia, Bulgaria, Albania	1944–1946

Belgium, Brittany in France, Ireland in the United Kingdom). Underlining the similarity between this process and the colonial situation, a number of scholars have referred to this dimension of the state-building process in Europe as "internal colonialism."[9]

9. For the phrase, see Lenin 1956: 172–77; Dobb 1947: 194; Hechter 1975: 30–33; Gouldner 1977–78; Jásci 1929: 185–212; Marczali 1910: 37–99. Numerous scholars have underlined the similarity between processes of nation-building and the colonial situation. Polanyi drew a parallel between colonial domination and the treatment of the laboring classes in Britain during the nineteenth century (1944: 157–59, 164, 290). Lenin used the term in an empirical study of Russian national development (1956: 172–77, 269, 363–65). Gramsci describes the establishment of northern colonial domination over the south in the course of Italian political and economic development (1957: 430). Braudel sees the process of national consolidation in

Colonialism involves reshaping the social and economic institutions of the conquered areas to the needs of the center. If a colony is "any territory where the conditions of life (social, economic, and political) are defined for the whole population in considerable measure by a minority different from the local majority in culture, history, beliefs, and often race" (*Encyclopaedia Britannica*, 14th ed., 1970, s.v. "Colony"), then processes of nation-building in Europe can be rightly characterized as internal colonialism.[10]

Internal colonialism shares many features with the external colonial situation. A militarily powerful core imposes physical control over culturally distinct groups. These groups are discriminated against on the basis of their language, religion, or other cultural forms. Often they are treated as objects of exploitation, "as a natural resource to be plundered," and with the brutality that states inflict on conquered foreign countries (Gouldner 1977–78: 41). The economy of the peripheral area is forced into complementary development to the core and generally relies on a single primary export. Juridical and political measures similar to those applied in overseas colonies are imposed in order to maintain the economic dependence of these areas. Members of the core monopolize commerce, trade, and credit. There is a relative lack of services and a lower standard of living.[11]

The Imperialism of European Nationalism

Nationalism and movements to form nation-states in Europe during the nineteenth century were thoroughly bound up with imperialism. In fact, it was because imperialist aims were so central to nationalism that subsequent processes of nation-building differed so little from empire-building. The aim of nationalism in Europe was not to form nation-states, but to resurrect or create empires. Nationalists and nationalist writers—Fichte, Treitschke, Mazzini, Garibaldi, D'Annunzio, Kossuth, Obradovich, Danilevsky—did not call for political independence of national com-

France as one in which the "interior" is "colonized by the periphery" of trading towns on the coastal and continental margins (1984: 3:42, 328–52). Eugen Weber points out that Fanon's account of the colonial situation in *The Wretched of the Earth* serves as an apt description of the conditions that existed in rural France at the beginning of the twentieth century (1976: 490–93). Dobb describes the internal development of the United States, Russia, Britain and France as a process of internal colonialism (1947: 194, 206–7, 209).

10. This defines only one type of colony, and so is not a complete definition.

11. Hechter 1975: 33. It might be argued that the external colonial situation is fundamentally different from the internal one because, in some cases, there existed more sharply defined racial or cultural differences between colonizer and colonized. However, racism and the assertion of cultural superiority were also, in some cases (e.g., the British, French, Italian), fundamental to internal colonialism, as will be shown later in this chapter.

munities within national frontiers. They demanded the resurrection of the historical empires of Byzantium and Rome, of Charlemagne, Caesar, Dushan, and Simeon. Where there was no imperial past to recall, nationalist writers and leaders called for the widest possible extension of national boundaries, regardless of ethnic considerations and in fundamental opposition to the national idea: Napoleon's empire and the Great Germany crusade; the Italian fascist crusade to recreate a Roman Empire; the Russian pan-Slav movement and, within the pan-Slav movement, a Greater Croatia movement; Greater Macedonia, Greater Serbia, Greater Bulgaria. Still others are the pan-Celtic movement to unite Gaels, Welsh, and Bretons, which was formed in the late nineteenth century; the Polish nationalist crusade to resurrect the supranational Polish Commonwealth; and the Lithuanian ambition to resurrect the Kingdom of Lithuania. There was also a pan-Scandinavian movement in the nineteenth century, but its aims were limited, apparently, to closer economic integration among the Nordic nations (Denmark, Iceland, Norway, Sweden, and Finland). A brief description of some of the nationalist movements in Europe during the nineteenth and early twentieth centuries—the French, German, Italian, Russian, Polish, Hungarian, Czechoslovak, Croatian, Serbian, Bulgarian, Romanian, and Greek—should serve to illustrate the close association between imperialism and nationalist ideas and movements.

At the end of the eighteenth century, Napoleon fused *French nationalism* with the Roman imperial idea and, as the alleged heir of Charlemagne, united France, western Germany, Italy and the Low Countries in a new empire. Though nationalists outside of France initially welcomed French armies,[12] it soon became evident that Napoleon's goal was the creation of a multinational empire. At the peak of its power (1810), France directly governed all Germany west of the Rhine, Belgium, the Netherlands, and North Germany eastwards to Luebeck, much of Italy, and parts of the Illyrian provinces.

German nationalism was centrally concerned with the notion of German

12. When the French invaded the United Provinces in January 1795, the Patriot Party welcomed them while the Prince of Orange went into exile. A Batavian Republic was proclaimed, with genuine support from a large part of the people. In 1806, however, Napoleon decided to make his brother Louis king of Holland, and in 1810 Holland was annexed to France. In Poland, those who did not accept the partitions as final placed their hopes of restoration in Napoleon. In 1806 Napoleon, with Polish volunteers fighting in his army, entered Poland in the course of his war against Prussia and Russia, and by the Treaty of Tilsit in July 1807 a much reduced and semi-independent Polish state was resuscitated in the form of the Grand Duchy of Warsaw, composed of most of the Polish lands formerly taken by Prussia. In 1809 its territory was increased by part of the lands taken by Austria, which was defeated by Napoleon with Polish help. In 1812 Napoleon's invasion force in Russia included nearly 100,000 Polish troops.

cultural, political, and military supremacy. It stressed the need to unify the German nation scattered across large parts of other states in central and eastern Europe. German nationalists sought territories with wholly non-German populations as well.

Friedrich List, whose book, *The National System of Political Economy* (1841), had a tremendous impact on German nationalism, wrote that the German nation

> cannot be considered complete so long as it does not extend over the whole coast, from the mouth of the Rhine to the frontier of Poland, including Holland and Denmark. A natural consequence of this union must be the admission of both these countries into the German Bund, and consequently into the German nationality, whereby the latter will at once obtain what it is now in need of, namely, fisheries, and naval power, maritime commerce, and colonies. Besides, both these nations belong, as respects their descent and whole character, to the German nationality.[13]

German nationalists put forth claims to territory regardless of whether the population directly concerned really desired to change its sovereignty. One example was the annexation by Germany of French Alsace-Lorraine in 1871 against the will of the population, who in spite of race and language, wished to remain politically French. The action was justified by Heinrich von Treitschke, as follows:

> These territories are ours by the right of the sword, and we shall dispose of them in virtue of a proper right—the right of the German nation, which will not permit its children to remain strangers to the German Empire. We Germans, who know Germany and France, know better than these unfortunates themselves what is good for the people of Alsace, who have remained under

---

13. List 1885: 177. List (1789–1846) played a significant role in organizing the *Zollverein*, which laid the basis for the German Reich. List, as Luxemburg wrote, is "the real messiah of the national unity of Germany." The nationalism of Fichte and other figures associated with German romanticism evolved as a reaction against Napoleon's armies and died out after the restoration. The "gospel" of List in the thirties and forties based the "national rebirth" on industry and trade, on the theory of the "domestic market" (Luxemburg 1976: 160–61). Fichte, who appears to have held similar views, argues for closing the state commercially: "May we at last recognize that while the airy theories about international trade and manufacturing for the world may do for the foreigner, and belong to the weapons with which he has always invaded us, they have no application to Germans, and that, next to unity among ourselves, internal independence and commercial self-reliance are the second means to our salvation" (in Engelbrecht 1968: 121).

the misleading influence of the French connection outside the sympathies of new Germany. We shall restore them to their true selves against their will.[14]

The ideas of Treitschke, as well as of List and Ernst Moritz Arndt,[15] inspired the development of the the pan-German movement. The movement was primarily concerned with the expansion of Prussian-German power through the incorporation of other German-speaking peoples, even against their will, into a greater Germany. Many pan-Germans demanded even more: the union of the Swiss, the Dutch, and even the Scandinavians with Germany in a great racial Nordic brotherhood.[16]

A clear line of continuity runs from the nationalist ideas of Treitschke, List, Arndt, and the pan-German movement, to Nazi imperialism in the years before and during World War II. The goal of Nazi Germany during these years was the establishment of a colonial empire in Europe, in which an Aryan elite would be served by masses of non-Aryan slaves. The Nazis' theory of the "economics of large areas" (Grossraumwirtschaft) envisaged a Grossraum for German economic expansion based on a regional specialization of economic functions with corresponding racial types. The central industrial core, inhabited by Aryans, would be surrounded by extensive regions in eastern Europe, which in the Nazi view provided unlimited space for producing agricultural products and industrial raw materials and were inhabited by inferior Slavic peoples.

Italian nationalism became bound up with a mission to "complete the Risorgimento" (unification movement) through expansion into contiguous and overseas territories. This was a theme of Giuseppe Mazzini no less than it was of Mussolini. Mazzini called on the "Italian Nation" to fulfill their destiny, their special "mission," and to exercise world leadership as they had done in antiquity and in the Middle Ages, for the sake of mankind.[17] Writing in his newspaper, *La Roma del Popolo*, in 1871, Mazzini set out an imperialist international policy

14. In Macartney 1934: 100. Heinrich von Treitschke (1834–96) was editor of the review *Preussische Jahrbücher* and a member of the German Reichstag. For an English translation of his work, see Treitschke 1916. For a discussion of his views and influence, see Hausrath 1914 and Davis 1915.

15. Arndt (1769–1860) was one of the most powerful agitators for the national uprising of the Germans against the French. He maintained that the Germans excelled over all other nations because they had preserved their racial purity and spoke the purest language. Arndt focused on language as the factor constituting a nation; all German-speaking people had to be united in a common fatherland. For a discussion of his views and their influence on German nationalism, see Pundt 1935.

16. The classic work on the Pan-German League is Wertheimer 1924.

17. Mazzini 1890: 1:290; 3:27, 33. This was also a theme of the Italian dramatist Vittorio Alfieri (1749–1803), who had an immense influence on nationalist writers and statesmen in Italy throughout the nineteenth century. Alfieri believed that leadership in civilization belonged to the Italians. In his "Exhortation to Liberate Italy from the Barbarians," he recalled the world

to lay open to Italy every pathway leading to the Asiatic world, and to fulfill at the same time the mission of civilization pointed out by the times, through the systematic augmentation of Italian influence at Suez and Alexandria, and by seizing the earliest opportunities of sending a colonizing expedition to Tunis.

He argued that

> in the inevitable movement of European civilization upon Africa, as Morocco belongs to Spain and Algeria to France, so does Tunis, key of the central Mediterranean, belong to Italy. Tunis, Tripoli, and Cyrenaica form a part—extremely important from its contiguity with Egypt, and through Egypt and Syria, with Asia—of that zone of Africa which truly belongs to the European system. And the Roman standard did float upon those heights in the days when, after the fall of Carthage, the Mediterranean was named our sea. We were masters of the whole of that region up to the fifth century. France has her eye upon it at the present, and will have it if we do not.[18]

Garibaldi, another leader of the Risorgimento, demanded that Italy "complete" it by liberating the "unredeemed" lands (terre irredente) still under Austrian rule. This demand was echoed by those who were in favor of Italy entering World War I.[19] Francesco Crispi, one of Garibaldi's "thousand" in 1860, preached the necessity of Italian expansion in the Mediterranean and the establishment of a "Greater Italy" (Cardella 1928–29). It was Crispi who, as prime minister in the late 1880s and early 1890s (1887–91, 1893–96), secured Italy her first footholds in Tunis and Abyssinia. Gabriele D'Annunzio (1863–1938) hoped these footholds in Africa were the prelude of Italy's advance on the world. In 1919 he led a band of storm troopers on the city of Fiume and held the city for fifteen months in defiance of the Italian government and of Italy's treaty obligations.[20] The fascists, in their crusade to recreate a Roman Empire, summoned the nation to "continue the Risorgimento," to fulfill Mazzini's vision of Italy's "mission," and to uphold the glory and epic heroism of Garibaldi.[21] Mus-

---

dominion of Rome, the intellectual and artistic supremacy of Italy, and the civilizing influence of Italy at various times in the past (Alfieri 1859: 10:108–10). See Megaro (1930: 130–48) for a discussion of the breadth and depth of Alfieri's influence on Italian writers, statesmen, and society.

18. For an English translation, see Mazzini 1877: 579.

19. See Salvemini 1915; Battisti 1915; Battisti 1914. See also Corradini 1915.

20. For D'Annunzio's defense of his Fiume expedition, an ode to Italy's prestige and glory, see D'Annunzio 1919.

21. The romantic historians of the nineteenth century tried to prove a natural unity of Italian history since the Middle Ages. The fascists developed an interpretation that traced the

solini, sharing Mazzini's hope for a "Third Rome" that would exercise world leadership as the Rome of the Caesars and the Rome of the Popes had done, declared on 25 October 1932 before an audience in Milan: "The Twentieth Century will be the century of fascism, the century of Italian power, the century during which Italy will become for the third time the leader of mankind" (in Kohn 1955: 81).

Russian nationalism in the nineteenth century centered on the doctrine of pan-Slavism, a doctrine which, in Russia, justified the imperial expansion of the Russian state.[22] Russian pan-Slavism bore all the features of imperialism: it glorified the nation's past, created myths of national and racial superiority and of a messianic mission granted by providence, and called for the expansion of the state. The Russian novelist Fyodor Dostoevsky (1821–81) was one of the leading spokesmen of pan-Slavism. Contrasting Europe's rotting civilization with the great Russian nation which was destined to renew the world, he wrote that "the Russian people is immeasurably higher, nobler, more honest, more naive, abler; full of a different idea, the highest Christian idea, which is not even understood by Europe with her moribund Catholicism and her stupidly self-contradictory Lutheranism" (Dostoevsky 1923: 29). According to pan-Slavism, it was the mission of the Slavs to lead humanity. For Dostoevsky, it was necessary to establish "the supremacy of the great Russian race over the whole Slav world," before the Slavs could take the place of the West in the mission to lead humanity (1923: 41). In what became the standard work of Russian pan-Slavism, *Rossiia i Evropa* (1871), Nikolai Danilevsky argued that Russia must create and lead a Slav federation in order to destroy "the rotting west" for the benefit of all mankind. Included in this federation were to be Russia (with Galicia, the Ukrainian parts of Bukovina and of Hungary, and the Carpatho-Ukraine added), Trieste, Gorizia, Istria, the major part of Carinthia, Czechoslovakia, Romania, Hungary, Bulgaria, Greece, and Constantinople.[23]

Polish nationalism claimed independence not only for the Polish-speaking districts of Russia, Austria, and Prussia, but for all the land within the historic frontiers of their medieval empire, including Lithuania

---

Risorgimento back to the Romans (see Rota 1948: 1:x) or to the House of Savoy in the Middle Ages (Volpe 1925).

22. Not all of Russia's territorial ambitions were directed at Slavic lands. Asian territories were also claimed on strategic or economic grounds.

23. Danilevsky is cited in Kohn 1946: 132. Similar plans were proposed by Rostislav Fedeeyev. In his *Opinion on the Eastern Question* (1871), Fedeeyev declared that Russia must either advance to the Adriatic or retire behind the Urals—it was her destiny to unify all the Slavs of Europe. The Slav nationalist leader Jan Kollar (1794–1852) called for the unity of all Slav peoples and prophesied their future greatness, peopling the territory from the Elbe to the Pacific Ocean, from the Arctic Sea to the Mediterranean.

and White Russia (Leslie 1963). The Poland which Polish nationalists sought and won from the Peace Conference following World War I was a resurrection of the supranational seventeenth-century Polish Commonwealth. The conference originally laid down a provisional frontier between Poland and Russia known as the Curzon Line which was in general accord with the ethnographic situation. However, in the early months of 1920, the Poles, desiring to push the Russian frontier as far east as possible, began an invasion of Russia. In May they succeeded in occupying Kiev. In March 1921, the Treaty of Riga concluded between Russia and Poland gave Poland an eastern boundary which, except for the territory that had become the new Republic of Lithuania, corresponded roughly with the one she had just before the partition of 1795 (Seton-Watson 1945).

Hungarian nationalism, as embodied in Lajos Kossuth's program of 3 March 1848, envisaged not a Magyar nation-state, but incorporation of Croatia-Slavonia, Transylvania, and the so-called Military Frontier in the Kingdom of Hungary. National independence for Hungary within the Dual Monarchy (1867–1918) won for the Magyars the right to rule over a population of thirteen million, out of which eleven million were mostly non-Magyar serfs who were forbidden to purchase land, and who paid all the tithes to the clergy, most of the taxes to the state, and various payments in kind to their landlords (Maurice 1887: 80–81). Hungarian national independence divided Carpathian Slovaks from their brothers, the Sudeten Czechs; the Germans of Bratislava, Temesvár, and Transylvania from the Austrian Germans; and the Croats and Dalmatian Serbs from Croatia and the Slovenians.

Czechoslovakian nationalism was primarily concerned with forcing the Germans into complete political and cultural dependence on the Czechs. The Czechs claimed the historic rights of the "Crown of Saint Wenceslaus" because in Bohemia, Moravia, and Silesia taken as a unit they were more numerous than the Germans, while in Austria as a whole they were in a minority (Macartney 1934: 142–43). Toward this end, the Czechs also aspired to separating the German population of Sudetenland from the Germans of the Alpine countries (Luxemburg 1976: 164).

The Czecho-Slovak national delegation at the Paris Peace Conference claimed Bohemia, Moravia, and Austrian Silesia—the "lands of the Bohemian Crown"—though Czechs constituted only about two-thirds of the population of Bohemia and Moravia and in Silesia were actually in a minority. The German population in these areas claimed the right to unite with German Austria, but after Czech troops occupied the disputed territories, the conference recognized the Czech claim and even granted the Czechs additional German and Austrian territory. Also included in Czecho-Slovakia were considerable blocks of territory that were purely Magyar in population, and the district known as Sub-Carpathian Russia, which was inhabited mainly by Ruthenes.

Balkan nationalisms came to the fore in the early nineteenth century. None of the Balkan nationalist movements, or their Great Power sponsors, were interested in dividing the Ottoman Empire according to the principles of nationality. Expansionist ideas were at the core of Balkan nationalism. *Croatian nationalism,* expressed by the Illyrian movement, aimed at the unification of the Croatians and the rest of the southern Slavs.[24] Croatian revolutionaries in 1848 demanded the union of Croatia with Dalmatia, Rijeka, and the Croatian littoral. *Serbian nationalism,* according to a program formulated in the 1840s, envisaged expansion of Serbian activities to encompass Bosnia, Herzegovina, Montenegro, northern Albania, and Croatia. This "Greater Serbia" idea was summarized in the Nacertanie (Project) of the Serbian politician Ilija Garasanin in 1844; it guided the national policy of Serbia until 1918. To guard its own independence and to bring about the unification of all Serbian people, Serbia should, according to the *Nacertanie,* restore its medieval Balkan empire through liberation of Bosnia and Herzegovina, union with Montenegro, and securing of an outlet on the Adriatic. Since Austria was opposed to such schemes, Serbia was to seek the support of the western European powers.[25] At the end of 1860, a *Serbo-Croatian* agreement had been drafted for a common federative state consisting of the Serbs, the Croats, and the Bulgarians. In September 1866, the scope of this collaboration was expanded to include efforts toward the achievement of liberation of all Slavs from Ottoman and Austrian domination. The Circular of the Belgrade Central Committee for the Unification of the Southern Slavs Addressed to Committees Abroad, issued in March 1867, indicated the extent of the common southern Slav state: it was to include Serbia, Bosnia, Herzegovina, Montenegro, northern Albania, Macedonia, Bulgaria, a large part of Thrace, Croatia, Srem, Dalmatia, Istria, Carniola, and the northern parts of Styria and of Karst (Djordjevic and Fischer-Galati 1981: 124). The movement was to be started in Bosnia, in the summer of 1867, by means of an insurrection. The insurgents were to establish a government, convoke an assembly, and proclaim union with Serbia.

Bulgarian nationalism envisioned the resurrection of the medieval empire of Tsar Simeon. In the nineteenth century, Bulgaria fought and lost three wars to regain it. A Greater Bulgaria was briefly established by the Rus-

24. The territory inhabited by Yugoslavs outside Serbia was fairly well defined: Bosnia, Herzegovina, Croatia, Slavonia, Slovenia, Montenegro, and Dalmatia. All were subject to the Austro-Hungarian government, Croatia and Slavonia being actually administered by the Magyar government.
25. See sources in Djordjevic and Fischer-Galati 1981: 251 n. 20.

sians in a treaty concluded with the Turks at San Stefano after the Russo-Turkish War of 1877. A subsequent Great Power agreement revised this treaty, however, and established a smaller Bulgarian state. After 1878, Bulgaria directed its external activities toward regaining the Greater Bulgaria of San Stefano. It worked primarily toward the incorporation of eastern Rumelia, and secondarily toward the annexation of Macedonia. In 1880, on the initiative of political parties in Bulgaria and eastern Rumelia, a secret Central Bulgarian Committee was created. In September 1885, the committee organized and launched an insurrection, followed by a coup. A proclamation by a provisional government established the union of eastern Rumelia and Bulgaria. This union was eventually recognized by the Great Powers (Black 1943; Jelavich 1958).

The *Romanian national* movement called for the unification of the Principalities of Moldavia and Wallachia. The Principalities were united under Ottoman suzerainty at the end of 1857. But Romanian nationalism sought more than the union of Moldavia and Wallachia. It also hoped to annex Transylvania and Bessarabia. The ultimate goal of the Romanian war of independence from the Ottoman Empire (1877–78) was the establishment of a greater Romania. In the course of World War I, Romania was able nearly to double her territories. The new frontiers were almost those of the province of Dacia to which the Roman Emperor Trajan sent colonists in the early second century A.D., and from which Romanians trace their lineage.[26]

Greek nationalism was directed by the Philiké Hetairia, an organization created in Odessa in 1814 that sought Greek emancipation from Ottoman rule. In October 1820, plans were devised that tied an uprising in the Peloponnesus with action in Serbia and in the rest of the Balkans. It was thought that the uprising would lead to a general revolution and result in the establishment of a Greek Balkan empire (Botzaris 1962: 102–9). But the insurrection which the Hetairia had planned materialized only in the Romanian Principalities and Greece. This insurrection was the prelude to the Greek Revolution, which began in March 1821. In 1829, Greece was declared an independent monarchy under the protection of Russia, England, and France.

But Greek communities remained outside the Greek state. This Greek diaspora, in Epirus and Thessaly, certain parts of Macedonia, Thrace, southern Bulgaria, Smyrna, central Europe, Italy, southern France, and

---

26. This was not the final chapter in the Greater Romania crusade. In the 1920s, a populist, revolutionary right emerged, a forerunner of the populist movement later identified with the Iron Guard, which sought to rally the masses for a national Christian crusade for the preservation of the integrity of Greater Romania. This movement enjoyed, from its very inception in the twenties, a significant amount of support from disgruntled intellectuals, students, and bureaucrats. See Roberts 1951; Weber 1965.

northern Africa, was economically a much stronger force than that of Greece itself, and became a focus of attraction for the Greek state as the economic and financial difficulties connected with the building of that state mounted. Greek national action became increasingly directed toward territorial expansion and led, eventually, to the formulation of the Megali Idea (Great Idea), the ideological cornerstone of Greek national politics until recent times (Petropulos 1968: 455–57). The Megali Idea was based on the notion of the resurrection of the glory and power of the Byzantine Empire. It traced the frontiers of Hellenism from the Balkan mountains in the north as far south as Cape Matapan; from the Adriatic Sea in the west to the Black Sea in the east.[27] In 1862, the National Assembly granted representation in parliament to all Greeks residing outside the territorial limits of Greece proper (Djordjevic and Fischer-Galati 1981: 115–16). The Megali Idea culminated in the twentieth century when, on 4 August 1936, General Johannes Metaxas established a fascist regime, inaugurating the "Third Hellenic Civilization," with the Spartan salute as its symbol (Daphnas 1955).

Nation- and Empire-Building within Europe

The older states of western Europe were formed by conquering groups who colonized territories and subjugated, massacred, expelled, or forcibly assimilated the native populations. Later, national movements were formed by groups that, as the self-declared representatives of ethnic or cultural nations, and with funds and military assistance provided by existing states, organized crusades to acquire territories for which they had created and advanced cultural or other claims. Where territories contained ethnically heterogeneous populations, claims were often based on "historical rights" going back to medieval or even ancient times. Additional claims often enlarged the original territory on the basis of strategic or economic considerations. These territories frequently contained either the most ethnically heterogeneous or the most homogeneously foreign population of the territories claimed by the state. Once statehood was achieved, the ruling nation in the new multinational entity often finished the work, usually already well under way, of expelling, exterminating, or forcibly

27. Premier Colettis (1844–47) explained the program of integral Hellenism to the Athens Assembly on 15 January 1844. According to him, there were two great centers of Greek peoples—Athens and Constantinople. The former was the capital of Greece, the latter that of Hellenism. The Kingdom of Greece may, in fact, comprise only the poorest peoples of the Greek nation, but that nation includes also the inhabitants of Jannina, Salonika, Adrianople, Crete, Samos, and Constantinople (Djordjevic and Fischer-Galati 1981: 104).

assimilating ethnic minorities and other portions of the population with separate territorial claims or with the power to challenge the rule of the dominant group. A series of brief sketches should serve to illustrate the universality of this process in Europe.

The creation of *Great Britain* began with England, and from the sixteenth century, England was created and directed by London, with its provincial economies becoming satellites of the capital (Braudel 1982: 2:365). England then expanded into Ireland, Scotland, and Wales, where Celtic populations hostile to English culture were subjugated by military conquest and forcibly united with England in different ways. The English exercised dominance over the commerce and trade of the Celtic lands, forcing their economies to respond to the needs of the English market. Ireland, where the English viewed the native population as savages (Hill 1967: 131) and appropriated three-quarters of the land to their own advantage, was totally subjugated to the English market (Plumb 1950: 179; Hechter 1975: 84–95; Cullen 1968: chaps. 2–4). Ireland, as well as Scotland and Wales, sank into the position of a "peripheral" country (Hechter 1975: 147–50). In 1968, these areas still ranked generally lower than England in employment, housing, education, health, environment, and personal income (Hammond 1968).

France was formed through the sometimes violent subjugation and incorporation of numerous territories by a political-military core, the Île de France, comprising Paris and its environs. France conquered Normandy in 1204 (which had been united with England since 1066). The French state expanded into and, by 1271, subjugated Occitania, in which there lived essentially a different people, with a different (Mediterranean) culture and a different language (langue d'oc). By 1500, the French state had expanded into Burgundy, Brittany—a region of Celtic culture, and Aquitaine.

These areas remained subordinate to the Île de France throughout subsequent centuries. In the eighteenth century, Montesquieu wrote: "In France there is only Paris—and a few outlying provinces Paris hasn't yet found time to gobble up" (in Tocqueville 1955: 12). At the end of the century, Tocqueville (1955: 72) wrote, "It is no exaggeration to say that Paris *was* France." The metropolis attracted to itself "all that was most vital in the nation." To the Marquis de Mirabeau the provinces existed in "a state of dependence on the capital, their inhabitants treated as a sort of inferior species" (in Tocqueville 1955: 73). "Paris," wrote Turgot, "swallow[s] up all the riches of the state" (in Braudel 1984: 328). Unequal exchange between Paris and the provinces ensured that Paris would continue "to grow more handsome and more populous . . . at the expense of the rest of the country" (Braudel 1984: 328).

Breton nationalist writers maintain that for centuries Brittany has existed as a domestic colony of Paris, which in partnership with a Gallicized local elite treats the Bretons as a socially, culturally, and morally inferior stock (Caerleon 1969; Tremel 1968). They argue that Breton railroads were deliberately designed to facilitate the movement of cheap Breton labor into metropolitan France, that Brittany has been systematically stripped of its natural resources, kept in a deliberately retarded state of economic development, and compelled to serve as a captive market for the consumption of artificially high-priced French-manufactured goods. These factors combine to produce rural poverty and subsistence living for the masses of Bretons (Loughlin 1985).

The story of *Spain* begins with the Reconquista (1085–1340), which regained the Iberian peninsula from the North African Almoravid Empire. In the centuries that followed, Spain, like France, grew by absorbing kingdoms markedly dissimilar in cultural and legal traditions and institutions, either through dynastic marriage (Castile, Aragon) or annexation by force (Navarre, Granada). *Portugal,* like Spain, built itself up in the Reconquista, and by similar means expanded to its present frontiers.

The creation of *Germany* was achieved under the direction of Prussia and through the military conquest, enforced cultural assimilation, and economic subordination of racially distinct peoples living in territories annexed from Poland, Denmark, and France. The acquisition of Schleswig-Holstein from Denmark, of Alsace-Lorraine from France, and of parts of Poland through military conquest, was followed by forced cultural assimilation. In Alsace and Lorraine the French language was eliminated or strictly limited in schools and universities. In Schleswig and in Polish territories under German rule the same policy was adopted with native languages there.

The unification of *Italy* was brought about by a process of "Piedmontization," the conquest and annexation by Piedmont, a territory not even considered by most of its inhabitants to be part of Italy,[28] of other provinces on the Italian peninsula. Some Italian provinces associated with Piedmont as a means of gaining autonomy from other overlords (e.g., Sicily from Naples), but they were annexed by Piedmont against their will (Smith 1971: 33). The new Italian state was a country divided into a highly developed north, with many features similar to industrialized areas of Britain and France, and a much poorer agrarian south. The south was treated as an area for quasi-colonial exploitation by the north,[29] and south-

28. In fact, the Piedmontese traveler who went to Florence, Rome, or Venice, used to say that he was going to Italy (Graf 1911: 5–6).
29. The north, Gramsci wrote, was an "octopus" which enriched itself at the expense of the south, "its economic increment in direct proportion to the impoverishment of the economy and the agriculture of the South" (1971: 71).

erners were considered by many northerners to be a biologically inferior race of barbarians.[30]

Russia expanded outward from a Russian political core, creating what was essentially a colonial empire. Outlying areas of the empire (e.g., Uzbekistan and Armenia) were turned into suppliers of agricultural raw materials to be processed in central Russia. In 1913 industries processing agricultural produce (cotton, seed oil) comprised over 80 percent of the industrial output of Uzbekistan, while heavy industries accounted for only 2 percent. Food and leather industries accounted for the rest (Plotnikov 1969: 315–17). Russia treated the populations of these areas much as the European powers treated the natives of their overseas colonies (Macartney 1934: 85). Today, most of the population of the non-Russian nationalities is working-class (Gouldner 1977–78).

The Creation of States in Europe by the Great Powers

It is generally thought that the states of the contemporary Third World differ from European states because their boundaries were established to suit the administrative, economic, and strategic interests of the Great Powers. But like states in contemporary Third World regions, states created in Europe during the nineteenth and twentieth centuries were also established to suit such interests. The frontiers established after 1815 and the states created later in the nineteenth century (Belgium, Greece, and Italy) and after World War I (Czechoslovakia, Hungary, Yugoslavia, Poland, the Baltic countries) were all designed to forward the regional interests of the Great Powers.

At the end of the Napoleonic Wars in 1815, the Congress of Vienna redrew the map of Europe with utter unconcern for ethnic or national divisions and solely to advance the interests of Russia, Austria, Prussia, and Britain. Austria was given parts of Italy; Russia gained Finland; Prus-

---

30. This was a widespread current of thought. Alfredo Niceforo argues (1901) that the Southern Italians are biologically inferior; similar arguments were put forth by Guiseppe Seri, Enrico Ferri, and Paolo Orano. In another work, Niceforo writes: "Within the single womb of a political Italy two societies exist, wholly different in their level of civilization, in their social life, in their moral colour: northern Italy on the one hand, and southern Italy on the other; in a word, *two Italies*, quite distinct. While one of these two Italies, that of the north, can be seen to possess the physiognomy of a more diffuse, fresher, more modern civilization, the other Italy, that of the south, possesses a moral and social structure which recalls primitive, perhaps even barbarian times, with a social structure typical of inferior civilizations." Niceforo argues that the government's aim should be to civilize the south, and that in the south "the powers of free administration, for which they are unsuited," should be withdrawn from the hands of "local autonomous groups unfitted for self government;" on the other hand, in the north the government "must grant ample liberty for evolution and autonomous action" (1890: 296–99).

sia received considerable accretions of territory in Germany; all three powers took shares of Poland. The establishment of the state of *Belgium* in 1831 was the first change in these arrangements. In the settlements of 1815, the Dutch Netherlands and the former Austrian Netherlands had been united under one sovereign. England had occupied Dutch colonies during the Napoleonic Wars and was unwilling to surrender them, so the Dutch were given the Belgian Netherlands as compensation. Austria gave up the Austrian Netherlands in exchange for concessions in Italy and Bavaria, and because it hoped a united Netherlands would serve as a buffer against France (Pirenne 1900: 4:231, 234). But in August 1830, a rising occurred in Brussels and the Dutch garrison was expelled. Occupied at home with their own domestic problems, none of the Great Powers was available to assist the Dutch king in putting down the rebellion (a joint anglo-French force later intervened to preserve an agreement reached by the Powers). Seeking to prevent the intervention of the others, however, the Powers (Britain, France, Prussia, Austria and Russia) met at an international conference held in London in January 1831 and there signed a protocol establishing the separate state of Belgium—an uneasy, sometimes hostile, and occasionally violent union of Catholic, French-speaking Walloons and Protestant, Flemish-speaking Flemings.

Almost simultaneously, *Greece* was established as an independent country, after a movement and a subsequent war for Greek independence which had been aided throughout by the Great Powers. They were motivated by military and strategic considerations, by the economic and political position of Greece in the eastern Mediterranean, and by Anglo-Russian rivalry (Crowley 1930). *Italy*, the next independent state to appear on the map of Europe, relied in every phase of its unification movement—1859, 1866, and 1870—on foreign help. Nationalist movements in *the Balkans* were successful only where the interests of the Great Powers favored them: chiefly, where Russia and Austria sought to encroach on the Ottoman domain or to thwart each other's territorial ambitions (e.g., Serbia, Bulgaria, Romania). Where national movements found no effective support from the powers, they were unsuccessful (e.g., the Hungarians in 1848 and the Poles in 1831, 1846, and 1863).

The states carved out of the dissolved Austro-Hungarian and Russian Empires by the western powers after World War I were also intended to serve the economic and strategic interests of existing powers and their allies. Nearly all the new states were ethnically heterogeneous.[31] They

31. Hungary is a notable exception. The price Hungarians paid for complete independence from Austria was the cession of two-thirds of the population and three-fourths of the territory of their former lands. By the Treaty of Trianon in 1919, the Slovak and Ruthene countries were lost to Czechoslovakia; Transylvania and several areas of Hungary proper, together with part

were created primarily with the purpose of preventing German or Austrian imperial resurgence and of erecting an impassable barrier between Russian communism and western Europe (Tihany 1976: 211, 222, 225–26; Albrecht-Carrié 1972: 406–11, 426; Barraclough 1967: 218; Benns 1930: 318–22). *Lithuania, Estonia,* and *Latvia* achieved statehood following the war due to the allied policy of cordon sanitaire, the quarantine designed to insulate Europe from the westward spread of communism from Russia.[32] Lithuania's population was approximately 2 million, and 16 percent were minorities.[33] An independent Latvia appeared for the first time in history in the area of formerly Russian- and Swedish-dominated Livonia and Courland. Latvia's population was 1.84 million in 1925, of which only 1.35 million were Lettish-speaking Latvians. The remaining .5 million consisted of Russians, Lithuanians, Germans, and Jews (League of Nations 1926: 104–5). When the independent state of *Finland* was established after World War I, the population of the Aaland Islands, which had been united with Finland under Russia from 1809 to 1917, and which consisted almost entirely of Swedes, demanded union with Sweden. Nevertheless, the Islands were assigned by the League of Nations to Finland (Benns 1930: 220–23).

The treaties of Versailles and St. Germain in 1919 resurrected the old 1772 multinational Kingdom of *Poland*. Out of a population of 27.2 million in 1921, 69 percent were Poles, and 31 percent consisted of Ukrainians, Jews, Germans, White Russians, Russians, Lithuanians, and Czechs.[34] Poland's frontier with Russia was fixed by treaty on the basis of the military status quo and left large districts inhabited by White Russians within the Polish frontiers. Danzig and the area immediately surrounding it, which was purely German, were given to Poland on economic grounds. In November 1919 the Supreme Council granted Poland a twenty-five-year mandate over East Galicia, a large district inhabited mainly by Ruthenes,

---

of the Banat, were lost to Romania; the rest of the Banat, Backa, and parts of Hungary proper went to Yugoslavia. In 1922, the German-speaking western fringe was ceded to Austria. As a result, Hungary retained a population of 7.9 million, among whom the proportion of the Hungarian ethnic element rose, due to the loss of the multinational peripheries, from 51 percent in 1910 to 90 percent in 1920. Only two minorities, Germans and Slovaks, numbered more than 100,000 each. See Tihany 1976: 221.

32. After World War I, not only the Little Entente (Czechoslovakia, Romania, and Yugoslavia) but the whole zone, including Poland, and the defeated states of Hungary and Bulgaria, were part of the French strategy of maintaining a political-ideological quarantine area of western-oriented states to prevent the spread of the Bolshevik contagion. See Tihany 1976: 208–23; Albrecht-Carrié 1972: 406–11; Barraclough 1967: 218; Benns 1930: 318–22.

33. League of Nations (1926: 106) tabulates the minorities as follows: Jews, 8 percent; Poles, 3 percent; Russians, 2.5 percent; and others, 2.5 percent.

34. The non-Polish population numbered: 3.9 million Ukrainians; 2.1 million Jews; 1 million Germans; 1 million White Russians; and Russians, Lithuanians, Czechs, and other groups, each numbering less than a hundred thousand (Seton-Watson 1945: 430).

who are racially and linguistically identical with Ukrainians and bitterly hostile to the Poles; in March 1923 the Conference of Ambassadors assigned East Galicia to Poland in full sovereignty. In the new state of *Czechoslovakia*, only 65 percent of the population of 13.6 million were Czechs and Slovaks. The rest of the population consisted of Germans, Hungarians, Ukrainians, Russians, Jews, and Poles.[35]

Albania, established in 1913 by the Great Powers to keep Montenegro, Serbia, and Greece from controlling the Adriatic Sea, had boundaries that separated some 400,000 Albanians from their fellow countrymen (Tihany 1976: 180–86, 208–9). The Serb-Croat-Slovene kingdom, later to be called *Yugoslavia*, was created in 1918 as the nation-state of three nationalities. Out of its total population in 1919, however, about 16 percent were non-Slavs. These included Germans, Hungarians, Albanians, Romanians, Turks, Jews, and Italians.[36]

Charles Tilly has distinguished two different processes of state formation in Europe: (1) the extension of the power and range of political centers; and (2) the deliberate creation of new states by existing states. The first of these two processes he describes as "the extension of the power and range of a more or less autonomous political unit by conquest, alliance, bargaining, chicanery, argument, and administrative encroachment, until the territory . . . claimed by the particular center extended either to the areas claimed by other strong centers or to a point where the costs of communication and control exceeded the returns from the periphery." The second process is "the more or less deliberate *creation* of new states by existing states. A relatively pure example," he notes, "is the carving of Yugoslavia and Czechoslovakia out of the trunk of the Austro-Hungarian Empire" (Tilly 1975d: 616).

But the process of state formation of both new and old states in Europe was essentially the same. In cases where boundaries of new states were set by older ones, there invariably was a preexisting claim to the territory, established by the same process of "conquest, alliance, bargaining, chicanery, argument, and administrative encroachment" that shaped the development of the older states themselves. This was certainly the case with Czechoslovakia and Yugoslavia—relatively pure examples, Tilly says, of his second process of state formation. As we have seen, the frontiers of Czechoslovakia were fixed by treaty, in part on the basis of claims

35. According to the census of 1921, these numbered: 3.1 million Germans; 745,000 Hungarians; 461,000 Ukrainians and Russians; 180,000 Jews; and 75,000 Poles. See Mamatey and Luza 1973: 40.
36. The non-Slav population of Yugoslavia included: 513,472 Austro-Germans; 472,409 Hungarians; 441,740 Albanians; 229,398 Romanians, Vlachs and Cincars; 168,404 Turks; 64,159 Jews; 12,825 Italians (Banac 1984: 58).

established by military conquest. The boundaries of the Serb-Croat-Slovene kingdom (later renamed Yugoslavia) were fixed by treaty at Versailles in 1918, on the basis of claims established through nearly eighty years of military activity, bargaining, and alliances between the southern Slavs, on the one hand, and the Balkan states and Great Powers, on the other.

Conclusions

Against the evidence assembled in this chapter, it might be argued that the structures and processes of state formation in Europe and colonialism in the Third World may look the same but are not equivalent, being comparable neither in their character nor their effects. Some might claim, for instance, that although the process of state-building in Europe was identical with that of imperialism, European nation-building was motivated by cultural (including ethnic and historical) considerations, and that this distinguishes it from imperialism. National cultures did not, however, constitute natural divisions within Europe, and in fact had no existence prior to the desire to establish claims to territory, the right to national sovereignty, or the right to rule over other groups. So-called national cultures were created for political ends in the states formed in Europe during the nineteenth century (e.g. Italy, Germany, and Greece), and in the nationalist movements that arose during the century within the Ottoman, Hapsburg, and Russian Empires (the Romanian, Croatian, Slovenian, Serbian, Hungarian, Czechoslovakian, Bulgarian, Finnish, Polish, and Albanian movements), and within existing nation-states (the Welsh, Scottish, Catalan; Basque in both France and Spain; Jurassic in Switzerland; Alsatian, Breton, Corsican, and Guadeloupan in France; South Tyrolean in Italy; Frisian in the Netherlands; Greenlandish in Denmark). Others might claim, however, that whatever the origins of these movements, eventually there evolved among the populations implicit consent for the states that resulted. Such consent would be difficult to document, however, since (as Chapter 7 will show) the franchise remained highly restricted in nearly all European states until well into the twentieth century.

The assertion that state formation in Europe and colonialism in the Third World did not equally involve exploitation is based on a tradition of scholarship and custom, both in the west and in the nonwestern world, designed either to foster the notion of western superiority or to reinforce the notion of Third World victimization. If the terminology associated with this tradition is translated into comparative language, it can be readily seen that the experience of Europe and the Third World was, with respect to the structural aspects of colonialism and the experience of domination and exploitation, in no way different. It might be argued that rule by an indigenous state, whatever the circumstances and effects of that rule, is not equivalent to foreign conquest and domination. But "legitimation as well as other, weaker forms of consent are important only where people already have significant social power. Only if the subordinate classes have acquired significant power does it make any difference whether a state is legitimate in their eyes or not" (Rueschemeyer et al. 1992: 66).

It might also be argued that the foregoing discussion has left out of account cases where nationalism has had as its aim delivering some group (defined as the nation) from oppression by some other group (defined as foreign). But while this is decidedly a part of nationalism in some instances, and while benefits may be gained for some portion of the population by acquiring freedom from foreign rule, more often than not nationalism frees the mass of a population from one oppression only to deliver them to another.[37] Most studies of nationalism tend to disregard postindependence oppression by conationals as irrelevant to their inquiry. But such persecution tends to be a concomitant of successful nationalist movements and of nation-building, and differs little if at all, in its character and consequences, from persecution by foreigners.

State-building in Europe, as this chapter has shown, proceeded with utter disregard for ethnic considerations and in fundamental opposition to the national idea. States in Europe were created through a process that bore all the characteristic features—political, economic, cultural, and military—of colonialism and imperialism. Nation-states were really multinational territories acquired through imperial expansion. State-building and imperialism had the same objective and the same end: control over the resources of a territory, including its population, their activities, and the goods they produced. As the following chapters will show, the impact of processes of state-building on large populations within Europe was similar to the impact of colonialism on Third World populations.

37. Immediately following the independence of Ecuador, the people found the perfect phrase to describe the period initiated with emancipation from Spain: "Last day of despotism and first of the same." As Cueva notes, "Popular wit was right on target, inasmuch as independence was going to mean for the exploited classes no more than a substitution of the metropolitan officer with the native agent on various levels of national life" (1982: 3).

Nationalism, the Aristocracy, and the State

It is often assumed that nineteenth-century European nation-states represented the coming to power of a new, liberal, industrial capitalist bourgeoisie. It is also assumed that the establishment of nation-states in Europe marked the emergence of rationalized, autonomous state institutions that advanced state or national interests. Against these prevalent views, I will show in this chapter that nineteenth-century European nation-states instead inaugurated the rule of the traditional nobility.

In most of Europe, the nobility was the national class and played the leading role in nationalist movements and efforts to establish nation-states. These states were not autonomous actors in the processes of economic and political development and change that took place in Europe during the nineteenth and early twentieth centuries. In fact, nationalism in Europe was a reaction by traditional elites to the growing autonomy of absolutist states and to monarchical attempts to rationalize and liberalize state structures. Nationalism was centrally concerned with eradicating state autonomy and with bringing institutional, economic, and ideological sources of autonomous state power under the control of traditional elites. Nationalism ensured that civil servants would be drawn from local privileged groups; it also eliminated extrasocietal sources of military power. Foreigners and minorities were deprived of their economic power and position, and their role in finance, commerce, and trade was reduced. Nationalism gained control of industrial development and channeled it into noncompetitive, ascriptive, monopolistic forms. It encouraged and supported a revival of religion and used the ideological and cultural apparatus of the church to ensure the continuity of rural, preindustrial, feudal, and autocratic structures of power and authority.

The Nation-State in Nineteenth-Century Europe:
Bourgeois or Aristocratic?

According to both liberal and classical Marxist historiography, nation-states were created in Europe by and for a rising new capitalist bourgeoisie. In the liberal view, nationalism and its embodiment in the nation-state represent the coming to prominence of a new, more rational and liberal bourgeoisie. The nation-state was an expresssion of the principles of popular sovereignty,[1] national self-determination, and democracy, and it provided the political framework for the establishment of liberal institutions and the gradual extension of liberalism.

But as numerous historians have shown (Howard 1979; Tilly 1975c), the creation of states was resisted by most of the European population and was made possible only through violent and protracted struggles. Nineteenth-century nationalist movements excluded large segments—usually the vast majority—of the population. Nationalist leaders depended for their support on wealthy, elite elements and made little effort to appeal to the masses. In most cases the masses took no part in nationalist movements.[2] In the French Revolution, the unskilled, the wageworkers, and the landless peasants were found neither in positions of leadership nor in large numbers among the rank and file. Throughout the nineteenth and early twentieth centuries, France continually confronted the problem of turning "peasants into Frenchmen" (Weber 1976). In Italy, Germany, Poland, Hungary, Romania, Bulgaria, Serbia, and elsewhere, nationalist movements met with peasant suspicion, distrust, or indifference.

It might be argued that eventually the states produced by national movements gained the consent of their populations. But democratic rights were not extended to other classes or nationalities after "national" independence was won (see Chapter 7). What the historical record reflects, in

1. The notion that states were created by popular will became a central feature of the national mythologies that developed in the nineteenth century. For example, Fichte maintained that Germany came into being through a free contract of all people among themselves. Fichte gives the name Staatsbürgervertrag to the social pact by which the state was created. According to Fichte, every social relation within the state is based on contract. There is also the property contract (Eigentumsvertrag), the protection contract (Schutzvertrag), the union contract (Vereinigungsvertrag), and another series of contracts between economic groups. The entire life of the state is based on contracts. See Fichte 1845: 3:95; in Engelbrecht 1968: 32.

2. See Djordjevic and Fischer-Galati 1981: 111–12, 162–63; Tihany 1976: 163; Gramsci 1971: 100–103; Smith 1971: 219–20; Pech 1969: 153–54; Macartney 1968: 387; Hobsbawm 1962: 156; Kohn 1961: 33, 60; Reddaway 1941: 2:378, 383; Seton-Watson 1934: 221.

fact, is that between 1789 and 1945, European states were continually torn by ethnic and class conflicts, civil wars, and revolutionary violence.[3]

The French Revolution did not represent the triumph of bourgeois ideas and values.[4] The century that followed was not an age of bourgeois liberalism and democracy, but of militant nationalism. This nationalism extolled the values and the traditional ways of life of the socially conservative peasant mass. Far from being a bourgeois movement, nationalism was determined to exclude from any significant share of power or wealth the foreign and minority groups which, in Europe and elsewhere during the nineteenth and early twentieth centuries, formed a significant portion of the bourgeoisie. The process of nation-building in Europe was undemocratic, illiberal, violent, and aggressive. In fact, nation-states did not represent an extension of liberty or an advance in human welfare. In many respects they were less liberal, less tolerant, and more oppressive than the absolutist states and empires that they replaced.

Classical Marxist accounts of the rise of nation-states emphasize two elements: (1) the victory of the rising capitalist bourgeoisie in its struggle with the "feudal" aristocracy, and (2) the establishment of a political framework for its class rule and for the development of capitalism.[5] Lenin provided the basic formulation:

> Throughout the world, the period of the final victory of capitalism over feudalism was linked up with national movements. The economic basis of these movements is that in order to achieve complete victory for commodity production the bourgeoisie must capture the home market, must have politically united territories with a population speaking the same language.[6]

3. I analyze these conflicts in a forthcoming book.
4. To the extent that France was a bourgeois state in 1815, this was the work not of the revolution, but of the ancien régime. The centralized administrative apparatus of the French state and the breakup of large estates was already underway long before 1789. Some students of the subject maintain that the number of landed proprietorships in France was scarcely smaller before 1789 than it is today. See Johnson 1979: 155.
5. The Marxist view of nationalism was systematized not by Marx and Engels, but by their successors. The classic Marxist work on the subject is Bauer 1907.
6. Lenin n.d.: 4:250. What came to be the standard formulation of Bolshevik views was Stalin's pamphlet *Marxism and the National Question*, based on an article which he wrote at the request of Lenin in 1913. Stalin defined nationality in terms of five essential features: a stable, continuing community; a common language; a distinct territory; economic cohesion; and a collective character. Nationality assumes positive political form as a nation under definite historical conditions, belonging to a specific epoch—that of the rise of capitalism and the struggles of the rising bourgeoisie against feudalism. Stalin ascribed the advent of the nation to industry's need of a common national market with a homogeneous population. See Stalin 1942: 9–12. Bloom (1941) surveys the writings of Marx on nations and nationalism. Shaheen (1956) reviews Lenin's and Stalin's views on nationalism. Davies (1967) examines prerevolutionary Marxist contributions on the subject. Boersner (1957) reviews contributions following the revolution through to the end of the 1920s. See also the brief survey by Löwy (1976).

Rosa Luxemburg (1976: 162) expressed more clearly the interrelationship of these elements. She argued that nationalism is rooted, in part, in the desire of the bourgeoisie to assure for itself an internal or domestic market for its own commodity production. But besides a "native" market for its commodities, the bourgeoisie needs, for the proper development of capitalism, the whole apparatus of a modern capitalistic state:

> a strong military, as a guarantee of the inviolability of this "fatherland," as well as a tool to clear a path for itself in the world market; . . . a suitable customs policy; [and] suitable forms of administration in regard to communications, jurisdiction, school systems, and financial policy. . . . The bourgeoisie needs for its normal existence not only strictly economic conditions for production, but also, in equal measure, political conditions for its class rule.

For Marxist historians, the French Revolution is the pivotal event in the rise of the nation-state. It was the revolution that brought the capitalist bourgeoisie to power. The revolution represented the inevitable moment of adjustment when the rising industrial and commercial class refused any longer to accept its subordinate status within a society and state whose values and policies reflected the obsolete demands of a decayed feudal order. Increases in colonial and domestic trade and the expansion of governmental activities had swelled the ranks of lawyers, lesser magistrates, civil servants, men in commerce and trade, nontitled property owners and other professional classes. These groups formed the Third Estate. When, in June 1789, the aristocracy and upper clergy tried to assert their ancient right to outvote the Third Estate two-to-one, the Third Estate declared itself the National Assembly and as such the sole representative of the nation.

Within Marxist historical writing, the notion that the French Revolution was initiated by a rising capitalist bourgeoisie, and that it redounded to the benefit of this class (and hence of capitalistic society) has been challenged by a revisionist school of thought.[7] However, despite differing views on

7. For the Marxist interpretation, see Soboul 1962. The classic study is Lefebvre 1947. The most recent contribution to this literature is Rudé 1989. Useful reviews of this literature can be found in Doyle 1980; Ellis 1978. The most prominent spokesmen of the revisionist school are Cobban and his followers, in England, and Furet in France. Cobban argues that the French Revolution was made by "declining" professionals and royal officials rather than "rising" capitalists, merchants, and manufacturers in the interest of capitalist development. In the end, their actions benefited landowners in general. The revolution actually retarded the development of capitalism in France: the French Revolution was "to an important extent one *against* and not *for* the rising forces of capitalism" (Cobban 1971: 168; see also 54–67). For a review of studies bearing on Cobban's thesis, see Cavanaugh 1972 and Dawson 1972. The revisionist

the role of the bourgeoisie, and the degree to which they benefited from the revolution, it is generally recognized that the old feudal classes in France were not eliminated in the revolution. In fact, in the restoration that followed not only were they able to return to their titles and to much of their land, but they were able to consolidate their position as a governing class as well.[8]

Marxist scholars once accorded to the bourgeoisie the central role in the *English revolutions* of the seventeenth century, usually considered to be the first full manifestation of modern nationalism. In recent years, however, a number of these scholars have revised their earlier views.[9] In the early seventeenth century, three groups developed that eventually coalesced in opposition to the rule of Charles I (1625–49): the Puritan divines, led by men who had been persecuted under the reign of Mary Tudor (1553–58); lawyers, many of whom had a guildlike interest in the common-law courts rather than in the prerogative courts of the king; and prominent landed gentry in Parliament, who sponsored Puritan clergy through their control of church benefices and employed lawyers in their lawsuits. Many of Charles's opponents were both legally trained and Puritans. A combination of religious inspiration, vested interest, and high social standing in the counties and in Parliament brought about powerful opposition to the king (Bendix 1978: 595).

For Karl Kautsky, the history of *German national unification* seemed to provide a perfect illustration of the connections between national movements and the class interests of the bourgeoisie. The basis for the German national movement, Kautsky argued, was above all the need to unify all the German territories (which were divided into several dozen feudal statelets with customs and tax barriers) into one great, integrated, capitalistic "fatherland," establishing a broad foundation for mechanized manufacturing and big industry.

---

position is summarized in articles by Furet (1971) and Lucas (1973). The most recent addition to this literature is Schama 1989, which argues that the revolution was an attempt to arrest rather than hasten the process of modernization.

8. Marx writes in the *Eighteenth Brumaire* that, under the second Bonaparte, the state machinery was completely independent of the bourgeoisie and of bourgeois society (1963: 121, 122, 131).

9. The standard Marxist accounts are Hill 1940 and Stone 1972. Stone later argued for a more complex model of causes (1981) but maintained that the result of the events of the 1640s was a bourgeois revolution. Hill (1981) also revised his earlier view, conceding that the revolution was not brought about or intended by the bourgeoisie. But Stone, like Hill, agrees that the revolution nonetheless established the political supremacy of the bourgeoisie after 1688. For an early argument concerning the limited role of the bourgeoisie in the revolution, see Hexter 1961. More recently the argument has been made by Clark (1985, 1986).

> The history of the industrial and commercial unification of Germany is so completely intertwined with the fate of Germany's political unification, that the history of the Customs Union [Zollverein], which reflected all the political developments and happenings in Germany, passes over, with perfect continuity, into the history of the birth of the present German Reich. (in Luxemburg 1976: 162)

The Customs Union, born in 1834, grouped seventeen minor states around Prussia; one after another, the remaining states also joined this union. In 1871, when the North German Union transferred its customs rights and duties to the newly formed Reich, the Bundesrat and Reichstag were established, in effect, to take the place of the Zollbundesrat and the Zollparlement. However, despite the fact that commercial and political unification proceeded concurrently, it was not the bourgeoisie that played the central role in the movement for German national unification. That movement was dominated, from the start and throughout, by the Prussian Junkers, a class of landowning aristocrats who controlled the imperial government.

Nor did a new political and economic bourgeoisie lead the movement for *Italian national unification*. Aristocratic control of that movement had, by the 1890s, prompted a Marxist critique of the "failure" of the Risorgimento. Engels condemned the new state for its compromises with the old feudal order: "The bourgeoisie, which gained power during and after national emancipation, was neither able nor willing to complete its victory. It has not destroyed the relics of feudalism, nor reorganized national production along the lines of a modern bourgeois model."[10]

The bourgeoisie played a minimal role in the *Polish national movement*, as the Polish Marxist, Rosa Luxemburg, recognized (1976: 176). "With us Poles," she wrote, "the national idea was a class idea of the nobility, never of the bourgeoisie." According to Luxemburg, the Polish bourgeoisie, far from being the "national" class, was a "foreign excrescence" on Polish society. It was concerned, not with establishing a domestic market, but with exploiting the opportunities offered by the international market.

> The bourgeoisie . . . was with us, from the very beginning, a clearly antinational factor. This was due not only to the specific origin of the 19th-century bourgeoisie, alien and heterogeneous, a product of colonization, an alien body transplanted into the Polish soil. Also decisive was the fact that Polish industry from its beginning, already in the 1820s and 1830s, was an export industry, even before it managed to control or even to create a domestic market within Poland. (Luxemburg 1976: 175–82)

10. Engels 1895: 23–24; see also Engels 1894. The Marxist interpretation of the Italian Risorgimento as a "failed revolution" acquired its definitive form with Gramsci 1949.

Luxemburg considered this set of factors to be peculiar to the Polish case, but these features of Polish society were actually characteristic of other eastern European societies as well.

In much of central and eastern Europe, the bourgeoisie consisted of foreign colonists—usually German, Jewish, or Greek, but also Polish and Italian—that were nationally, as well as socially, different from the surrounding population. As noted in the previous chapter, up to the second half of the nineteenth century, and sometimes even into the early twentieth, many towns in central and eastern Europe were German, Jewish, Greek, or Italian enclaves within Slav, Magyar, or Romanian societies. In Poland, Bohemia, and the Slavonic districts of southeastern Austria, the towns were for many centuries exclusively German. Well into the nineteenth century all the larger towns of Hungary were essentially German. Commercial life and industry were controlled by ethnic Germans in Estonia and Latvia. Jews constituted the main urban class in Romania and Poland, as well as in parts of Lithuania.

A foreign bourgeoisie could hardly claim to represent the nation, and in fact they constituted an international class. Their prosperity was based on their having an international network at their disposal; their primary interest, therefore, was in maintaining the autonomy of the cities and the links among them, rather than in establishing national markets. The industrial or trading groups that grew up in particular provinces of the Hapsburg Empire "clearly preferred the great markets open to them" to the little markets of national states. As we have seen, even the indigenous bourgeoisie rarely played a prominent role in nationalist movements. Polish industrialists, "with all Russia at their feet," sat out the revolutionary national movements of the nineteenth century. The commercial classes in Italy preferred the "larger prosperity of trading all over the Mediterranean" to the possibilities of a national Italian market (Hobsbawm 1962: 166–67). They sat out the revolutions of 1830 and 1848. The bourgeois elements who took part in the later unification movement were those who were dependent on the monarchy, the church, and the landholding aristocracy (Gramsci 1971: 55–102). If prosperous, the bourgeoisie owed its prosperity to international trade and was not attracted by the more limited possibilities offered by a national market; if weak, it was dependent on the aristocracy. In most of Europe, the nobility was the nationalist class.

The State Autonomy Thesis

According to the state autonomy thesis, the state is to be understood as a set of administrative and coercive structures or institutions that are wholly, relatively, or potentially autonomous from social forces. The development of autonomous state power is the result of the progressive differentiation and rationalization of state structures. Most theories of state autonomy offer a variation of the same theme. Compelled by modernization (Huntington 1968), industrialization (Gellner 1983), class conflict in capitalist society (Therborn 1978; Wright 1976; Poulantzas 1973a, 1973b, 1975, 1976), the division of labor in the world capitalist system (Wallerstein 1974a: 51, 93–95, 237, 269, 349), or international conflict and advances in military technology (Downing 1992; Kaiser 1990; Parker 1988; Skocpol 1979: 203; Hintze 1975), differentiated political centers emerge whose distance from society and control of resources give them autonomy relative to social forces. Successive forms of the state—absolutist and national, for example—are understood as representing progressive phases in this evolution. Thus, according to this view, the emergence of nation-states represents an evolutionary advance in the growth of rationalized, differentiated, and autonomous state structures.

In Marxist theory, the modern capitalist state is created by and for a rising capitalist bourgeoisie, is controlled by the capitalist class, and is principally an agent of capitalist class rule.[11] Nation-states, according to Marxist theory, consolidated the rule of the capitalist bourgeoisie. Nationalism was motivated by the desire of the bourgeoisie to secure for itself an internal or domestic market for its own commodity production, and to establish the political and legal framework necessary to insure its class rule and the development of capitalism.

Confronted by the fact that in many cases there is no evidence that the capitalist class, or any section of it, controls the government or determines government decisions, Marxist theorists have been concerned in recent years to explain why and how the capitalist bourgeoisie dominates without controlling state institutions—why it remains separated from the means of coercion and why the state, nonetheless, operates to its benefit.[12] These explanations have converged on the notion of the "relative autonomy" of the state from direct control by the dominant class.[13]

The relative autonomy thesis contends that capitalism requires an independent state to absorb class conflict, prevent the politicization of produc-

---

11. The view of the state as the instrument of a ruling class (defined by its ownership and control of the means of production) was fundamental for Marx and Engels. The classic formulation by Marx and Engels is in the *Communist Manifesto:* "The executive of the modern state is but a committee for managing the common affairs of the whole bourgeoisie" (Marx and Engels 1970: 18). For the basics of the Marxist theory of the state see Engels 1950; Lenin 1932; Miliband 1973a: 128–50; Tucker 1970: chap. 3.

12. In Kautsky's famous phrase, "the ruling class does not rule" in capitalism. See Bloch 1977.

13. See, e.g., Poulantzas 1976, 1975, 1973b; Therborn 1978; Wright 1976. For a Marxist critique of the relative autonomy thesis, see Miliband 1973b.

tion relations, and avert endemic tendencies to economic stagnation and crisis.[14] The ruling class grants the state relative autonomy in order that it might moderate competition among capitalists, both internally and internationally, for the good of the capitalist class as a whole.[15] The autonomous state also provides legitimacy, which is less costly than coercion, particularly as the workers constitute the overwhelming mass of the population.[16]

Non-Marxist theories of the state center on the assumption that the state is founded on a basis of social power separate from that of social classes and possibly in competition with it. The state's control of its bureaucracy and its monopoly of the legitimate use of coercion within the territory over which it claims sovereignty, which developed as a rational response to various world-historical processes, render economic elites dependent upon the state. The development of nation-states is seen as an evolutionary advance in this process of rationalization.

Some theorists view the differentiation of an autonomous governing subsystem as a rational response to the tensions that arise in the course of modernization. With the breakdown of traditional authority relations, the difficulty of achieving "political community" among increasingly conscious and active social groups, and the consequent tendencies to anomie and alienation, state institutions emerge to reduce social tension and to institutionalize a new form of consensus (see, e.g., Huntington 1968: 8–9, 36–38, 397). A variation on this theme views rationalization as arising in

14. Some theorists have sought to show that the notion of a relatively autonomous state does not necessarily contradict the notion of the state as concerned to serve the purposes and interests of the dominant class or classes. Poulantzas's formulation of the "relative autonomy of the state" (1973b: 247) reflects the view that the state might have a substantial degree of autonomy but that it remains, for all practical purposes, the state of the ruling class. "The relation between the bourgeois class and the state is an *objective relation*. This means that if the *function* of the state in a determinant social formation and the *interests* of the dominant class *coincide*, it is by reason of the system itself: the direct participation of members of the ruling class in the State apparatus is not the *cause* but the *effect* and moreover a chance and contingent one, of this objective coincidence" (Poulantzas 1973b: 245).

15. State structures and functions are not simply controlled by dominant classes alone, but are shaped by the class struggle between the dominant and subordinate classes—a struggle that goes on within the objective limits of the given economy and class structure as a whole. Poulantzas argues that capitalist relations of production and the labor process create a "material frame of reference" within which organizations and individuals must function (Poulantzas 1978: 64; see also Wright 1976; Therborn 1978; Offe 1975, 1974; Offe and Ronge 1975).

16. Neo-Marxists have argued that the ideological and cultural apparatus of the modern state is an instrument in the hands of the ruling class, generated for consumption by, and subordination of, other classes. The state is a concrete institution that serves the interests of the dominant class, but that seeks to portray itself as serving the nation as a whole, thereby obscuring the basic lines of class antagonism. These theorists place great emphasis on ideology, consciousness, legitimacy, and the mediating role of institutions and ideas. See, e.g., Habermas 1976; O'Connor 1973; Offe 1976.

the process of industrialization. Ernest Gellner (1983: 46) argues, for instance, that the growing complexity of society in the process of industrialization, which depends more and more upon scientific knowledge, technical capacity, and administrative expertise, "can only function with a mobile, literate, culturally standardized, interchangeable population." Nationalism reflects the objective need for homogeneity in the industrialization process and thus emerges as a means of rationalizing production along these lines. "Ethnicity enters the political sphere as 'nationalism' at times when cultural homogeneity or continuity . . . is required by the economic base of social life" (Gellner 1983: 94).

Immanuel Wallerstein's world systems theory connects state forms and the growth of state power with the functional and geographic division of labor that develops within the world capitalist system. According to Wallerstein, strong bureaucratic states came into being in western Europe after the sixteenth century to protect the key interests of the new capitalist classes. The absolutist state, he argues, is the political form first assumed by the nascent capitalist system. The state protected the new organization of the economy and the new social elites dependent on that organization; it hastened the shift from agriculture to industry, fostered the search for new markets, and assured control of the seas.

The emergence of nation-states represents a rational response to the needs of the new world system. This system, Wallerstein argues, needed both strong and weak states: weak states were needed in the periphery to allow imperialist exploitation by core states; strong, national states developed in the core areas of the world economy to protect the capitalist classes who dominated those societies.[17]

Other theorists focus on the development of military force as the central process in the growth of different state forms. The general argument is that the creation of a centralized bureaucratic state apparatus was a rational response to the need for protection within an anarchical international environment. To sustain an effective military capability and meet the challenge of the rise of standing armies and the development of ever more technically sophisticated weaponry, the state must rationalize its operations in order to extract the necessary resources from society. This leads to a vast administrative system both to collect the resources and to ensure that the society is capable of producing them. Over time state institutions become differentiated from society because they have a monopoly on

17. Weak states were needed to allow the "effective operation of transnational economic entities whose locus was in another state." Without strong, national states, "the capitalist strata would have no mechanisms to protect their interests, guaranteeing their property rights, assuring various monopolies, spreading losses among the larger population, etc." (Wallerstein 1974a: 355).

military power and because it is their function to protect the polity, and they thus gain autonomy from social forces.

Numerous scholars (e.g., Downing 1992; Kaiser 1990; Hintze 1975) have argued that the threat of invasion or the desire to act efficaciously in the international system prompted rulers to maintain and increase military establishments. These increases required higher levels of taxation, which in turn required a more extensive bureaucracy. In a recent work that elaborates this argument, Charles Tilly (1990: 14–15) argues that "extraction and struggle over the means of war created the central organizational structures of states." States at the periphery of the international system lacked capital and had powerful landlords, so their rulers extracted military force through coercion; states at the center with urbanized merchant economies and a strong concentration of capital were able to purchase military might. National states with considerable capital and extensive resources developed powerful standing armies as a result of bargaining between the rulers and competing power blocs within society. This bargaining also resulted in the creation or strengthening of representative institutions.

Theda Skocpol has argued that nationalism gave the state a greater capacity to provide protection. The state's first and foremost function, according to Skocpol, is to extract resources from society in order to protect itself from its enemies—the most threatening of which are other states. Successful protection demands that the state acquire from society goods and services on a far more massive scale than royal agents had ever been able to command under the ancien régime. The nation-state "created by the revolution in the name of the People," proved better able to secure the goods and services necessary for its survival than the state in the ancien régime (Skocpol 1979: 203).

In all these theories, the nation-state emerges as a more rational method of organizing production or defense, and thus it represents a progressive stage or phase in the development of the modern rational state. In the process of rationalization, structures of authority become differentiated from other structures. This frees the state from the control of particularistic subgroups and insures that it will remain an instrument of clear, rational thought.[18] Historically, this differentiation is supposed to have taken the form of the divorce between the monarchy and the aristocracy (e.g., Parsons 1966).

A fundamental error in both Marxist and non-Marxist theories of the state is the assumption that a rising new capitalist bourgeois class came to

18. An early formulation of the thesis is Durkheim's: once the steadily increasing division of labor has made the state a "distinct organ of society," it can then "stand above all other interests," above "castes, classes, corporations, coteries of every sort, and every kind of economic person" (Durkheim 1975: 177).

power in Europe during the nineteenth century. The notion that the owners of capital were a fundamentally new class[19] created the problem for Marxist theory of a ruling class that does not rule, and compelled Marxist theorists to grapple with the question of the autonomy of the state. Non-Marxist perspectives that associate nation-states with greater rationality in securing protection and in producing goods, or with liberal institutions, popular sovereignty, and democracy, present a thoroughly ahistorical view.

Contrary to both Marxist and non-Marxist theories, it was the traditional feudal elite that were the principal owners of capital.[20] If we recognize that this class remained the dominant class, despite the development of new productive forces, and that it was not replaced by some previously dominated class, the problem of explaining the disjuncture between political and economic power disappears.[21] The fact that nation-states consolidated the power, not of a new liberal bourgeois class, but of the traditional nobility, explains the incongruity that existed between liberal bourgeois values and nationalism in nineteenth- and early-twentieth-century Europe.

The rupture between the monarchy and the aristocracy did not result in the establishment of bourgeois rule or in greater state autonomy. Rather, it

19. Because the emergence of the capitalist state coincided with the disappearance of serfdom, Marx and Engels assumed that feudal relations had also disappeared. This assumption was consistent with Marx's famous formula: "The mode of production of material life conditions the general character of the social, political and spiritual processes of life. . . . In broad outline the Asiatic, ancient, feudal and modern bourgeois modes of production can be designated as epochs marking progress in the economic development of society" (Marx 1970: 21–22).

20. It might be argued that the class nature of this traditional feudal elite was transformed so that, despite the fact that the same families remained in power, a new class was constructed out of them. But relations of production were not radically transformed. While rural labor was made "free" in the sense that workers were no longer in possession of the means of production, and though landlords were now producing for a market, many landlords continued to extract surplus product from labor through feudal controls rather than market-mediated exchanges. Though the institutional nature of production was changed in terms of consumption and distribution, relations of production remained the same since landlords continued to employ feudal controls over labor. Thus their class nature was not wholly transformed. The word "capitalist" does not appear to have referred originally to a new class of men. According to Braudel, the word dates from the mid-seventeenth century and was originally a pejorative term to describe the already rich, similar in tone to men of means, millionaires, moneybags. By the end of the eighteenth century, the word referred to wealthy people who used their wealth in order to obtain more. It did not pertain to investors or entrepreneurs, but to those who pursued wealth for its own sake (Braudel, 1982: 234–37).

21. Engels's oft cited description of the relatively autonomous state really asserts only the state's autonomy from "capitalists" and workers, not from the traditional elite: in the new German Empire under Bismarck, "capitalists and workers are balanced against each other and equally cheated for the benefit of the impoverished Prussian cabbage junkers" (Engels 1950: 290–91).

impelled the aristocracy to seek to gain control of the state apparatus. This it did by means of nationalism, which arose in reaction to the efforts of absolute monarchs to rationalize tax structures and to introduce liberal reforms. It was a rearguard movement of the privileged classes, meant to restore the union of state and aristocracy, to reduce the leveling effects of bureaucratic absolutism, and to limit the growing autonomy of the state.

Nor did the rationalization and differentiation of the political sphere occur as a result of the imperatives of the international system, that is, as a more rational means for securing protection under conditions of anarchy. States in Europe were built up within an international society; they arose as a means of protecting the property and privilege of dominant groups within this society against local foes. Interdependent changes in state structures were not the result of competition among them and of the need to protect themselves from each other, but rather resulted from the fact that solutions developed locally were shared by states facing similar internal challenges. State formation in Europe took place within an essentially cooperative international environment that provided legitimation and protection for successive forms of local rule. In Europe in the nineteenth century, the threat most frequently came from within, not from without. In fact, throughout the nineteenth century, it was the international system that provided the military force for keeping domestic order. In the age of nationalism and the development of nation-states, the international system, far from representing a threat to the sovereignty of states, provided rulers with the means of maintaining internal order.

Absolutism and the Struggle of the Aristocracy against State Autonomy

A crisis in feudalism that threatened to destroy serfdom and thus to undermine the feudal mode of production[22] led to the reorganization of the feudal framework in the absolutist state.[23] That state was above all the result of a coalition of feudal lords, which combined feudal seigneuries in the hands of a single seigneur for the protection of aristocratic property

22. The crisis involved widespread peasant riots in western Europe from the thirteenth to the fifteenth centuries. See Hilton 1951. A compact review of various interpretations of the crisis of feudalism is in Wallerstein 1974a.

23. According to Perry Anderson, absolutism was essentially "a redeployed apparatus of feudal domination, the new political carapace of a threatened nobility." The rule of the absolutist state "was that of the feudal nobility in the epoch of transition to capitalism" (Anderson 1979: 18, 42).

and privileges. The central bureaucracy operated to reproduce, on a national scale, the feudal mode of extracting profit. Although the state did strip the aristocracy of some of its political powers, it did not seek to bring about any far-reaching changes in the system of social and economic domination, which was basically beneficial to the rural aristocracy. The monarch lived largely on the taxes of peasants, and the nobility was exempted almost entirely from taxation.

Under absolutism, the feudal nobility continued to own the bulk of the fundamental means of production in the economy, and to occupy the great majority of positions within the total apparatus of political power. In France the local seigneur appointed the bailiff, the registrar and other legal and judicial officers, the attorneys, notaries, seigneurial sergeants, constabulary, and forest wardens. He received dues for providing care and safety within the walls of the town and for military protection; dues exacted from those who sold beer, wine, and other beverages; dues on fires, levied on each fireside, house, or family; dues on passing flocks of sheep; and a sixth, fifth, or fourth of the price of every piece of ground sold and of every lease exceeding nine years. Landlords had monopolistic control of mills, ovens, slaughterhouses, and wine presses. They obliged the inhabitants to use these or pay for their support and demolished all structures that might enter into competition with them.[24] Under feudalism, the authority to wage war, to tax, and to administer and enforce the law had been privately owned as a hereditary right by members of a military landed aristocracy. Under absolutism, the king's great vassals continued to own important elements of public power as hereditary and legally recognized property rights. From the beginning to the end of the history of absolutism, the feudal nobility was never dislodged from its command of political power (Anderson 1979: 40).

In the sixteenth century, absolutist rulers attempted to end internal customs dues and break up entailed estates, and to eliminate complex feudal regulations and customs which hampered economic progress. Faced with this threat to their power and privileges, the feudal nobility resisted; in response, rulers sought to gain autonomy over the nobility. Animated by the ambition to break the power of the feudal lords, and to unify their dominions under a centralized, bureaucratic rule, absolute monarchs sought to rationalize bureaucracies and to make them operate independently of local power groups. In the seventeenth century Frederick William I of Prussia, Frederick III of Denmark, Charles XI of

---

24. Taine 1962: 21–24. Feudal or manorial dues, as extensive as those in France, continued to be payable throughout Prussia well into the nineteenth century. See Bleiber 1966: 20–21, 37–88, 45–46, 59–60. For a summary in English, see Reddy 1987: 170–71.

Sweden, and Peter of Russia inducted commoners and ethnic minorities into the state bureaucracy. This triggered an often violent conflict between the state and traditional elites over control of state institutions. Absolutist rulers also endeavored to acquire control of the army through the use of mercenaries, and to raise revenues through the use of foreign and minority industrialists and commercial classes. In France, Louis XIII (1610–43) replaced aristocratic governors with royal officials (intendants) and tried unsuccessfully to eliminate the purchase of offices and courts based on class (parlements). Louis XIV (1643–1715) granted the Huguenots an important role in creating the financial basis for the development of mercantilism. A revolt by the nobility in 1648–53 against these developments failed, and as a result, the upper nobility was deprived of political power, though they did retain their ownership of land, exemption from taxation, and special judicial status.

In the eighteenth century, absolutist rulers, faced with growing fiscal crises, attempted to foster economic growth by increasing agricultural productivity and urban commerce. Rulers sought to raise revenue by heavily taxing the peasantry, by borrowing from private financiers, and by the sale of offices. When these measures proved insufficient, however, rulers increasingly sought to eliminate many of the fiscal privileges of the landed and wealthy elite. These elites resisted every measure of reform, and after 1715 were constantly at odds with the royal administration. In France, Louis XV (1715–74) created a standing army in 1726 to smash the autonomy of the towns and to prevent rebellions against economic reforms. He nationalized all army regiments, establishing a monopoly of the use of force and doing away with personal armies under the command of various local authorities (Badie and Birnbaum 1982: 108). Despite these inroads, under Louis XVI (1774–92) the aristocracy was able to retain their power and gradually to win a large share in administration (Lefebvre 1947: 19). Eventually they sought control both of the central power and of local administration.

The power position of rulers and their capacity to define goals and to support demands has always depended on the autonomous control of resources. A king could gain autonomy from the local nobility only if he was in a position to establish his own army and bureaucracy and to pay both from his own treasury (Weber 1978: 2:1057, 1092). One way of gaining revenue was to extend market privileges and found cities, in order to obtain high ground-rents and subjects capable of paying high taxes. In the seventeenth and eighteenth centuries, rulers increasingly favored a policy of attracting foreign ethnic or religious groups, both to raise revenues and to undermine the position of resident groups. In Poland, Bohemia, and

Hungary, German colonists were granted royal charters permitting them to acquire property and to pursue trades under their own German law.[25] The kings of Poland invited masses of Jews from western Europe, as well as Germans, into Polish territories. Catherine the Great encouraged substantial German colonization on the Volga and the Black Sea to offset the power of local Tartar communities. The Hapsburgs recolonized lands acquired from the Ottomans with Germans and other minorities to inhibit and contain the Magyars (Pearson 1983: 11). In the eighteenth century, they offered German colonists free land, free houses, and tax exemptions in the Banat (in the Vojvodina). By 1790, German immigrants owned more land in the Banat than any other group (Lampe and Jackson 1982: 64–67).

These policies eventually created a threefold national and social class structure in some areas of eastern Europe: the original conquering races (Magyars, Germans, Swedes, Turks, and Poles) which formed an upper class of landowners and administrators; the conquered serfs (Czechs, Slovaks, Slovenes, Vlachs, Ruthenes, White Russians, Finns, Lithuanians, and the non-Turkish races of the Balkans)[26] who tilled the land; and midway between the two in legal status, the middle class of German, Polish, or Jewish colonists (Macartney 1934: 82–83). In certain parts of Hungary, for instance, the landed gentry were Magyars, the urban middle class German-speaking, the peasants Croat or Slovak natives.

Rulers also gained autonomy through the direct regulation of economic resources and activities. For instance, in France rulers adopted an interventionist policy with regard to industry that worked primarily to make the productive apparatus dependent on the state or subject to its control (Nef 1967: 58–60). First under Richelieu and then under Colbert, the state set up manufacturing enterprises, offered subsidies and privileges as a way of orienting production, and regulated both foreign and internal trade. Later, states obtained outside sources of revenue by allowing a high degree of foreign ownership of industry and a variety of dependency relationships with international capital involving credit, ownership, technology, and marketing.

Another source of power for rulers and ruling groups is control of the population. Charismatic leaders achieve autonomy because they are able to gain control of the population and thus deprive traditional power-holders

25. The German colonists, the new class of burghers, "was an immediate necessity in the political balancing act" (Tihany 1976: 48).
26. The upper classes of the conquered population tended to assimilate culturally to the conquerors. For instance, when the Poles became the ruling class north of the Carpathians, the nobles of Ruthene origin became Polonized. As a result, there were Polish serfs, but there were no Ruthene nobles.

of their major resource. The problem, however, becomes one of institutionalizing, or in Weber's term, "routinizing" charismatic power. Until the emergence of nation-states, the church had been the most successful instrument for institutionalizing control of the masses, but the eighteenth century philosophes made the church the object of continual attack. The rulers of Europe—Frederick II of Prussia, Catherine II of Russia, Joseph II of Austria, Charles III of Spain, Gustavus III of Sweden, and others—read the works of the philosophes and were strongly influenced by them (Gagliardo 1967: 21–23). Everywhere in Europe rulers sought to restrict the church's authority. In 1762, France closed down the Jesuit schools and proceeded to secularize education, placing it under state control. The Jesuits were expelled from France (1764), Portugal (1759), and Spain (1767). By 1772, Pope Clement XIV was forced to give way to the rulers and suppress the Jesuits altogether.

The French Revolution and the rise of nationalism and nationalist movements in Europe reversed this trend. Beginning with the revolution in France, there was a massive resurgence of religion throughout Europe (see Chapter 4), as the church and the aristocracy closed ranks against forces of change that had accelerated under the rule of absolutism. The resurgence of religion in Europe would provide the ideological and cultural apparatus and the institutional vehicle for solidifying the hegemony of the traditional national elite.

Nationalism fused with religion to provide a fundamental basis for national identity and nation-building in the nineteenth century. French Catholics believed that France's special mission was a Christian one, and that a return to the faith was a means of preserving its national unity and reviving its greatness (Zeldin 1970). In Spain and Poland, there was a total fusion of religion and nationality. The main organ of Scottish nationalist identity was its church. The rising of United Irishman in 1798, which had been initiated by Protestants in the north, took on a Catholic character in the south, where it included forced conversions of Protestants. Orthodox Greece achieved its independence from the Ottoman Empire in an uprising that fused religion and nationalism. In Bulgaria and Romania national identity was plainly associated with Orthodoxy. Catholic Croatia and Orthodox Serbia represented unions of religion and nationhood within the state of Yugoslavia after World War I. In the nineteenth century, being Russian and being Orthodox was the same thing. In Switzerland, the Protestant-Catholic War of 1847 consolidated the link between Protestantism and the maintenance of Swiss unity. In Croatia, Ireland, Cyprus, Greece, Poland, Belgium, and Slovakia, bishops spoke for nations. The earliest nationwide movements in Ireland—the campaigns for Catholic emancipation in the 1820s and for repeal of the union in the 1840s—

depended heavily on the work of the clergy (Newsinger 1979: 463).[27] A bishop led Cyprus during its independence struggle, as well as after it. The Slovak People's Party, founded in 1913, was led by a priest, Hlinka; in 1939, an independent Slovakia emerged under Hitler's protection with a Catholic priest, Tiso, as president.

Nationalism was centrally concerned with the struggle for control of the population. The rising danger to the social position of elites was linked specifically and directly to the loss of such control: in France, local administrative reforms and the replacement of church schools with state education; in the Hapsburg state and in the Balkans, monarchical reforms that sought to release the peasants from feudal burdens. Nationalism identified the main sources of national life with the traditional forms of life of the rural population.[28] It extolled the socially conservative peasant mass as the genuine mainstay of the national culture. The nationalist nobility revived peasant costumes, dance, and celebrations; old German or Italian aristocratic families concealed their knowledge of Latin, French, or German, and began to speak Tzechish or Slovenian when they were in the country (Naumann 1916: 88). In sum, nationalism sought to bring potential bases of autonomous state power—bureaucratic, military,[29] economic, and social—under the control of local aristocracies and privileged groups allied with them. This was the central aim, and the central achievement, of nationalism in Europe during the nineteenth and early twentieth centuries.

Nationalism and the Victory of the Aristocracy

Historically, the word "nation" (from Latin natio) was used to designate a restricted social class category—the nobility and the clerical elite (on this, see Zernatto 1944: 352, 355–63); it never refered to people, states, or masses.[30] A movement that arose among the Princes of the Church in the

27. Even at times when relations between the clergy and the revolutionary wing of Irish nationalism became strained (e.g., during the Fenian risings and conspiracies in the 1860s), Catholicism remained associated with the nationalist cause.

28. Renner observes that in Austria-Hungary during the nineteenth century, a number of cities changed their nationality, becoming Hungarian or Czech rather than German. German cities, especially Vienna, absorbed an immense influx of nationalities and assimilated them to the German nation. The peasant population is the one that remains national. The peasantry firmly adheres to its nationality as to any tradition, while the city dweller, especially the educated one, assimilates much more easily. See Renner 1902; in Luxemburg 1976: 260, 262.

29. For a discussion of absolutist attempts to make bureaucracies and armies autonomous from local elites, see Halperin 1993.

30. Separate words existed to describe the whole population: populus, peuple, people, popolo, and pueblo (Seton-Watson 1977: 8).

thirteenth century to curtail and restrict the supremacy of the pope resulted in the establishment of representative councils of bishops and prelates called nationes.[31] Nationes thereafter came to mean above all a select or elite representative body.

From the fifteenth century we find the term "nation" used in this way in Europe. For instance, Transylvania in the fifteenth century had three *nationes* recognized by law and represented in the Transylvanian Diet: Hungarian, Székély, and Saxon. Since the Székély and Saxons had no serfs in their communities, the whole population was to some extent represented (Seton-Watson 1977: 8). The Hungarian natio referred, however, not to the generality of the people inhabiting the territory of Hungary or those of Hungarian speech, but only to persons of noble status. In the sixteenth century, Luther distinguished the "nation" of the bishops and princes from the "people" subject to their rule (Hertz 1947). The Peace of Satzmar of 1711, which ended the fighting between Hapsburg and Hungarian forces, referred to the parties involved in the settlement as the Hapsburg dynasty and "the Hungarian nation": here "nation" meant "the barons, prelates, and nobles of Hungary, an exceedingly small part of the population" (Kedourie 1960: 14). The Polish "nation" under the old commonwealth consisted, in law as well as in fact, of the nobility (szlachta), a class which comprised about a tenth of the population (Snyder 1964: 123). The nobility before the French Revolution considered themselves to be a separate nation from the classes below them (Barzun 1932: 228–51).

Eventually, a "nation" was understood as that body of persons who could claim to represent, or to elect representatives for, a particular territory at councils, diets, or estates. By the eighteenth century, "nation" referred to those wealthy and educated classes who considered themselves alone capable of government, prestige, and power. In the 1760s, the French parlements (bodies of magistrates drawn from the privileged classes) announced that they constituted a single united magistracy representing the whole country. Thereafter, the term "nationalist" applied to the parlements (Palmer 1944: 105), and hence "nationalism" referred to the idea of representation by aristocrats (Zernatto 1944: 361).

The French Revolution introduced the vocabulary and rhetoric of nationalism throughout Europe. The revolution, which was initiated by the aristocracy in the name of the nation and of national sovereignty (Lefebvre 1947: 30, 36, 51), represented the culmination of the struggle of the aristocracy against absolutism and state autonomy (Breuilly 1982: 57–61). Throughout the succeeding century, the fusion of state and society ensured

---

31. Nationes of this kind first are found at the Council of Lyon (1274). They are especially significant at the Council of Constance (1414–18).

the economic and political survival of traditional elites and the continuity of traditional relations of authority.

Nationalism in Europe

The history of nationalism in Europe traces a course through the nationalist revolutions in England (1688), France (1789), Serbia (1804–13), Greece (1821–29), and Belgium (1830), the development of Hungarian, Czech, and Romanian nationalist movements (1840s), and the German and Italian movements for national unification (1860s). In England and France, elites sought to gain control of the government of their own states in the name of the "nation." Serbians, Greeks, Belgians, Hungarians, Czechs, and Romanians sought to create independent states by carving out pieces of existing states. Germany and Italy were formed by a series of seizures of territory by small, but ambitious and militarily dominant, states. These nationalisms will be discussed below, followed by brief references to the remaining European states—the Netherlands, Portugal, Spain, Switzerland, Russia, Poland, the Baltics, Ireland, Bulgaria, Albania, and the Scandinavian countries. Some have nationalist histories similar to the ones detailed below, whereas others have histories that appear to fit with none of those to be discussed. A few have no history of nationalism at all.

The *English revolution* of 1688 is usually considered to be the first full manifestation of modern nationalism. Charles II (1660–68), who had been educated at the court of Louis XIV, attempted an imitation of French absolutism and encountered similar difficulties. He struggled to impose tax and judicial reforms against the opposition of the English bourgeoisie. The Glorious Revolution of 1688 eliminated a crucial means for the assertion of monarchical power by securing for the nobility the right of approval over taxation and the assurance that no standing army would be raised. This revolution was "an early compromise" that preserved "the old remnants of feudalism. The old forms of medieval England were not shattered or swept away, but filled with new content" (Luxemburg 1976: 232).

The *French Revolution* began as an aristocratic attempt to recapture the state. The absolute monarchy had preferred to fill official posts with technically competent and politically harmless middle-class men. Throughout the eighteenth century, however, in France as in many other countries, the nobility encroached steadily upon official posts. With footholds established in the local and central administration, they gained fiscal and tax exemptions that helped push France to the verge of bankruptcy. As Georges Lefebvre points out, "Technically the crisis was easy to meet: all that was necessary was to make everybody pay" (1947: 23). By the late

1780s falling real wages, rising inflation, increasing feudal burdens and bad harvests made it impossible to squeeze more from the common people. Faced with financial crisis, Louis's finance minister, Turgot, proposed a reform program that included the abolition of feudal rights and of guild restrictions and the introduction of a general property tax. The parlements defeated the program, but Turgot's successors, Necker and Calonne, took up the plans again, insisting that it would be necessary to tax aristocratic incomes, abolish some guild restrictions, and lighten the feudal burdens of the peasantry.

But proposals to stimulate economic activity and increase the taxable wealth represented more than a threat to noble tax privileges. At stake was the growth of state autonomy, for as Lefebvre notes, "if a budgetary balance could be restored, and maintained through the growth of national wealth, there would be no more need of erratic fiscal expedients and the king would escape from the control of the parlements" (Lefebvre 1947: 24–25). Thus, the aristocracy refused to pay without an extension of their privileges and forced the king to recall that relic of feudalism, the Estates General. They demanded the king recognize that the aristocracy alone had the necessary rank to advise him and to command in his name, and that he grant them a monopoly of employments compatible with that rank (Lefebvre 1947: 15).

Despite the existence of other sources of grievance and discontent, the aristocracy was the only organized group within society that had the means of gaining control of the state, and the only group that sought to do so. Eventually, all classes combined under the leadership of the aristocracy to overthrow the absolutist Bourbon regime and demand a constitutional order. The bourgeoisie sought not a revolution, not a fundamental change in social structure, but inclusion in the ranks of the aristocracy. The financiers were foreigners and Protestants for the most part, especially Swiss, Dutchmen, and Englishmen (Lefebvre 1947: 42). The powerful merchants eventually formed the framework of the constitutional monarchist party. Members of the liberal professions—lawyers, judges, solicitors, notaries and barristers, schoolmasters, printers, and booksellers—sought an expansion of economic opportunity, an opening of careers blocked because of their nonnoble origins. The working class complained above all about scarcity and high prices and demanded employment or increases in wages. The motive force in peasant revolts was usually material want. Their purpose was not to dislocate the administration of the ancien régime.

The transformation of the monarchy into a constitutional government was a reform on which nobles and bourgeois agreed. Division only took place when the aristocracy refused to surrender all the privileges of its position and insisted, in June 1789, on receiving special and separate representation in the Estates General and in the future government of the country. In the restoration that followed the revolution, the aristocracy were able to return to their titles and to much of their land, and to their monopoly of high office in government, church, and army. Though the landlords were formally abolished as an estate, they continued to be at the core of the dominant class throughout the subsequent century.

The *Serbian revolution* was the first major national revolutionary activity to occur in the Balkans. In the initial stages (1804–13), the revolution assumed the form of a limited struggle against the Janissaries (Dahis), who had defied the authority of the Ottoman Porte by forcibly taking over the province's fiscal regime. When the scope of the uprising expanded in a manner detrimental to the interests of the Porte, Ottoman armies were despatched to crush the rebels. After a second Serbian uprising in 1815, an agreement signed by the Serbian leader Milos Obrenovic and the Ottoman Vizier for Serbia provided for the restoration of tax collection by the Serbian notables. Milos used tax revenues to bribe the Ottoman commissioner, who negotiated a formal grant of Serbian autonomy in 1830 and recognized Milos as prince. An added gift of 300,000 piastres to the sultan clinched the deal. More bribery in 1835 secured for the Serbian government exemption from other obligations to the Porte (Lampe and Jackson 1982: 112). Serbian independence was used by Milos and his partners to consolidate their commercial position locally. They monopolized the rural market by denying peddlers access to trade passports and denying rural shops permits to operate. The collection of tariffs, the issuing of licenses for internal as well as external trade, pricing and credit arrangements, monopolies on transport, and the exclusion of foreign traders, were all used blatantly for personal advantage (Lampe and Jackson 1982: 111–19). Of all the Serbian nationalist organizations advocating insurrection, unification, and the formation of a large state, none sought to appeal to the masses (Djordjevic and Fischer-Galati 1981: 127). Though commoners such as Gaj and Mažuranic were among the leading figures in *Croatian nationalism*, the movement could not have succeeded without a significant portion of the nobility, and it avoided any challenge to the nobility's social interests (Banac and Bushkovitch 1983).

Nineteenth-century *Greek nationalism* originated with the Patriarchate and the Phanariote oligarchy (from the wealthy Greek colony in the Phanar section of Constantinople). In the eighteenth century, the Ottoman Porte had become increasingly dependent, financially and politically, on the Phanariote Greeks, particularly in the Romanian provinces and in Serbian territories. Hoping for greater revenues through increased Phanariote economic activity, the Porte helped the Greeks usurp ecclesiastical posts and urban commercial centers of the native clergy and of the local commercial classes elsewhere in the Balkans (Stavrianos 1961: chap. 3). Despite these advantages, Russia, intent on expanding southward into the Balkans, was able to tempt the Greek primates and commercial leaders with promises of redistribution of Ottoman lands and capital to the Greeks, in exchange for their support of Russia's crusade against the Porte (Djordjevic and Fischer-Galati 1981: 56–60).

A secret revolutionary society, the Philiké Hetairia, was organized in Odessa in 1814 with the connivance of the tsar. In 1821, the Hetairia began the war for Greek independence with a revolt in Moldavia and in the Morea.[32] An agreement among the powers of Europe, registered in the London Protocol of 3 February 1830, established an independent Greece with a Bavarian prince, Otto I, as its king. In 1843, a bloodless coup forced Otto to dismiss his Bavarian advisers, appoint a new ministry, and convoke a national assembly dominated by native oligarchs and nobles. Thereafter, the Greek national government adopted the Patriarchate's *Megali* Idea of reviving the Byzantine Empire and attempted to broaden its definition of Greek national frontiers to include territories containing large numbers of Serbs, Bulgarians, Macedonians, and Latin Vlachs, largely on the basis of the authority exercised by the Patriarchate in Istanbul over these people.

Belgian nationalism was the project of the more privileged elements within the Dutch Netherlands. In 1830, both the Walloons and Flemish peoples of Belgium rose up against rule by the Dutch. The leaders of the movement were members of the upper bourgeoisie and, as was the custom of their class, admirers of the French language and French culture and despisers of the Flemish language and the Netherlandish culture (Clough 1930: 48). The wealthy Francophile leaders of the Belgian nationalist movement offered the Belgian crown to a royal heir of France (when he refused, they offered it to a German prince), and French was proclaimed as the only official language of the state of Belgium in one of the first acts of the provisional government of the new state. Though more than half the population spoke Flemish (57 percent in 1846), French was the language of those who at that time wielded political and economic power. The proclamation gave rise to a struggle for emancipation spearheaded by the Flemish Movement, whose aims were political and economic as well as cultural (De Vries 1976: 1–2). In the conflict that developed between the Walloons and the Flemish, the Walloons sought to retain their dominant status, despite their fewer numbers, and the Flemings demanded a greater share in political, administrative, and economic life commensurate with their numbers.

---

32. See Dakin 1973; Woodhouse 1952. For the ecclesiastical role in the Greek national movement, see Frazee 1969. For the vicissitudes of the *Megali* Idea, see Driault and Lhéritier 1925.

As with French nationalism, *Hungarian nationalism* was initiated by the nobility in reaction to monarchical reforms. At the end of the eighteenth century, Joseph II (1765–90) attempted to reform the empire. In 1781 and 1785, Joseph II decreed the abolition of serfdom and of the guilds, and toleration for the denominations. The Hungarian nobility were able, however, to block serious land and tax reform, as well as state investment to aid the mass of peasants. Measures intended to improve the peasants' lot were rescinded completely after Joseph's death.

The peasants bore the entire burden of support for the state and the public services, as the nobles were exempt from any kind of taxation. Throughout the eighteenth century, this exploitation led to continual, often violent, tensions between the peasantry and the nobility. In order to force the aristocracy of Hungary, Transylvania, and Poland to accept administrative reforms, Joseph II threatened to support an uprising of the peasantry against the aristocracy (Fejtö 1948: 16). This strategy was later used by the Austrian government against the Polish nobility in Galicia when they revolted against Austrian domination in 1846 and had, at that time, a powerful effect on the nobility, not only in Hungary but in Austria's Italian lands as well (Kieniewicz 1948–49). During the 1848 revolution, Francis Joseph (1848–1916) sought to crush the Magyar nationalists by backing a rebellion of the minorities under Magyar domination. Playing off the Slavs (who were demanding independence from Hungary) against them, Francis Joseph sent a Croatian nationalist force against the Magyars (July through September 1848). Following their defeat in 1849, the Hungarian nobility lost their exemption from taxation.

In order to forestall a revolutionary rising of Magyar peasants and workers and of national minorities during the Austro-Prussian War of 1866, the Magyar nobility accepted the Ausgleich, or Compromise of 1867. This compromise secured Magyar hegemony over the Slav majority and gave the Magyar nobility a position of equality, in some respects of privilege, in the new state of Austria-Hungary. The Magyar nobility ruled over all of the Hungarian part of the empire until 1918 and pursued a policy of Magyarization towards the Slav majority under its domination, in repudiation of the Hapsburgs' tolerant Law of Nationalities (1868). After the turn of the century, improved representation was extended to non-German minorities within Austria by the Moravian Compromise of 1905, the Bukovina Compromise of 1910 and the Polish-Ruthenian Compromise of early 1914. Liberal elements within the government were spreading the principle of Ausgleich as far and as rapidly as politically feasible until the very outbreak of World War I.

Czech nationalism emerged in reaction to the same reform measures that fueled the Hungarian nationalist movement. The reforms of Joseph II threatened the ancient Czech laws that for centuries had protected the feudal rights of the Bohemian nobility. In 1848, however, democratic and socialist revolutionary ferment in the Czech provinces threatened to put an end to the privileged position of the nobility "from below." In March of that year, artisans and guild and factory workers formed an assembly to draft a list of demands for social reform, including the right of labor to organize and wage controls. The assembly called for a committee, composed of representatives of all classes, including members of the nobility, to draft a petition to be presented to the Austrian emperor. The resulting petition, which came to be known as the Twelve Articles of Saint Wenceslas, included the demand for the complete equality between Bohemia's Czech and German populations in the schools and in government service. But after the petition was drafted, the noble elements in the assembly took control of the enterprise. The petition finally presented to the emperor made no mention of improving the peasants' lot or abolishing statute labor and the landowners' judicial powers, nor did it refer to the workers' demands for labor organization, the guarantee of work, and fixed wages. When a movement was formed to draft a second, stronger petition, the Governor President of Bohemia, Count Rudolf Stadion, created another body, a "National Council," which effectively suppressed the Saint Wenceslas Committee and put an end to any representation of the common people and its demands for social reform in the Czech national movement, which eventually became a counterrevolutionary force in the revolutionary events of 1848–49. Thus despite the reforms of Joseph II and despite tensions between the nobility and the monarchy,[33] the threat of revolution from below ensured that up to 1918 the nobility was indifferent to the national question and remained "true Bohemians and good Austrians, loyal to God, King, and Country" (Klima 1949: 284).

German nationalism was dominated by the Prussian landowning aristocracy, the Junkers. For centuries the Hohenzollern rulers and the Junkers had maintained a tacit alliance: the crown ruled the state, and in exchange the nobility occupied positions of honor and profit within the state (Carsten 1954: 272). Rulers secured the support of the landed aristocracy by granting them a monopoly on land, consolidating serfdom, exempting the nobility from taxation, and incorporating them into the administrative structure of the state (Finer 1975: 136). But these measures fiscally strained the cities. When measures of reform were resisted in 1667, Frederick William of Brandenburg-Prussia (1620–88) used troops to impose taxes on the towns, suppress the traditional self-government of the municipalities,

33. For instance, when the central government attempted in December 1846 to replace statute labor and feudal rights by certain taxes in order to lighten the burden carried by the peasants, there was a storm of protests.

and destroy the representative Estates (Braun 1975: 270–71). His successor, Frederick William I of Prussia (1688–1740), instituted far-reaching educational, fiscal, and military reforms; his son, Frederick II (1740–86), introduced legal reforms and sought to extend freedom of religion to all his subjects. Despite these measures, the Prussian nobility not only managed to hang on to its old privileges of landholding and patrimonial justice, but obtained as a new privilege the principal claim on the state's positions (Rosenberg 1958: 66–70, 76, 137–38, 151, 168–73, 209–28). In the nineteenth century, it was the Prussian Junkers who led the movement for German national unification and controlled the machinery of government after unification.[34]

In the *Italian nationalist* wars of independence against Austria in 1848, the Piedmontese aristocracy took the conduct of the war, and the unification of Italy, out of the hands of the Mazzinians, radicals, and moderates. For the aristocracy, national unity was a means of fortifying established interests in Piedmont by enlarging the principality and eradicating the peril of "red republican" anarchy sweeping Italy (Whyte 1975: 423). The aim of the Piedmontese was to replace Austria as the ruling force in Italy. This was shown by its hasty annexation, not only of Austrian Lombardy-Venetia, but of the independent duchies of Modena and Parma, followed by the annexations of Piacenza and of Milan.[35] In 1859, national unification proceeded with the annexation by Piedmont of Emilia and Tuscany. The following year, the final phase of the war for national unification, led by the Piedmontese army, resulted in a transfer of power in the south and the

---

34. See, for instance, Stern 1977a; Dahrendorf 1967; Veblen 1915. In a recent volume on nationalism, Greenfeld (1992: 293–310, 358–78) argues that German nationalism (in contrast to English, French, and Russian nationalism) was a middle-class phenomenon. Focusing on the cultural dimension of German nationalism, Greenfeld argues that while the nobility in Germany embraced French culture, the German Bildungsbürger became suffused with *ressentiment* of France and all things French when frustration with their subordinate position within German society was exacerbated by confrontation with French cultural superiority. It was the *ressentiment* of this element within German society that fueled and directed German nationalism. Greenfeld's argument is compelling but difficult to assess, since her evidence focuses exclusively on culture and the middle classes, and excludes consideration of political, social, economic, and military elites and their relationship to nationalism. Certainly, the aristocracy came to loathe all things French after Napoleon's invasion and the introduction of reforms based on the French example. Following the 1848 revolutions, German nationalism becomes even more exclusively aristocratic and is centrally concerned with imperialism and protectionism.

35. A plebiscite was held to determine whether or not Lombardy and the duchies should be annexed by Piedmont. The alternatives presented were not annexation, on the one hand, and the formation of some sort of independent state, on the other. The choice was either being defended by Piedmont against Austria, or being abandoned to Austria. The people voted for annexation.

establishment of the Kingdom of Italy under the rule of King Victor Emmanuel.

Nationalist revolutions and movements in the Balkans during the nineteenth and twentieth centuries were led by nobles and notabilities in reaction to the Tanzimat (reorganization) reforms undertaken by the Ottoman Empire. In the nineteenth century, the Ottoman state passed a series of measures, collectively known as the Tanzimat, to liberalize the status of the peasant and to allow the merchants economic freedom. Elites, intent on defending their feudal privileges, sought to gain support from the masses in their struggle against the Ottoman Empire through religious and ethnic-national identification.

Balkan nationalist movements and their Great Power sponsors (in pursuit of their own interests in the area) portrayed Balkan nationalism as a movement of oppressed Christians against Turkish Moslem overlords. But most rebellions were either revolts by the nobility against Ottoman reforms designed to benefit the peasants, or uprisings of peasants against their own (ethnic) Mohammedanized nobility—local notables who had become Moslems after the fifteenth century in order to retain their land and other privileges. In Bosnia and Herzegovina, for example, the local Mohammedanized Serbian feudal nobility ruled over the country in an oppressive fashion. In the 1840s, the Ottoman Porte attempted to remove the Bosniak nobles from local military positions, to eliminate requirements for forced labor, and to codify the owner-tenant relationship. The Mohammedanized and Turkicized landowning classes in the provinces resented these reforms. At the same time, among the Christian population there was widespread dissatisfaction due to the slowness of the Porte in applying and implementing reforms to improve their social and economic status. It was the revolts of the nobles against the Sultan's reform measures, however, that eventually metamorphosed into the nationalist revolutions and movements in the Balkans in the nineteenth and twentieth centuries.

Romanian nationalism was the project of the Romanian notabilities (voevods and boyars) seeking to safeguard their traditional noble privileges.[36] Reform measures passed by the Ottoman government to liberalize the status of the peasants in the provinces inspired the local rulers of Wallachia and Moldavia to side with Russia in the Ottoman Empire's war with Russia in 1711. As a consequence, after the war the Sultan decided to replace these local rulers with reliable Greek families from the Phanar district in Constantinople. In order to consolidate their own control over

36. Djordjevic and Fischer-Galati 1981: 38–43. The Russian and South Slav boyar—"noble"— is a Turanian word adopted from the nomad aristocracy of the steppes, first designating the Bulgar ruling class (Dvornik 1962: 121).

the economic and political life of the provinces, the Greek hospodars sought to destroy the pro-Russian and pro-Austrian boyar groups. The rapid promotion of fellow Phanariotes to boyardoms and the implementation of decrees favoring the peasants at the expense of their masters incensed the Romanian aristocracy (Djordjevic and Fischer-Galati 1981: 56). As a result, the Romanian aristocracy looked with great favor on the Russian occupation of the provinces in 1769. The Moldavian aristocracy requested and obtained Russia's guarantee of its "historic feudal privileges," and enjoyed them under Russian suzerainty in an autonomous Moldavia ruled by a boyar oligarchy. In Wallachia, the boyars demanded outright incorporation of their province into Russia, hoping that the provisions of Russia's Charter of the Nobility would be extended also to them (Djordjevic and Fischer-Galati 1981: 61).

In the nineteenth century, the Ottoman Tanzimat reforms precipitated renewed rebellion on the part of the Romanian nobility. During the revolutions of 1848, the boyars in Moldavia and Wallachia sought an extension of their political rights as a safeguard of their noble privileges (Djordjevic and Fischer-Galati 1981: 111–12; Roller 1948: 302–3). The leaders of the Romanian revolution essentially sought to secure extended political rights for the bourgeoisie and lesser aristocracy. Romania was recognized as an autonomous principality within the Ottoman Empire by the European powers in 1862. The united principalities gained full independence in 1877 and were ruled by essentially Francophile wealthy Wallachian boyars, educated in Paris and based in Bucharest (Lampe and Jackson 1982: 25).

Bulgarian nationalism arose within the Ottoman Empire but in opposition to its Russian governor-general (Prince Dondukov) and his Russian-controlled administration. The Treaty of Berlin in 1878 established the modern Bulgarian state. The Bulgarian throne was offered to the German Prince Alexander of Battenberg, who formed his first government from the ranks of the notables. *Albania,* in 1921, was carved out of the Ottoman Empire with aid from Italy and Austria, both of them seeking to thwart the expansion of Slav influence in the Balkans. In 1925, a republic was proclaimed following a rebellion of large landowners, one of whom, Ahmed Bey Zogu, became president. He was later proclaimed King Zog I.

Other nationalist movements predated the nineteenth-century movements that are the subject of this review. *Switzerland* was formed in the thirteenth century in a struggle against the Hapsburgs and acquired its present borders in 1815. The *Netherlands* was created out of the Hapsburg Empire in 1648, after a long bloody war of independence. The war began with a revolt by the high aristocracy against the introduction of modern centralized administration. In other states, nationalism arose in the nineteenth century as a result of foreign occupation. *Polish nationalism* began as a reaction of the nobility to the partition and occupation of their country by Austrians, Prussians, and Russians. The establishment of the state of *Sweden* resulted from the efforts of the local aristocracy to oust Danish invaders in 1520. A noble, Gustavus Vasa, led the revolt against Danish dominion, established his own rule over the country, and then proceeded ruthlessly to lay the bases of a monarchical state in Sweden. *Finland* was united with Sweden from the early Middle Ages until 1809, and then was a Russian grand duchy until 1917. A period of repression from 1910 to 1916 stimulated the growth of national sentiment and the Finns seized the opportunity of revolutionary chaos in Russia in 1917 to proclaim their independence (July 1917).

Nationalist sentiment played no part in the establishment of Portugal and Spain as independent states, but arose much later and only in response to foreign occupation. *Portugal* was formed when the Iberian peninsula was reconquered from the Moors in the twelfth century, and it was ruled as the private domain of successive monarchs. During the Napoleonic Wars, the occupation of Portugal by the French triggered a popular uprising and the expulsion of Napoleon's forces. Liberal and republican revolts in 1820, 1836, 1891, and 1910 were not billed as nationalist revolutions and failed to overturn the traditional order. *Spain* was formed by the sixteenth century from a union of kingdoms with markedly dissimilar cultural traditions and institutions. This process was not considered one of national unification. A revolt against French occupying forces in 1808 might properly be called Europe's first truly nationalist revolt, in the sense of a local popular uprising against foreign invaders.

Other national movements were separatist movements. *Irish nationalism* can be traced to the struggles of the Irish beginning in the twelfth century to free themselves from the yoke of English rule. In 1923 an independent Irish Free State was recognized by the English and granted the same dominion status as Canada. The last formal ties with the British crown were broken in 1948. Under pressure from Sweden, *Norway* declared her complete independence from Denmark in 1815 and her union with the Swedish crown as an independent kingdom. The decision by the Norwegian parliament to dissolve the union with Sweden in June 1905 was confirmed by a plebiscite and accepted by Sweden a few months later. *Denmark*, which appears not to have had a nationalist movement, formed an independent state after the fifteenth century. The *Baltic states*—Lithuania, Estonia, and Latvia—were carved out of the Russian Empire following World War I as a result of the allies' desire to create a defensive line of friendly states to bar the westward spread of communism from Russia.

Conclusions

A common set of elements appears in the nationalist movements and revolutions discussed in this chapter. In most cases, the nobility was the national class and led the movements to form national states. In most cases, the nationalist struggle was motivated by considerations related to the safeguarding of the prerogatives of the traditional nobility, rather than to considerations of culture and race per se. In most cases, the catalyst to national revolt was bureaucratic reform undertaken by absolutist states that challenged the prerogatives of the traditional nobility: the threat of liberal reform triggered the French Revolution; the liberal policies of Hapsburg monarchs gave rise to Magyar and Czech nationalism; Ottoman reforms precipitated Balkan nationalisms. Often the rising danger of revolt from below (Czech, Hungarian, Italian) threatened to open up a second front against the nobility. In some cases, popular struggles for social reform temporarily fused with the national struggle (Italy, France, Czechoslovakia). But in most cases, national struggles had little, if anything, to do with popular sovereignty or social reform. After the establishment of nation-states, the "nation" continued to represent a restricted social-class category. Elites did not seek, nor would they accept, major social and political changes. The instruments of the nation-state were used primarily to enrich and protect the traditional elite.

Nationalism was a movement by privileged classes to systematically eliminate various bases of potential state autonomy. The vocabulary of nationalism, once constructed, became available to all groups for all purposes. Nationalism is used by everyone, as Miroslav Hroch has shown (1985). So while analysts should take nationalism seriously on its own terms, they must also seek to separate rhetoric from reality. Though disadvantaged groups joined nationalist movements in order to acquire democratic rights, as Eric Hobsbawm (1990) and others have argued, and nationalist leaders used the rhetoric of freedom and democracy to mobilize support, the outcome of these movements provides no justification for the association of nationalism in Europe with democracy or freedom.[37] Nationalist movements in Europe were initiated, led, and brought to successful conclusions by the nobility, with the intention not of extending liberties to other classes or groups but of thwarting threats to their own privileges

37. Statements made here regarding the non-association between democracy and nationalism are not positive/logical, but historical/empirical. The arguments presented in this chapter, while perhaps applicable to nationalist movements in other regions and other times, are most likely not applicable to nationalist movements involving the seizure or colonization of land by foreigners and the struggle of indigenous peoples to regain their land and rights. These are relatively straightforward cases which can probably be satisfactorily understood without systematic comparative research and theory-building.

and prerogatives and making more secure their own domination over lower classes and ethnic minorities.

The first nationalisms were conceived in opposition to monarchical reforms. Centralized bureaucratic reform was an essential catalyst of nationalist revolt. Absolutist states had grown up within an international society dominated by a feudal landowning and clerical elite. Eventually, rulers sought to gain autonomy from these elites by developing and bringing various resources and institutional bases of power under the control of the state. When rulers attempted to introduce liberal reforms that threatened to undermine the power of the nobility, the nobility sought to control state institutions and possible sources of autonomous state power. Nationalism was the means by which the nobility pursued and gained this objective.

Animated by the ambition to break the power of the feudal lords and of the Estates, and to unify their dominions under a centralized bureaucratic rule, absolute monarchs had pursued a policy of induction of ethnic minorities for the furtherance of imperial authority. Nationalism targeted foreign and minority elements. It transferred economic power to a dominant "national" group through restrictions on land ownership and through confiscation of properties owned by groups now defined as foreigners or minorities within the national territory. Other restrictions followed to limit the mobility of labor and capital within the national territory. The state apparatus was used to form national markets within and in opposition to the international economy; it served to regulate, control, and restrict the mobility of productive factors internationally and domestically, in order to protect local groups.

Throughout the nineteenth century, state policy created the conditions that permitted the survival of various forms of protection and monopoly. The medieval guilds had been thoroughly absorbed within the institutions of the ancien régime. Their abolition was therefore central to the establishment of state autonomy. Guild and corporate structures were never fully abolished, however. Corporate structures were used both to prevent the popular sector from gaining access to the state and to open up channels of access for dominant groups (see Chapter 6). By gaining privileged access to the state, dominant classes were able to extract unequal advantage from the state and from all the resources at its command.

In Europe, nationalism and its embodiment in the nationalist state represented the victory of the traditional aristocracy. With this victory, the state, far from becoming an autonomous actor, was placed more firmly in the hands of dominant class interests. Nationalism ensured that civil servants would be drawn from local privileged groups. It also eliminated extra-societal sources of military power and deprived foreigners and minorities of their economic power and position. As subsequent chapters will show, the institutions and policies established as a result of nationalist revolutions and movements effectively blocked both the rise to power of new classes and the development of state autonomy.

The emergence of nation-states did not represent a progressive phase in the rationalization of state structures and the growth of state autonomy. The class forces that had worked to establish nation-states were able to block subsequent efforts by governing elites to institutionalize sources of autonomous state power. Some theorists assume that as the state becomes more powerful, it can supersede class interests or can override them in its own interests. But in Europe, the state did not gain autonomy from dominant classes until after the destruction of the traditional class structure in the world wars of the twentieth century. Thus, the growth of state power in the nineteenth century was used to give dominant classes privileged access to national resources, to guarantee the political and economic exclusion of the popular sector, and to prevent the traditional elite from falling victim to the market. In fact, as the next chapter will show, the traditional elite survived as a powerful force in Europe until the twentieth century.

The Erroneous
Class Succession Thesis

Many scholars claim that the social structures typically found throughout the contemporary Third World are not at all like those that characterized European societies during the course of their industrial development. The general assumption is that in the Third World dependent development prevented the indigenous bourgeoisie from acquiring either political or economic hegemony, while in Europe a strong, independent bourgeoisie emerged in the nineteenth century and played an important role in the development of both industrial capitalism and democracy there.

In an influential analysis of Latin American development, Fernando Henrique Cardoso and Enzo Faletto describe two class structures characteristic of Latin American societies. The first, a structure of "oligarchic-bourgeois domination," centers on the alliance of a national bourgeoisie of local producing groups (plantation and mine owners, merchants, and bankers) with local traditional oligarchies and bureaucratic-military states usually opposed to "any effort to convert the dominant paternalism into a more efficient bureaucracy." The second structure, found in countries where mining and plantation enclaves are predominant, is characterized by a weak bourgeois sector and oligarchic groups of large landholders linked to the enclave sectors. Their analysis of these structures, the authors state, "does away with the idea that class relations in dependent countries are like those of the central countries during their early development" (Cardoso and Faletto 1979: 22, 66–73). For what their study and others show is that in the Third World, the industrial capitalist bourgeoisie, if it develops there at all, is either too weak to challenge the power of traditional elites (e.g., Chase-Dunn 1975) or is itself a vital part of the system of domination that perpetuates dependency relations (e.g., Portes 1985; P. Evans 1979; Baran 1957).

In contrast to the alliance of the national bourgeoisie, landowning classes, and the state in contemporary Third World development, industrial development in Europe, according to most accounts, was "promoted and led by an independent capitalist middle class which fought against the old aristocracy as well as against the restrictive power of the state" (Chirot 1977: 223). Some scholars assume that the struggle between the capitalist bourgeoisie and the old aristocracy resulted in the victory of the capitalist class in the course of the nineteenth and early twentieth centuries (e.g., Chirot 1977); others assume that a process of "bourgeoisification" destroyed the old landed class by fusing it with or subordinating it to the new capitalist classes (see, e.g., Cannadine 1990: 391–444; Blum 1978: 422–24; Maier 1975). Still others contend that the European feudal landowning class became a capitalist landed aristocracy in the sixteenth century and so by the nineteenth century there was no feudal aristocracy because its class nature had become thoroughly transformed.[1]

Against these views, this chapter argues that up until the period of the world wars, the traditional aristocracy in Europe retained its wealth and power and played the dominant role in industrial capitalist development. Almost nowhere in Europe was there a strong independent industrial capitalist bourgeoisie in the nineteenth and early twentieth centuries. Often the bourgeoisie either was a foreign class within European societies, or was weak and regionally confined, and consequently dependent on the state or the landholding aristocracy. The old aristocracy absorbed and dominated new wealthy elements and imposed their standards of behavior on them. Landlords and capitalists were not separate and contending classes in Europe during the nineteenth century, but factions of a single dominant class. Traditional and landed elites remained hegemonic within this class until well into the twentieth century, providing leadership and exerting overriding influence even when they were not dominant.

The political and legal framework of modern capitalist states in Europe, as I showed in Chapter 3, was designed by and for traditional elites, and throughout the nineteenth century it worked to strengthen the old order,

---

1. See, e.g., Wallerstein 1974a on the transformation of the feudal landed elite in Europe during the "long sixteenth century." For a further elaboration of the argument and its implications, see the debate between Dobb and Sweezy concerning the transition from feudalism to capitalism in early modern Europe (Sweezy 1954), and between Frank (1967) and Laclau (1971) on Latin American development.

rather than to weaken or liberalize it.[2] In all European countries, most leaders belonged to the landowning aristocracy and state policies were generally consistent with its immediate interests. As a result, industrial capitalist development in Europe was shaped, not by a liberal, competitive bourgeois ethos, but by the conventional mores and organizations of traditional rural society.

The Fusion of the Bourgeois and Landed Elite

It is often assumed that the French Revolution and the repeal of the English corn laws represented a critical turning point in the evolution of class power in Europe: the end of landed power and the beginning of bourgeois hegemony. But in the course of the nineteenth century, landowners and industrial elites—including the landowners and manufacturers of England—became part of a single pan-European elite.

After the French Revolution, émigrés began to return to France, and by 1799 former exiles were living throughout the country. In 1790, the revolutionary governments had sold most of the estates owned by the clergy and many of those owned by the nobility. But these lands were sold to the highest bidder, so most of it was bought by wealthy people who already had land of their own. In fact, in the redistribution of noble land effected by the revolution, the total land owned by the nobility dropped from one-quarter to one-fifth.[3] Thus, though estates changed hands, the structure of landholding remained much the same (Tocqueville 1955: 25).

As the state regained the hierarchical structure that it had had under the ancien régime, returning nobles took up office under Napoleon. After 1806, officeholders were often either drawn from the ranks of new nobles or were themselves ennobled. Napoleon revived the institution of nobility in 1806, and by the end of the Napoleonic Wars he had created 31 dukes, 388 counts, 1090 barons, and about 1500 knights. These he endowed with fine chateaux in the Ile de France and entailed estates from his private domain or from foreign conquests. The old nobility scorned these new notables at first. Old and new aristocracy eventually became fused, how-

2. This theme is treated at length by Max Weber. See, for instance, Gerth and Mills 1946: 228–32.
3. Magraw 1983: 24–25. Formerly it was supposed that the multiplicity of small proprietorships which is the distinguishing feature of rural France today was wholly a consequence of the revolution. Research has shown that, on the contrary, the breaking up of the agricultural lands of France into little holdings was already underway long before 1789. Some scholars maintain that the number of landed proprietorships in France was scarcely smaller before 1789 than it is today. (See Johnson 1979: 155, on the Russian scholar Loutchinsky.)

ever, as common fears and common enemies increasingly united them socially and politically. Thus it was that, following the Napoleonic Wars, the old feudal classes not only returned to their titles and to much of their land, but in fact became the governing class.[4]

In England, the repeal of the corn laws was far less a consequence of the strength of rising new industrial classes or the weakness of declining landed ones, and had far less impact on the social structure of rural England, than is often supposed. "Ultimately," as John Morley wrote in his life of Cobden (1882: 215; in Bairoch 1993: 20), "it was because of the very wet summer and autumn of 1845, together with the potato crop in Ireland, that the Corn Laws were repealed. . . . It was the rain that rained away the Corn Laws." The wide range of divergent interests and opinions that joined the crusade for repeal of the corn laws had come together for that sole purpose and afterward dissolved. After the repeal of the corn laws, Richard Cobden tried to rally forces around a campaign for free trade in land: the breakup of estates, the diffusion of land ownership, and the end of landlordism. However, the campaign rallied all landowners and wealthy business men together in opposition to it, and as a result helped to fuse the old landed gentry and the new industrialists into a new ruling class (Thompson 1963: 284–85). This process of fusion was effectively achieved following the revolutionary events of 1848.

In east-central Europe, the development of an export-oriented agriculture strengthened the large landowners and reinforced their social domination. As the production of wheat, cereals, and other foodstuffs for foreign (mainly English) markets at the end of the eighteenth century raised land values, landlords began to squeeze the peasants off the land. By the mid- to late nineteenth century, they had converted the peasantry into a subordinate, landless tenantry. The rise of world grain prices in the nineteenth century steadily increased the prosperity of Prussian and other east European landlords and enabled them substantially to enlarge their holdings. Throughout the nineteenth century they successfully undermined attempts to make the peasants independent of their control and minimized the impact of reforms that might have created an industrial competitor for their labor force (Blum 1978: 406–9, 429–30; Tipton 1976: 119; Rosenberg 1966: 225–28).

In Germany, industrialization reinforced the preindustrial political and social order (Stern 1977a: 45; Dahrendorf 1967: 46–60; Rosenberg 1966: 44; Veblen 1915: 199, 204–9). Between 1820 and 1850, the traditional nobility

4. The fortunes of the French nobility during and after the revolution are sympathetically recounted in Montagu 1970: 29–60. Even Marx recognized that in France under the second Bonaparte the state machinery was completely independent of the bourgeoisie and of bourgeois society (1963: 121–22, 131).

consolidated its leading position within the administrative services and its monopoly of the top positions in the army.[5] Then, during the 1850s, "the Prussian nobility rose to its political flowering" (Tönnies 1912: 1057; in Stern 1977a: 55). In the middle of the century, Engels noted that, except in the Rhineland, there was no independent, politically conscious bourgeoisie to be found in Germany. "The feudal nobility in Germany had retained a great portion of their ancient privileges. The feudal system of tenure was prevalent almost everywhere. The lords of the land had even retained the jurisdiction over their tenants." They had preserved "almost all their medieval supremacy over the peasantry of their demesnes, as well as their exemption from taxes." This feudal nobility "was considered, officially, the first 'Order' in the country. It furnished the higher government officials, it almost exclusively officered the army" (Engels 1969: 12). At the beginning of the twentieth century, Max Weber observed that a politically conscious German bourgeoisie had not yet emerged (Weber 1958a, 1958b) and he wrote of the "feudalization" of the German bourgeoisie (Mommsen 1984: 91–100). The feudal nobility retained their hegemony through the first decades of the twentieth century. Their positions at court, in the government, and in the military, their hold on provincial and local administration, epitomized by their continued heavy presence as Landräte or country councillors, provided them with sufficient political power to forestall their ultimate decline until after the world wars.[6]

As in France, the traditional elite regained its status in Italy and was restored to power following the Napoleonic Wars.[7] We have seen that the

---

5. "In 1859 two thirds of all lieutenants, three quarters of the senior officers, nine tenths of the generals were noblemen. Their actual influence in the army was even greater, since the bourgeois element was largely concentrated in the technical branches" (Holborn 1969: 137).
6. David Blackbourn and Geoff Eley have argued that a successful bourgeois revolution of the sort that supposedly failed to occur in Germany in 1848 never took place anywhere else in Europe (1984: 51–61; see also Collins 1995). Their work has added fuel to the debate which began in the late 1970s over the German *Sonderweg*. The notion of a German *Sonderweg* (which, before World War II, had positive connotations) refers to supposed aberrations of German history which had precluded the development of liberal democracy in Germany, including the absence of a bourgeois revolution, its strong statist tradition, and the role of the Prussian military. Blackbourn and Eley argue that these supposed peculiarities of German development are not peculiar at all, but were consistent with the experience of Britain and other European countries. Their arguments comparing German to European development in the nineteenth and early twentieth centuries might be seen as an analogue to mine comparing European to non-European industrial capitalist development.
7. Many of the nobility had lost money or property during the wars, however, and were unable to retrieve their economic position. In Naples efforts were made to resuscitate the nobility by restoring the system of entail and primogeniture, but few big estates were able to keep clear of heavy mortgages. The big landlords increasingly lived in Rome and farmed out their estates to wealthy merchants. Only in Tuscany and, more particularly, in Piedmont were the nobility able to regain both their social and economic preeminence (Montagu 1970: 117–20).

Piedmontese nobility played the key role in the Risorgimento, and they continued to dominate the Italian state following unification and throughout the nineteenth century. Though mercantile and professional elements entered into government and administration after the Risorgimento, the social status of Italy's traditional nobility remained unchanged. In the 1890s, Marxist critiques condemned the "failure" of the Risorgimento to destroy the old feudal order. The bourgeoisie, wrote Engels, had been "neither able nor willing" either to destroy "the relics of feudalism" or to reorganize national production "along the lines of a modern bourgeois model" (Engels 1895: 23–24).

In Spain, the aristocracy grew in strength and numbers during the nineteenth century. Five revolutions failed to bring about a transformation of the social structure, and reforms failed to dismantle the nobility's great latifundia in the southern part of the country. Forced sales of ecclesiastical holdings through auction (desamortización) enabled wealthy urban residents to buy up holdings owned by urban ecclesiastical institutions. Since the new owners rented out the land to peasants as the church had done before, local land distribution and local social structures—minus the clergy as a separate landed class—were preserved (Carr 1966: 274–75).

Though the buyers of the church lands were urban residents, the new landed elite that took shape was not bourgeois, either culturally or economically. Many of these urban residents were members of landed families who had moved to the cities. Moreover, marriages between the landed elite and urban families absorbed the latter into the culture and political objectives of the landowners.

> Not all owned land before, but throughout Spain they all formed part of a social structure long geared to agriculture as the final source of income. As the century progressed the really large properties everywhere often went to distant men of wealth, especially in Madrid, some of them speculators, some merchants, some government officials, and some also landowners. . . . The landed elite soon absorbed socially and culturally those outsiders who bought large holdings. (Herr 1977: 103, 108–9)

The Spanish system of sale thus concentrated land in the hands of a new class of absentee landlords that tended to identify with the landowning aristocracy and thus maintained traditional agrarian patterns (Nadal 1973). Successive revolutions also failed to bring about a transformation of the traditional social structure in Portugal. During the nineteenth century, the mercantile and landowning nobility grew stronger. Land tenure in agriculture remained neofeudal at least up to World War II (Holland 1979).

In the Balkans, the development of a market economy and the expansion of production did not produce a new elite or new relations of production. Throughout the area, the nobles and great landowners dominated virtually the whole of agricultural and manufacturing production (Braudel 1982: 270–72). There was no major transformation of agriculture and industrial-urban development.[8] In fact, feudal features appeared, in some places for the first time, alongside the emerging market economy.

The agricultural depression that began in the 1870s inspired Europe's landowning classes to adopt industrial interests on a large scale. Since the aristocracy owned most of Europe's land they also possessed the lion's share of its mineral resources—tin and copper, lead, iron ore, and coal. Most of England's wealthiest aristocrats in 1914 depended to a great extent on nonagricultural sources of income. In large part, the wealth of dukes, earls, and marquesses was owed to coal, which in 1914 was still the world's prime source of energy (Rubinstein 1981: 194; Spring 1971: 30–37).

Of the eleven richest Prussians in 1913, six were Upper Silesian aristocratic industrialists. The mining and industrial center of Silesia was the world's greatest zinc producer, and its coal deposits were exceeded in Europe only by those of the English Midlands. In the two decades before 1914, profits from Silesian coal and zinc soared (Lieven 1992: 130–31). The great aristocrats were crucial for Silesian development (members of the German nobility developed the iron and machine-building industries and played a prominent role in linen manufacture as well). As the only people who could supply both capital and entrepreneurship, they were joined, but never supplanted, by a handful of rich bourgeois.

Following the depression of the 1870s, and increasingly during the 1880s and the 1890s, there was a general movement by landowners to spread their assets by investing on the stock exchange. Increasingly, the great estate and the large corporation became bound together by overlapping and common economic interests. By 1896, more than one quarter of the British peerage held directorships, most of them in more than one company (Montagu 1970: 170). Younger sons of the nobility went into the professions. In the 1880s, almost without exception, the most successful lawyers came from titled and landed families (Cannadine 1990: 250).

When the Hapsburg Empire abolished forced labor[9] during the Revolution of 1848, many landlords converted themselves into great capitalists,

8. See the discussion of the Ottoman provinces in Chapters 2 and 3. Lampe and Jackson point out that Ottoman institutions prior to the emergence of a market economy were neither precapitalist nor feudal, and they suggest that the phrase "command economy," with its connotation of centralized government control of production and full access to any surplus for supporting the state, fits far better (1982: 12–13). In the Ottoman provinces it was only with the emerging market economy that feudal features first appeared. Elsewhere in eastern Europe there emerged what is called the Second Serfdom, or refeudalization. See, for instance, Blum 1957; Gestrin 1962; Rosenberg 1966: 28–29, 44, 226.
9. The "robot" system had required tenants to put in a fixed amount of work with their own teams of animals on their landlords' lands.

using the compensation money paid them by the state to invest in new agricultural machinery, sawmills, and sugar-beet factories. A few noblemen became entrepreneurs and industrialists, mining coal, manufacturing paper, and investing in spas and hotels. In Bohemia, nobles played the leading part in the development of heavy industries, sugar refineries, and the glass and textile industries (Langer 1969: 48). After 1918, when the laws of entail were abolished in the former Hapsburg lands and heavy taxes laid on city property virtually eliminated private incomes from house rents, aristocrats began increasingly to supplement their reduced incomes by speculating on the stock exchange.

At the same time that the aristocracy was investing in and developing industry and entering the professions, the most enterprising and successful members of the merchant class were lifted into the aristocracy. These gravitated to the land and there assumed the privileges and authority of nobles. Few bourgeois fortunes remained invested in trade or industry for more than two or three generations. Capital accumulated in business was continually drained off into land, office, and the trappings of aristocratic status. So seriously were trade and industry weakened by this trend that the state began to stipulate that patents of nobility were conditional on continuance of the family enterprise. On the whole these efforts to keep the bourgeois a bourgeois were not successful.

In England, only the ownership of property brought with it political rights. As a consequence, social barriers between the nobility and the bourgeoisie were much less important. Financial and industrial occupations were also more viable socially and did not lessen the prestige of land ownership (Spring 1977: 13; Habbakuk 1967: 12, 15). The dominant class thus became an "active symbiosis of two social strata, one of which supported the other economically but was in turn supported by the other politically" (Schumpeter 1947: 136–37).

The Hegemony of the Landed Elite within the Dominant Class

Within the dominant class, the landed elite was the hegemonic element, imposing their own particular interests and ethos on the class as a whole. They retained this capacity until World War II. Throughout the nineteenth century, the nobility in Europe was an expanding, not a declining class.[10]

10. From 1871 to 1918, the German emperor created over a thousand new nobles. The English peerage, always considerably smaller than its continental counterparts, was increased by the creation of two hundred new peers between 1888 and 1914 (Tipton and Aldrich 1987a: 77). The number of Spanish aristocrats grew considerably in the nineteenth century. In Spain there were 118 grandes and 535 other titled nobles in 1787. By 1896 the numbers had risen to 207 and 1206, roughly double the totals of 1787 (Herr 1977: 99).

In fact, with the creation of new peerages, the hereditary peerage grew more rapidly than ever before. While these new creations brought in bankers and businessmen, the great majority still originated from traditional stock (Montagu 1970: 172). It was not until 1905 that the creation of nonlanded peerages began on a lavish scale, and not until 1945 that peerages were given to those who had no large income (Cannadine 1980: 21). Out of the 246 new peerages granted in Britain between 1886 and 1914, some 200 individuals entered the nobility for the first time. More than a third of these (70) represented new industrial wealth, but three-quarters of those were sons of men who had acquired landed status. Another third had risen in the professions and diplomacy, but a good proportion of those were younger sons of the nobility and gentry. Hence in terms of their family backgrounds, more than half the new peers still came from landed circles (Thompson 1963: 294).

As for the new wealthy elements, these were absorbed and dominated by the old aristocracy. The traditional elite was successful in accommodating, absorbing, and containing newcomers largely because the new elements did not form a counter-elite to challenge it but sought only to join. Many of the new rich—South African millionaires, international financiers, grocery-chain proprietors—were eager to adopt the conventions of the old aristocracy and to promote its institutions and values (Guttsman 1954: 22). Thus at the end of the nineteenth century, "a certain amount of new wine had been poured into old bottles, and the bottles had not cracked" (Thompson 1977: 37).

In Germany, traditional aristocratic modes of life and values exercised hegemony over new elites. Rich entrepreneurs bought up landed estates, and once on those estates, emulated the style of life there. They had their portraits painted and their family trees refurbished; they sought out distinctions, orders, titles, and ennoblement (Stern 1977a: 60). "The change in ownership personnel did not seriously impair the cohesion of the Junker squirearchy, since, as a rule, social mobility was accompanied by rapid assimilation between the newcomers and the old established elements. But as to political leadership, social mores, and ideological outlook, it was the old landed nobility which continued to set the standards that governed the life of the landed aristocracy as a whole" (Rosenberg 1966: 221). As late as 1914, Robert Michels observed that the German bourgeoisie sought to be accepted by the nobility in order to be dissolved in it (Michels 1914: 143; in Stern 1977a: 64).

Industrialization in eastern Europe did not eliminate the nobility from its commanding position. Until the end of World War II, the political and social history of eastern Europe "was in large part the history of the continued dominance, political and social, of the nobility and the attempts of others to unseat or restrict it" (Banac and Bushkovitch 1983: 1). The nobility continued to control an enormous portion of the land. Where many of them invested in industry, as in Bohemia, the new economic order merely perpetuated the noble dynasties on a renewed basis. The nobility played a leading role in the Hapsburg bureaucracy, the army, and especially in the court circles that continued to be an important factor in the political life of the empire until its demise in World War I (Banac and Bushkovitch 1983: 1).

The Italian nobility had, for centuries, been an amalgam of agrarian and mercantile families. While wealthy merchants acquired landed estates and titles, the old feudal families branched out into commerce and trade. But the gradual fusion between them took a "nobiliar form" (Mayer 1981: 123). Throughout the nineteenth century, the elite retained a feudal rather than a bourgeois character (Gramsci 1949; Engels 1894).

The hegemony of the landed elite within the dominant class is evidenced by their occupancy of positions within the state apparatus—in the executive and in the cabinets of presidents and prime ministers—as well as in parliament and other local and national legislative bodies. During the nineteenth century, officials throughout the various components of the state system were drawn from agrarian elites directly, or the occupants of these positions were absorbed into the agrarian elite.

The class power of the landed elite was also evident in the direction of state policies regarding issues that at different times were sources of political rivalry between landlords and capitalists: free trade versus protection, public investment in infrastructure, differential taxation on landed property and capital, the alienability of landed property, the mobility of wage labor, the prices of foodstuffs, and controls on agricultural commodities and capital goods. State policies with regard to these issues protected landlords from experiencing significant political setbacks until after World War II.

Political Leadership

The political leadership of all European countries was drawn from the ranks of the aristocratic landowning classes. In England, the state remained an "administration of notables" until the twentieth century (Weber 1978: 2:1974). Having won the repeal of the corn laws, industrial manufacturers in Britain had no interest in challenging the political and social leadership of the landed elite. The British landowning elite were a hereditary political class, "men with the self-confidence to govern and legislate, men with the independent means and the leisure needed for membership of the House." The expense involved in being a member of parliament ensured that "as long as they pursued sensible policies with reasonable regard for the interests and opinions of others," businessmen, shopkeepers, and tradesmen would be content to entrust their representation to the landed elite (Thompson 1963: 276–77). Thus, despite franchise changes in the 1830s and 1880s, top jobs and key positions remained in the hands of the landowners (Thompson 1977). Until 1905, every British cabinet, whether Conservative or Liberal, was dominated by the traditional landed elite, with the brief exceptions of the Liberal ministries of 1892–95. Of the eighty-one ministers in the cabinets during the period 1832 to 1866, sixty-four were aristocrats, twelve were lawyers, five were primarily businessmen (Thomas 1939: 4). Between 1868 and 1886, two-thirds of the forty-nine cabinet members were either from landowning families or from families closely linked with the aristocracy in the church, the services, and diplomacy. In 1900, the cabinet included Robert Arthur Talbot Gascoyne-Cecil, ninth Earl and third Marquess of Salisbury, whose illustrious ancestor had served Queen Elizabeth; the Marquess of Lansdowne, Secretary for War, whose subsidiary title went back to 1181 and whose grandfather had been Prime Minister under George III; and the Duke of Devonshire, the Lord President of the Council, who owned 186,000 acres in eleven counties, and whose ancestors had served in parliament since the fourteenth century (Montagu 1970: 158). In 1924, at least half the cabinet were landowners; in 1937 the aristocratic contingent was not much smaller (Cannadine 1990: 207). It was not until 1908 that the first prime minister took office who did not own a landed estate (Herbert Henry Asquith). In 1914, the Foreign Office and diplomatic service were still strongholds of the landed classes.

The social composition of Parliament remained the same throughout the nineteenth century. The House of Lords was the preserve of the landed aristocracy. The supreme embodiment of institutionalized aristocratic power and hereditary political privilege, it retained the unchallenged right to veto virtually all legislation initiated in the Commons until 1911. In 1911, there were more than 570 hereditary members of the House of Lords, and not more than one-eleventh came from the business world, although perhaps as many as one-sixth were first generation peers from nonlanded backgrounds (Thompson 1963: 297). The Commons remained an assembly of the younger sons of the nobility and placemen of influential magnates. Landed families continued to furnish a majority of the House of Commons until 1885 (Thompson 1963: 276).

It has been argued that the French aristocracy "disappeared from the political arena as a coherent and effective political group" in the Revolution of 1830 (Moore 1966: 106). But during the Second Empire (1852–70) the bureaucracy fell completely into the hands of the traditional ruling classes and was reduced to a "parasitic excrescence." In elections held in February 1871, over two-thirds of the deputies elected to the Chamber of Deputies were local notables from old aristocratic families (Cole and Campbell 1989: 48–54). The state bureaucracy still recruited from the privileged social strata at the beginning of the Fourth Republic in 1945 (Badie and Birnbaum 1982: 113–14).

The German bureaucracy remained under the control of the aristocracy throughout the nineteenth century (Weber 1978: 2:1974; Rosenberg 1966: 43, 44, 199, 217, 218). In 1910, nobles occupied nine out of eleven cabinet positions, the upper legislative house, 25 percent of lower legislative seats, 55 percent of all army ranks of colonel and above, 80 percent of ambassadorships, eleven out of twelve administrative headships, twenty-three out of twenty-seven regional administrative headships, and 60 percent of all prefectures (Goldstein 1983: 252). In 1913, 75 percent of the upper house in the Prussian Landtag, and over a fourth (119) of the 443 members of the lower house were nobles (Blum 1978: 420). The Catholic Center Party, the largest party in both the national and Prussian legislatures until 1912, had aristocrats lead its Reichstag faction.

Though Sweden did not have a powerful landed upper class, in the late nineteenth century it nontheless "rivalled Germany in the perpetuation of late medieval political forms" (Lipset 1983). Sweden's "highly status-conscious nobility," which dominated the officers' corps and the upper ranks of the bureaucracy, looked to imperial Germany "for its models in social organization and culture" (Rueschemeyer et al. 1992: 92). In 1908, nobles occupied six out of eleven cabinet positions, 35 percent of commissioned officers in the armed forces, thirteen out of twenty-three county governorships, and a very sizable proportion of the upper governmental bureaucracy. In the mid-1920s, the nobility still dominated the higher echelons of Sweden's bureaucracy (Samuelsson 1968: 214).

Right up to the eve of the revolution of 1917, the Russian governmental apparatus was dominated exclusively by the nobility (Beetham 1974: 199). In 1890, new legislation increased noble representation in the zemstvos, so that nobles came to make up 55.2 percent and 89.5 percent respectively of the district and provincial zemstvos. An imperial decree in June 1907 enabled the nobility, who formed less than 1 percent of the population, to hold more than half the seats in the Third and Fourth Dumas (Blum 1977: 91).

State Policies

State policies were generally consistent with the immediate interests of the landlords. As a result, landowners did not experience significant political

setbacks with respect to tariffs, labor legislation, land reform, state alloca-
tions, tax policy, or internal terms of trade until after World War II. Protectionism, rather than free trade, characterized the nineteenth century in
Europe. The period 1860–79 represents the only free-trade interlude in an
otherwise protectionist century (see Chapter 6). The protectionist trend
after 1879 continued until 1914.

While tariff policy varied throughout Europe and fluctuated during the
nineteenth century, nowhere and at no time was agriculture left without
substantial protection. Germany maintained tariff protection in favor of
East Elbian grain producers from the mid-1870s onward. It was only by the
aid of tariffs and other special favors that German agriculture maintained
even the semblance of prosperity after 1870 (Ogg 1930: 200). France
developed a comprehensive system of agricultural protection from the
1880s on (Meredith 1904: chaps. 4 and 5).

Agriculture was also protected by state tax and pricing policies. When
states found it necessary to control the prices of grain and other food
staples in order to reduce the wage bill for industrialists, legislation put a
floor under agricultural prices to prevent them from dropping too low and
cutting into the profits of large landowners. Wholesale and retail price
controls on agricultural products and taxes on their export were also offset
by low agricultural land taxes.

The landowning elite was able to preserve the existing pattern of land
ownership by blocking efforts at agrarian reform. Land reform was not
successfully undertaken in Europe until after World War II. On the eve of
World War I, the system of great estates remained largely unaltered in
Britain (Cannadine 1990: 142), and agrarian reform was one of its major
problems. As Lloyd George repeatedly affirmed, land was the greatest and
the least controlled of all monopolies in England. The great landowners
kept vast stretches of fertile land in a state of total undevelopment and
fixed the conditions under which the remainder of the land could be
utilized. In 1914, large estates and labor shortages were still major problems for Germany. In Italy and Spain there was little change in the conditions surrounding large holdings and the numbers of landless workers
prior to World War I (Clough 1952: 576).

Landowners saw to it that labor organization was effectively prohibited
or efficiently controlled. They maintained the social and political isolation
of agrarian labor, exempted their resident tenants and other workers from
labor legislation, and prevented them from securing the right to organize,
until after World War I. While the agrarian and industrial elite were seldom in complete agreement with regard to economic policies, they were of
a single mind about maintaining patriarchal labor relationships. The corporatist arrangements that emerged throughout Europe during the inter-

war years are testimony to the political and social consensus shared by these groups (see Chapter 6). Occasionally the Catholic Center Party (the largest party in the Reichstag until 1912) supported liberal legislation, but only to the extent that it left traditional rural life unaffected. For instance, it advocated workers' protection but argued against extension of the legislation to agricultural workers, on the ground that it would disturb the "patriarchal relationship" which still existed on the land (Evans 1981: 88).

In Russia, Tsar Alexander II (1855–71) was forced by pressures beyond his control to order the freeing of the serfs. The nobles were made to turn over about half of their land to the now free peasants, but were well compensated.[11] However, the liberation of the serfs in Russia, as elsewhere in Europe (e.g., Prussia and Silesia in 1810), did not destroy the power of the landowning class, but only reformulated the terms under which it operated. After emancipation the political rights of the landholders were extended (without a corresponding expansion of the rights of other groups). Laws continued to guarantee them preferential treatment in court proceedings, a special role in preserving law and order at the village level, the authority to entail property above a certain size, and a tax rate on land that was about half that levied on peasant land (Blum 1977: 80). Despite these advantages, and partly due to the fact that more and more landowners were becoming absentee proprietors, the wealth and status of the nobility had declined by the 1880s. It became a central aim of the government of Alexander III (1871–94) to reverse this trend. The government established a Land Bank for the Nobility in 1885 to provide them with cheap credit. It created the office of Land Captain (zemskii nachal'nik) in 1889 to restore to the nobility its authority in the countryside, with powers over the peasants as extensive as in the days of serfdom (Charques 1965: 32).

The Bases of Landed Power in Europe

The hegemony of the landed elite within the dominant class rested on their secure power base in rural areas. In 1914, most of Europe was still rural and "pre-eminently pre-industrial" (Mayer 1981: 187, 301). Agriculture

11. The emancipation statute ordered the peasants to compensate the landowners for the land that they had relinquished. The state advanced 75 to 80 percent of the cost of the land to the landowners in the form of special government bonds. The peasants were to pay back the state for this advance over a period of forty-nine years. The statute stated that landowners were to be indemnified only for the loss of their land and were to receive nothing for the loss of the person and labor of their serfs. The state evaded its own legislation, however, by setting the price of the land allotted to the peasant at 20 to 90 percent above its current market price. See Gerschenkron 1965: 722–43.

was still the single largest and weightiest sector in all the continental countries. Even after World War I, France drew her wealth principally from agriculture and approximately half of her population was engaged in agricultural pursuits (Ogg 1930: 185). In 1914 almost half of western Europe's working population was still employed in agriculture (including fishing and forestry), and rural dwellers still made up the largest part of the population in all the countries of continental Europe except Germany. In many western European industrial countries, the absolute numbers of those employed in agriculture did not decline dramatically until after 1945, when mechanization of production increased significantly. Thus it was that the great landowners' monopoly of most arable and irrigated land and their control of the rural population—of its vote as well as its labor power—guaranteed them a continuing base of political and economic power.[12]

Rural Europe before 1945

Until World War I, agrarian relations in Europe were relatively stable, resting on paternal (i.e., authoritarian and hierarchical) relations between the landowner and the resident laborers. While new industrial elites were struggling against a militant, highly self-conscious, and politically radical working class in the mines and factories, landowners were secure in their hold on agrarian labor until after World War I. In 1914, European aristocracies still had the support of their rural base—not only the peasantry but the tenant farmers who were crucial subelites in the countryside (Lieven 1992). In fact, landowners continued to enjoy a secure base of social and political power in rural Europe until World War II (Thompson 1963: 337; Cannadine 1980: 21).

Landowners were able to preserve their control of local government until after World War I, and in some places beyond. In Britain, rural government and justice was dominated by the exclusively aristocratic Lords Lieutenant of the counties. These Lords Lieutenant had a decisive influ-

---

12. Karl Kautsky's study (1899) of capitalism and agriculture challenged the classical Marxist view that, as peasant economies were transformed by capital, the peasantry would become assimilated to petty commodity production and cease to exist. Kautsky recognized that the peasantry might endure within the general framework of capitalism and that precapitalist and noncapitalist forms of agriculture were, in fact, persisting within capitalist societies of his day (1899: 1–3). This triggered a controversy over the "agrarian question" among his contemporaries. In fact, the agrarian question—whether Marx had overemphasized the extent to which capitalism would wholly transform society—became a central issue within European socialist parties. However, as Alavi and Shanin point out, Kautsky's work "has been neglected by twentieth century theorists not only in the context of European rural history but also, and especially, in that of changes in the contemporary peasant societies of the third world" (1988: xi).

ence on the appointment of Justices of the Peace—unpaid oligarchs, predominantly landowners, who ruled the countryside. The Local Government Act of 1888 installed elected county councils in place of the justices; however, the first elected county councils were composed predominantly of members of the upper class (Keith-Lucas and Richards 1978), and in many areas of England, the aristocracy and gentry continued to dominate local government through these new councils.[13] In France, village mayors, departmental councillors, deputies, and senators were usually drawn from the ranks of the landowners (Wright 1964: 14–18).

The Prussian Landrat, the key figure in local government in Prussia until 1914, was both an official of the central government and the representative of the landowners. Until 1872, the Landrat was selected by the king from candidates elected by landowners. After 1872, the government changed the electoral college in order to make the selection somewhat more democratic. Despite the change, however, in 1914 well over half of the Prussian Landrate were still noblemen (Spring 1977: 14; Lieven 1992: 215–16).

The landlords' police power was suspended to some degree by regulations for administrative districts (Kreisirdnung) introduced in 1872 and by the rural community regulations (Landgemeindeordnung) of 1891. But the landowners continued to play the dominant role in the districts. The three-class voting system in Prussian elections enabled landowners to weaken the most offensive measures (Puhle 1986: 85). Moreover, the institution of estate districts (Gutsbezirke), which gave Prussian estate owners considerable administrative functions and jurisdictional privileges over the population of their districts, were not abolished until December 1927. At that time, there were still almost twelve thousand estate districts, with a population of some one and a half million (Gerschenkron 1943: 105–6). In 1914, 83 percent of Prussia's provincial prefects (Oberpräsidenten) and over 50 percent of the chief territorial administrators (Regierungspräsidenten) were nobles (Lieven 1992: 219; Armstrong 1973: 77). The great landowners thus governed Prussia until World War I.

In 1914, local administration in Russia was dominated by district marshals, the elected heads of the district nobility. In the absence of any sort of state-appointed subprefects to coordinate government at the local level, the district marshals were used to fill the gap. Sweden was divided into twenty-five administrative provinces, each with a Landsting (assembly) under the presidency of a member designated by the crown. All members were elected directly by voters, who on the eve of World War I, were

---

13. Lieven 1992: 206; Spring 1977: 14. For studies of the politics of British local government before the world wars, see Robson 1931; Sharp 1969; Chester 1951; Griffith 1966.

essentially drawn from the property-holding class (Ogg 1914: 601). In Spain, the landed and other elites maintained local authority through the mechanism of caciquismo. The caciques saw to it that local administrators and judges carried out policies consistent with the interests of those to whom the caciques were subservient (Herr 1977: 112–17; Kern 1973).

The landowners were successful in translating the social and political authority which they enjoyed at the local level into political power at the national level. Throughout the nineteenth century, urban areas were grossly underrepresented in national elections relative to rural areas (see Chapter 7).[14] For instance, in France during the Third Republic, more than 30,000 of the communes had populations of less than 1,500. Each of these had one senatorial elector, while Paris (with a population of almost 3 million by 1914) had only 30 electors (Wright 1964: 213 n. 2).

Though many agricultural laborers were given the vote before World War I, they were economically dependent upon the goodwill and charity of landlords and farmers. As a result, the great landowners were able to manipulate the votes of rural inhabitants. Bismarck, in fact, pressed for an extension of the suffrage because he thought this would strengthen landed interests against financial interests. Conservative interests elsewhere in Europe did the same (e.g., in the Netherlands).

In Prussia, landless laborers depended on the landowners for their incomes, homes, and food. As there was no secret ballot, landowners were able to control the behavior of their dependents at the polls. Squires led their peasants to the polls and watched them carefully. Owners of large estates withdrew their trade from merchants or artisans who voted for liberals. Government officials used official funds and licensing powers to reward and punish the appropriate people (Weiss 1977: 76). Local troublemakers were persecuted or dismissed from official posts. Liberals or radicals were not allowed onto the estates to canvass or pass around their ballot papers. Right up to 1914 "the only ballot paper an estate laborer was likely to see was the Conservative one, handed to him by his foreman outside the polling booth." Open-air rural meetings were illegal, and landlords, their police, and the Landräte could deny opponents access to the village hall (Lieven 1992: 222). County commissioners, recruited from the ranks of local landowners, were expected to deliver their home districts to the Conservatives at election time. After the 1890s, the German govern-

---

14. In the Scandinavian countries, urban areas were generally overrepresented in the legislatures, reflecting the influence of bureaucratic-mercantile interests. In Austria, urban areas and interests were also overrepresented to ensure that political dominance would remain in the hands of the disproportionately urbanized German elements rather than the overwhelmingly rural Slavic areas.

ment became even more dependent on the Conservatives in both the Reichstag and the Prussian Landtag (Tipton 1976: 966).

Many agricultural laborers were given the vote in Britain in 1884, but they remained dependent upon the goodwill and charity of landlords and farmers. Farm laborers seen at Labour meetings were subject to prosecution (*Labour Organizer*, March 1924, 9). At the same time, the Conservative (Unionist) party relied upon the English aristocracy, the clergy, and the squires in the rural sections of England to put pressure upon tenants and farm workers to support Conservative candidates (Gosnell 1930: 24–25). Until 1945, priests and large landed proprietors in France saw to it that voters did their duty on election day (Gosnell 1930: 55). The Russian nobility had nearly unlimited sway over the persons and belongings of their serfs, and broad local civil, police, and judicial authority, even after the Emancipation Statute of 1861.

Working farmers and the peasantry took little active part in political life before the 1930s, even at the local level (Wright 1964: 14–18). Few peasants anywhere could think of competing with the town bourgeoisie or large landowners for elective office. German peasants, threatened and unable to cope with rapid socioeconomic change, retreated behind the political leadership of the Junkers.[15] In the Agrarian League (Bund der Landwirte), the dominant agrarian interest group in Prussia from 1893 to 1914, landowners controlled the organizational committees and the financially independent bureaucratic structure. In 1908 league members constituted an absolute majority of representatives in the Prussian lower house (Puhle 1986: 92).

Between 1884 and 1914 local or regional farmers' syndicates organized by "local crusaders from the landed aristocracy or the bourgeoisie" were established in every section of France. The leaders of agrarian syndicalism were large landowners "who were largely motivated by a desire to insulate the peasantry from radical ideas and preserve a bloc of voters committed to political and social conservatism" (Wright 1964: 18–19). The syndicates were federated in 1886 as the Union Centrale des Syndicats des Agriculteurs de France. Republican leaders of the center and left organized their own syndicates in the countryside in response to this right-wing

---

15. Gerschenkron 1943. Patron-client politics, with its mutual benefits to each party, are usually at the root of the ability of landlords to influence peasants in a conservative direction in their electoral preferences. Huntington (1968: 443–44) cites evidence of this in Germany and England, as well as Brazil, Turkey, and Ceylon. There is some evidence that latifundia peasants may vote with their landlords against agrarian reform. In these cases, the peasantry is persuaded by the landlords that agrarian reform would mean the distribution of large landholdings among all the peasants in the area, and not simply among the residents. This has been suggested for parts of Peru and became an important issue in the Chilean reform process (Drew 1969: 78; Kaughman 1972: 119–23).

syndicalism; however, the membership of these organizations did not equal that of the right-wing syndicates until 1917 (Wright 1964: 21).

The major landowners everywhere continued to enlarge and consolidate their holdings during the nineteenth century. The proportion of land held in the great estates grew every year until 1873 (Montagu 1970: 168). In most of Europe, landed property continued throughout the century to be the most important form of wealth. At the end of the nineteenth century, the great landowners were still the largest group of wealth-holders in Britain, and the richest of these were far richer than the wealthiest British businessman until the twentieth century (Rubinstein 1977).

There is an intimate relationship between wealth and power. Whether or not the wealthy elite actually occupy the seats of government, wealth enables them to assemble multiple resources when their interests are threatened. Because of the support they could mobilize when necessary for favored candidates and established political figures, the important landowning families were also able to press with great success for the appointment of their own representatives to executive positions in government. Wealth enabled landowners to fund authoritarian parties and movements, and to threaten governments with investment slowdown and capital flight. Where dominant classes did not determine the actual decisions made by governments, their resources limited the options available to the state and thus its autonomous capacity to impose collective goals distinct from the private goals of the dominant classes.

Throughout the nineteenth century, successive conservative governments in France followed policies that favored the powerful and propertied. When faced with economic crises, the salaries of lesser officials were decreased, taxes were lowered, and public spending, especially for social welfare, was cut. To protect the franc and to avoid taxing the wealthy, conservative governments preferred to borrow rather than pay costs as they arose. Thus short-term bonds were sold to an extremely wealthy minority. This meant that governments which introduced measures of social reform could be, and often were, brought down by the threat of the financial community to pull its money out of government bonds. Thus, conservative forces were able to control state policy, whether or not they actually occupied top governmental positions. In 1936, a Popular Front government dominated by socialists was elected. But in June 1937, French capitalists brought down the government by their refusal to purchase government bonds. In Italy, and for the same reasons, conservative agrarians crippled the executive branch of government in the years before 1914 (Tipton 1974: 964).

Political leadership, both at the national and local levels, remained in the hands of large landowners or traditional bureaucratic elites. The aristocracy "absorbed the brains from the other strata that drifted into politics" and "continued to man the political engine, to manage the state, to govern" (Schumpeter 1947: 136–37). Rising industrial and commercial interests did not dominate cabinets, governmental bureacracies, legislatures, or local government until after World War II.

State policies were generally consistent with the immediate interests of the landlords. In fact, landlords did not experience significant political setbacks or suffer any erosion of their hold on agrarian labor until the world wars. Agrarian reform was not a serious item on the agenda until then. Because of tariffs and agricultural subsidies from the government, as well as tax and pricing policies, agricultural production was not subordinated to the market until after World War II.

Labor legislation effectively prohibited the organization of agrarian labor until World War I. Even after the war, labor organizers had limited access to the peasantry and rural labor. In England, the Labour Party was still unable to gain significant strength in rural areas. Labour propagandists were refused halls or embarrassed by the presence of the local squire in their audience. In 1929 the Labour Party did not carry a single predominantly rural district (Gosnell 1930: 19).

Wages of agricultural workers were kept depressed until World War I. In England, the report of a Land Enquiry Committee, appointed in 1912 to investigate wages, hours, housing, and conditions of land tenure, showed that more than 60 percent of adult agricultural laborers received less than the amount necessary for the maintenance of a laborer and his family. The average wages on the land were lower, the hours longer, and the housing and other conditions of living worse, than in any other large industry. Laborers could not combine. If they attempted to do so, they could be turned out of their homes (Ogg 1930: 174). A statutory minimum wage was not achieved for rural workers until 1917 (Read 1964: 217–19).

Until World War I, the traditional elite was successful in presenting their class interest as the general interest. In France, agriculture was portrayed as the natural and proper employment of the nation's labor and the production of bread grains as the basis of the nation's health. The East Prussian agrarian elite, by opposing all outside threats to the region's economic structure, including government grants for industrial development, maintained and increased the region's dependence on the declining agricultural sector (Tipton 1976: 119). The agrarian movement developed an ideological justification for this program: the crisis of eastern agriculture was expanded to a general crisis of the entire German economy and Germany's place in the world (Gerschenkron 1943: 28–32, 75–76). "When German agriculture collapses," declared von Moltke, "the German Empire will collapse without a shot" (Ogg 1930: 200). The whole course of public policy was based on the assumption expressed in this dictum. Only by the aid of protective tariffs and other special favors did German agriculture maintain even the semblance of prosperity (Ogg 1930: 200).

The Church

One of the most important bases of power of Europe's traditional elite during the nineteenth and early twentieth centuries was the church.[16] Traditional elites were bound by common interests to the clergy, and they depended on the ideological and cultural apparatus of the church to ensure the continuity of rural, preindustrial, feudal, and autocratic structures of power and authority. It is commonly assumed that in the eighteenth century the Enlightenment and the French Revolution accelerated a process of secularization that had been ongoing since at least the mid-seventeenth century, and that in the nineteenth century technological progress and changing patterns of economic relationships worked to complete that process. What is often overlooked is that during the nineteenth century a revival of religion "in its most uncompromising, irrationalist, and emotionally compulsive forms" swept through Europe (Hobsbawm 1962: 271). The Catholic Church, which throughout the century remained "the greatest international organization of that or any other day" as one historian wrote in 1944 (Petrie 1944: 165), provided this revival with a powerful ideology of uncompromising resistance to the modern world. Throughout the century the Church resoundingly and forcefully condemned the separation of church and state, freedom of conscience, freedom of books (Mirari Vos, 1832), liberalism and the liberal state (Quanta Cura and Syllabus of Errors, 1864; Immortale Dei, 1878), industrialization, capitalism, republicanism, democracy, and socialism (Quadrigesimo Anno, 1931; Divini Redemptoris, 1937), and called for a return to medieval Christian principles (Rerum Novarum, 1891).[17]

Before this religious revival, the authority of the church had become increasingly separate from and subordinated to state power. This trend had begun after the Peace of Westphalia in 1648, which terminated the Thirty Years War. As the authority of the church declined, there was also a decline in religious observance (Kantorowicz 1957: chap. 3; Bendix 1978: 27–35). By the end of the seventeenth century, there was widespread dechristianization among the upper classes, and the eighteenth century

16. Two forms of the word "church" will be used in this discussion: (1) *Church* refers to the Catholic Church in Europe, and is also used in the title of a specific religious establishment, such as the Church of England; (2) *church* refers to both the Protestant and Catholic churches in Europe, and is used in statements meant to apply to religious establishments generally.
17. The English texts of the papal encyclicals that spell out these anathemas can be found in Koenig 1943.

saw this trend on the rise in rural areas in France (McLeod 1981: 11). In England, too, ordinary religious practice declined—the result, among other things, of the end of state-enforced church attendance after 1690. Ernst Troeltsch concludes that by the end of the eighteenth century religion—both Catholic and Protestant—was "going through a process of decay and even of destruction" (Troeltsch 1960: 1012). In Catholic Europe, rulers sought to restrict the church's authority. During the eighteenth century, rulers expelled Rome's special servant, the Society of Jesus, from Portugal (1759), France (1764), and Spain (1767).

These trends culminated at the end of the eighteenth century when the revolutionary regime in France attempted to subject the Church completely to the authority of the state. The Napoleonic Wars spread this movement throughout continental Europe. In France, the state seized Church lands, abolished tithes and fiscal immunities which had favored the Church, dissolved all religious orders, reordered diocesan boundaries, and turned the clergy into state employees. In addition to these measures, the state ceased its enforcement of Church attendance, imposed deist or atheist ritual substitutes for Christianity, and adopted a new calendar that counted its years from the abolition of the French monarchy in October 1792, rather than from the birth of Jesus.

As the work of the revolution continued, French clerics and aristocrats closed ranks and, using religious symbols and sentiment to activate and mobilize the masses, set in motion a counterrevolution. Louis XVI took an oath dedicating his country to the Sacré Coeur; the insurgents of the Vendée uprising in Brittany wore the emblem of the Sacré Coeur on their sleeves (Heyer 1969: 178). By 1796, religious symbols and ideology had fused with counterrevolution and generated a full-blown religious revival. As the revival spread, there was "a general explosion in favor of Catholic worship" which left the authorities "increasingly impotent" (Cholvy 1978: 461; quoted in McLeod 1981: 5). In dechristianized areas, villagers demanded the reopening of churches, and throughout France processions and pilgrimages were revived. In 1801, Napoleon signed a concordat which reinstated the church in France.

Following the French Revolution, there emerged in Europe a militant ultramontane Catholicism. The Jesuits, who were restored to France following the revolution, were its principal exponents. Its chief aims were to broaden the popular appeal of the Church and strengthen its defenses against hostile forces. In France, where the movement began, ultramontane clergy led revivalist meetings in public squares and held masses to purge the sins of Jacobinism. They imposed a weekly attendance at mass, a novel experience for most Catholics. They built bigger and more richly decorated churches; made more use of music, incense, banners, and processions in their ceremonies; encouraged the use of beads, scapulars, and medallions; and revived cults like that of the Virgin Mary. The ultramontane movement spread beyond France, to other Catholic countries and to Catholic communities within predominantly Protestant states. The re-Catholicization of Ireland by the ultramontane movement was considered by the movement to be among its greatest triumphs (Gilley 1988: 238).

There was a phenomenal revival of pilgrimages, processions, and venerations of saints everywhere in Catholic Europe. New saints, and thus new places of pilgrimage, were continually being created. There was a steady increase in the number of churches and a phenomenal revival of religious orders. The numbers in religious orders rose in France from 37,000 to 162,000 between 1851 and 1901 (McLeod 1981: 49); in Belgium, from 12,000 to 18,200 between 1846 and 1890 (Boulger 1904: 167); in Spain from 15,000 to 68,000 between 1861 and 1920 (McLeod 1981: 49). There was also a revival of Catholic missionary activity both in Europe and beyond, which was given a new international outreach after 1850 in Asia and the Pacific and in the French empire in Africa.

A revival also occurred within the established Protestant churches following the French Revolution. Protestant sects, which had been large and influential in the tumultuous seventeenth century but had lost considerable ground in the eighteenth, grew into a mass religion. Germany's Protestant Awakening and the revival of orthodox Calvinism in the Netherlands were part of this movement. At the same time, the Methodist movement in England, which had less than 60,000 adherents before the French Revolution, increased its membership to 143,000 in 1811, and to 600,000 in 1850 (McLeod 1981: 37; Hobsbawm 1959: 129). The Free Kirk movement initiated a religious awakening in Scotland in defense of the "Crown Rights of the Redeemer" against secular tyranny (Gilley 1988: 235–36). Numerous other movements arose whose "harsh and pristine puritanism" (Hunter 1976: 101) and literalist understanding of Scripture became the foundation of modern fundamentalism.

The last decade of the eighteenth century and the first decades of the nineteenth saw the beginning of systematic Protestant missionary activity. Some organizations were founded for the purpose, and others rededicated themselves to the missionary effort: the Baptist Missionary Society (1792), the London Missionary Society (1795) the Netherlands Missionary Society (1797), the Church Missionary Society (1799), the British and Foreign Bible Society (1804), Wesleyans (1813–1818), the Basel Missionaries, the Berlin and Rhenish societies (1820s), the Church of Scotland (1824), the United Presbyterians (1835), the Swedish, Leipzig, and Bremen societies (1830s), and the Norwegian society (1842) (Hobsbawm 1962: 264–65). There was an astonishing mass conversion to Protestantism during the first half of the century. Protestant churches appeared in remote areas and long neglected parishes sprung back to life.

The church's mass support in Europe was built up primarily through a vast and growing network of charitable organizations which made available to the poor social services not provided by the state. Among the most successful of these was the Société de Saint Vincent de Paul, which was founded in France in 1833. The Société supplied the poor with soup kitchens, cheap food, old clothes, help with rent, warm public rooms in winter, affordable housing, employment agencies, free medical and legal advice, holiday camps, old people's homes, catechist teaching, orphanages, apprenticeships, adult classes, clubs, allotments, libraries, and pilgrimages. As was typical of church-sponsored charitable organizations throughout the century, the attitude of the Société toward the poor was paternalistic and traditional; it was primarily concerned, not with curing the causes of poverty, but with "resisting liberal ideas" and preserving Catholics from compromise in religion and politics (Zeldin 1970: 108).

The religious revival in Europe was initiated by the clergy during the French Revolution, largely in defense of Church interests. After 1815, religious-political parties and connections developed throughout much of Europe with the principal objects of opposing the secularization of European society and of making the machinery of the state serve the interests of the church. Among the interests the church sought to defend was the preservation of itself as a state religion. The introduction of religious toleration at various times, in France, Britain, Germany, Scandinavia, and elsewhere, threatened the character of the church as the state religion and hence its status as the sole religion enjoying the privilege of public worship. In France, the Catholic ultramontane clergy condemned the state for allowing Protestants, Jews, and freethinkers to exercise equal rights with Catholics. The issues of Catholic emancipation and disestablishment were fiercely debated in Britain throughout the nineteenth century. After the German government began to dismantle its anti-Catholic legislation in 1866, an Evangelical League, formed "for the defense of German Protestant interests" against "false parity and tolerance concepts," became active in election campaigns and other aspects of public life, and continued its activism both under the empire and in the Weimar Republic (Evans 1981: 93).

Measures to introduce civil marriage and divorce became a leading grievance of the church and were fiercely contested. New systems of mass schooling created by the state were condemned as well. The Church exhorted the faithful to reject the idea that "Catholics may approve of the system of educating youth unconnected with the Catholic faith and the power of the Church" (Pius IX 1864: 2:48) and encouraged their political involvement in defense of confessional education. Conflict over education remained a central issue in Belgian politics after 1847 and throughout the rest of the century. In the Netherlands, militant Calvinists and the large Roman Catholic minority organized themselves politically in the 1870s to fight for state support for their own schools. The introduction of civil marriage and state-controlled education in Austria impelled the Church to involve itself more directly in politics and to align more closely with the political right. Vested religious interests in education remained a constant obstacle to the development of general education in England during the nineteenth century; as a result, England was the last of the western European states to establish a national school system.

Religious-political parties and connections were powerful elements in national politics. Germany's Catholic Center Party was almost totally identified with the defense of Church interests. The Catholic Party in Belgium was asked to form a government in 1870. The Church had a powerful voice in French politics after 1815, and it became more powerful as the century progressed: in 1871, French Catholics won their biggest electoral victory since 1789. The Calvinist Anti-Revolutionary Party in the Netherlands, formed in 1878, successfully secured state sponsorship for religious schools and became an important source of support for forces on the right. The Catholic Church in Austria was a powerful force in Austrian political life and directly involved itself in national politics through its Social Christian Party. Britain's Conservative Party identified itself with the Anglican Church and was committed to the defense of its interests throughout the century. In Tsarist Russia, the Orthodox Church was an extension and branch of state power, and its clergy took an active part in party, electoral, and parliamentary politics (Mazour 1951: 44–74).

Politically active religious parties were sustained throughout the nineteenth century by a variety of groups, for the pursuit of political ends not solely or directly related to the church or the defense of corporate church interests. During the French Revolution, the traditional aristocracy had joined forces with the Church to defend the institutions upon which their power and privileges depended. The church and the traditional landowning elite were natural allies since both were major property owners. On the eve of the French Revolution, the Catholic Church owned outright roughly 10 percent of the surface of France (Geffre and Jossua 1989); in England, the Anglican clergy were among the chief beneficiaries of the Enclosure Acts (between 1760 and 1850), and for the most part they identified with wealthy landowners throughout the nineteenth century (Gilbert 1980: 71). The church was also a highly desirable ally, as its symbolism, emotionalism, wealth, and organizational power made it an ideal instrument for political operations.

Following the Napoleonic Wars, the formerly dechristianized French émigré nobility returned to the Church en masse. They also had themselves appointed to high positions in the Church: seventy of the ninety bishops chosen under the restoration were nobles (Moody et al. 1953: 177). In England, recruitment of the clergy to the established church was in the hands of the landowners throughout the nineteenth century (Thompson 1974: 198–207). The Protestant Awakening in Germany found its most devoted following among large estate owners. In Pomerania many landowners transformed their estates into Christian communities, where they not only preached and distributed Bibles, but undertook to rule their tenants like biblical patriarchs (Shanahan 1954: 118). In most parts of France attendance at mass was largely confined to rich Catholics. In England, attendance at the established churches was highest among the upper class: counts of church attendance in London in 1902–3 showed that Anglican congregations averaged 4 percent of total population in the poorest districts, but 22 percent in wealthy parishes (McLeod 1981: 27; McLeod 1973: 31).

The aristocracy as a class remained committed to the defense of the church as a social and political institution throughout the century. Thus, religious control over education became one of their most ardent causes. In France, the nobility looked upon the Catholic schools as "a means of conserving their values from one generation to another, and of insulating their children from anti-religious influences and the principles of 1789" (Zeldin 1970: 70). Thus, the idea of an education based on isolation from external influences, originally worked out by the Catholic teaching orders of the ancien régime, acquired new force in the nineteenth century. The preservation of confessional education became a key political issue not only in Catholic countries, but in Protestant ones as well.

The dominance of the traditional nobility in state administrations and in national legislatures ensured that the state, which had previously sought to restrict the expansion of church power, would join with the church after 1815 to suppress the revolutionary forces which continued to sweep through Europe. The Comte de Provence, who was pretender to the French throne and, until 1797, a philosophical skeptic, wrote in that year to the bishops of an "inner connection that exists between Throne and Altar" and of "the necessity of the mutual support of the one by the other" (Heyer 1969: 131). The formula "throne and altar" was to dominate European society and politics for the remainder of the century. The sanctity of Christianity was invoked by traditional constituted authority: the Holy Alliance that Austria, Russia, and Prussia formed in 1815; the restored Bourbon monarchies of France, Spain, and Naples; and conservative governments throughout Europe. Charles X (1824–30) brought the Jesuits back to France, gave Catholic leaders a powerful voice in political appointments, and passed a bill that made profaning sacred vessels or consecrated wafers a capital offense (Weiss 1977: 53). Spain (1851, 1859), Austria (1855), Württemberg (1857), and Baden (1859) signed concordats ceding to the Church control of book censorship and education, canon law, and marriage; a separate penal system for the clergy; and protection of church property and monastic foundations.

When the state failed to uphold church interests, the church moved against the state. For instance, when Louis Napoleon seized power in a coup in 1852, the Church placed its its vast communications network at his disposal and helped him to suppress all resistance. But when he assisted Piedmont in its struggle against the Papal States in 1859, the ultramontane clergy declared war on him and exhorted French Catholics to prepare for another Vendean war to unseat him and restore the Bourbons to power. The Société de Saint Paul involved itself in plans to assassinate him; one of its clandestine presses printed instructions for the home manufacture of gunpowder (Zeldin 1970: 150).

In Greece, Serbia, Romania, and Bulgaria, churches joined in or led uprisings against the state (Hapsburg or Ottoman) when reforms designed to centralize administration and lighten the burdens of the peasantry threatened traditional privileges. The Old Believer movement in Russia attempted during the Napoleonic Wars to form an alliance with Napoleon against the tsar, and thereafter became a focus of resistance to the state (Dunn and Dunn 1964). Churches helped to bring down governments in Portugal (1933), Austria (1934), and Spain (1936).

As traditional elites monopolized gains from economic development, tensions increased between the upper and middle classes and led to the emergence of dissident, nonconformist, or radical religious movements. Since the electoral systems severely restricted the political participation of all but the most wealthy (see Chapter 7), these movements provided a means by which the middle and professional classes could express political opposition to their exclusion from the existing order and attract mass support from the multitude of urban poor—particularly in cities like London and in the port towns where vast accumulations of immigrants lived in crowded slums.

These new Protestant movements were largely middle class in character (Gilley 1988: 236) and essentially conservative. Like the established churches, they were hostile to religious minorities, and they sought to impose totalitarian controls over the faithful and to isolate them from contact with the world of unbelievers (McLeod 1981: 36). Intense conflict between the state churches and these new movements emerged, particularly after the 1830s. But in the 1880s, as the upper and middle classes united against the rising tide of socialism, conflict within the church abated. In England, wealthier members of the nonconformist churches defected to Anglicanism, and the membership of the nonconformist churches began to decline (McLeod 1981: 12, 69). In France, a "return toward faith" by both upper and middle classes was due, according to Tocqueville, to the role of religion in "the government of the masses," and "the fear of socialism" which affected the middle classes in much the same way as the French Revolution had affected the traditional landowners (1866: 6:178).

As socialist activity became more violent, frequent, and widespread, the church in Europe moved farther to the right. During the interwar years in Germany, France, Austria, Portugal, Spain, Poland, Belgium, Holland, Italy, Norway, and Sweden, corporatist regimes or structures were established whose organizational basis was the clerico-corporatist social order defined by the Catholic Church in Rerum Novarum and which, in a variety of forms, embodied all of the themes that the church had used throughout the centuries to oppose the breakdown of traditional society.[18]

In Italy, the Church relaxed its ban on Catholic participation in politics in the hope of stemming the tide of socialism; in 1929, it formalized its support of fascism in the Lateran Treaty. A clerico-fascist regime came to power in Austria in 1934 and ruled until the country united with the German Reich in 1938. As socialist forces grew stronger in Spain, its most widely read religious periodical, the Messenger, called for a "crusade" to make Spain fully Catholic again (McLeod 1981: 52). The constitution of Spain's Second Republic (1931–36), which declared a separation between church and state, the confiscation of some Church properties, and the exclusion of the religious orders from education, set the stage for a bloody civil war between left and right. The victory of fascism over the republic in that war was regarded by most Catholics as a Christian triumph (Carr 1966).

The Catholic Church helped to bring about the collapse of Portugal's republic and the establishment, in 1933, of an authoritarian regime under Salazar. In Germany, despite the overt atheism of Nazism, only a small minority of Protestants and Catholics opposed Hitler's rise to power. The Catholic Center Party voted to pass the Enabling Act granting Hitler dictatorial powers, and then officially dissolved itself. After 1933, many Catholic organizations were merged with Nazi organizations (Evans 1981: 395). In France, authoritarian movements, particularly Charles Maurras's monarchist Action Française, were supported by the vast majority of

18. See Berghahn 1988; Sutton 1982; Elbow 1953; Bowen 1947; Gulick 1940.

French bishops (Buthman 1939; Soucy 1972);[19] in the 1940s, the church supported the Vichy regime. Clerico-fascist regimes were established in the 1940s in Croatia and Slovakia.

Throughout the nineteenth and early twentieth centuries, the church and the nobility worked together to preserve the structures and institutions of traditional society. Even where, early in the century, the nobility and the church were at odds with each other—for instance, in Italy, where the existence of rival secular and papal governments split the aristocracy from the Church, or in Spain, where popular hostility to the Church made it a poor vehicle for preserving traditional society—they eventually closed ranks. Later, divisions within the church and between the upper and middle classes dissolved or were submerged as the threat of socialism increased. The tensions engendered by the rise of socialism increasingly polarized European society and led eventually to the world wars. Religion was thoroughly interconnected with these conflicts and integral to their development.[20]

After World War II, the political power and role of the church in Europe began to decline. Churchgoing had been a medium of news, contacts, and recreation, and a vehicle of welfare and charity. As the state began to take over the social welfare role of the church and charities were secularized, and as the press and nonreligious social clubs developed, church membership and attendance decreased. After World War II, religious issues no longer occupied the large place they had held in politics throughout the previous one hundred and fifty years.

Conclusions

In this chapter we went searching for the rising bourgeoisie of Liberal and Marxist lore and found, instead, cooptation and assimilation of bourgeois elements by the traditional nobility. In most European societies "the social and political pre-eminence of pre-industrial ruling groups continued even

19. Although the Church condemned the Action Française in 1926, it later relaxed its ban against Catholics joining it.
20. "All the Churches lost ground substantially during World War I. The decline was arrested in the 1920s, when even in proportion to the still-growing British population most Churches virtually held their own. But by the early 1930s indices of total membership and membership density (membership as a percentage of adult population), were again in decline. The Second World War exacerbated this trend, and the recovery which followed in the late 1940s and early 1950s was minimal even in comparison with the short-lived upturn after the First World War. Worse was to follow, however. Since 1960 declining membership, attendance, Sunday-school participation, baptisms, confirmations, and numbers of candidates offering themselves for the professional ministry have presented a consistent picture of massive crisis" (Gilbert 1980: 71).

when their economic fortunes declined, and the subordinate social and political role of the 'middle classes' continued even when their economic fortunes rose" (Bendix 1977: 420–21). Except perhaps in Switzerland and the Low Countries,[21] the absence of a politically and economically power-ful bourgeoisie was a characteristic feature of industrial development ev-erywhere in Europe. Throughout the nineteenth century, the nobility suc-cessfully accommodated, absorbed, and contained various commercial and industrial elements that arose during the century. No counter-elite, no independent capitalist bourgeoisie, emerged to challenge its power. The rising bourgeoisie became assimilated to the aristocracy rather than form-ing a separate class, and within this augmented class, the landed elite remained hegemonic until the era of the world wars. Landed property continued to be the most important form of wealth. In most of Europe, not only wealth, but social and political power, remained firmly in the hands of the landed class. Thus, the traditional elite was able to play the leading part in economic and political development in Europe throughout the nineteenth century. In fact, as I will show in Chapter 6, industrial develop-ment in Europe was characterized not by the bourgeoisification of rural Europe but by the increasing feudalization of the urban industrial sphere.

21. A number of scholars have noted the weakness or absence of a landed upper class in the small western European countries (Katzenstein 1985; Rokkan 1970). But even in Scandinavia and the Low Countries, areas with considerable peasant landholding, the nobility monopo-lized political power.

Dependency and Development
in Europe

Development in the contemporary Third World has been shaped by colonial and traditional structures and forces, and it is characterized by dualism and monopoly, a lack of internal structural integration, and dependency on outside capital, labor, and markets. These are well documented aspects of Third World development. Frequently, Third World "dependent" development is contrasted to a more benign and "independent" European development, as in this statement: "Instead of undergoing an independent process of capitalist development, [other regions] found themselves incorporated into the emerging Europe-centered capitalist system as colonies, dependencies, or clients of one sort or another. It was in this way that capitalism as we know it today started in its very earliest infancy as a dialectical unity of self-directed center and dependent periphery" (Sweezy 1982: 211). However, the assumption that Europe experienced an independent development distinctly different from contemporary Third World dependent development is erroneous.

In this chapter I delineate the key elements of the dependency thesis and describe the features that should characterize independent development. I show that industrial capitalist development in Europe conformed more closely to the model of dependent development than to that of independent development.

Dependent and Independent Development

The term "dependent development" is meant to describe certain characteristics of Third World economies and those processes that are causally linked to underdevelopment. No definition of dependent development is likely to meet with universal agreement, but any definition needs to be particularly sensitive to two issues. The first relates to the definition's completeness. An inclusive definition is likely to include elements that some scholars think are nonessential or irrelevant; narrower definitions may exclude elements that other observers consider crucial. The definition I adopt here errs on the side of inclusiveness. All of its elements are found throughout the Third World, though not, in most cases, together. All of its elements were also characteristic of industrial capitalist development in Europe before 1945. The second issue involves the need for a dynamic and relational definition of dependent development. It is not sufficient to show, for instance, that elements associated with dependent development were present in European cases at various points in time. Rather, they must have been characteristic of and integral to long-term processes of growth and must in some way have been related.[1] The features that comprise dependent development are:

1. a history of colonialism;
2. the condition of being less-developed and not yet well-integrated nation-states in an international environment dominated by more-developed and homogeneous states;[2]
3. dualism (i.e., the lack of integration of various parts of the domestic economy due to strong linkages between portions of the economy and foreign economies);
4. dependence on a narrow range of export goods and a few trading partners;
5. dependence on the foreign supply of important factors of production (technology, capital);
6. specialization in the production of raw materials and primary crops (more generally, limited developmental choices that constrain a country's capacity for setting its own developmental course);
7. inequality (both of income and of land-tenure structures) and a growing gap between elites and masses;
8. absence of an independent indigenous capitalist bourgeoisie and a dominant role for the state in development;
9. formal but inauthentic, partial, and unstable democracy.

1. Thus, Cardoso stresses that dependent capitalist development refers "necessarily and simultaneously" to various elements. These elements—"socioeconomic exploitation, unequal distribution of income, the private appropriation of the means of income, and the subordination of some economies to others" (Cardoso 1977: 17)—are included in the definition adopted here.
2. I follow here the distinction drawn by Caporaso (1978) between "dependence" and "dependency." See Chapter 1.

In other chapters I have shown that some of these elements were present in European development: a history of colonialism (Chapter 2); poor integration as nation-states (Chapter 3), and the international environment within which states in Europe developed (Chapters 1 and 2); the absence of a strong indigenous and independent capitalist bourgeoisie in Europe (Chapter 4); and formal but partial democracy (Chapter 7). The other elements are discussed below.

What is independent development? The dependency and neoclassical literatures suggest the following (I exclude elements discussed in other chapters):

1. the development of a domestic market for the products of national industry;
2. a diversified industrial structure with numerous linkages, including economically strategic capital goods industries;
3. diversification of the export structure, of trade partners, and of sources of capital and technology;
4. "national" control over the investment of capital and the accumulation process.

These elements, I shall show, were not features of European development in the nineteenth and early twentieth centuries. They eventually did come to characterize European development, but not until after World War II.

According to dependency theory, the story of dependent development in the Third World begins with the colonial and imperial policies of European powers.[3] Colonialism recast Third World economies in a specialized, export-producing mold, thus creating fundamental and interrelated structural distortions that continue to thwart development. The most characteristic distortion is the dual economy (Sunkel 1993). Dualism is typical of the colonial economy, in which an intrusive modern economic sector fails to transform the rest of society, and slave and feudal relations combine and coexist with capitalist and state-owned enterprises. After decolonization, dualism is perpetuated by various forms of neocolonialism.[4] Dualism is *not* meant to describe natural or more or less automatic processes of unbalanced growth between rural and urban, or between successful and less successful, sectors of the economy; it is the result of conscious policies

3. See, e.g., Murdoch 1980; S. Amin 1979; S. Amin 1974; Williams 1978; Caldwell 1977; Cardoso 1972; Rodney 1972; Emmanuel 1972; Stein and Stein 1970; Furtado 1970.
4. The dual economy model was developed to explain the economies of colonial countries where an island of western economic institutions and organizations was surrounded by an archaic community with primitive institutions and an underdeveloped economy. See Boeke 1953. See also Gonzàles-Casanova 1965, for a discussion of neocolonialism and dualism. For an introduction to dualistic theories, with bibliography, see Meier 1970: 125–288.

pursued by owners of wealth. There is no investment beyond the enclave—profits are either reinvested there or exported. Improvements in technology do not diffuse outward to agriculture or to cottage industry. Society is structurally divided by different rules, processes, and institutions.

Dualism engenders dependence on a narrow range of export goods and a few trading partners, leading to unstable growth patterns geared to the ebb and flow of the international market and to a high degree of foreign input into decisions affecting the national economy. Dependence on a few export goods and markets limits a country's developmental autonomy. Dualism also creates dependence on foreign capital. In particular, foreign direct investment places important sectors of manufacturing, agro-industry, mining, and commerce in the hands of foreign-owned enterprises. It thus involves a sociopolitical presence not entailed in trade dependency, one that further limits a country's autonomy. The technology used in the dynamic sector is more or less unadapted from developed countries and is "inappropriate" to the needs of developing countries.[5] The lack of fit between this technology and the social structure of developing countries encourages monopolistic practices, exacerbates a highly uneven distribution of income, marginalizes large sections of the population, and perpetuates structures of dependency.

Dependent countries have highly unequal distributions of land tenure and of income (Coatsworth 1993: 26–27; Dos Santos 1970; Frank 1970, 1967). In many instances, these inequalities get worse with economic growth (Coatsworth 1993: 24; Chase-Dunn 1975; Bodenheimer 1971b). A particular pattern of class relations is among the most important of the structural distortions that characterize dependent development (Portes 1985; Cardoso 1979). Where foreign capital penetrates deeply into the industrial sector, the national bourgeoisie is weak or nonexistent (Nash 1984; Cardoso and Falleto 1979; Frank 1972b; Baran 1970, 1957). Colonial powers reinforce traditional elites, often maintaining them in power by direct military incursions or covert but violent interference (Kautsky 1980; Emerson 1960). In general, colonialism enriches traditional elites[6] or creates new dominant classes. After independence, local elites remain clients of these powers, basing their domestic rule on a coalition of interests favorable to the international connection (Bodenheimer 1971b). Internal forms of colonialism maintain a "dynamic of inequality" and prevent

5. See S. Amin 1977; S. Amin 1974; Kay 1975; Alavi 1975, 1964; Stewart 1974; Cardoso 1972. Liberal development economists have made similar analyses of the implications for Third World societies of their imported technologies. See, for instance, Singer and Ansari 1977.
6. Rather than dispossessing local elites, colonial powers usually work in alliance with those elites to advance economic goals of mutual benefit. See Kautsky 1980: chap. 3.

the emergence of egalitarianism (Gonzàlez-Casanova 1965: 35; Emerson 1960: 342). As a consequence of the weakness of the indigenous bourgeoisie, the state plays a more important and more coercive role in industrialization in the late developers (O'Donnell 1977). In most developing countries, the mass of the population is excluded from the political life of the nation.[7] Where democratic forms of government are found, they tend to be partial and highly unstable.

These features of dependent development are well documented for the countries of the contemporary Third World. However, the development literature has generally failed to recognize that these features were also characteristic of European industrial development.

Development in Nineteenth- and Early-Twentieth-Century Europe

European countries have experienced forms of colonial exploitation similar to those found in the countries of the contemporary Third World. During the nineteenth and early twentieth centuries, several states experienced direct colonial control: Norway, Finland, the Hapsburg territories (which after World War I became the states of Czechoslovakia and Yugosalvia), Italy, Hungary, Poland, Ireland, Greece, the Baltic states, Romania, Bulgaria, and Albania. Many Europeans elsewhere experienced colonial domination through processes of nation-building which, as I showed in Chapter 2, proceeded by means of military force, economic domination, and cultural assimilation.

Many parts of Europe were also subject to indirect control. In the Balkans and in eastern and southern Europe, in particular, western European powers obtained extensive concessions, including highly uneven trade agreements. By the beginning of the twentieth century, loans and credits granted by France, Germany, and Austria had brought the Balkan countries into their creditors' spheres of interest. But although this export of capital had an important military-political aspect, investments did little to lift the economies of the Balkan countries from an underdeveloped, preindustrial level. They remained agrarian suppliers to the more industrialized states (Berend and Ránki 1974: chap. 6).

Elsewhere, indirect control was established by means of foreign concessions. In Spain, for instance, exemptions to the regulations for limited companies allowed foreign countries almost complete liberty to found every type of company by issuing shares (Nadal 1973: 545). The mining and smelting of lead was entirely in foreign hands, and foreigners dominated pig iron production and zinc and copper mining. Foreign companies

7. See O'Donnell 1979; Schmitter 1971; Chalmers 1969; King 1968; Cardoso and Faletto 1969.

built railways in Spain as an instrument of extraction and of international trade, to facilitate export of mining products, rather than as an instrument of internal development. Neither railway construction nor the mining industry had a significant impact on other sectors of the economy before 1914. At the outbreak of World War I, Spain was still a mainly agricultural country (Carr 1966).

Dualism characterizes colonial economies and is thought to be uniquely typical of contemporary Third World development. In fact, dualism was an integral feature of many European societies in the nineteenth and early twentieth centuries. Internal colonialism created in Europe the same structural distortions that overseas colonialism is thought to have created in the contemporary Third World.[8] All the states of Europe manifested some degree of economic dualism. Every country had a core area that was economically more dynamic and that exercised political and cultural sway over more backward areas. Regional inequality remained prominent in most European countries until the end of World War II. Jeffrey Williamson has shown that rising disparities in regional income and increasing north-south dualism were typical of many European countries during the nineteenth century. Growth was often accompanied by the emergence of large, depressed regions—regions that were relatively progressive exporters of agricultural products in earlier periods. Regional inequality became increasingly severe from the 1860s to World War I (Williamson 1965).

In *Great Britain*, dualistic structures developed in the Celtic periphery. England created a diversified industrial economy, but production in Wales, Scotland, and Ireland became excessively specialized. In the Celtic fringe, industrialization was geographically confined to a highly limited number of counties that formed industrial enclaves in nonindustrial hinterlands. These enclaves were oriented to and dependent on English and international markets. Large sectors of the Celtic periphery remained nonindustrial.

Dualism was a prominent feature of development in *France* at least from the eighteenth century. Edward Fox has described eighteenth-century France as two Frances: one, the new France, which imported England's Industrial Revolution and developed a mature capitalist society; the other, the old France, which still lived by subsistence agriculture. These two

8. In fact, as the analysis of dualism in Stavenhagen 1968 suggests, the term "internal colonialism" describes more accurately than "dualism" the relationship of developing urban centers or productive agricultural areas in Latin American countries to their backward, underdeveloped regions. What exists in Latin America is not two independent social and economic systems, which is what the term "dualism" suggests, but two worlds bound together into a functional whole, a relationship in which "the backward, underdeveloped regions of our countries have always played the role of *internal colonies* in relation to the developing urban centers or the productive agricultural areas" (Stavenhagen 1968: 14–18).

"identifiable and discrete" societies (Fox 1971: 178) "continued to coexist and maintain their separate identities well into the twentieth century" (98). In 1827 Baron Charles Dupin described the striking contrast between the wealthier north—"enlightened France"—and the least economically and culturally developed parts of France (Brittany, the Loire valley, and the center of France)—"benighted France" (Dupin 1826; in Chartier 1978: 531). The nation was, he wrote, divided into two distinct economic universes, in terms of value of agricultural and industrial products, per capita income, and public revenue. The south sent agricultural products to the north, whereas the north sent back manufactured products to the south (Dupin 1827: 1:1; in Chartier 1978: 534).

Within the industrial areas, structural change was extremely limited before 1851. Growth occurred through the production of more goods—by an extension of existing methods of production rather than by technological innovation. Modern forms of production were exceptional and coexisted with the establishments typical of preindustrial economies. After 1851, economic development began to shift in the direction of modern production. By 1870, however, traditional industries such as textiles, clothing, leather, building, and woodworking still represented 85 percent of the gross product; more modern industries such as fuel and minerals, metallurgy, and engineering accounted for only 10 percent (Price 1981: 97).

As economic development concentrated industrial activity in the north and northeast, other regions experienced deindustrialization and economic stagnation. Most of the Midi, Brittany, the mountainous areas of east-central France, and the southeastern and southwestern margins of the Paris basin were characterized by archaic agriculture, low levels of commercialization, the survival of only residual industry, and demographic decline (Price 1981: 237–38). After 1870, enormous regional disparities emerged. In 1947, Jean-François Gravier could still describe France as an "island" of prosperity, centered on Paris, surrounded by "the French Desert."[9]

In *Belgium*, industrial development and economic expansion took place during the nineteenth century mainly in the Walloon section. The Flemish-speaking areas of Belgium, earlier the center of Belgium's economic life, became economically and culturally backward and dependent on the financial center of Brussels. Wages were considerably lower in the Flemish areas until after World War I. Extreme poverty characterized the Flemish

9. Gravier 1947. The "French Desert" was home to the underprivileged 70 percent of the population whose average taxes amounted to less than 250 francs per head in départements like Haute-Loire and Lozàre. By contrast, the 2.5 million inhabitants of Paris were prosperous enough to generate a figure of 1,676 francs per head, four times the national average of just under 400 francs (Coates et al. 1977: 32–34).

provinces after the mid-1840s (Mokyr 1976: 239). During the interwar years, Flemish nationalists drew attention to the "colonization of Flanders by Frenchified Brussels capital, based on Brussels and Walloon political power" (Elias 1969; in Kossmann 1978: 636). Not until after World War II did backward Flemish areas begin to develop (De Vries 1976: 29; Davin 1969).

While its industrial expansion made it a military and industrial power in Europe, *Germany* was still a country where large sectors of the economy were characterized by landless peasants, struggling artisans, impoverished shopkeepers, and hungry journeymen. As Germany concentrated on advanced and expensive technology, introducing large-scale plants and fostering investment-goods industries (Gerschenkron 1962), many manufacturers clung tenaciously to hand processes and domestic production. In 1907, nearly a third of people engaged in mining and manufacture were self-employed or worked in enterprises of five persons or fewer. Dispersed home production was common in clothing and textiles, leather and woodwork, toy manufacture, food processing, and a host of minor metal trades (Landes 1969: 330). In 1914 personal income in the province of East Prussia stood at about the same level as the average for all of Prussia in 1892. Berliners in 1907 received almost three times the income of persons in East Prussia.[10] Death rates and infant mortality rates were consistently above the national average. Low income and poor living conditions were the most commonly cited reasons for emigration.[11]

The *Austro-Hungarian Empire*'s great industrial cities and glittering court elite contrasted sharply with its Slav regions where subsistence agriculture barely sustained an impoverished peasantry (Tipton and Aldrich 1987a: 34). Of the 28 million inhabitants of the "hereditary provinces," 11 million, nearly 40 percent, lived in Galicia, Bukovina, and Dalmatia, but only 15 percent of industry was in these regions. The Bohemian and Austrian provinces had per capita production and consumption levels 30 to 40 percent higher. In Galicia, Bukovina, and Dalmatia, 80 to 85 percent of the population worked in agriculture. The average in 1910 for Bohemia and Austria was 38 percent and 42 percent respectively (Berend and Ránki 1974: 121–22, 134). In 1914, income and output showed enormous regional differences that to a large degree mirrored ethnic differences. Per capita income in Lower Austria (850 crowns) and Bohemia (761 crowns) far exceeded income in Galicia (316 crowns), Bukovina (310 crowns), and Dalmatia (264 crowns) (Good 1984: 150). Slovakia, though well endowed with the mineral resources needed for heavy industry, remained chiefly a

10. Tipton 1976: 112. The figures are computed from data in Orsagh 1968; Goeldel 1917: 24; Statistisches Reichsamt 1932: 32–33, 72.
11. See the sources in Tipton 1976: 112.

supplier of raw materials and labor for industry in Hungary and else-where. In 1913, Slovakia produced well over half of Hungary's iron ore, iron pyrites, copper ore, and antimony ore (Busek and Spulber 1957: 297), yet Slovakia remained a backward agrarian area with a weak industrial sector.

The dualism between the developed north and the rural south in *Italy* has traditionally been the distinguishing feature of Italian society. In 1861, when the nine states of Italy united to form the Kingdom of Italy, there were enormous differences between the north—where land ownership much resembled the northwest European pattern—and the south, with its enormous church and secular estates and millions of landless peasants. In 1859, 0.1 percent of all southern landowners held 28 percent of all the land; 39 percent was in parcels up to 1.4 hectares in size, and was held by 94 percent of all landowners (Siegenthaler 1973: 370). Ninety years later, in 1951, southern Italians had per capita incomes just over half the average of the rest of the country, high unemployment and underemployment, over half the work force engaged in agriculture, a small manufacturing sector composed mainly of artisan "subsistence" units, large inequalities in the distribution of wealth, low investment, and a history of mass emigration (Vito 1969: 211). In *Switzerland*, the share of manufactured commodities in total exports was over 75 percent on the eve of World War I, but most Swiss were peasants. In 1920, only 26.7 percent of the population lived in urban areas (Hughes 1975: 173, 274; Crafts 1984).

Industrial development in *Poland* in the nineteenth and early twentieth centuries was concentrated in three "islands" around Lodz, Sosnowiec, and Warsaw (Luxemburg 1977: 19–26). At midcentury, the Scandinavian countries had enclave economies, in which the towns benefited from in-creasing trade and rising income, whereas the countryside remained more or less unaffected (Jörberg 1973: 426–27). *Finland* was perhaps the most extreme case. In the course of the nineteenth century, the southwest re-gions of the country experienced a relatively rapid and successful com-mercialization, but industry in eastern Finland stagnated. In the 1850s the sawmills there produced about two-thirds of Finland's sawn goods; by the end of the century, they produced only 12 percent, as the southern prov-ince of Viipuri came to control 80 percent of the sawmill production of eastern Finland (more than 50 percent of the country's total sawmill pro-duction), through six commercial houses. By 1915 timber companies had purchased 20 percent or more of the land of eastern Finland owned by the state. Rural poverty was much greater in the east than in the southwest. In the east, 19 to 20 percent of the population were homeless compared to 9 percent for the whole country (Alapuro 1979: 351). Dualism was also characteristic of Norway, Sweden, and Denmark. At the beginning of the nineteenth century, *Norway's* society and economy comprised: (1) an urban community of rich merchants and officials (and numerous servants, workers, and beggars), based on a money economy, market exchange, and profitable investment; and (2) a noncapitalist, family-household peasant economy producing for subsistence. Economy and society were characterized by relatively isolated, patriarchal and partly self-sufficient peasant households and communes, with an upper tier of peasant proprietors and prosperous tenants and a lower class of highly dependent servants and crofters (Osterud 1978: 111–12).

In the state of *Czechoslovakia,* created after World War I, the Czech provinces and Slovakia constituted two distinct economic regions. National income per capita in Slovakia was 45 percent lower than in Bohemia. In the Czech provinces 37 percent of the total labor force was employed in industry and less than 30 percent in agriculture, but in Slovakia the corresponding figures were 16 percent and 64 percent (Turcan 1969: 243). In 1945 Slovakia was still a backward agrarian area with an impoverished rural population and a weak industrial sector.

In the early twentieth century, *Russia's* industries were "scattered islands in a sea of agrarianism" (Berend and Ránki 1982: 154). On the eve of World War I, however, Russia had the fifth largest industrial complex in the world (after the United States, Germany, Great Britain, and France). Until 1914, Russia's economy and society showed all the characteristics of dual development found in contemporary Third World countries. Industrialization was created by foreign investors. Technicians and industrialists were mainly foreigners. All export trade was in the hands of foreign merchants and entrepreneurs. By 1914, 90 percent of mining, almost 100 percent of oil extraction, 40 percent of the metallurgical industry, 50 percent of the chemical industry, and 28 percent of the textile industry were foreign-owned (Munting 1982: 34).

Although Russia was the fourth-largest industrial power before 1914, its per capital level of industrialization was less than one-quarter of Germany's and less than one-sixth of Britain's (Kennedy 1987: 234). Eighty percent of the population derived its livelihood from agriculture. The great move toward modernization was state-inspired and addressed military needs—railways, iron and steel, armaments, and so on. To pay for imported foreign manufactures and to pay interest on the enormous foreign debt (by the early twentieth century, Russia had the largest foreign debt in the world), the Russian state had to ensure that agricultural exports, especially wheat, steadily increased, even during famines, as in 1891. As late as 1913, 63 percent of Russian exports consisted of agricultural produce and 11 percent of timber (Munting 1982: 31). A slow increase in farm output did not imply a better standard of living for the deprived and undernourished peasantry. By 1913 the average Russian had 50 percent more of his income appropriated by the state for current defense than did the average Englishman, even though the Russian's income was only 27 percent of that of his English contemporary (Lieven 1983: 13). As late as 1913 the nation's literacy rate was only 30 percent, lower than that of mid-eighteenth-century England (Kennedy 1987: 238).

In *Spain* and *Portugal*, export sectors formed isolated enclaves within the economy (Berend and Ránki 1982: 127, 140). Foreign demand promoted investments primarily in the export sectors. Much of local manufacturing was foreign-owned. Salaried staff, some in modern industries and many in the government bureaucracies, enjoyed living conditions comparable to those of their counterparts in richer countries, while the rural population lived at subsistence levels. Between 1830 and 1914, cotton was Spain's leading sector and the leading cotton region, Catalonia, was for most of that period the sole manufacturing area. The rest of the country, with few exceptions, remained anchored in a backward agriculture based on cereals. The nobility's great latifundia in the south, with landless peasant masses, coexisted with and contrasted to the northern areas where free-holding was the rule. In Portugal, dependence on more advanced countries, particularly Britain, followed an almost classical pattern. In the early nineteenth century English merchants dominated the export of wine. Foreign investment was in sectors that had only a minimal spin-off effect. Huge foreign loans also failed to stimulate the Portuguese economy, and the payments of interest and principal became an ever heavier burden (Sideri 1970).

Industrial development in the Balkans favored narrow sectors within impoverished agrarian economies. Industrial development in *Greece* was typical. There, capitalist enterprises using wage labor constituted only a small island in a sea of family-based artisan units. In 1922, the economy was still largely agricultural, with noncapitalist modes of production found in all sectors. Massive spending did little to help manufacturing. There were very few organic links with the rest of Greek industry, since most materials, even those that could have been produced locally, were imported. The key manufacturing sectors (metallurgy, chemicals) were left to foreign capital (Evangelinides 1979). In *Romania*, 60 percent of total foreign investment before 1914 was concentrated in the oil industry and had little effect on other sectors of industry. Likewise, in *Serbia* the rapid development of a few industries, funded with foreign capital, had relatively little effect on the development and transformation of the economy as a whole (Berend and Ránki 1974: 107–9).

In most of eastern Europe, the Balkans, and parts of southern Europe, modern capitalism in big industry and finance existed side by side with traditional agrarian sectors characterized by large feudal estates and peasant smallholders. In almost every branch of industry noteworthy for development before 1914, a few large firms acquired a dominant position with the support of foreign capital (Berend and Ránki 1974: 310–11). The development of a market economy and the expansion of production failed to transform agriculture or even urban industry. In fact, feudal features appeared, in some places for the first time, alongside the emerging market economy.

During the nineteenth century, once-prosperous regions became backward, among them Brittany, parts of central and southeastern France, eastern Finland, and Transylvania. A regressive devolution took place in some rural areas of Germany, the Netherlands, and Scandinavia. Southern Italy and the Slav areas of Austria-Hungary became increasingly backward in relation to more advanced areas (Riggs 1964: 24–26; Badie and Birnbaum 1982: 25–64). In Italy, Spain, and Portugal, large landed estates that were operated by hired workers and tenants, and with labor dues and obligatory services for the landlord, persisted until the 1930s. In Hungary, feudal landholding controlled most of the country's agricultural resources before 1945.

During the nineteenth and early twentieth centuries, some degree of economic dualism existed in every country in Europe. Everywhere a core area, economically more dynamic, exercised political and cultural sway over backward areas. Modern industrial sectors, oriented to and dependent on international markets, formed enclaves within nonindustrial, mainly agricultural hinterlands. In the contemporary Third World, this dualism is reflected in the unequal distributions of agriculture and industry in labor and GDP (see Statistical Appendix, Tables 5 and 6), whereas in Europe it is more evident in the disaggregated data used in studies of regional inequality. See, for example, Table 3.

Monoculture dependency was also a feature of European economic development; many countries of Europe were unable to make progress in diversifying their exports of primary products until well into the twentieth century. This tendency was particularly characteristic of the Balkans, but also of northern Europe and Russia.

The Scandinavian countries were all highly dependent upon income from exports of a small range of goods (see Table 4): Sweden relied on timber and iron, Finland on timber, Denmark on agricultural products, Norway on fish, timber products and shipping; they were all dependent, as well, on a few trading partners. Norway's economic growth after 1870 depended on exports of fish and timber, and on income from shipping (Jörberg 1973: 429). At the beginning of the twentieth century, agricultural exports, mainly livestock and dairy products, accounted for about 90 per-

Table 3. Regional inequality (Y)[a] in Europe before 1945

SWEDEN	Stockholmstad	Gotlands
1930	264.2	58.1
1944	181.8	71.3
FRANCE	Paris region	Britanny
1864	175.1	62.1
GERMANY	Hamburg	East Prussia
1926	154.8	69.5
1936	134.8	73.2
ITALY	Piedmont	Sicily
1928	155.6	69.7
1938	165.3	71.3
NETHERLANDS	North-Holland	Drenthe
1938	141.2	50.0

[a]Y = per capita income of region relative to national average.
Source: Williamson 1965.

cent of Denmark's exports (Jörberg 1973: 398). Finland's export sector was extremely narrow: wood industry (71 percent) and agricultural (17 percent) products constituted about 88 percent of total exports. The sector was externally oriented, was wholly dependent on a few foreign markets, and had relatively few linkages with other sectors of the economy (Jörberg 1973: 421, 423–25; see, also Alapuro 1979: 347–48). All the Scandinavian countries were dependent on a few trading partners. During the 1870s, 60 percent of all products produced by Finland's metal and engineering in-

Table 4. Food items, agricultural raw materials and timber as percent of exports in pre–World War II Europe

Country[a]	Percent of exports
Denmark	90
Finland	88
Sweden	65
Russia	75
Albania	84
Bulgaria	83
Greece	84
Romania	69
Yugoslavia	77

[a]Scandinavia, 1910, Russia, 1913, Balkans 1926–30.
Sources: Lampe and Jackson 1982: 368–69; Jörberg 1973: 395, 398, 421; Munting 1982: 31.

dustry and over two-thirds of the textile products were exported to Russia. Practically all forest industry products were exported to western Europe. Britain accounted for some 60 percent of Denmark's export market in 1900 (Jörberg 1973: 395).

German agriculture was wholly dependent on the vagaries of foreign markets. When English landlords succeeded in imposing tariffs on East Elbian grains, German Junkers shifted to production of the wool demanded by the expanding English textile industry. With the suspension of the English corn laws in 1846, the Junkers once again concentrated on production of grains for export. In 1910, 66 percent of Austria-Hungary's trade was carried out with four countries: Germany (42 percent), Great Britain (14 percent), the United States (6 percent), and Russia (5 percent). Sixty-two percent of Belgium's trade was carried on with these countries and France (Mitchell 1975: 569, 573). Belgium experienced boom periods and depressions because of the country's dependence on foreign trade. As its dependence increased, it felt, to an ever increasing degree, the ups and downs of international business cycles. Between 1873 and 1895, Belgium suffered an acute crisis as a result of competition from American grain (Chlepner 1945: 179, 183).

Some scholars argue that different kinds of production (e.g., plantation vs. industrial) are a far greater determinant of subsequent development than the diversification of exports and trade partners (monoculture and trade dependence). A country that exports ten plantation crops to ten partners may not be better off than a country that exports two industrial goods to two partners. Dependent countries are classically those whose histories of involvement with the international market have led them to specialize in the export of a few primary products. Because these few products are absolutely central to the process of accumulation in the dependent country, economic fluctuations in the center may have severe negative consequences for the periphery. But, as was shown above, in Europe many countries depended on the export of a few primary products until the twentieth century.

Moreover, in 1913, among the eight or nine richest countries in the world, five—Argentina, Canada, Australia, New Zealand, and the United States—were exporters of primary goods. During the nineteenth century, more than two-thirds of United States exports were composed of primary goods, and a large share of these were raw materials, principally cotton (Bairoch 1993: 140). In Canada, the gains from a succession of export staples (furs in the seventeenth and eighteenth centuries, timber in the late eighteenth and nineteenth, grain and minerals in the nineteenth and twentieth) generated the earnings necessary to make possible balanced growth along a wide front of activity. This was true too of Australia (wool, meat, wheat, minerals), the United States (tobacco, cotton, wheat, minerals), and Sweden (timber, iron ore and semifinished bar iron, copper).

In 1913, although exports were represented largely by a few primary products, average export levels in Argentina, Chile, Cuba, and Uruguay were above those of France and Sweden (Banks 1971); those of Brazil, Colombia, Mexico, Peru, and Venezuela were not far below (Maddison 1991: 1). Moreover, in the decades before World War I, the annual rates of growth of exports from Argentina, Brazil, Ecuador, Peru, Colombia, Mexico, and Uruguay were greater than those for Belgium, France, and Great Britain (see Statistical Appendix, Tables 7, 8a and b, and 9).

In addition to the distinction drawn between the structures associated with the production and export of primary and industrial products, scholars also differentiate between domestically controlled systems and enclave systems dominated by foreigners. Cardoso and Faletto (1979), for example, describe two dependency situations: dependency in enclave situations and dependency where the productive system is nationally controlled. Each affects the process of capital creation, expansion, and accumulation. In enclave economies foreign invested capital originates in the exterior, is valorized through exploitation of local labor forces, and realized through the sale of staples in external markets. In Europe, enclave economies were found in Finland, Wales, Ireland, Scotland, the Netherlands, Russia, Spain, Portugal, and parts of Great Britain, France, and the Austro-Hungarian Empire. In economies controlled by a local bourgeoisie, accumulation is "the result of the appropriation of natural resources by local entrepreneurs and the exploitation of the local labor force by this same local group. The starting point for capital accumulation is thus internal." Insofar as the products of the local productive process consist of staples and food products, "the international market is required to realize the final steps of the capital circuit" (Cardoso and Faletto 1979: xviii–xix). In Europe, these economies included those of Sweden, Denmark, Norway, Finland, Russia, Greece, Portugal, Spain, and the Balkan states.

Given appropriate policies on the part of governments and a social structure that allows the implementation of those policies, a foreign-financed enclave can contribute to the development of the whole economy through payments made to the government, as well as by low-cost resources made available to the rest of the economy and by the demand made on other goods and services. Whether the foreign-owned sector acts as an engine of growth for the entire economy has largely to do with the various uses to which governments put the taxes, royalties, and so forth received as direct payments from the foreign investor.[12]

---

12. Numerous Middle East economists have made this case. Issawi has argued that foreign

Conventional accounts of Third World development hold that the impetus to modernize in the now developed countries was the result of endogenous cultural and institutional transformations, while change in contemporary developing countries results primarily from exogenous stimuli— the diffusion of Western institutions from the early modernizers. But every country in Europe relied upon more advanced areas in the development of modern capitalist conditions, and their dynamic sectors were linked to international, rather than domestic, markets.[13] All developing countries in Europe were dependent for technology, financing, markets, and basic imports on an international economic system dominated by more-developed countries.

The economic and political breakthrough that occurred in England and France at the end of the eighteenth century put every other country of the world into a position of "backwardness." The economic transformation of England had provided a model for France, while the political revolution of France had become a major focus of political debate in England. As I noted in an earlier chapter, advanced countries of the past like Holland, Spain, and Sweden became followers of Britain and France.

Foreign capitalists in London, particularly Dutch and Hanseatic bankers and merchants, for centuries managed trade on England's behalf. The English woolen industry was built up by immigrants from Flanders in the fourteenth and fifteenth century. Until the sixteenth century, Hanseatic merchants were granted privileges in London to establish joint stock companies and to manage industry and trade. Foreign manufacturers established the first papermaking factories and cannon foundries in England in the sixteenth century (Clough 1952: 174, 178–79, 185).

After 1815, every major iron and engineering works in Belgium and France, every early railway, and many textile mills and other enterprises, operated with British help. Between 1815 and 1848 Europe was flooded with British experts, investments, and technology (Hobsbawm 1962:

---

trade (1) did not generate underdevelopment, (2) generated growth in some sectors, and (3) failed to stimulate growth generally because of largely internal factors. Issawi points out that the import capacity of Middle East countries expanded far more rapidly than their GNPs, and he suggests that their foreign exchange receipts were adequate and that trade was not the major constraint on growth and development (1982: 42). The crucial question is "how political elites confront the problems of income distribution, sectoral investment, and national savings. To understand these one must in turn examine closely class alignments, the degree to which the state is rooted in a given class or stratum, and the developmental strategies of those who retain power as the major causal factors in the generation of external dependency" (Waterbury 1983: 32; but see also Sayigh 1978; Kerr 1981; G. Amin 1974).

13. Though Friedrich List was all the rage in Europe, it was not his theory of the domestic market (see Chapter 2) but his protectionism that caught the fancy of conservative forces— and this was protectionism for purposes of monopoly, not for purposes of transforming agriculture.

chap. 2). Every new German industry used British technology and many used French capital and entrepreneurship. Englishmen established or helped to establish factories in France, Belgium, and various parts of Germany. Still later, Frenchmen did the same in Russia and all over Europe. By the last quarter of the nineteenth century, Europe saw the emergence of multinational corporations, as firms from the more advanced countries established subsidiaries in the Balkans, Russia, and eastern Europe in order, among other reasons, to get behind the tariff barriers (Lewis 1978a: 159).

Foreign capital played a significant role in the development of most European countries. British capital was important in France and Belgium. British and French capital participated in the development of German industry and banking and in the building of Germany's railways. French and German capital was significant in Austria's development. French investments also helped to industrialize Spain, Italy, Russia, and the Balkans. German capital built modern transport systems in Sweden and other Scandinavian countries. German and Swedish capital was invested in the first large-scale sawmills and pulp and paper factories in Finland. Foreign capital played an important part in building Norway's industry and railroads. In 1870, more than half the mining industry in Norway was owned by foreigners (Jörberg 1973: 431). Sweden's rate of growth in the fifty years before World War I was substantially dependent on the influx of foreign capital (Heckscher 1954: 247–48; Cameron 1961: 489–90).

Foreign capital became the principal factor in the economic transformation of the countries of eastern and central Europe in the closing decades of the nineteenth century (Berend and Ránki 1974: chap. 5). Austria's state loans, industrial investments, and railway construction depended on the goodwill of the masters of the Frankfurt-Paris money markets. About one-third of the bonds and shares issued in Austria were held outside the country at the turn of the century (Berend and Ránki 1974: 96–97).

Fifty-five percent of the shares of the big banks in Hungary were foreign-owned, and about half of industrial investments were linked to the activities of foreign capital. Around 1900, 42 percent of the share capital of Hungarian manufacturing industry was completely under foreign control, while another 18 percent was controlled jointly by foreign entrepreneurs and Hungarians. In 1913 foreign capital held 55 percent of Hungarian government securities, 44 percent of the priority bond of railways not owned by the state, and 56 percent of debentures and municipal bonds (Berend and Ránki 1974: 102–3). By 1938 there was no branch of industry in Czechoslovakia in which foreign capital was not directly invested (Teichova 1974: 40–45).

In the late 1930s direct foreign capital participation in Polish industry amounted to 44.2 percent of the total capital of all joint-stock companies in

Poland. Foreign capital participation in limited companies was 89.7 percent of the total. In mining and metallurgy, foreign capital participation came to 71 percent in joint-stock companies and 93.1 percent in limited companies; in the electric power industry to 81 percent in joint-stock companies and 99.1 percent in limited companies; in the chemical industry to 60 percent in joint-stock companies and 87 percent in limited companies (Teichova 1974: 17).

Until 1939 the greater part of industry and banking in Romania was in the hands of French, British, and American capital. Before World War I, 95 percent of the capital invested in the oil industry was foreign. The situation was roughly similar in gas and electric power production (95.5 percent foreign capital), in the sugar industry (94 percent), the chemical industry (72.3 percent), and the timber industry (70 percent). Of the total foreign investment, 60 percent was concentrated in the oil industry and had little effect on other fields of industry or on the national economy (Teichova 1974: 23; Berend and Ránki 1974: 107).

In Serbia, the first major iron works (Metallurgic Combine Smerderlovo) was founded with British capital, and the copper mines of Maidenpek with French capital. French capital was also active in coal mining and in the cement business. The rapid growth of these industries had relatively little effect on the development and transformation of the economy as a whole (Berend and Ránki 1974: 107–9). After the establishment of Yugoslavia, foreign capital had an even stronger hold over that economy. The share of foreign investment in the total nominal capital of all Yugoslav joint-stock companies in 1937 was about 61 percent. Total participation of foreign capital in Yugoslav banking was approximately 75 percent in 1937 (Teichova 1974: 23). Foreign financiers held 82.5 percent of government securities and 44 percent of the share capital. Foreign capital accounted for 69 percent of the total capital in mining, 83 percent in electrical power, and 70 percent in the chemical industry (Berend and Ránki 1974: 237, 316–17).

Much of the capital for Russia's industrialization came from direct foreign investment. Foreign capital played an important role in railways, iron and steel, coal mining, petroleum extraction, and after the turn of the century, big banks. By 1914, 90 percent of mining, 60 percent of pig iron production, almost 100 percent of oil extraction, 40 percent of the metallurgical industry, 50 percent of the chemical industry, and even 28 percent of the textile industry were foreign-owned (Munting 1982: 34; Machay 1970: 24–37; Sontag 1968: 531).

Most European countries depended heavily on foreigners for their industrial technology, and as in the Third World today, there was a significant gap between the imported technology and local social structures. This was certainly the case, for instance, with Germany, as Thorstein Veblen makes clear in these observations, written in 1915:

> Germany combines the results of the English experience in the development of modern technology with a state of the other arts of life more equivalent to what prevailed in England before the modern industrial regime came on; so that the German people have been enabled to take up the technological heritage of the English without having paid for it in the habits of thought, the use and wont, induced in the English community by the experience involved in achieving it. Modern technology has come to Germany ready-made, without the cultural consequences which its gradual development and continued use has entailed upon the people whose experience initiated it and determined the course of its development. (Veblen 1939: 85–86)

In Russia, which in the nineteenth century possessed the world's largest army, modern artillery divisions rode through village streets whose inhabitants knew nothing of modern technology. In the industrial areas of Belgium and France, a significant number of skilled workers were foreigners (Strikwerda 1993a: 1122). More than two-thirds of the labor force in the industrial area of French Lorraine were foreign (Vignes 1913: 685–86). Germany employed approximately a million foreign workers (Bade 1985: 133). By 1910, at least one-quarter of Ruhr miners were Polish, and many others were Italian and Dutch (Herbert 1990: 21).

As I have shown in Chapter 4, almost no European state had a strong, independent, and indigenous industrial capitalist bourgeoisie. In fact, everywhere in Europe, as in the Third World today, the state played a central role in economic development. Alexander Gerschenkron has argued that economic development in England was a totally spontaneous process due to the high level of capital accumulation, and that it proceeded without any inducement or assistance from the state (Gerschenkron 1962: 14). But this disregards colonial exploitation and world trade—both mediated by the state—as sources of accumulation. Domestic accumulation in England was so great because, among other factors, the state had been active in the advancement of navigation and trade and in the acquisition of colonies.[14] State legislation shaped the direction and structure of foreign trade, which was of great importance in the process of growth for Britain, by differential duties, the regulation of shipping, colonial economies, and the attempted

14. To say that state-sponsored colonialism aided accumulation and development in Britain is not to concede that colonialism was necessary for British development. Colonialism may have initially played a positive role in British development, but it became detrimental to British growth later on.

exclusion of rival trading nations like the Dutch and the French. The state also intervened in and strengthened the enclosure movement, and later promoted through protectionist legislation the growth of new and rising industries (Mathias 1969: chaps. 3, 4, and 5).

In France, a clear line of continuity runs from Colbertian mercantilism (1661–83) and the establishment of state-run royal manufactories, to the elaboration of a national policy for "the encouragement of industry"[15] under Napoleon I, to the policies inspired by the Saint-Simonians under Napoleon III. The state constructed a network of railroads, pursued mercantilist economic policies, and protected domestic industries (Supple 1973: 311, 317, 327–29; Price 1981: 159–68).

Similar provisions were made in the Hapsburg monarchy, particularly from the time of Maria Theresa, in Belgium (Supple 1973: 328–30), and at a later date in Italy (Mori 1979). In Prussia, Frederick the Great pursued a policy of public aid and investment benefiting textile and chemical factories. The economic role of the Steurräte and Fabrikinspektoren and the Bismarckian policy of economic and industrial expansion continued the line of state activity in development (Henderson 1958; Pounds 1959). In eastern Europe, the state played a major role in mobilizing and securing foreign financial resources (Berend and Ránki 1974: chap. 4). The industrial takeoff of tsarist Russia was accomplished by state agencies, which not only established infrastructure and banking institutions but also worked to encourage investment via fiscal policy (Gerschenkron 1962: 119–52). The same is true of industrial development in the Scandinavian countries (Jörberg 1973).

Almost universally, national governments in Europe were involved in building railways and ports, and in the expansion and control of credit institutions (Cameron 1972). National governments unified their countries politically, removed institutional barriers to the growth of market systems, and substituted government demand and foreign inputs for missing developmental prerequisites such as capital, skills, and a home market for industrial goods (Morris and Adelman 1988: 123–24). Governments eliminated legal and political barriers to trade among regions and reduced the cost of economic transactions generally—making it cheaper to exploit new economic opportunities. Governments explicitly used ideology to strengthen voluntary compliance with the existing property system and to persuade society of its legitimacy (North 1981).

It appears, then, that the state played an important part in Europe's

15. The Société d'encouragement pour l'industrie nationale de la France was formed under government patronage in 1902.

industrial development, that the central role of the state in economic development is historically normal, and that it should not be considered unique to the contemporary Third World. It might be argued, however, that in the contemporary Third World, the state plays a uniquely repressive role. Gerschenkron (1962) claimed that the authoritarian state tends to be characteristic of later industrializers because it participates in the effort to mobilize capital and repress wages. Similar arguments have been made by Guillermo O'Donnell, David Collier, and Peter Evans with respect to Latin America. There a repressive-entrepreneurial (Collier 1979) or "bureaucratic-authoritarian" (O'Donnell 1979: 85–111; 1978b: 34–54) state tries to build national consensus around a policy of economic growth and social stability—the latter conceived in terms of labor docility, low wages, and political demobilization—in order to create a good investment climate for big business. Peter Evans (1979: 50) argues that the "dependent capitalist state . . . is a state whose repressive protection of the interests of the dominant class is blatant, yet it excludes most of the national bourgeoisie from political participation just as it excludes the mass of the population." But the state in Europe before World War II (as I argued in Chapter 2 and will argue further in Chapter 6) also operated for the protection of the interests of the dominant class; the state in Europe brutally repressed labor organization and (as I will show in Chapter 7) excluded the mass of the population from participation in economic and political life.

The degreee of inequality of distribution of personal income in Europe before World War II was comparable to that prevailing in Latin America today (see Statistical Appendix, Table 3). In Europe during the nineteenth century, as in the Third World now, the majority of the population lived in poverty. Of the European population as a whole during the 1815–50 period, approximately one-third lived below the level of subsistence and "on the brink of starvation" (Langer 1969: 182).

In 1897, five million Britons owned two-thirds of the national income, while the other thirty-five million subsisted on the rest (Romein 1978: 195). In 1914, less than 5 percent of the population above the age of twenty-five still owned more than 60 percent of the national wealth (Clough 1952: 671). Surveys of poverty in London made in the late 1880s indicated that no less than 30 percent of the population was living below the poverty line at any given time. An estimated six out of seven workers experienced destitution at some time in their lives, and this was particularly common in large families and among the elderly. Only the top 15 percent of the working class could expect, barring accident, illness, or depression, to ride above the poverty line (Gillis 1977: 269). There was a very considerable emigration from Switzerland between 1820 and 1925 because of widespread hunger in the countryside and the destruction of artisan jobs as a result of the replacement of handlooms with power looms. In the cities, industrialization created desperate suffering among the poor (Luck 1985: 428).

In Lille, the upper class rose from 7 to 9 percent of the population between 1820 and 1873–75, but its share of wealth left in wills grew from 58 to 90 percent. The lower classes, rose from 62 to 68 percent of the population during that time. Its share of the testamentary wealth fell from 1.4 percent in 1820 to 0.23 percent in 1873–75 (Hobsbawm 1979: 245). In 1933, 1.7 percent of the inheritance-tax payers owned 34 percent of the wealth inherited that year (Clough 1952: 673).

In Prussia, the top 5 percent of the population received more than one-fourth of the income in 1875; the top 20 percent received 48 percent. In 1911, wealth was even more concentrated (see Clough 1952: 673). In 1913, the top 5 percent of the population received nearly a third of the income; the top 20 percent received 50 percent. The richest 1.5 percent of the population of Sweden owned 55 percent of the country's private wealth. Of the Hungarian population 7 percent received over one-third of the national income (Goldstein 1983: 240). Throughout Europe during the nineteenth century, as in the developing world today, the majority of the population grew poorer. At the turn of the century, the gulf between rich and poor townsmen was greater than in any previous or subsequent period of European history (Romein 1978: chap. 13). European countries also had highly unequal land tenure structures in the nineteenth century, as may be seen from Table 5, which provides turn-of-the-century data for landholdings in Europe (1892–1907). The monopolization of industry was also a characteristic of European development in the nineteenth century, and it became increasingly so after the beginning of the twentieth century. This will be the focus of discussion in Chapter 6.

It is now time to review the features that comprise independent development, as implied by dependency and neoclassical arguments, and as discussed at the beginning of this chapter. When we examined the history of European development, instead of diversified industrial structures with numerous linkages, we found a monoculture of national production and dualism; instead of diversification of export structures, of trade partners, and of sources of capital and technology, we found overall trade, trade-partner, capital, and technological dependence. European countries did not have an indigenous capacity for the development of technologies appropriate to their industrialization strategy. Most European countries (including Britain, Holland, Flanders, and Italy) adopted from abroad an already developed technology. Continental Europe made a comparatively modest contribution to the technological improvements

Table 5. Landholdings in Europe before World War I

	Distribution of land holdings				Concentration of land holdings	
	Less than 5 ha		100 ha & over			
	% of landholders	% of area	% of landholders	% of area	% of population	% of land
Austria (1902)	72	—	.7	50	—	—
Denmark (1901)	53	62	4.0	33	3.5	33
England (1897)	—	—	—	—	.4	90
France (1892)	85	30	2.0	43	2.4	43
Germany (1907)	74	61	.4	23	.4	23
Hungary (1895)	73	42	.5	42	.5	42
Poland (1905)	48	42	.9	44	.9	44
Romania (1905)	77	25	.6	49	.6	49
Average	69	44	1.4	41	1.24	46

Sources: Blum 1978: 437; Clough 1952: 671.

that it adopted from England. The developed countries did, and often still do, depend heavily on foreigners for their industrial technology.

As for national control over the investment of capital and the accumulation process, throughout the nineteenth century economic power in Europe became increasingly concentrated (see Chapter 6). By the first decades of the twentieth century, monopolies and international cartels had come to control the economies, and increasingly the governments, of the various states, and national policy became essentially the product of their influence. The investment strategies pursued were designed to increase the wealth of a narrow elite which monopolized most of the land and industry of Europe. Elites preferred to develop investment opportunities abroad in order, among other things, not to damage their monopolistic market positions at home.[16]

In Britain, the pursuit of private investment profits overseas had, by the twentieth century, become inconsistent with the long-run social productiv-

16. The neglect of domestic development in favor of foreign investment was related to the monopoly conditions that prevailed in Europe before 1945. Foreign investment is a strategy of monopolistic or oligopolistic industry to expand or defend barriers to entry which are repeatedly challenged or eroded. However, it is also a *result* of barriers to entry or excess capacity due to domestic monopolies. Under conditions of monopoly, excess capacity, which is the result of earlier economies of scale or fluctuating demand, does not tend to be squeezed out of the industry, because high-cost firms are not thrown out of the market. Excess capacity discourages new investment, particularly in industries where its existence is well known because the number of firms is small. Thus the monopolist or oligopolist finds little inducement to plow back his profits into his own enterprise (Baran 1957: chaps. 3 and 4).

ity of the British economy. Capital was diverted to foreign use at the expense of domestic industry. In some respects London institutions were more highly organized to provide capital to foreign investors than to British industry;[17] capital flowed between London and the far reaches of the empire, but not between London and the industrial north. "A limited number of firms in a limited number of industries could get access to the London new-issues market—railroads, shipping, steel, cotton (after 1868), along with banks and insurance companies. And some attention was devoted to refinancing existing private companies. For the most part, however, the flow of savings was aimed abroad and not to domestic industries" (Kindleberger 1964: 62). The technical performance of British industry would have been improved if there had been a full employment of home resources, if foreign lending had been on a smaller scale, and if investors had exploited opportunities at home (Lewis 1978a: 176–77; Lewis 1972; Trebilcock 1981).

France, the second largest investor, was technologically backward and clearly in need of much larger home investment. In fact, the French on the whole did not invest domestically in large-scale industrial enterprises during the nineteenth and early twentieth centuries. Foreign lending built up rapidly in the 1850s. It flourished from 1879 to 1881, 1896 to 1913, and 1919 to 1930. The industrial banks were mainly interested in underwriting foreign bonds rather than in lending to domestic industry (Collas 1908; Baldy 1922). The Crédit Mobilier, founded in 1852, quickly turned from loans to industry to securities promotion abroad. After its demise in 1868, the next generation of banks, notably the Banque de Paris et des Pays-Bas and the Union Parisienne, followed the same pattern. Crédit Lyonnais quickly changed from an industrial bank to a deposit bank and soon turned from industrial lending to rents and foreign loans (Bouvier 1961: chap. 6). Three years after its founding in 1863, it started to restrict its loans to industry and to lend abroad. The merchant banks also concentrated mainly on the sale of foreign securities, rather than on securities for domestic industry (Bigo 1947: 124).

French capital exports, according to widespread opinion, slowed down French expansion.[18] Yet French investments helped to industrialize considerable parts of Europe, including Spain and Italy. France financed the construction of American ports and made massive investments in Turkey,

17. Committee on Finance and Industry, 1931: 171.
18. Cairncross asserts that French industry was "starved for capital" (1953: 225). The issue was a matter of debate from at least the 1830s. See Cameron 1961: 123, 152; for citations, see also Landes 1954: 260 n. 9. Sée believes that foreign lending was a handicap to French development after 1896, especially loans to agriculture (1942: 360). Lévy blames foreign lending for capital shortage, especially in the chemical industry and in urban transport (1951–52: 228).

the Balkans, and above all Russia.[19] There is little evidence that this capital brought the country the optimal return, either in terms of interest earned or in a rise in foreign orders for French products. By 1914, France's total industrial potential was only about 40 percent of Germany's. What coal, steel, and iron were produced was usually more expensive, coming from smaller plants and poorer mines (Kennedy 1987: 222).

Instead of the development of a domestic market for the products of national industry, there was a very limited diffusion of industry, persistent dualism, and increasing poverty. Industrial production in Europe, like the production of primary goods in Europe during the nineteenth century and in parts of the Third World today, was largely for an external market. Industrial goods and technology were exported to other countries, there to generate dynamic but restricted focal points of development, linked not to other sectors of the domestic economy but to similar industrial enclaves in other countries.

The case of Great Britain is instructive. By the end of World War I, textiles, coal, iron, steel, and shipbuilding, which all bulked large in the British economy, had slipped behind international competitors and proved unable to adapt to changing techniques and conditions. In order to make exports more competitive while at the same time avoiding new investment, British mine owners sought to reduce costs by lowering wages and increasing hours. Continued attempts to reduce British prices by reducing wages rather than increasing investment led to labor unrest (Tipton and Aldrich 1987a: 169, 171).

Ever since the 1870s other countries had been equipping themselves with industries more up-to-date than those of Britain. The British export of manufactures was adversely affected in the 1880s and 1890s by the decline in the rate of growth of world trade in manufactures. But it was affected even more by the industrialization of the new countries, and the effect was more permanent. In 1876–80 the British share of world exports of manufactures was 38 percent; in 1911–13, when world trade as a whole was buoyant, the British share was only 27 percent. The principal reason for the relative stagnation of British industry was that Britain had ceased to be the workshop of the world. She had become too dependent on international trade. Henceforth, if industrial production was to recover its vigorous growth, there would have to be much more emphasis on the home market.

Having ceased to be able to command an abnormal share of world trade in manufactures, Britain temporarily maintained her balance of payments by achieving an abnormal share of the world's shipping, insurance, and other

19. See Trebilcock 1981; Cameron 1961. Kindleberger (1984) provides a summary of the extensive literature on French banking and overseas investment.

commercial services. It is most doubtful whether such a position could have
been maintained permanently. . . . Sooner or later . . . other countries would
have begun to develop their own shipping and similar services, just as they
had developed their own manufactures. (Lewis 1949: 75–77)

In the 1920s various inquiries showed that stagnation was due to loss of
export markets, and that unemployment was concentrated in the export
trades. Machinery was created to facilitate the transfer of labor from export
trade areas into others, but since no special effort was made to stimulate
production for home consumption, employment opportunities outside the
export trade areas did not expand rapidly enough to absorb the export
unemployment (Lewis 1949: 80). It has been argued that the range of
choices available to early developing countries was greater than that available to later developing countries. Yet, despite the broader range of choices
available to England and France and other early developers, the consequences of the various roads taken were essentially the same.

Dependency theorists contend that dual structures and other characteristics of dependent development are unique to the contemporary Third
World and arose as a result of European exploitation. It appears, however,
that these structures are common to European and Third World development. In Europe, there were also strikingly diverse institutional and economic consequences of capitalist penetration: some countries experienced
widely spread growth, though less widespread and much later than is
usually supposed; in most, modern industrial sectors oriented to and dependent on international markets formed enclaves within nonindustrial,
mainly agricultural and backward hinterlands. Shares of manufactured
commodities to total exports varied from under 11 percent for Greece,
Denmark, Norway, and Portugal to over 74 percent for Britain, Switzerland, and Germany, with the rest of Europe somewhere in between (Crafts
1984: 448). In 1913, the gap between rich and poor countries within Europe
was wider than the gap between European and Latin American countries.
At the beginning of the nineteenth century the three richest countries in
Europe had an average GNP per capita some 45 percent above that of the
three poorest. By 1860 this gap had increased to about 160 percent, and by
1913 it stood at about 240 percent. Portugal, which was probably among
the five richest countries around 1800, was among the three or four poorest
in 1913 (Bairoch 1976: 286).[20]

The similarities of European and Third World development do not rest
on the experience of eastern Europe. Until World War II, Switzerland was a

---

20. The five richest countries around 1800 were the United Kingdom, the Netherlands (including Belgium), Switzerland, Portugal, and France. In 1913 the three richest countries were
the United Kingdom, Switzerland, and Belgium.

poor and overwhelmingly rural country, with a standard of living half that of England's (Hughes 1975: 173, 274). In Belgium, the Netherlands, Denmark, Sweden, Norway, Finland, and parts of Great Britain and France, the course of development in the nineteenth and twentieth century conformed more closely to the model of dependent development than to that of independent development.

Conclusions

Dependent industrial capitalist development is not a myth; independent development is. Domination, exploitation, and dependence were as much a part of the historical experience of the developed countries as they are of contemporary development. Developing countries, both past and present, have been dependent for technology, financing, markets, and basic imports on the international economic system dominated by more-developed countries. The dualism thought to characterize contemporary development was an integral feature of European societies in the nineteenth and early twentieth centuries. All countries adopted from abroad an already developed technology and various political institutions while retaining their indigenous archaic, feudal, or traditional social structures. The developed countries did, and often still do, depend heavily on foreigners for their industrial technology. All of the presently developed countries were increasingly dominated by international capital in the course of their development. Every developing country has had its fortunes tied to the development of the whole system.

The social rigidities common to many of the underdeveloped countries of today were also a characteristic feature of many of the present-day developed countries in the early stages of their economic development. Industrial development has tended historically to reinforce traditional elites; it neither weakens nor liberalizes them. The central role of the state and the absence of a powerful middle class are historically commonplace and not unique to the Third World. Differences in consumption patterns between classes have marked both European and contemporary Third World economies. The tastes of elites have always been in some sense alienated from those of the common people and have always been heavily influenced by the dominant culture of the day. Increasing inequalities of income typified industrial capitalist growth in the developed countries.

Domination, exploitation, inequality, cultural distortions, authoritarianism, national disintegration, and formal but inauthentic democracy are universal attributes of industrial capitalist development. They are not unique to countries in the contemporary Third World. By implying that the economic growth of Third World countries is different from that of western countries, dependency theories underplay the intrinsic costs of industrial development. There have been certain common problems in the construction of industrial societies and, historically, a common set of responses to those problems. The recognition that the same problems and responses recur in widely separated settings should reduce the intellectual need to erect separate explanatory frameworks for each setting.

Between Feudalism and Capitalism:
Industrial Development in Europe
before the World Wars

In the Third World, capitalist penetration accelerated some of the preconditions for capitalist expansion while at the same time fostering a political and social coalition dedicated to the defense of existing feudal structures. In place of a class structure dominated by a dynamic industrial bourgeoisie, as supposedly emerged in Europe during the nineteenth century, there is a "political and social coalition of wealthy compradors, powerful monopolists, and large landowners" dedicated to the defense of the existing social order. These alliances produced government policies that limited greatly the diffusion of growth in the nineteenth century. The "restrictive impact of monopoly capitalism" helped to slow and actually stop the transformation to industrial capitalism. Economic surplus, appropriated in lavish amounts by monopolistic concerns, was "used in a manner very much resembling that of the landed aristocracy": it was largely spent on excess consumption with the remainder "invested in the acquisition of rent-bearing land, in financing mercantile activities of all kinds, in usury and speculation" (Baran 1957: 177, 194, 195).

The same phenomenon, however, characterized industrial capitalist development in Europe. The expansion of market institutions in Europe proceeded simultaneously with measures and policies designed to check the market with respect to labor, land, and money, and which ultimately acted to retard economic growth. Capitalist development in Europe was shaped, not by a liberal, competitive ethos, but by monopoly and by rural, preindustrial, feudal, and autocratic structures of power and authority. It was characterized not by the bourgeoisification of the rural sector, but by the feudalization of the industrial sphere.[1]

Industrial development in Europe took place within a system of restrictions designed to limit competition. Various forms of economic protection including tariffs and cartels, as well as restrictions on labor organization, enabled a small elite of landowners and wealthy industrialists to monopolize land as well as the entire field of industry and trade. At the outset of industrial development in Europe, land was almost the only source of wealth, and most of it was in the hands of a tiny fraction of the population. As industrialization proceeded, landholdings became increasingly concentrated. Tariffs were used to protect and enrich both the landowning class and wealthy industrialists. Agricultural tariffs gave landed elites a practical monopoly of the home market. Industrial protection made possible the creation of cartels and trusts, which enabled industrialists to unite more effectively against labor and to control the market.

As Europe developed, the industrial sphere became increasingly penetrated by feudal forms of organization. In some places, traditional corporatist structures—guilds, and patronage and clientelist networks—survived and grew stronger. In 1889 Engels (1971: 396) described the situation this way:

Everything connected with the old government of the City of London—the constitution and the administration of the city proper—is still downright medieval. And this includes also the port of London, the leading port in the world. The wharfingers, the lightermen and the watermen form regular guilds with exclusive privileges and partly still don medieval costumes. These antiquated guild privileges have in the past seventy years been

1. A debate between Boris Porchnev and Roland Mousnier in the 1960s brought these terms into prominence. Porchnev argued that during the sixteenth and seventeenth centuries there took place, not an "embourgeoisement of the nobility," but rather the feudalization of the bourgeoisie (1963: 577, 580). Mousnier argued that, on the contrary, the remnants of the feudal order tended to do battle with the bourgeois element that grew up under absolutism, rather than to ally with it (1964: 82–83; for a review of the debate, and other contributions to it, see Wallerstein 1974a: 283–97).

A similar debate has emerged concerning the evolution of classes and class relations in Europe during the nineteenth and early twentieth centuries. Arno Mayer (1980) describes this period as one of persistent aristocratic domination or "feudalization," while David Blackbourn and Geoff Eley (1984) characterize it as a period of increasing consolidation of bourgeois domination or "embourgeoisement."

While it may not be possible to attach to these terms an exact socioeconomic definition, several criteria are used, both in Chapter 2 and here, to distinguish the former from the latter. These include the continuing social and political hegemony of the traditional landowning elite; the persistence and valorization of precapitalist and aristocratic institutions and ways of life; and the subordination of the needs of industrial capitalist development to the preservation of traditional ways of life, social organization, and relations of production.

crowned with the monopoly of the dock companies, and thereby the whole huge port of London had been delivered up to a small number of privileged corporations for ruthless exploitation. And this whole privileged monstrosity is being perpetuated and, as it were, made inviolable through an endless series of intricate and contradictory Acts of Parliament, through which it was born and raised, so that this legal labyrinth has become its best rampart. But while these corporations presume upon their medieval privileges in dealing with the commercial public and make London the most expensive port in the world, their members have become regular bourgeois, who besides fleecing their customers, exploit their workers in the vilest manner and thus profit simultaneously from the advantages of medieval guild and modern capitalist society.

While in some places traditional corporatist structures survived and grew stronger, elsewhere, new corporatist structures were created. These structures enabled wealthy people to preserve and reinforce the existing relations of power and distribution of wealth within society, and to exclude the mass of the population from any possibility of gaining significant institutionalized economic, social, or political power.

Land Ownership in Europe

Landed property remained the most important form of wealth in most of Europe throughout the nineteenth century. In 1815, a few hundred aristocratic families owned 25 percent of all the land of England and Wales, and a similar number of magnates owned about one-third of the Hapsburg Empire. Five families owned 15 percent of Hungary, while about fifteen families owned over one-third of the Danubian Principalities. In the Nordic countries, the consolidation of landholdings by midcentury left a fifth of the population of Sweden and Norway and two-fifths of the Finnish population landless (Langer 1969: 12). The Danish and Swedish nobilities, each of which constituted less than 1 percent of the population, owned about one-third of their countries' lands. The Spanish nobility, about 5 percent of the population, owned over half of their country. Similar concentrations of landholdings were found in Ireland, eastern Germany, the southern parts of Portugal and Italy, and Russia.[2]

2. England possesses the most thorough survey in the nineteenth century of a nation's landowning structure. Between 1874 and 1876 the government published, in what is generally known as the "New Domesday Book," the results of a special census identifying landowners and indicating the location and size of their estates. See Great Britain, *Parliamentary Papers*, vol. 72 (1874), "Return of Owners of Land, 1872–73." The raw data of the parliamentary returns

In England and Wales, open fields and common lands were abolished by legal procedure, chicanery, or pressure, continuing the process begun with the enclosure movements (between 1760 and 1840 and also earlier, during the Tudor period). In eastern Germany, most of the Hapsburg Empire, Russia, and the Danubian Principalities of Moldavia and Wallachia, the nobility was either the only class allowed to own land or had monopolized this right for so long (in Russia until 1801, in Prussia until 1808) that they held virtually all privately owned land. The vast majority of peasants or serfs in these areas held only usufructuary rights to portions of the nobles' estates. In payment for these rights, they were required to work a certain number of days per week on nonusufructuary land owned by the nobles. After 1815, though theoretically serfs could, except in Russia, leave their land without the lord's permission, legal and monetary obligations to the lord bound them in practice to the soil.[3]

No continental elite in the nineteenth century owned so large a part of its landed territory as did the English. The new Domesday Book revealed that, in the 1870s, about 80 percent of the land of the United Kingdom was owned by some 7,000 persons. In England, 25 percent of the land was owned by 363 landowners, usually titled, who held estates of 10,000 acres and more. Another 30 percent was in the hands of 3,000 owners, usually untitled gentry, who held estates ranging from 1,000 to 10,000 acres. Alto-

---

were abstracted and organized by Bateman 1971. In the final edition of his work, originally published in 1883, Bateman listed all landowners owning 2,000 acres or more, and indicated their total holdings county by county. For English statistics, see also Montagu 1970. For French statistics, see Grantham 1975; Zeldin 1973. Prussian statistics for the years 1882, 1895, and 1907 may be found in Grünberg 1922; Born 1976; Berdahl 1972; Muncy 1973, 1944. For Russian statistics, see Pavlovsky 1930.

3. Prussian peasants were made personally free in 1810, "but their property holdings remained subject to most of the labor and money dues that had previously attached to their persons. . . . As in the rest of the east, there was little capital available to the peasants to help them buy their way out of feudal dues even when the law allowed it; the amounts of land or money to be paid by the peasants in such buyouts were set in the first instance in local courts whose judges were picked by the local Junker. . . . In law, buyouts were supposed to require ceding no more than half the land; but in practice, a piece of land in Silesia that had been fully freed of feudal dues sold for as much as ten times the price it would have fetched before being freed." Feudal money dues were still required of peasants in Prussia after they were made free. These included the basic *Handdiensttage,* manual labor days; *Jagdgeld,* to keep the lord from hunting on one's plot; *Springeld,* for using a spinning wheel; *Weberzins,* for using a loom; *Schutzgeld,* to compensate the lord for costs in case one were arrested and imprisoned at his expense; *Laudemium,* a 10 percent levy on any land transaction whether or not the land had been freed of other dues through a buyout; and *Grundzins,* payable yearly on all land within the estate, owned or rented. Debts to shopkeepers, bakers, innkeepers, and merchant-manufacturers were a major impediment to movement. Junkers also contrived to impede mobility by demanding certificates of morality from anyone who moved to a new estate. For a Junker to prevent someone from leaving his own estate, therefore, he had only to deny him such a certificate (Reddy 1987: 170–72).

gether, these elites owned at least 55 percent of English land (Bateman 1971: 515).

Throughout the century, the larger landowners continued to enlarge and consolidate their holdings. In 1897, 175,000 people owned ten-elevenths of the land of England, and forty million people the remaining one-eleventh (Romein 1978: 195). In 1900, less than 1 percent of the population owned more than 40 percent of the land of Austria, Hungary, Romania, Germany, and Poland; less than 4 percent of the population owned 25 percent of the land of Denmark and France. Ten percent of landowners held 85 percent of Italy; less than one percent of the landowners controlled over 40 percent of the land of southern and central Spain (Goldstein 1983: 240).

The growing land hunger in Europe was reflected in the massive emigration that began in the final decades of the century. Between 1870 and 1914, 35 million Europeans left the region. About 75 percent of the 10 million who left before 1890 departed from northwestern Europe; about 65 percent of the 25 million who emigrated during the following 25 years came from southern, central, and eastern Europe (Goldstein 1983: 246).

In 1912, a semi-official Land Enquiry Committee report showed that more than 60 percent of the adult agricultural laborers of the kingdom received less than the amount necessary for the maintenance of a laborer and his family on workhouse fare. The average wages on the land were affirmed to be lower, the hours longer, and the housing and other conditions of living worse, than in any other great form of industry (Ogg 1930: 174).

In Prussia's eastern agricultural regions, the flow of emigrants intensified as dependent cultivators were displaced by the consolidation and mechanization of the large Junker estates and by the disintegration of German wheat production (Wolf 1982: chap. 12). In 1914, large landholdings and impoverished rural wage earners were still one of the principal problems of Prussia (Ogg 1930: 195). Displaced peasants and agricultural laborers from southern Italy, the Austro-Hungarian Empire, and the Balkans left for the New World after 1890. During the crisis of agriculture beginning in the 1870s, the sale of public-domain and church lands enabled large landowners to add to their holdings. As the crisis deepened, wealthy landowners began to move their liquid wealth into industry (Smith 1969: 159). Small cultivators, however, were squeezed out by falling prices for agricultural products and could escape the squeeze only by moving elsewhere (Schneider and Schneider 1976: 120–25). Of the more than four million that left Italy permanently between 1861 and 1911, the majority from southern Italy, four-fifths were agricultural laborers and construction workers (Sereni 1968: 353). Russian landlords sold one-quarter of their entire landholdings to the peasants in 1905, but the land hunger was only temporarily satisfied. Agrarian discontent was one of the mainsprings of the Bolshevik Revolution in 1917, and agrarian riots formed one of its most serious phases.[4]

Protection in Europe and the Myth of Free Trade

It is often claimed that the nineteenth century was an era characterized by laissez-faire policies in Europe, but the historical record does not support the assertion. Protectionism, rather than laissez-faire, characterized nineteenth-century Europe. Except for a time during the 1860s, no laissez-faire policies were to be found in Europe during the nineteenth century. There were attempts, sectors, ideologies, but no genuine laissez-faire practice anywhere for very long. Throughout most of the nineteenth and early twentieth centuries, traditional landowning classes and industrial elites were successful in securing protective tariffs. These and a variety of other measures and policies enabled them to monopolize the home market and to enrich themselves at the expense of the general population.

At the beginning of the nineteenth century, Napoleon's Continental System (1806–10) provided a large protected market for France's noncompetitive industries. The purely protectionistic aims of the system were as important to Napoleon as was its apparent objective of conquering Great Britain. Napoleon not only neglected this latter objective by failing to form an economic combine of continental Europe, he even directed his system against the countries of his own continental vassals and allies (Heckscher 1964: 257–59). A licensing system was developed to export French industrial products, and commercial measures were instituted against the allies of France, mainly in the interest of the French silk industry (Heckscher 1964: 267).

Tariff policies, together with the general circumstances of the Napoleonic Wars, brought into existence in France a small but influential class of ironmasters and textile manufacturers who were determined to keep British goods out and retain the substantial monopoly of the French market which they had acquired. After the war, high tariffs for industry were retained or adopted, and "a system designed to ruin England in time of war was extended to all other countries in time of peace" (Ogg 1930: 270–71).

Prohibitive customs tariffs to keep the price of bread extremely high (the

4. Trotsky gives an account of the merging of Bolshevik aims with the ongoing agrarian discontent. See Trotsky 1937: 3:48–51. Ogg (1930: 311–12) provides a list of the agrarian riots and uprisings which continued throughout 1917. Kennan (1960: 34) notes that the Bolsheviks, capitalizing on this discontent, stole the agrarian program of the Socialist-Revolutionary Party, to which Kerensky nominally belonged.

corn laws), were imposed in Britain after the Napoleonic Wars. These measures promoted the interests of the landowning classes, but were clearly detrimental to the living standards of the industrial working class (Barnes 1965: 148, 210–13; Clark 1951). Other western European states introduced similar legislation in order to protect agriculture against the cheap wheat available for export in countries such as Germany and Poland (Fairlie 1965). In France, legislation in 1819 made importation of grain subject to a fixed duty and a surtax varying according to the amount by which the home prices should fall below a certain level; the legislation allowed for the suspension of importation altogether under certain circumstances. Although tariff policy fluctuated throughout the remainder of the century, at no time was agriculture left without substantial protection.

The 1860s represents the only free trade interlude in an otherwise protectionist century. During the late 1850s and the 1860s there was a general lowering of barriers to international trade. Restrictions and levies on the traffic of international waterways were lowered on the Danube (1857), the Rhine (1861), the Scheldt (1863), the lower Elbe (1861), upper Elbe (1863 and 1870), and the Danish Sound and the channels between the Baltic and North Seas (1857). Currencies were simplified with the adoption of the German thaler in 1857 and the uniform Austrian florin in 1858, as well as the Latin monetary agreement among France, Belgium, Switzerland, and Italy in 1865. A series of commercial treaties provided for a substantial diminution of tariff rates between leading industrial nations of Europe: Britain-France (1860); France-Belgium (1861); France-Prussia (1862), and by extension France-Zollverein (1866); Prussia-Belgium (1863, 1865); Prussia-Britain (1865); and Prussia-Italy (1865) are only some of the agreements concluded during the decade. These trade agreements were unique in the European economic history of the nineteenth century. They were barely achieved when the tide turned.

The most fundamental factor in the overthrow of the short-lived liberal system of the 1860s was the depression of 1875–80, which was general throughout western Europe and affected both industry and agriculture. In the 1870s, protective tariffs in both agriculture and industry were reintroduced and increased from previous levels. In addition, remedies were sought for shrinking markets and increased competition through the creation of large economic blocs: in Germany, the mid-European customs union; in England, the Imperial customs union.

By 1875, the protectionist revival in France had taken on the character of a nationwide reaction. During the decade 1881–90 it centered on the demands of the agriculturists for high tariffs. The elections of 1885 were contested almost entirely upon the question of agricultural protection. Following the election, legislation was enacted that introduced or increased duties on wheat, barley, oats, cattle, meats, and other agricultural products. In 1892 France introduced the Méline tariff which, in its effort to protect farm incomes and preserve social stability, slowed down the drift from the land and supported inefficient producers. In 1910 a new tariff law, passed to meet the demands of the manufacturers, increased minimum rates and imposed taxes on many new articles (Ogg 1930: 279). The tariff measure, while designed primarily to meet the demands of industry, perpetuated, and in some instances increased, the rates on agricultural products (Ogg 1930: 277).

In Germany, an alliance of agricultural and industrial interests was formed for the reciprocal safeguarding of tariffs. In 1873, at the demand of the agricultural elements, who desired cheap machinery, the iron duties had been lowered; other taxes were lowered as well. By 1877, 95 percent of all imports entered the country duty-free. By 1879, however, Germany turned once again to protectionism and followed that course uninterruptedly through World War II.

In Italy, the owners of large grain-producing estates in the south began to demand protective tariffs in the 1870s. Agriculture could have become more competitive in international markets by specializing in fruits, vegetables, and dairy products suitable to the Italian climate. But such a shift would have required a change in social structure in the grain-growing areas, away from the traditional forms of sharecropping, which predominated, and towards more capital-intensive smaller farms. The local elites in those districts resisted such a change; they preferred to grow grain behind the tariff wall, using the labor of the numerous landless peasants and a low level of technology (Tipton and Aldrich 1987a: 29).

From the late 1870s on, domestic markets in Europe underwent steady closure and constriction. By the turn of the century protection had been adopted in all western countries and the trend was accelerated during World War I when a number of governments put into effect a comprehensive policy of import restrictions. In Germany, those who called for agricultural protection advocated, as well, the creation of a mid-European customs union. Combining smaller areas within a uniform tariff system would enable agricultural interests to expand and secure their markets. Agrarian congresses in Berlin (1880) and Budapest (1884) debated the issue.[5] Enthusiasm dissolved when Hungarian landowners became hostile to Balkan imports and the Reich-German Junkers became sensitive to imports from the Monarchy. However, the idea of a mid-European customs

5. A Frenchmen, G. de Molinari, opened the discussion in 1879, suggesting to Bismarck a unified Europe Centrale to comprise France, Holland, Belgium, Germany, Austria-Hungary, and Switzerland. The Zollverein had brought such prosperity to Germany, he argued, that a broader customs union would foster European prosperity, enhance the prospects of peace, and encourage gradual abolition of trade barriers throughout the world (Molinari 1879; in Meyer 1955: 60).

union continued to attract the attention of theoretical economists despite the opposition of special economic interests. Many wrote on the subject.[6]

Publications on Mitteleuropa, and the crescendo of discussion and writing on the subject aroused much apprehension in the west.[7] By early 1916, it was firmly believed in high policy-making circles of the Allies that a German desire to create Mitteleuropa had been one of the fundamental causes of the war and constituted the major objective of the German government. During 1916 the Allies met twice at Paris to consider the impending threat of an economic Mitteleuropa, and they agreed to continue the economic war against the Central Powers even after the cessation of hostilities.[8]

After the war, Germany was forced by several developments to reconsider her position as a commercial power: the peace settlement (which was devised to injure German overseas trade),[9] the fear of a pan-American

6. For a detailed account of these discussions see Bosc 1907: 311–57. Most prominent was Gustav Schmoller, editor of the most important prewar German economic journal, who also saw a definite need for some type of mid-European defense against the other economic colossi (1900). In 1885 Lujo Brentano published an analysis indicating a strong trend in the world towards a few huge economic regions, each dominated by a great power. He found that Germany's only hope for securing ample markets and sources of raw materials lay in a customs union of the two monarchies and the Balkans (Brentano 1885). Friedrich Naumann's book, *Mitteleuropa*, was the literary event of 1917. "It was the most important book published in Germany during the war and the greatest success from a publisher's point of view since Bismarck's memoirs" (Meyer 1955: 206). Translations were soon published in France, Britain, Italy, Sweden, Switzerland, and the United States.

7. In May 1917, Lord Balfour sent President Wilson copies of all the secret treaties of the war period which bound Britain, and also enclosed a statement of remarks he had recently made to the Imperial Council. Among these latter comments was his stated belief that prewar German policy had earnestly striven to pave a land route to India, and that the wartime Mitteleuropa was the logical fulfillment of earlier dreams. See Meyer 1955: 251–52.

8. A conference of Allied politicians met in Paris in March 1916 and decided to convene an economic conference to examine in detail inter-Allied economic cooperation in war and peace. This conference opened in Paris on 14 June 1916. The chief results of its deliberations were agreement on closer cooperation in the blockade of the Central Powers, on the exchange of natural resources, and on the protectionist measures to be adopted vis-à-vis German trade during the demobilization phase. There was also a general resolution on the long-term prospects of economic cooperation after the war. Agreement was reached on two types of measures: (1) tightening of the blockade, particularly by controlling trade of the neutral nations; and (2) contemplation of steps to continue economic pressure on the Central Powers after hostilities ceased, by cooperative resistance against German exports (abolition of most-favored-nation agreements) and by denying the mid-European powers access to raw materials under control of the Entente nations. These resolutions were passed over the vigorous protests of the Russians, who stood to lose 40 percent of their prewar grain markets, and the mixed reactions of the British, who at that time feared being forced off free trade (Great Britain, H.M.S. Stationary Office, 1916); Nolde 1928: 57–58, 152–70.

9. By the treaty, Germany lost its sovereignty and influence over the whole of its former overseas possessions, and the persons and property of her nationals in those parts were deprived of legal status and legal security (arts. 119, 120, 257). Germany was also required to renounce all rights and privileges it may have acquired in China (arts. 129, 132), Siam (arts. 135–37), Liberia (arts. 135–40), Morocco (art. 141), and Egypt (art. 148). The text of the treaty

customs union, the rise in Russian import duties, prospects of a severe increase in French protection, and similar tendencies in a number of lesser states. As a result, Germany turned from a prewar Weltpolitik toward the Nazi program to create a self-sufficient, thousand-year Reich in *Mitteleuropa*. France returned progressively to a protective system based upon duties that could be increased at frequent periodic intervals by an inter-ministerial commission. This allowed higher rates to be levied upon German and Austrian goods without recourse to a parliamentary overhauling of the tariff. The Belgian emergency tariff of November 1921 contained a similar arrangement for protection against certain German manufactured goods (Ogg 1930: 697).

England in 1915 imposed heavy import duties on manufactured products (the McKenna Duties). The original purpose of these duties was to discourage home consumption of foreign-made goods during World War I, but they came to be regarded as a necessary part of the protective armor that was gradually constructed around British industry toward the end of the war and afterward.[10] Postwar proposals for the revival of protectionism focused on the erection of a tariff wall against the entire non-British world and the establishment of an Imperial customs union, consisting of Great Britain and all of her colonies and dependencies.

The 1920s and 1930s were years of crisis for agricultural producers. Disruption in traditional producing areas in northern France, eastern Europe, and the Balkans had led during the war to a large extension of cultivation in the Americas. Eventually, as output rose, prices declined and farmers clamored for protection. Reconstruction of western European industry and the resumption of industrial development in eastern Europe not only restored old capacity but also increased potential output, the new plants being larger and more efficient than their prewar predecessors. As in the case of agriculture, producers demanded protection. Tariffs were increased, and direct controls, quotas, prohibitions, and bilateral agreements further restricted the flow of trade.

The Cartel Movement

With increasing protection, there was an increase in the growth of monopoly in Europe after 1870. Tariffs enable cartelization[11] by preserving in-

can be found in Temperley 1920: vol. 3.

10. Further duties were imposed by the Safeguarding of Industries Act (1921). Britain raised existing tariffs in 1931, imposing a general 10 percent tariff on all imports in 1932, and substantially increased the rates on particular items in subsequent years (Tipton and Aldrich: 1987a: 227).

11. For example, the German iron duties in 1873 not only enabled cartelization of the iron industry, but also facilitated the rail cartel.

ferior industries; cartelization, in turn, tends to perpetuate tariffs.[12] Thus, the same parties waging the fight for protective tariffs backed the formation of cartels (Maschke 1969: 227). Cartels are associations of independent enterprises for purposes of monopoly.[13] Monopoly is generally understood to mean a position in law or in fact enabling the monopolist to produce or sell particular goods to the exclusion of all competitors. In addition to cartels, there also developed a number of different types of "combines"—concerns that grouped a sizable fraction of the productive units in a given trade in various degrees of amalgamation.[14] The combination generally combines separate enterprises, hitherto in competition, for purposes of obtaining higher profits (Levy 1927: 219). Both cartels and combinations aimed to control the market by eliminating competition, fixing prices, sharing out supplies, buying raw materials en bloc, and cutting out middlemen with the help of special distribution centers. International cartels operated in the same way. They were formed to protect members' domestic markets and give them exclusive rights in certain export markets. After World War I, international cartels became increasingly significant in Europe (Maschke 1969: 56).

The foundations of the modern cartel movement were laid in the crisis of 1873 and during the subsequent depression years. In all countries of Europe where large-scale industry had developed, firms attempted to eliminate competition by agreement and thus improve their economic position. By 1900, most German enterprises were run by cartels; some of the most important branches of German and Belgian industry had been combined into cartels, and the same process was taking place in Russia. Powerful trusts began to emerge in large numbers in England after World War I (Romein 1978: 180–91).

There were no special provisions dealing with industrial or commercial combinations before World War II. In Great Britain, a Profiteering Act introduced in 1919 lapsed in 1921. A Cartel Decree (Kartellverordnung) issued in Germany in 1923 required that agreements to combine be exam-

12. The question whether international cartels can exercise a decisive influence on the tariff policy of the states concerned, was taken up by the Economic Consultative Committee, set up by the World Economic Conference of 1927. The committee concluded that "combines are often concluded on the basis of the commercial possibilities resulting from the protection afforded by the existing tariffs, and a change of tariffs modifying these possibilities would be regarded as jeopardizing the combine itself" (League of Nations 1931a: 29).

13. As such, cartels are distinct from industrial, technical, or trade associations which aim only to promote the interests and efficiency of some special industry and do not aim at monopoly. The earliest definitions of cartels referred to the limitation of competition by adjustment of output to demand, not to monopoly (Kleinwächter 1883: 143). By the turn of the century, however, monopoly was always described in definitions as the essential object of association (Liefmann 1897: 7).

14. Mergers, concerns, and trusts are different kinds of combinations that are distinguished by the manner in which they are organized.

ined on a case-by-case basis to determine whether an abuse of economic power existed; judgments, however, generally varied with changes in the economic and political situation (Landes 1969: 245–46; Maschke 1969: 134–37). Cartel laws were put into force in Hungary (1931), Poland (1933), and Romania (1937); however, these provided only for compulsory registration and state control.

Cartels were most numerous and effective in *Germany*. In 1897, the German Supreme Court recognized the right to combine in order to raise unduly low prices. In 1889, Germany had some 100 cartels; it had 300 by 1900, and 600 by 1914. By 1914, practically every German industry of importance was affected directly or indirectly by cartels (Curtis 1931: 402–3). The Rhenish-Westphalian Coal Syndicate, formed in 1893, controlled the entire coal industry of Rhineland-Westphalia and, in effect, the coal supply of all northwestern and much of central Germany. The steel industry was controlled almost entirely by the Steel Works Union, formed in 1904 (Ogg 1930: 223–24). The cartels and syndicates in the coal and iron industries, in the amount of capital represented and in their influence upon industry generally, outweighed in importance all the rest put together (Dawson 1913: 118). There were no industries of any consequence, except shipbuilding, which were not affected profoundly by combinations. After Germany, *Austria* had the most cartels, many of which were associated with the corresponding German ones; in these cases, one cartel covered both countries (Curtis 1931: 411). In *Belgium* cartels were also developed largely on German models. As in Austria, many of them were linked to corresponding German cartels. Belgium's most important industries, like coal mining, iron and steel, glass, and cement, were organized for joint action at a comparatively early stage. There was a regional association in the coal industry as early as 1841. A formal cartel providing for the fixing of prices, joint selling, and indemnification for dumping was organized in 1896. The Belgian coke producers organized a joint selling bureau or comptoir in 1894 and entered into an understanding with the Ruhr coke syndicate regarding the division of markets. Practically every phase of the iron and steel industry was cartelized long before the outbreak of World War I (Curtis 1931: 411).

In *France*, the cartel generally took the form of a comptoir, which involved price fixing but not, as a rule, restriction of output. In industries lending themselves to large-scale production—sugar, petroleum refining, iron and steel, heavy chemicals, plate glass—there was market control. The oldest and best-known cartel-like organization in France was the Comptoir Métallurgique de Longwy, organized in 1876 as a joint selling organization for the steel and pig iron producers of Lorraine. In the textile industry, the Comité Française de la Filature de Coton was founded in

1899. During World War I the comptoirs either disappeared or were used by the government for controlling industry. But after the armistice, many of them, especially in the iron and steel industry, were revived (Curtis 1931: 410–11).

In industry as a whole there was a marked movement towards concentration, both technical and financial, after the 1860s. Mergers and take-overs by the large iron and steel firms began in the 1840s, and by the 1860s had become common. In 1847 the seven largest firms controlled 37.5 percent of French iron and steel production; by 1860, the eight largest firms controlled 53 percent. In 1912, the ten leading iron and steel companies controlled 70.5 percent of the total capital in those French industries. By 1914, concentration in coal was also dominated by ten very powerful companies. The basic chemical industries were dominated by five companies, and four of these were controlled by the Société de Saint Gobain. The aluminum industry also consisted of five enterprises, but the market was controlled by only two of these (Caron 1979: chap. 7). A few spectacular mergers took place in the aluminum industry in the 1920s. In 1925 the Kuhlmann Company took over the Société Nationale des Matières Colorantes, which had been founded during the war. In 1928 the Etablissements du Rhône and the Société Poulenc merged to form the Société Rhône-Poulenc (Caron 1979: 284).

Cartelization of industry in *Great Britain* began with the "shipping rings" established between 1870 and 1880. In England, however, cartels were overshadowed by combinations which, during the interwar years, were actively encouraged by the British government. Between 1917 and 1927, combinations were established in the English iron and steel industries that exercised all the functions of a monopoly (Levy 1927: 233). In some cases (e.g., coal and cotton) "cooperation" between producers was imposed by law. "Such arrangements involved regulating prices and fixing quotas of production in such a way that even the least efficient firms were able to retain 'their' share of the market. Competition being thus set aside, inefficiency was perpetuated" (Youngson 1976: 169–70). But mergers, which fused all phases of a business into a single new company, overshadowed both cartels and other types of combinations. Examples include the Coates sewing-thread firm, which absorbed rivals until in 1919 it controlled 95 percent of the British sewing-thread business, and the Dunlop Rubber Company, whose mergers meant that in 1925 it produced 90 percent of the total British rubber output. The great munitions company, Vickers-Armstrong, was also created by a merger in 1927. After 1945, when a Monopolies Commission and Restrictive Practices Court was set up in Great Britain to deal with restrictive agreements, "the deluge of restrictive agreements shaken from the branches of British industry confirmed the

Table 6. Cartels and combinations

Country	Industries
Great Britain	cement, iron, coal, steel, industrial spirits, whiskey, wallpaper, electrical goods, cable, salt, cotton, sewing thread, bleaching and dying, calico printing, artificial silk, chemicals, railways, tobacco, rubber, munitions, alcohol, yeast, matches, copper mining, insurance, bookselling, textiles, cement, porcelain, carpets
France	sugar, petroleum refining, plate glass, iron, steel, heavy chemicals, pig iron, coal, chemicals, aluminum, porcelain, salt, soap, petroleum, button, paper, textiles
Germany	iron, steel, chemicals, electrical goods, potash, cement, coal, dye, synthetic nitrates, rayon, salt, explosives, textiles, paints and lacquers, fertilizer, pharmaceuticals, shipbuilding, weaving, wire cable, zinc, copper, brass, nickel, lead, brick and tile, aluminum, foodstuffs, sugar, distilling, paper, toilet paper, bicycles, merry-go-rounds, railway carriages and wagons, ceramics, shipping and transport agencies
Belgium	coal, coke, iron, steel, glass, plate glass, zinc, cement
Switzerland	silk, cotton, lace, lime, velvet, beer, brick, granite, tannery, milling, milk, chocolate, films, vinegar, paper, wood pulp, chemicals, breweries, cement, electricity, watches, cable, rubber, aluminum, matches
Scandinavia	timber products, iron ore, electrical goods, glass, machines, molybdenum, copper, carbide, bricks, soda, cement, limestone, granite, flour, cellulose, paper, soap, peat, spirits, artificial manures, meat, cotton, chocolate, margarine, carbonic acid, tar, jute, canned goods, tin plate, textiles, superphosphate, shipping
Italy	cotton textiles, iron, sugar, marble, paper, sulphur, steel screws, pumice stone, artificial manures, silk, spirits, citric acid, milling, glass
Spain	iron, wire, wire nails, screws, rolling stock, pyrites, coal, copper, lead, timber, resin, cement, mirror glass, table glass, paper, resin, cement, mirror glass, table glass, paper, rubber, goods, cotton weaving, jute weaving, rice, beer, woollen weaving, artificial manures, soap, nitrite, sugar, flour, meat, canned goods
Hungary	iron, metal, stone, clay, coal mining, steel screws, spirits, mineral water, carbonic acid, petroleum, carbide, soda, beer, sugar, glue, dyes, borax, tartaric acid, tanning materials, magnesite, artificial manures, matches, bricks, cement, candles, coffee substitutes, incandescent lamps, cable, cotton, cloth, woven goods, leather
Czechoslovakia	lignite, railway materials, iron, string, spirits, steel, chains, cable, insulating materials, jute, cloth, screws, tubes, copper, brass, aluminum goods, mineral oils, carbide cement, asbestos, bottles, table glass, bricks, glue, cellulose, paper, sugar, chemicals, mining, ceramics, rubber, textiles, wood
Romania	petroleum, pig iron, nails, lime, glass, paper, spirits, wood, wooden pegs
Bulgaria	sugar, tobacco, spirits, oil of roses
Poland	coal, iron, wire, tubes, chains, enamel goods, glass, zinc, cement, porcelain, paper, sugar, cotton, leather, spirits, flour, candles, paraffin, naphtha, superphosphate, pharmaceutical products, perfume, cotton, sulfuric acid
Russia	coal, iron, copper, cement, sugar, matches, tobacco, salt, spirits, mirror glass, paper, chemicals, cellulose, buttons, petroleum, glue, rubber, asbestos, glass, cotton, calico printing, book printing, agricultural machinery

Sources: Liefmann 1933: 25–30, 40–41; Curtis 1931: 411; Berend and Ránki 1974: 311–13; Lampe and Jackson 1982: 492; Clough 1952: 642; Tipton and Aldrich 1987a: 29; Levy 1927: chap. 9; Teichova 1974: 60.

view that cartellike trade associations had been essentially pervasive" (Caves et al. 1968: 307). The trend was much the same elsewhere in Europe, as can be seen in Table 6.

Cartelization, which had been a salient feature of eastern European economies before the war, became more extensive during the interwar period. *Hungary* had about 100 cartels before 1914; by 1938, it had 357. These controlled 41 percent of total industrial production, including 60 percent of the iron and metal industries, 83 percent of the stone and clay industries, and 100 percent of coal mining (Berend and Ránki 1974: 312). In *Romania*, 94 cartel organizations uniting about 1,600 firms represented 50 percent of the invested capital, 53 percent of the machinery, and 23 percent of the production value in 1938 (Berend and Ránki 1974: 311). In *Yugoslavia* the number of cartels grew from 30 in the 1920s to 80 in the 1930s, at which time they controlled 25 percent of investments. In *Bulgaria* cartels controlled 20 to 30 percent of industrial production by the 1930s (Berend and Ránki 1974: 313). In *Poland* there were 11 cartels in 1919; by 1936 there were 266 (Berend and Ránki 1974: 313).

The formation of trusts and cartels became one of the most characteristic features of European industrial organization during the late nineteenth and early twentieth centuries. Throughout Europe, large firms sought stable sources of labor and raw materials and assured access to markets at profitable prices. They also attempted to influence government policy regarding labor organizations, tariffs, and colonial expansion. This influence was formalized in the corporatist structures and relations that were established in many countries throughout Europe after World War I.

Corporatism

The corporatist structures that emerged in many European countries following World War I represented a further move away from industrial competition. In the course of the war, large corporations had increasingly made use of the state apparatus to solve economic problems, especially in the field of armaments. The wartime interaction of industry and state set the stage for the institution of corporatist arrangements during the interwar years. During the war, Lenin had spoken of the transition from the "monopoly" stage of capitalism to the "state monopoly" stage (Lenin 1932: 5). Liberals interpreted the wartime changes as having effectively harnessed the economy to noneconomic, national or social goals, a view embodied in the term "war socialism" common at the time. However, colossal profits were earned between 1914 and 1918. A comparative study made during the war showed that corporations achieved profits several times greater than those of prewar years (Fuchs 1918; in Hardach 1977: 106).

Profits were achieved not only by firms immediately concerned with the production of war material (arms, munitions, and powder and explosives), but also by those engaged in basic industries (mining, iron and steel, chemicals), and in branches of manufacturing such as leather and motor vehicles (Kennedy 1987: 105–7).

After World War I, corporatist institutions were established in Portugal, Spain, Austria, Poland, France, Belgium, Holland, Italy, Norway, and Sweden. The major theme in the corporatist reorganization that followed World War I was the need to shield industry from market forces (Maier 1975: chap. 8; Neumann 1944: chap. 3). Corporatist arrangements displaced power from elected representatives or career bureaucracies to the major organized forces of European society and economy—cartels and trusts, as well as various associations of business and industrial leaders— "sometimes bargaining among themselves, sometimes exerting influence through a weakened parliament, and occasionally seeking advantage through new executive authority" (Maier 1975: 9).

"Corporatism," a term once used exclusively to refer to fascist and authoritarian regimes in Europe during the interwar period, has more recently been elaborated and applied to the liberal-democratic states of contemporary Europe. "Corporatism" here, however, is meant to denote a form of politico-economic interest-group representation that is the antithesis of liberalism. It is a form of state economic control that operates by means of cooperative arrangements between private business and government. In contrast to post-World War II corporatism in Europe, it allows no independent representation of labor.[15] "Corporatism" refers to the legal and administrative instruments projected by the state to structure corporatively the representative organizations of specific social groups, to regulate formally and define the scope of their activities, and to convey through authorized channels their interests and demands to the state.

The ideas underlying interwar corporatism in Europe were not products of the twentieth century. They originated in the early nineteenth century in the works of Adam Müller (1797–1882) and Franz von Baader (1765–1841). Müller, an employee of the Austrian government in the last years of his life, championed the medieval system of estates, a "natural inequality" of occupational and personal status in which the clergy and nobility occupied the highest ranks and the peasantry was made an appendage of the nobility. Baader proposed an "organic state" which retained and expanded the old guild system to mediate between the individual and state authority (Bowen 1947: 31–38).

15. The literature on corporatism is too vast to summarize here. Migdal (1983) does it succinctly. The distinction between the so-called neo-corporative arrangements found throughout post-World War II Europe and prewar corporatism will be elaborated in Chapter 8.

Corporativists found support for their views in the encyclical Rerum Novarum issued by Leo XIII in 1891. The encyclical proposed an organic state and the union of labor and capital in the same associations rather than unions exclusively for labor.[16] After 1891, corporativism came to be recognized as the preferred theoretical ideal of the church for social and economic organization. Pope Pius XI explicitly committed the papacy to corporativism in 1931 with the publication of Quadragesimo Anno.

A variety of corporate forms were developed or strengthened during the nineteenth century. The medieval guilds and corporate structures, which had been thoroughly absorbed within the institutions of the ancien régime, were never fully abolished. They were suppressed in 1776 by Louis IV's finance minister, Turgot, but were restored after his fall (Lefebvre 1947: 45). In 1791, the National Assembly suppressed the guilds and all other corporations of artisans and workmen. It forbade all combinations, strikes, and agreements between workmen to refuse to work or between employers to refuse to give work except on specified conditions.[17] Under Napoleon, however, quasi-corporations of guildlike character were established and allowed to dominate a number of important fields of industry. Restrictions on labor and trade unions, however, remained in place for most of the century.

Throughout the nineteenth century, "nostalgia for effective corporate organization remained in the restorationist and Catholic right" in France (Crouch 1986: 192; see also Williamson 1984: chaps. 2 through 5). In Britain, the "mixing of state and society" in such institutions as the voluntary magistrate and the elite London clubs, which were private places where public business was transacted, served as a "functional equivalent of corporatism" (Crouch 1986: 194). Corporatist structures were used to control and impede industrialization in the Hapsburg territories, and guild structures remained relatively intact in Denmark. The corporate institutions established in Portugal in the 1930s were built up on an older corporatist-patrimonialist system that had long governed the structure of political

16. Some trace the genesis of these ideas to early utopian socialists, particularly Owen and Saint-Simon. Robert Owen (1771–1858), a manufacturer and philanthropist, advocated the organization of men in groups which should own and use in common all the instrumentalities of production necessary for the welfare of the members of the group. His fundamental consideration, however, was the poverty of the working class. Owen maintained that the development of machine production, when organized entirely for private profit, must mean the poverty and degradation of the working class, and that accordingly some corrective upon this tendency must be applied. See Owen 1969. Claude Henri de Rouvray, Comte de Saint-Simon (1760–1825), argued that the state should assume control of the production and distribution of goods (Saint-Simon 1802). Like Owen, Saint-Simon was fundamentally concerned with the cause of greater equality of distribution.

17. In the *Decree upon the Organization of Trades and Professions* of June 14, 1791. Text in Anderson 1904: 43–45.

institutions and behavior in Portugal (Wiarda 1977: 8; Williamson 1984: 105).

In Germany, "as the middle classes pressed more and more strongly for parliamentary institutions that would enlarge their influence in national affairs, organic estates doctrines . . . became articles of common faith for conservatives and traditionalists" (Bowen 1947: 71). In the 1850s, the court and the aristocracy in Prussia shored up their rule by giving state aid and self-regulatory powers to thousands of guilds and reestablishing aristocratic manorial rights. Corporatist conceptions of state and society advanced by representatives of the clergy and the nobility throughout the nineteenth century reflected their irreconcilable hostility to the growing pressures for secularism and democracy. The chief preoccupation in these conceptions was to find a way to preserve and justify the privileged position enjoyed by the clergy and nobility.

Bismarck advanced corporatist schemes in order to combat economic liberalism and democratic collectivism. Between 1880 and 1890, his efforts to promote the development of corporative political and economic institutions became closely bound up with his project to undermine the position of Parliament (Berghahn 1988: 110–12). He introduced a plan to supplement or replace the Reichstag by establishing a National Economic Board. Though the plan was defeated, a board of this kind was established in Prussia and for several years functioned as an advisory body on economic and social questions. The idea remained alive and nearly forty years later it became the subject of heated constitutional debate at Weimar.

Bismarck's corporatist sympathies were also reflected in his amendments of 1881, 1884, and 1886 to the Trades Law of 1869. The Trades Law, which had been adopted by a liberal parliament of the North German Confederation, had abolished all the surviving legal sanctions on which the craft guilds depended for the enforcement of their regulations. Bismarck's amendments revived a number of those sanctions and made the right to engage in certain occupations dependent on governmental or guild authorization; their effect was to strengthen and extend guild organization in some fields against factory organization and hamper the trade union movement (Bowen 1947: 149–56).

In Spain and Italy, extensive patron-client networks ensured that state elites would develop little autonomous self-definition and orientation. In Spain, caciques were used by the landed elite to thwart policies which threatened their predominance. In Central Italy, these networks centered until the 1950s around mezzadria landlords who monopolized contacts with the regional and national system and the resources it commanded through direct participation in national political life and control of local bureaucratic jobs (Eisenstadt and Lemarchand 1981).

Corporate forms persisted due to their usefulness to dominant industrial and capitalist interests. Rather than engaging in competitive political action, these interests sought to gain access to credit and fiscal facilities and other resources under the control of the state "by remaining entrenched in bureaucratic or palace politics where the informal network of family, regional, and factional solidarity is at the heart of the game" (Leca 1990: 183). Upper classes favor economic freedom "only up to the point that some of them succeed, through the purchase of privileges from the political authority or simply through the power of capital, in obtaining for themselves a monopoly for the sale of their products or the acquisition of their means of production, and in thus closing the market on their own part" (Weber 1978: 1: 638).

Throughout the nineteenth century, state policy created the conditions that permitted the survival of various forms of corporatism and monopoly. Corporate structures were used both to prevent the popular sector from gaining access to the state and at the same time to open up channels of access to the state for dominant groups. By gaining privileged access to the state, dominant classes were able to extract recurring unequal advantage from the state and from all the resources at its command.

While corporate structures gave dominant classes privileged access to the state, the popular sector was contained through electoral restrictions, limitations on the right to strike, and the corporatization of unions. Autonomous protest action or campaigns for suffrage were treated as major threats to authority. In an environment in which the state and dominant groups were fused through corporatist arrangements, "every attack on the employers' prerogatives was seen as a challenge to the state." Thus, "right up to the Second World War, nearly every major strike turned into a bloody confrontation" (Kumar 1983: 165).

Corporativist schemes everywhere were concerned with labor control. Corporatism attempted to recreate traditional, paternalistic, and rural ways of life and relations of authority in the industrial sphere. Many of the corporatist arrangements that eventually emerged in Europe recalled key features of feudal society: the fundamental antagonism between landlord and peasant, the exercise of power over the peasantry through economic exploitation and politico-legal coercion, and the ideological vision of an organic society of orders.

The aim of fascist corporatism was to ensure that economic modernization would be contained within traditional hierarchical social forms (Linz 1984: 105–6; Crouch 1986: 193). The Vichy regime in France created a comprehensive network of corporate committees and councils whose aim was made explicit by Petain: "Step by step we will progress toward the establishment of a corporatism which, taking into account the evolution in the social and economic domain, will recall in many respects the close solidarity which formerly existed among the remarkable conscientious workers of our old families" (Elbow 1953: 183).

The first major setback for labor under the interwar corporatist regimes was the limitation of factory representation. In France the movement for such representation hardly got started; in Germany the councils were legally restricted in scope; in Italy they were eliminated by fascist union leaders in concert with industrialists (Maier 1975: 582). The foremost problem of concern to French corporatists after World War I was the existence of strife between employers and employees, manifested particularly in the form of strikes. French corporatists viewed this conflict as a mortal threat to the capitalist system. They believed that every time a strike or a threat of one occurred a breakdown of the whole machinery of production was imminent (Elbow 1953: 196). Among the key objectives of Italian fascism was the control and discipline of labor. It destroyed the free trade unions, the shop committees, and the system of union contracts which in 1931 applied to ten million office employees; instituted centralized trade union control and prohibited strikes; and severely reduced wages.

In Germany, Italy, Portugal, Spain, and Austria, corporatism culminated in variants of fascism after World War I. Corporative institutions were also established in France, Sweden, Belgium, Holland, Norway, and Poland. National Socialism in Germany and fascism in Italy were subsidized largely by heavy industry and bankers (Guérin 1939: 23–40). These movements were supported by the business leaders who were seeking a way to smash the labor unions and extend their control over the entire national economy. The aim of fascist movements in both countries was to stamp out democratic liberties, destroy the labor organizations, and hand over the state to pliable politicians (Guérin 1939: 24–25). By 1930, most of the great industrialists had supplied the German National Socialist Party with material resources on a scale suffient to enable it to score a major electoral victory and to gain 107 seats in the Reichstag (Guérin 1939: 24–25).

In *Germany,* the program of the National Socialist Party, spelled out in 1920, included the creation of estate and occupational chambers for the execution of statutes enacted by the legislative authorities. Some National Socialists later used these proposals to elaborate comprehensive programs for a reorganization of the German economic system on a corporative basis. Among their first acts after coming to power in 1933 was to transfer the property of the trade unions and their affiliate organizations to the state. Under National Socialism, the German system of private corporative monopoly capitalism operated to benefit a small group of powerful industrial, financial, and agrarian monopolists, and to deprive the large mass of workers and salaried employees of any kind of organization or means of articulating their views (Neumann 1944: 634).

In *Italy*, the conservative Italian Nationalist Association's plans to develop the Italian economy by means of a regimented corporatist system were adopted with the accession of the Nationalists to positions of prominence in the regime in 1925 (the Fascist Party and the Nationalist Association having agreed to unite in February 1923). The great industrialists were particularly hard hit by the Depression because their enormous fixed capital burdened them with extremely high fixed costs, which they had to carry even when their plants lay idle. The regime instituted one of the highest tariff barriers in the world. The protectionist system, including customs duties on imported goods and the issue of licenses for the production of certain goods, provided for monopoly control of the internal market by big capital and guaranteed it high profits (Schmidt 1939: 165–66). The 1928 Royal Decree on Approval of the Electoral Law effectively eradicated representative government. The electoral system was replaced by a system of accepting or rejecting a single national list of candidates chosen by the Fascist Grand Council, aided by the syndicates and other organizations under party supervision. The suffrage was also restricted (Williamson 1984: 93–96).

In Franco's *Spain*, membership in occupational corporations (sindicatos verticales) which grouped workers and employers together was compulsory for all. The officials of these corporations were government appointees who belonged to the Falange. There was no political party other then the Falange, and the Cortes was organized as a corporative chamber. Strikes were a criminal offense.

In *Portugal*, corporatism was inaugurated with the Constitution of 1933, which proclaimed Portugal to be a republican and corporative state, and with the passing of a Labor Statute and numerous decrees establishing corporatist structures.[18] Between 1933 and 1950, small and medium businesses often were ousted from the field because they lacked access to government funds and assistance from which the larger concerns benefited, while in other cases legally enforced mergers were pushed through (Simas 1971: 29–30). The Labor Statute, which accompanied the Constitution and was an extension of it, contained language that was almost a direct translation of Mussolini's Carta del Lavoro and borrowed also from

18. Among the more important were Decree Law 23,049, which established a national system of gremios, or associations of employers' interests in industry and commerce; Decree Law 23,050, which established a national system of sindicatos, or workers' organizations, and a number of orders to give members of the liberal professions their own agencies; and Decree Law 23,051, which created a nationwide system of organizations in rural parishes consisting of both rural workers and landowners in a two-tier system of membership.

the papal encyclicals. The regime kept wages low and the provision of welfare for workers at a minimum (Williamson 1984: 120).

The clerico-fascist regime that ruled *Austria* until the German Anschluss in 1938 attempted to reorganize Austria on the basis of an estate system composed of an aristocracy, a clergy, industrialists, and merchants, to integrate industry into the political system, and to supplant parliamentary institutions (Gulick 1940).

In *France*, the Depression made it increasingly evident that controls were necessary and that regulation of production and prices could not be left completely in the hands of the individual entrepreneur. However, French corporatist thinking rejected state planning and demanded instead decentralized control by each industry organized corporatively. Corporatists recognized that social security was necessary but regarded state management, social insurance, and technical education as inefficient. The profession, through its corporations, should have the authority to look after the well-being of its members. Moreover, corporations should have a voice in the government either through a corporative branch of the legislature or an advisory national corporative council. French corporatists believed that the corporative organization of society would strengthen family life, the influence of the church, and loyalty to the nation (Elbow 1953: 198).

The big metal producers sought to organize and assert collective power. After 1864, the Comité des Forges, which grouped major steel industrialists, intervened to influence government tariff and social policies. World War I gave its leaders new power and responsibility, as state agencies in charge of raw material and production sought out unified industrial authorities with which to deal, giving the Comité des Forges authority, for instance, to supervise sales of steel abroad and the purchase of coal in London. By 1918 it was administering a system of industrywide levies and subsidies designed to equalize metal prices despite the differential costs for various producers. The Comité promoted a nationwide scheme of industrial self-regulation similar to the ideas for a planned economy current in Germany. Thirty-one "syndicates" were formed to constitute a Fédération Nationale des Syndicats, which was to serve as a government advisory organ. The Confédération Générale de la Production Française (CGPF), which grouped together business representatives, was inaugurated in 1919. During the war, the Comité des Forges formulated its own demands for the peace settlement. It asked for the cession of the Saar, the reannexation of Alsace-Lorraine, and the transfer of Luxembourg from the German Customs Union to a new Union with Belgium. During the war, the Comité also put in place plans for the long-term elimination of competition (Maier 1975: 73–74). After the war, the Comité sought to prevent any postwar German incursion into French steel markets. At the same time,

industry gained five years of duty-free entry for Lorraine and Saar products into Germany, and it won the right to incorporate the Saar economy
into its own customs frontier for fifteen years (at which time a plebiscite
would determine the political future of the region). The German-Lorraine
iron and steel concerns acquired by France were transferred at bargain
prices to the new French condominiums. French steel firms also acquired
seven of the nine major Saar steel firms (Maier 1975: 519–41).

After World War I, government subsidies made the state the "savior" of
certain sectors and certain types of enterprises. Initially, the French government used tax relief to subsidize certain sectors; after 1931, the state
itself came to the rescue of companies in difficulty by increasing its share
holdings (Caron 1979: 263). The state also intervened to organize markets
and thus give a certain amount of protection to producers in sectors un-
protected by cartels because of the dispersed nature of the markets. In
agricultural markets, an attempt was made to reduce the quantities of wine
and corn produced. In industry, attempts were made to set up professional
organizations, which foreshadowed and prepared the way for the corporatism of the Vichy government (Caron 1979: 263–64).

In *Sweden*, the process of corporatization began with the founding of the
Swedish Employers' Confederation (SAF) in 1902. Sweden's industrial
structure was highly concentrated and Swedish business carried out an
extremely militant and organized fight against unionization up to World
War I (Rueschemeyer et al. 1992: 92), Following years of conflict and bitter-
ness in the Swedish labor market (1909–36), the Saltsjöbaden Agreement
between the Swedish Confederation of Trade Unions (LO) and the SAF
placed labor under centralized control and laid the ground plan for a
corporatist system (Elder 1988).

Conclusions

Industrial development in Europe was shaped by monopoly. The highly
unequal system of land ownership that existed at the beginning of the
nineteenth century remained intact into the twentieth; the concentration of
landholdings, in fact, increased in many countries. Protection, for both
agriculture and industry, was found everywhere in Europe and increased
substantially from the last quarter of the nineteenth century through the
end of World War II. Industry also became highly concentrated. The
cartels, trusts, and combinations of various types found throughout Europe represented an industrial and commercial version of the enclosure
movements that had occurred centuries earlier. In general, the major
themes of economic organization, particularly after 1870, were the restric-

tion of output and division of markets in lieu of their expansion, the need to cartelize industry at home or bind it into price associations or pools, and the need for corporatist arrangements to shield industry from market forces.

Industrial concentration began to increase rapidly starting at the end of the nineteenth century; by the early twentieth century the cartelization of industry had become endemic throughout Europe. Trends towards industrial concentration culminated in the corporatist structures that emerged in Europe following World War I. Full-fledged corporatist regimes came to power during the interwar years in Germany, France, Austria, Portugal, Spain, and Poland. Corporative institutions were established in Belgium, Holland, Italy, Norway, and Sweden. These structures represented an attempt to apply the organization of feudal society to the industrial sphere, and in a variety of forms embodied all of the themes that the nobility had used, from the end of the eighteenth century and throughout the nineteenth, to oppose the breakdown of traditional society and the extension of political and economic rights to peasants and industrial workers (Bowen 1947; Berghahn 1988; Elbow 1953; Gulick 1940).

In Europe, industrial development proceeded within a straitjacket of monopolistic and dualistic structures designed by elites to preserve the traditional bases of their political and economic power, to monopolize gains from economic development, and to exclude other classes and groups from political and economic life. Elites kept peasants and rural workers poor and weak by blocking land reform and, through the creation of cartels and syndicates, monopolizing trade and industry. They also attempted to monopolize domestic markets and international trade through tariffs and various other controls. This obstructed rising entrepreneurs and foreign competitors, while keeping prices high at the expense of the consuming public. They instituted corporatist arrangements of a discriminatory and asymmetrical nature to place further limits on competition, so as to keep labor weak, dependent, and controlled and wages low. Monopolism, protectionism, cartelization, and corporatism were strategies fully suited for the maintenance of power by traditional feudal elites in Europe, reflecting their ethos and preserving their power.

The Myth of European Democracy
before the World Wars

It is often argued that in the Third World, where political exclusion and repression are the rule, processes characteristic of late and dependent development, and the peripheral status of the Third World in the global division of labor, have worked to prevent the development of democracy.[1] Alexander Gerschenkron (1962) argues that the characteristics of later industrializers in Europe tended to favor authoritarian government as part of an effort to mobilize capital and repress wages. Gerschenkron's argument was later developed by Albert Hirschman (1971) and Guillermo O'Donnell (1979; O'Donnell and Linck 1973) within the Latin American context. Theories of dependent development and world systems theory argue that economic dependence creates pressures toward authoritarian rule. These pressures are related, in part, to the class structure and low degree of national solidarity typical of peripheral societies. In addition, "the power of the core, both of core governments and of the large multinational core businesses, is so great, and its ability to seduce, corrupt, or otherwise influence policy in weak states is so high, that only relatively autocratic governments can resist" (Chirot 1977: 222–24).

It is frequently claimed that, in contrast to the political evolution of societies in the contemporary Third World, "in the early part of the twentieth century," most western European societies "were either political democracies, or well on the way toward becoming so" (Chirot 1977: 222).

---

1. For late development as the cause, see O'Donnell 1979; O'Donnell and Linck 1973; Gourevitch 1984, 1978; Hirschman 1971; Gerschenkron 1962. For dependent development see Thomas 1984; P. Evans 1979; Collier 1979. For the Third World's peripheral status see Chirot 1977; Wallerstein 1974a.

But stable, full democracy was established in parts of western Europe only after 1945. Until then Europe, in common with parts of the Third World today, experienced partial democratization and reversals of democratic rule. Political institutions in Europe were established by elites for the purpose of preserving and extending their social and economic power, and they were continually compromised and undermined by efforts to preserve privilege and to forestall the acquisition of power by subordinate groups and classes. Political participation was severely limited. Where liberal electoral politics were introduced, governments had difficulty maintaining them for sustained periods of time. Parliaments were dissolved, election results were disregarded, and constitutions and democratic civil liberties were continually thwarted by extralegal patronage systems, corruption, and violence.

Before 1945, what has uncritically been accepted as democracy in Europe was a severely limited form of representative government that excluded the great majority of adults from participation: men below the age of twenty-five or thirty-five and women. Given that the life expectancy in Europe before World War I was between forty-one (Austria, Spain) and fifty-five (Sweden, Denmark, Norway) years of age (see Goldstein 1983: 241), this meant that those who had the vote were men in the last third of their life; if the same system prevailed in the west today, the vote would be restricted to men over fifty-four years of age.

Nineteenth-century European democracy was everywhere constructed on the basis of a highly restrictive, means-tested suffrage that excluded the majority of the population from participation in the political process. Like democracy in the ancient world, it was really an "egalitarian oligarchy," in which "a ruling class of citizens shared the rights and spoils of political control" (MacIver 1932: 352). Universal adult suffrage would have enfranchised 40 to 50 percent of each country's population. In 1910, only some 14 to 22 percent of the population was enfranchised in Sweden, Switzerland, Great Britain, Belgium, Denmark, and the Netherlands.

The percentages enfranchised in 1910 were (Goldstein 1983: 241):

Finland	45	Sweden	19
Norway	33	U.K.	18
France	29	Denmark	17
Spain	24	Romania	16
Bulgaria	23	Russia	15
Greece	23	Netherlands	14
Serbia	23	Portugal	12
Belgium	22	Italy	8
Switzerland	22	Hungary	6
Austria	21	Germany	2

Where the suffrage did include members of the poorer classes, three-class and other weighted and plural voting systems, as well as open balloting and restrictions on and biases against working-class organizations and parties, made it futile for poor people to vote. Thus, the figures listed above do not reflect the actual number of people who were permitted to vote under the systems existing at the time.

In the 1950s and 1960s studies of political development tended, erroneously, to equate the existence of parliamentary institutions in the countries of the Third World with democracy. This is no longer the case. Today studies of Third World development pay greater attention to the bases, structure, aims, and scope of parliaments and other institutions of representative government that exist in the Third World, and to the forms of political activity and participation that they permit. However, the same tendency to equate the existence of parliaments with democracy has been and continues to be a feature of studies of European political development.

The development of parliamentary institutions in the nineteenth century did not affect the character of popular representation in Europe. In fact, before World War I, parliaments in Europe functioned rather more like royal courts than like the parliaments and other legislative bodies that exist today in the west. A French journalist writing in the 1920s described the situation this way:

> Under the old régime . . . birth in the nobility opened . . . the way to all high places. We had a revolution in order to change this situation. But it happens that nothing has been changed. As before, we have dukes, barons, marquesses, and counts who distribute among themselves all the important political places. The only difference is that now they belong not to the royal court but to that of the parliament. Having no special merits they are appointed to such positions only because of their birth within parliamentary circles. In this way there has appeared a new aristocracy in all respects similar to that of the old régime. (Sorokin 1927: 486)

In 1914, hereditary transmission of sociopolitical status was still widespread. For instance, the British House of Lords, a purely hereditary body monopolized by the great landowning families, had absolute veto power over legislation proposed by the House of Commons until 1911 (Lieven 1992: 205).

The purpose of this chapter is to show that democracy and political stability are not old and enduring characteristics of the European experience, but very recent acquisitions. "Democracy" is here defined as a political system in which there are found (1) free and fair elections of representatives with universal and equal suffrage; and (2) the institutionalization of opposition rights (freedom of association and expression, protection of individual rights against arbitrary state action). This definition borrows from Rueschemeyer et al. (1992: 43–44) who, however, include a third element in their definition: responsiveness of the state apparatus to the elected parliament. This element is dependent on the first two: where there are important electoral abuses, unelected or highly restricted upper houses with absolute veto power over all legislation, and the exclusion of working-class organizations and parties from the political process, the state's responsiveness to the legislature can hardly be considered a measure of popular representation. Since such abuses, restrictions, and exclusions characterized European political systems until World War I, and in some places beyond, this third element is largely irrelevant to the discussion.

As Rueschemeyer and his coauthors rightly point out, inclusive participation in the political process, with a right to vote that transcends class boundaries, is the central feature of democracy, though it is often treated as secondary to other dimensions. Thus, universal *male* suffrage is the historically critical benchmark in their study, because what is important is that electoral participation transcend class lines. This seems sensible, both in terms of its focus of concern and for purposes of comparative study.

Electoral Practices and the Suffrage

In nearly all European states the franchise remained highly restricted until well into the twentieth century. Among the electoral practices and restrictions that were most commonly used to block the exercise of free and fair elections were: high tax-payment and income qualifications, gerrymandering, disproportionate allocation of seats, weighted suffrage, plural voting, indirect voting, and open balloting.

Restrictions on suffrage were typically based on criteria of tax payment and income. In bicameral legislative bodies, these qualifications would normally be considerably higher for the politically privileged upper house. As a result, the nobility were overrepresented in the legislative assemblies that became standard parts of European governments in the era before World War I. In two-chamber parliaments most of the seats of the upper houses, which had veto powers over the actions of the lower house, were reserved for noblemen. But the lower houses often had many noblemen among their members as well (Gehrlich 1973).

The practice of gerrymandering and disproportionate allocation of seats

retained, for most of Europe, a clear overrepresentation of more conservative rural voters throughout the century. In Great Britain, the urban areas
were grossly underrepresented while scores of depopulated constituencies
(the so-called rotten boroughs) existed under the control of large landowners who were able to manipulate the votes of the inhabitants. Other
strategies for restricting the suffrage included weighted suffrage and plural voting. The Austrian Kurien and the Prussian three-class system were
two notable examples. Universal suffrage was granted, but the weights of
the votes given to the lower classes were infinitesimal in comparison with
those of the established landed or financial elite. Indirect voting, in which
ballots were cast not for legislative deputies but for electors, who in turn
selected representatives to parliament, was also used in many countries.[2]

Open balloting, usually by oral voting or by a show of hands, facilitated
the use of pressure and manipulation by governmental officials and local
elites, especially in rural areas. Open balloting was used in Hungary and
Prussia as late as 1914, in Denmark until 1901, and in Austria until 1906
(Goldstein 1983: 15–17). Even after the introduction of the secret ballot, it
was not difficult to manipulate elections by influence, bribery, and
intimidation.

In *France*, universal and equal suffrage was not achieved until after
World War I. Before the French Revolution, some towns were, to all intents
and purposes, small democratic republics, their officials being elected by
the townspeople and answerable to them alone. There was an active municipal life in which all took part. In 1692, municipal elections were abolished, and municipal posts were "put in offices," which meant that the
king now sold them. Though this dealt a serious blow to the independence
of the towns, right up until the revolution local government retained some
autonomy and democratic qualities (Tocqueville 1955: 41–42).

Napoleon virtually eliminated electoral politics and all meaningful political participation.[3] Under Napoleon, Tocqueville observed, "a government, both stronger and far more autocratic than the one which the Revolution had overthrown, centralized once more the entire administration,
made itself all-powerful, suppressed our dearly bought liberties, and replaced them with a mere pretense of freedom . . . . The much vaunted 'free
vote' in matters of taxation came to signify no more than the meaning-

2. Voting was indirect in Norway (1805–1906), Prussia (1849–1918), Russia (1905–17), Romania (1866–1907), Austria (1873–1907), and Finland (until 1906).
3. Napoleon abolished "any participation of the people in local autonomy and gave over the
entire power into the hands of officials assigned by the central government: prefect, sub-
prefect, and mayor. In the department, the Napoleonic prefect was, in a considerable measure,
a resurrection of the supervisor from the happy times of the ancien régime" (Tocqueville 1955:
220–21).

less assent of assemblies tamed to servility and silence" (Tocqueville 1955: ix–x).

The revolutionaries and republicans who became an elite in the new order opposed widespread political participation. They excluded the left from the political class and helped pave the way for the reintegration of the old nobility into an oligarchy of notables.[4] Less than a year after the outbreak of the revolution Mirabeau wrote in a confidential letter to the King:

> Only compare the present state of affairs with the old order and you will find that it has reassuring features and gives grounds for hope. The majority of the edicts issued by the National Assembly are obviously favorable to monarchical government. Is it not [well] to be done with parlements, with pays d'états, with an all-powerful priesthood, with privilege and the nobility? The modern idea of a single class of citizens on an equal footing would certainly have pleased Richelieu, since surface equality of this kind facilitates the exercise of power. Absolute government during successive reigns could not have done as much as this one year of revolution to make good the King's authority. (in Tocqueville 1955: 8)

The principles of the old order were revived and were endorsed by all successive governments (Tocqueville 1955: 60). The democratic constitution proclaimed in France in 1793, the first in the world to include universal male suffrage, was never put into practice and was revoked the following year (Hunt 1984: 117–19).

When, at the conclusion of the Napoleonic Wars, ultraroyalists ("ultras," as they came to be called) were returned by force of allied arms to rule over France, these returning former émigré aristocrats mounted an immediate campaign to reverse what results remained from the revolutionary era. Louis XVIII reclaimed the throne for the Bourbons (1814–24) with the help of foreign armies, triggering a spontaneous "white terror," as royalist gangs, often led by nobles, murdered thousands of former Jacobins, Bonapartists, Protestants, and Jews. In elections for the Chamber of Deputies in 1816, the ultras won 350 seats out of 392 (Weiss 1977: 50–51).

The death of Louis XVIII brought to the throne the most reactionary of

4. Hunt 1984: 233, 234. The ideas of the new leaders were best expressed by the widely read pamphlet, *Qu'est-ce que le tiers état?*, written by the Abbé Sièyes. "Himself elected to the Third Estate, Sièyes led the battle against nobles and clerics, guided much of the assembly's legislation, was a member of the government throughout the 1790s—and even stage-managed Napoleon's coup in 1799." But "Sièyes did not speak for the masses without property. He spoke for the bureaucratic, professional, and commercial classes . . . as well as for the small peasant proprietors suffering from feudal burdens" (Weiss 1977: 22). France would now be ruled by a legislative assembly elected by those adult males who owned significant amounts of property.

the ultras, Charles X. In the first election of his reign (1827), Charles disregarded the election results, dissolved the chamber, suspended freedom of the press, and declared a new electoral system that shifted electoral power gained by the professional, commercial, and industrial middle classes into the hands of noble and landed proprietors. These measures triggered a revolution among craftsmen, small shop owners, workers, and the unemployed, during which 200 soldiers and 2,000 citizens died.

Between 1815 and 1831, only some 90,000 citizens out of 32 million had enough property to vote, while only a third of these bothered to do so. There was no secret ballot; one-third of the deputies were government officials, and police, government and clergy could intimidate voters with ease (Weiss 1977: 51). Barrington Moore argues that the Revolution of 1830 finished the work of the Great Revolution and the "old aristocracy disappeared from the political arena as a coherent and effective political group" (1966: 106). But under the laws of 1831 and 1833, the franchise, previously limited to wealthy landowners, was expanded to include only a small minority of the most highly taxed commercial and industrial wealthholders. In fact, fewer Frenchmen exercised the franchise after the 1832 Reform Bill (4.2 percent of the population), than had exercised it at the end of the seventeenth century (4.7 per cent of the population) (Neale 1975: 91). Between 1831 and 1848, the number of electors was increased from 166,000 (a total of .5 percent of the population) to about 241,000 by reducing the tax requirement (Cole and Campbell 1989: 43; Goldstein 1983: 4). The government made sure that the high property qualification included industrial and commercial capital, so that the wealthy industrialists and bankers who had formed the opposition to the previous regime were satisfied. This left out the mass of the population as well as most of the salaried professionals. The regime remained essentially what it had been under the Bourbons, a regime of the notables, most of whom were owners of landed property (Cole and Campbell 1989: 43–44).

The Revolution of 1848 introduced universal suffrage for departmental councils. Conservatives won by a sizable majority, for the liberal agitators in the 1848 uprisings, once having gained the right to vote, had no interest in extending freedoms to the lower classes. In 1849, Louis Napoleon and the new assembly elected that year purged the government and army of republicans and disenfranchised some 3 million of those most likely to vote for the left (Cole and Campbell 1989: 45). Forbidden by the constitution from running for a second term, Louis Napoleon seized power in 1852 and swiftly suppressed some 100,000 who rose up against him. The French public was permitted to vote to approve the coup. Louis then set in motion reforms which put local administration even further back than the reforms of Napoleon I, and expanded the power of the prefects (by the laws of 1852 and 1861) so that they were completely independent of the government (Marx 1963: 121–23).

Elections were held in February 1871 to form a temporary governing body to negotiate peace terms following the Franco-Prussian War. Over two-thirds of the deputies returned were local notables and members of old aristocratic families (Cole and Campbell 1989: 48–49). They voted to move the government away from radical Paris to Versailles, the traditional home of monarchs. Radicals then declared Paris a self-governing commune. After they were defeated by the National Guard, thousands of rebels were shot without trial, and many more died a slow death in French penal colonies. Following the uprising, the powers of the departments were expanded to prevent further revolutionary movements. However, in 1874 the departments were again deprived of the right of electing their own mayors.

In 1873, the head of government, Adolphe Thiers, was forced from office by royalist politicians. Marshal MacMahon was elected to replace him for a seven-year term. In 1876, McMahon, ignoring the republican parliamentary majority, dismissed his republican prime minister and appointed a royalist aristocrat in his place. When the Chamber of Deputies defied him, MacMahon resigned. By the early 1890s, however, many large landowners and leaders of finance and industry, fearful of the rise of the left, had made their peace with the Republic. For similar reasons, even the Pope reconciled himself to the Third Republic. Under the Republic, traditional elites were able to retain their political dominance due to electoral practices which ensured the overrepresentation of more conservative rural voters: 30,000 of France's communes with populations of less than 1,500 each had one senatorial elector, while Paris (with a population of almost 3 million by 1914) had only 30 electors (Wright 1964: 213 n.2). Proportional representation was not introduced in France until 1945.

After the turn of the century, French society became polarized between the left and an increasingly anti-parliamentary right. At the end of World War I, France established a system that was highly unproportional and designed to work to the disadvantage of the socialists. The Communist Party polled over a million votes in 1928, or 11.4 percent of the total vote cast, but elected only 2 percent of the total membership of the chamber. The election law of 1927 was deliberately planned to accomplish such a result as it concentrated the Communist strength in a few areas (Gosnell 1930: 65). It was only in 1945 that a true form of proportional representation was introduced for the first time.

In *Great Britain*, massive rural risings impelled the government in 1832 to extend the franchise to a larger number of the rich (the Reform of 1832).

The reform added only some 217,000 voters to the existing electorate, increasing the number of voters from 435,000 to 652,000 and leaving 96 percent of the adult population without democratic representation. The reform did did little in subsequent years to change the social composition of the House of Commons, which continued, as before, to be an assembly of the younger sons of the nobility and placemen of influential magnates (Gillis 1977: 124–25). The upper house, of course, remained the preserve of the landed aristocracy. The Second Reform Bill in 1867 further increased the electorate by about 400,000, but even then not much more than one in thirty had the vote. Five out of six adult males, and nearly all the working class, were voteless.

The Third Reform Bill of 1884 granted most of the male population the vote, in principle. But until 1918, suffrage qualifications were so complicated in England that it was difficult to determine the number of qualified voters. Lodgers had to make an annual claim in order to keep on the register. Claims and objections were heard and passed upon by the revising barristers in the presence of party agents. This method of compiling the lists did not secure accuracy or completeness (Gosnell 1930). Though 88 percent of the adult male population should have qualified to vote in 1911, "complications and limitations in the registration procedures which were biased against the working class," meant that less than 30 percent of the total adult population of the United Kingdom was able to vote. "Moreover, in 1911, half a million of the eight million voters were plural voters and needless to say not many of them were working-class" (Rueschemeyer et al. 1992: 97; see also Blewett 1965; Maehl 1967: 10; Hanham 1970; Wright 1970: 103–10, 140–41; Therborn 1977).

World War I transformed Britain from an oligarchy into a democracy (Howard 1979: 103). Between the parliamentary election of December 1910 and that of May 1929, the electoral system of Great Britain underwent several profound changes. The 1913 Parliament Act, by limiting the power of the peers, removed the remaining institutional barrier within the state to the extension of the suffrage. The Representation of the People Act of 1918 completely changed the procedure for registration and nearly tripled the size of the electorate by simplifying the requirements for male voters and by extending the suffrage to women thirty years and over who qualified as occupants. In 1928 the suffrage was extended to women on the same terms as men. But plural voting, which survived in England until 1948 (O'Leary 1962), and other electoral abuses, still barred the operation of democratic politics. In 1931, the Labour Party received 9 percent of the seats in parliament with 30 percent of the vote (Carstairs 1980: 197). It was not until 1948 that the Representation of the People Bill abolished plural voting.

In *Prussia*, reforms initiated by Napoleon were halted, liberal constitutions abrogated, and liberals imprisoned or exiled. The Carlsbad Decrees of 1819 sought to silence liberal nationalists by assigning to each university a government representative whose task was to fire and blacklist all instructors, expel all students, and ban all secret societies of liberal persuasion. Presses were placed under strict censorship and a Central Investigating Commission was set up to harass any potentially dangerous groups or individuals.

Political parties first appeared in Prussia during the revolution of 1848. They remained committed to diffuse principles, however, rather than to programs calling for specific courses of action. Because of the lack of political freedom and the powerlessness of the Prussian Landtag, this general tendency persisted (Berdahl 1972). The Catholic Center Party, formed in 1852, ultimately became the largest party in the national and Prussian legislatures. The other major parties that emerged on the German political scene were the National Liberals, which began to lose strength after 1881, the Social Democratic Party (founded in 1875), and the German Conservative Party, which after 1876 devoted itself to the defense of eastern agriculture. In 1878, the press, political organizations, and meetings of the Social Democratic party were outlawed. Despite these measures, socialist votes doubled in 1890; by 1910, the Social Democrats had become Germany's largest party.

In 1850, Frederick William IV of Prussia granted a constitution which established a system of three-class suffrage. This system multiplied the number of votes at the disposal of the upper classes, giving a wealthy landowner or businessman a vote equal to that of thirty-five poor Berliners. The constitution promulgated by the German Reich in 1870 provided for Reichstag elections in which all German male citizens twenty-five years of age and over had the vote. Though in the following years there were great shifts in the population from the rural to the urban centers, no changes were made in the electoral law. Consequently, the votes of the rural electors had much more weight than those of the urban electors (Gosnell 1930: 69). Until 1914, the stagnant or declining small towns and rural areas of Prussia that supported conservatives were vastly overrepresented in the Reichstag.[5] At the end of World War I, Prussia's election system still featured, in addition to the three-class system, an oral voting system which enabled the large landlords to intimidate the poorer classes into inaction or acquiescence (Gosnell 1930: 169). The three-class system made it futile for the poor man to vote, as his group could never

5. See Goldstein 1983: 18–19. In the Scandinavian countries and in Austria, urban areas were generally overrepresented in the legislatures. See p. 101 n. 14.

hope to control a majority of the legislature. The new constitution of Prussia, adopted in 1919, did away with the three-class system. Parliamentary democracy was established in Germany after 1918, ended in 1933, and reinstated in West Germany following the defeat of the Third Reich in 1945.

In *Austria*, the upper house of the parliament was composed of princes of the imperial family, large noble landowners who inherited their seats, prelates, and life members appointed by the emperor. The members of the lower house were chosen by an electorate divided into four divisions, called curials. The 5,402 large landowners, nearly all of them noblemen, who in 1891 made up the first curial, chose 85 of the 353 deputies in the lower house, while the 1,387,572 rural voters who were the fourth curial elected 129. This system remained intact until 1907 (Blum 1978: 431).

The German minority feared that democracy would erode their power in the empire. Ultimately, this minority could only hope to maintain its privileged status and power by thrusting aside the moderate traditional conservatism of the Hapsburgs and replacing it with the extremism of the racist and authoritarian ultraright. The elections of 1907 marked the emergence of the ultraconservative Christian Social People's Party (CSVP), which became the largest political party in Austria. In 1907 it controlled Vienna, as well as most provincial capitals and numerous towns. With each extension of universal suffrage the CSVP increased its representation.

Austria established full universal suffrage and a parliamentary government after the fall of the Hapsburgs in 1918. Thus in 1920 Austria was a democratic and socialist republic. But this was only a temporary result of defeat in war. In Austria, as elsewhere during the interwar years, armed right-wing and semifascist groups sprang up. In February 1934, socialists were disarmed, disbanded, and jailed. The Austrian chancellor, Engelbert Dollfuss, then suspended parliament and proceeded to form his own clerico-fascist ruling party, the Fatherland Front. Turmoil and violence that year culminated in civil war. At its conclusion, a clerico-fascist regime governed the country by means of "emergency measures." The social laws affecting workers were withdrawn, trial by jury was largely abolished, freedom of the press was abrogated, and all democratic rights in Austria were wiped out (MacDonald 1946; Deutsch 1934: 11–13). Austria's present-day democracy dates from 1955.

Unified *Italy* took over the extremely narrow franchise of the Kingdom of Sardinia and retained this narrow suffrage until 1912, when the male vote was established. However, prefects and the mazzieri continued to control elections (Seton-Watson 1967: 147). Italy achieved universal manhood suffrage in 1919, when the vote was extended to all men over twenty-one who had served in the armed forces during the war. The free exercise of full and equal voting rights was established for both males and females in 1946.

In *Belgium*, the means-tested suffrage was so restrictive that only the fairly affluent bourgeois class had the vote. Belgium's 1831 constitution restricted the franchise for elections to the lower house and to citizens who paid direct taxes varying from 20 to 100 florins in different areas. The means test discriminated in favor of the rural areas, which were mainly peasant and Catholic. The constitution also required that elections be held in constituencies that formed divisions within each province. Because the constituencies rather than the provinces were the areas within which proportionality was to be achieved, the Catholics were strengthened where they were weak and reinforced where they were strong. The Catholics had a majority of seats in the chamber until 1914, but secured only a minority of votes in elections (Carstairs 1980: 49–50).

After the 1880s there was a system of male voting in which the heads of propertied families disposed of three votes. Constitutional amendments of 1893 introduced universal manhood suffrage at the age of twenty-five, but with plural voting allowed for certain categories of the electorate. This was called the vote capacitaire et censitaire, or the qualifications and property-assessment franchise. An extra vote was granted to married or widowed taxpayers and landowners, and two extra votes to those holding higher qualifications in education, or occupied in certain professions, or employed in certain offices. This was meant as a safeguard against the domination of parliament by the masses, and against the sweeping aside of the better educated and property-owning classes. The electoral reforms in the last days of the nineteenth century (29 December 1899) introduced a system that was heavily biased in favor of the Catholic party, and which allowed the Catholic party to remain permanently in power until 1914.

Switzerland established male suffrage in 1880, when a proper electoral register was drawn up for the first time, thus institutionalizing the male suffrage granted by the 1850 constitution. Switzerland did not adopt proportional representation until 1919, and women did not receive the vote until 1971.

The *Netherlands* had a narrow, property-based franchise until after World War I. A limited reform took place in 1887 which had the effect of increasing the electorate from about 2.5 percent of the population to 6.5 percent of the population. Another reform in 1896 increased the electorate to 12 percent of the population. In 1917, male universal suffrage was established, and the suffrage was extended to women two years later. Until 1917, when proportional representation was adopted, there were considerable discrepancies in the size of various constituencies, a situation that biased the vote in favor of the Catholic Party (Carstairs 1980: 61–66).

In *Denmark,* the peasants were enfranchised in 1849, but the votes of noble landowners and wealthy burghers were weighted to give them a majority of the seats in the upper chamber of parliament. That same year, Denmark established a bicameral constitutional monarchy with equal and nearly universal male suffrage for the lower chamber. A struggle with the upper chamber, dominated by an alliance of the landowning aristocracy with the big urban bourgeoisie, secured cabinet responsibility for the lower chamber in 1901.

Denmark did not have a secret ballot until that year. The system was favorable to the numerically largest party, the Venstre, which in 1901 received 67 percent of the seats of the Landsting (upper house) and Folketing (lower house) with 43 percent of the votes. Property qualifications were also high. In 1906 elections for the Landsting, the electors who met high property qualifications formed 7 percent of the electorate but returned more than 38 percent of the electoral college.

Equal suffrage was not introduced until 1915. A constitutional amendment in that year abolished the property qualifications previously required for Landsting elections and allowed all male and female citizens over the age of thirty-five to elect a college of electors. Women over twenty-nine years of age were admitted to the franchise for the Folketing for the first time in 1918, but under a hybrid system of proportional representation designed to increase considerably the representation of conservatives. In 1920 a single electoral system was introduced for the whole country (Carstairs 1980: 78–80).

In *Sweden,* an election reform in 1866 extended the franchise to about 5 percent of the population. The system enabled a rich elector to cast thousands of votes; in 1900, a rich elector could still cast 5,000 votes in county constituencies, and 100 votes in the towns. The franchise for the lower chamber was limited to those who met high property qualifications. In 1905, the franchise was extended to little more than 8 percent of the population (Carstairs 1980: 99). Males were granted equal voting rights to the second chamber in 1907. However, the first chamber, to which were attributed equal powers, was elected indirectly according to a system whereby the richest voters disposed of 40 votes. Between 1918 and 1921, universal male and female suffrage was established for both chambers of parliament, at the age of twenty-seven for the upper chamber and at the age of twenty-three for the lower, and plural voting was abolished for the upper chamber (Verney 1957: 21–22).

Finland had one of the most archaic forms of parliament in Europe until

1906, based on four separate estates of nobility, clergy, burgesses, and farmers, with an exclusive type of representation for the first two, and a highly restricted electoral franchise for the others. A general strike and workers' demonstrations in 1905 led to the establishment of a unicameral legislature elected by universal suffrage. Finland remained part of the Russian Empire, however, and its senate did not take on the functions of a parliament until after 1919.

In *Norway*, the electorate in 1882 was only 7.6 percent of the population. A constitutional amendment in 1884 extended the suffrage to citizens paying taxes on income above a certain level; this increased the electorate to 9.4 percent of the population. In 1897, legislation that introduced universal manhood suffrage at the age of twenty-five increased the electorate to 19.7 percent by 1900. Full universal suffrage was established in 1915. Unequal representation survived in some degree long after the adoption of so-called proportional representation in 1919, ensuring that city dwellers, who constituted only 10 percent of the population, were represented by one-third of the deputies in parliament (Carstairs 1980: 90–91).

In *Hungary*, the franchise excluded more than 90 percent of the population until 1914 (Anderson and Anderson 1967: 319–20, 326–27). In March 1913, the Diet passed a suffrage bill that extended the vote from about 6 percent to about 8 percent of the population, leaving Hungary with the most restricted franchise in Europe (Goldstein 1983: 297–302).

In *Russia*, suffrage laws for rural and urban government were revised in 1890 and 1892 respectively, drastically reducing the franchise in the cities and greatly limiting peasants' influence in the rural zemstvos. The peasants received the franchise in 1905. In the first two Dumas, elected in 1906 and 1907, 43 percent of the members were peasants. However, a decree of June 1907 restructured the franchise so that peasants comprised 22 percent of the assembly and the nobility, who were about 1 percent of the population, elected nearly half of its members (Miliukov 1917: 28–29). The new electoral law drastically reduced the representation for non-Russian nationalities and drastically increased the voting weight of the 100,000 great landlords, so that this 1 percent of the electorate was assured of about 50 percent of the Duma seats (Goldstein 1983: 285–86).

During the Napoleonic Wars, the Spanish Cortes presented *Spain* with a bourgeois constitution (1812) that did away with practically all noble prerogatives and abolished the Inquisition. The Bourbon restoration nullified these measures. In 1820, French troops helped the king and feudal elements defeat an attempt to restore the constitution and democratic civil liberties. Efforts in 1834 and between 1854 and 1856 to reinstate the bourgeois constitution were also defeated.

On the surface, Spain appeared to be a parliamentary monarchy, but while political parties alternated in power, they did not do so through normal voting procedures. On the whole, people did not vote at all. Deputies were returned by caciques after negotiations between the latter and the government, and among party or factional leaders in the government (Romero-Maura 1977: 53–54). While bureaucrats varied with revolutions and restorations, beneath the surface Spain was run by and for the caciques and their associates. Thus, a hierarchy of authority and administration arose that had no formal constitutional or legal recognition but became the effective network for enforcing the policies of those with social and economic power.

The landed and other elites maintained local authority and thwarted the democratic challenge by means of caciquismo. The purpose of caciquismo was to subvert the official hierarchies in order to effect privately determined policies. While corrupting elections was the most famous achievement of caciques, their primary duty was to see that local administrators and judges carried out policies determined by those to whom they were subservient. Judges rendered biased decisions, administrators granted favors, made arrests, and enforced the law selectively. Reforming administrators and honest judges found themselves unable to rise in the system (Herr 1977: 112–17; Kern 1973).

The state of *Greece*, the establishment of which had been the great liberal cause of the 1820s, was unable to sustain liberal institutions in the nineteenth century. In September 1843, a bloodless coup forced King Otto to convoke a national assembly dominated by the native oligarchs and notables. The western institutions adopted the following year were "little more than a facade behind which the Greek notables took over from the monarchy the effective control of affairs" (Langer 1969: 179–80). Rulers repeatedly violated the constitution. "Whenever any law thwarted the interests of powerful men, it was, if it were possible, set aside" (Finlay 1877: 5:208). Elections were corrupt, governments seldom lasted long, and both were frequently threatened by violence and bloodshed. Between 1864 and 1880 there were nine general elections and thirty-one distinct administrations; between 1881 and 1910 there were another twelve general elections and thirty-nine administrations (Woodhouse 1968: 172).

In *Romania*, high property and educational qualifications restricted the vote for members of the upper house of the parliament to two percent of the population. The lower house was divided into three so-called colleges, elected by different groups of voters. The first college, with 41 percent of the deputies, was chosen by about 1.5 percent of the electorate; the second college, with 38 percent of the deputies, was chosen by 3.5 percent of the electorate. The third, with 21 percent of the deputies, was chosen by the remaining 95 percent of the voters. Most of this 95 percent did not vote directly for their representatives but chose electors, who in turn chose the deputies (Blum 1978: 431).

Political institutions and electoral politics existed in the other *Balkan states* established after World War I, as well as in *Poland*. But political activity involved only a small elite. Elections were thoroughly corrupt. Voters were bought or intimidated, votes were forged, ballot boxes were lost or stolen (Seton-Watson 1945: 154–56). Public offices were used for little other than the pursuit of personal gain. The greatest fortunes were made not in industry and banking but in politics (Seton-Watson 1945: 148–50).

When World War I began, Norway was the only country in Europe with universal and equal suffrage. If we count male suffrage, as specified at the beginning of this chapter, then France can be added to this list of one. Great Britain had still not enfranchised the whole male working class. After the war, Denmark, Finland, the Netherlands, and Sweden also established full suffrage. Germany and Austria did too, but only briefly. By the time World War II began, Great Britain can be added to the list, though instances of plural voting remained.

The Institutionalization of Opposition Rights

Though labor governments came to power in Scandinavia, Britain, France, and Spain, a broad spectrum of public opinion in those countries and elsewhere still considered them essentially illegitimate. This perception was important in the manipulation of parliamentary politics by authoritarian movements as they rose to power during the interwar years in France, Spain, Austria, Hungary, Poland, Bulgaria, Romania, and Portugal. In most of Europe, socialist and communist parties did not become fully legitimate participants in the political process until after World War II.

The largest socialist party in Europe before 1917 was the German Social Democratic Party (SPD), but Germany under the Second and Third Reichs provided a harsh environment for socialist politics (Breitman 1981: 9). Socialist parties were outlawed in 1878, as were all associations, meetings, and publications having for their object "the subversion of the social order" or in which there was any trace of socialistic tendency. The law, which was enacted for four years, was renewed twice. Then in 1890, when it came up for renewal a third time, Bismarck proposed a new antisocialist law that he hoped would provoke the socialists, operating clandestinely, to acts of violence, thus allowing him to wipe them out altogether. The emperor disapproved, and Bismarck resigned. Though German socialists were allowed to campaign openly after 1890, an elastic interpretation of the penal law and bureaucratic chicanery ensured that strikes and general union activities would be dealt with as harshly as at the time of the Anti-Socialist Law (Hardach 1977: 177). The SPD remained a prime target for harassment up until World War I (Roth 1963: 315–19). Organizations such as the Central League of German Industrialists, the Colonial Association, the Pan-German League, the Agrarian League, and the Reich League against Social Democracy worked to make the SPD a scapegoat for all the ills of German society and to unify a broad spectrum of political and economic interests against the expansion of socialism in Germany (Groh 1973: 53–54, 66–69).

Throughout the nineteenth and early twentieth centuries, liberalism and liberal institutions were continually compromised and undermined by alliances with and attacks from the right. In an effort to preserve privilege and to forestall the rise of socialism, constitutions and democratic civil liberties were continually thwarted by conservative restorations and reaction, by extralegal patronage systems, by corruption, and by violence. After World War I, European governments suspended parliaments and outlawed opposition parties, censored the press and limited assemblies. In Italy (1922), Portugal (1926), the Baltic states (1926), Hungary (1919), Poland (1926), the Balkan countries (1923, 1926, 1929), Belgium (1926, 1935), Germany (1934), Austria (1934), the Netherlands (1935), Switzerland (1935), and Spain (1936), parliamentary democracy was destroyed.

During the interwar years and throughout Europe, the chief political objective for most conservative parties or interest groups was the exclusion of the socialists from any decisive influence on the state. "If the socialist left seriously presented its own economic objectives on the national level, alarmed conservatives fought back. They resorted either to decentralized but simultaneous boycotts of government bonds and money (as in France), or to concerted political opposition to taxation within the terms of coalition politics (as in Germany), or to extra-legal coercion (as in Italy)" (Maier 1975: 581). Socialist parties were shut down by right-wing governments in Italy, Germany, Austria, and Spain. Socialist parties were outlawed in Portugal (1926), Hungary (1919), Poland (1926), and the Balkan countries (1923, 1926, 1929). Socialists did not participate in cabinets in Belgium and Holland until 1939.

During the first decade of the interwar period, the German SPD and the German Federation of Trade Unions (ADGB) had worked to establish parliamentary democracy in Germany. But it was their entrance into coalition governments during the Weimar Republic and the refusal of non-socialist parties, organized business interests, and the military to cooperate with them, that caused the collapse of the republic. The SDP leadership placed the highest priority on the establishment of parliamentary democracy and were fully committed to cooperation between socialists and nonsocialists, but the presence of socialists in government made interparty cooperation impossible (Breitman 1981). After the National Socialists came to power in 1933, the houses, newspapers, and property of the SDP were seized and the party was dissolved as "subversive and hostile to the state."[6]

The first Labour government took office in Britain in 1923, but fell two years later as a result of its failure to prosecute an alleged communist editor charged with sedition. During the election campaign that followed, a red scare was aroused by the Foreign Office and played a decisive role in Labour's defeat. The party made a comeback in 1929, but in the bitter 1931 campaign, a coalition of Liberals and Conservatives, which eventually formed the new government, denounced Labour leaders for being Bolshevik fellow travelers and convinced a majority of the voters that the Labour Party represented "Bolshevism run mad" (McHenry 1940: 16–17).

In 1936, a Popular Front government dominated by socialists was elected in France. Leon Blum, who headed the government, was denounced as an agent of Moscow after carrying into law labor reforms that the wealthier classes regarded as revolutionary (Carr 1947: 264). A boycott of government bonds and money by French capitalists forced Blum to resign in 1937.

After 1945, socialists regularly participated in coalition governments in Austria, Switzerland, the Low Countries, and the Nordic countries. Labor and socialist parties formed governments and joined ruling coalitions in Britain and France. In Italy, the Christian Democrats brought the Independent Socialist Party into the government in 1963. In West Germany, socialists ruled in coalition with the Christian Democrats from 1963 to 1966 and formed the first left government in the history of the Federal Republic in 1969.

Parties representing the working class were not permitted to participate in the parliamentary process on an equal basis with other parties until after World War II. Though parties representing labor participated in government in several countries before 1945, their presence was strenuously and sometimes violently resisted by the right. It was only after 1945 that socialist and labor party participation in European governments was treated as fully legitimate.

---

6. Carsten 1967: 156. Industrial workers were almost totally absent from the supporters of National Socialism. National Socialism was supported by racist, völkisch, and extreme right-wing groups and parties, some of which had existed in Germany for decades. The members of these groups were artisans, tradesmen, civil servants, and white-collar employers. Support also came from paramilitary organizations formed after the war, former soldiers, and students. See Carsten 1967: 130–32.

Democracy and Class

Arguments in the dependency and the traditional development literature maintain that, while in Europe the industrial bourgeoisie played an important role in challenging the political power of traditional elites and was a prime force in the rise of political democracy, in Third World countries the industrial bourgeoisie is an important link supporting nondemocratic governments. In Europe, however, the industrial bourgeoisie was at the center of resistance to working-class political incorporation, except in Switzerland and perhaps also in France and Britain, where segments of this class played a positive role (Rueschemeyer et al., 1992: 98). Moore (1966) argues that the bourgeoisie is favorably disposed towards democracy, but in Europe the bourgeoisie in fact opposed the extension of suffrage to the working classes.

Democracy in Europe first arose as democracy for male members of the ruling class alone. As the industrial bourgeoisie grew in strength and numbers, it sought to wrest a share of political power from the ancien régime, and at the same time defend itself on the left against the pressures of social democracy. At the end of the eighteenth century, the wealthy urban bourgeoisie began to seek freedom from restrictions favoring landed wealth. When elements from within the industrial bourgeoisie showed themselves prepared to ally with the lower classes in order to achieve their objectives, the representatives of the landed elites were willing to grant to wealthy elements of the industrial bourgeoisie representation in parliaments. Once this was achieved, by the middle of the nineteenth century, these industrial elements closed ranks with the landed elite to prevent any effective extension of the franchise. Throughout the nineteenth century, this upper landed and industrial elite remained united in the determination to defend the institution of private property and to resist the pressure of the lower classes for representation and a democratic system.

No class that is economically and politically dominant will be eager to dilute its political power by democratization. The introduction of a parliamentary system was, for Europe's upper classes, a means of preserving their interests. Motivated by a desire to expand their own rights, the nobility initiated political action that opened the door to a flow of demands from other sectors within society; frightened at what it had wrought, the nobility then hastened to assist the monarchy in slamming shut the door once again. Thus the brief appearance of nobles at the head of revolutionary movements was a recurring phenomenon in Europe and elsewhere.[7]

---

7. See, e.g., France in 1789. In Russia during the Revolution of 1905, nobles in provincial

To the extent that the aristocracy which initially achieved a rudimentary electoral participation in these systems was a land-based aristocracy, rural participation—of its upper stratum—either coincided with, or even preceded, participation by an urban-based aristocracy or upper bourgeoisie. In the earliest extensions of suffrage to the peasantry (such as the Norwegian process studied by Rokkan 1967), it was the substantial, property-owning stratum of the peasantry that achieved access prior to the urban working class. Bismarck pressed for an extension of the suffrage, convinced that it would strengthen landed interests against financial interests because the landed elite controlled the behavior of their dependents and their workers at the polls (Weiss 1977: 76). In Belgium, the right had less to fear from universal manhood suffrage than did the Liberals. The Liberal vote was mainly bourgeois, but the right could count on the mass of peasant voters who were Catholics (Carstairs 1980: 51). Many Catholics in Belgium were more favorably inclined than the Socialists were to the introduction of women's suffrage. It was commonly believed that, under the influence of the priesthood, women would be more likely than men to support conservative and Catholic policies (Carstairs 1980: 55).

In general, however, the classes that benefited from the status quo, nearly without exception, resisted democracy. The industrial bourgeoisie, like the landed elite, was "generally supportive of the installation of constitutional and representative government, but opposed to extending political inclusion to the lower classes" (Rueschemeyer et al. 1992: 8). After the repeal of the corn laws, the old landed elite and the new wealthy industrialists were fused into a new ruling class dedicated to blocking free trade in land and extensions of the franchise. Most of the liberal agitators in the Paris uprisings of 1848 were middle-class intellectuals whose major desire was to have the same rights as the propertied bourgeoisie; they had no intention of offering the lower classes equal shares. Most German liberals could not accept even a simple democratic commitment. They felt that democracy must mean social democracy, mass leveling, and despotism. "From Macauley to Mises, from Spencer to Sumner, there was not a militant liberal who did not express the conviction that popular democracy was a danger to capitalism" (Polanyi 1944: 226).

It was the subordinate classes that fought for democracy, as Rueschemeyer and his coauthors (1992: 47) have argued. The urban work-

---

assemblies demanded representative government and universal and equal suffrage. In the face of massive peasant defiance and violence and revolutionary demands, Tsar Nicholas by his Manifesto of October 17 transformed Russia into a constitutional monarchy. But by 1906 the nobles, threatened by the prospect of reform, abandoned their brief flirtation with revolution and resumed their traditional relationship with the throne, which by the end of 1906 had regained much that it had yielded the year before.

ing class was the major proponent of democracy and the most consistently prodemocratic force. The prodemocratic character of working-class interests shows itself not only in labor's role in the original process of democratization, but also in the defense of democratic institutions in Europe in the 1930s.

Conclusions

Throughout the nineteenth and early twentieth centuries, commitment on the part of elites to democratic government was highly qualified. Political institutions in Europe were continually compromised and undermined by efforts to preserve privilege and to forestall the acquisition of power by subordinate groups and classes. Where liberal electoral politics were introduced, governments had difficulty in maintaining them for sustained periods of time. Constitutions and democratic civil liberties were continually thwarted by extralegal patronage systems, corruption, and violence. Parliaments were dissolved and election results were disregarded. In general, political institutions were designed to increase the power of traditional forces against the lower classes; in general, they were successful in achieving that end. In sum, democracy in Europe was late and restricted in its arrival. By the years immediately preceding World War I, Norway was the only country in Europe with universal and equal suffrage. Only after World War II did universal, equal, direct, and secret suffrage become the norm throughout western Europe.

There was in Europe a decisive disjuncture between the articulation of democratic principles by liberal elements of both the traditional upper class and the rising industrial bourgeoisie and support for their embodiment in concrete policies and deeds. This phenomenon is neither novel nor inexplicable. Rome, which never experienced anything but a narrow and oppressive oligarchy, gave birth to the Latin cult of libertas and "the most elegant threnodies for freedom in Antiquity." On the other hand, "Athens, which had known the most untrammeled democracy of the Ancient World, produced no important theorists or defenders of it." The reason, Perry Anderson suggests, is that in Rome there was no social conflict between literature and politics: power and culture were concentrated in a compact aristocracy. The narrower the circle that enjoyed freedom, "the purer was the vindication of liberty it bequeathed to posterity" (Anderson 1978: 73).

This disjuncture between the articulation of ideas in writing and in action was noted by Hippolyte Adolphe Taine during the French Revolution. Taine explains the phenomenon in terms of the structure of the human intellect, which he compares to a two-story house. In the upper story of the house, "abstract reasoning spins its arguments"; in the lower story, "an active faith reposes." Between them, communication is neither complete or immediate:

> A certain set of principles never leave[s] the upper story; they remain there in the position of curiosities, so many delicate, ingenious subtleties of which a parade is willingly made but which scarcely ever enter into actual service. If the proprietor sometimes transfers them to the lower story he makes but a partial use of them; established customs, anterior and more powerful interests and instincts restrict their employment. In this respect he is not acting in bad faith, but as a man, each of us possessing truths which he does not put into practice. (Taine 1962: 286–87)

To illustrate how the disjuncture between the two stories manifests itself concretely, Taine provides this anecdote (1962: 286) concerning an aristocratic delegate to the National Assembly:

> Mirabeau, on returning home just after having voted for the abolition of nobility titles, takes his servant by the ear and bawls out to him in his stentorian voice, "Look here, drôle, I trust that to you I shall always be Monsieur Le Comte!" This shows to what extent new theories are admitted into an aristocratic brain. They occupy the whole of the upper story, and there, with a pleasing murmur, they weave the web of interminable conversation; their buzzing lasts throughout the century.

Conclusions: Industrial Capitalist Development in Comparative-Historical Perspective

Many people claim that development in the Third World has been shaped by colonial and traditional structures and forces, and that it is characterized by dualism and monopoly, a lack of internal structural integration, and dependence on outside capital, labor, and markets. They are right. Frequently they contrast this development with a more liberal, internally focused, independent European development. Here they are wrong. In fact, all the structures we associate with dependency were as common to Europe before the world wars as they are to the Third World today—including dualism; dependence on a narrow range of export goods, on a few trading partners, and on foreign capital and technology; and specialization in the production of raw materials and primary crops.

The expansion of capitalism both in Europe and in the contemporary Third World produced a socioeconomic system that was capitalist in many institutional aspects of production but feudal in its social relations. In both places, the expansion of capitalism "reoriented partly or wholly self-sufficient economies of agricultural countries toward the production of marketable commodities," but "failed to replace feudal relations with capitalist relations." Both in Europe and in the Third World, the insertion of countries into what today is a global capitalist system involved the participation of limited groups and only very gradually broadened to include participation of the urban middle classes and the industrial bourgeoisie. As a result, on the eve of World War I both areas were living "in the twilight between capitalism and feudalism" (Baran 1970: 286). As late as 1912, Britain's Lloyd George could still declare a national land campaign to "break down the remnants of the feudal system" (Cannadine 1990: 70). It was not until World War I that processes of rapid and radical change set in motion the final "passing of feudalism" in Europe. As C. F. G. Masterman wrote a few years later, because of the war "the Feudal System vanished in blood and fire, and the landed classes were consumed" (1923: 48).

In Europe, the traditional landowning elite survived the age of absolutism, gained control of the apparatus of the state through nationalist movements and the establishment of nation-states, and shaped and directed the course of economic and political development in Europe until the era of the world wars. Industry developed in Europe within a straitjacket of dualistic and monopolistic structures designed to preserve the power and position of traditional classes. Various forms of economic protection and monopoly, as well as restrictions on labor organization and on political participation, enabled a small elite of landowners and wealthy industrialists to monopolize land as well as the entire field of industry and trade. This system produced a pattern of socioeconomic and political development that in the Third World context (but not in the European) has been called dependent development. Industrial production was largely for an external market; dynamic but restricted focal points of development were linked, not to other sectors of the domestic economy, but to similar industrial enclaves in other countries.

State institutions were designed to increase the power of traditional forces against the lower classes. While dominant classes had privileged access to these institutions and to all the resources at their command, states brutally repressed labor organizations and excluded the mass of the population from participation in economic and political life. Traditional forms of protection and monopoly—medieval guilds and corporate structures— were never fully abolished; these, together with newer corporatist structures, ensured that industrial development would increase the wealth and power of traditional landowners. New wealthy industrialists were drawn from the aristocracy, or quickly became assimilated to it. As a result, the structure of traditional society remained intact in Europe until the beginning of World War I.

Traditional agrarian structures in Europe were largely preserved during the nineteenth century. Most land was in the hands of a tiny fraction of the population, and land ownership became increasingly concentrated in the course of the century. Land concentration, by limiting modernization and technological improvement of rural production and producing an unequal distribution of income, eventually slowed the growth of industrial production (Morris and Adelman 1988: chap. 5). Sustained and vigorous growth in industrial production requires the development of an internal market (Lewis 1949: 75–77, 80). This in turn implies the efficient use of resources, which entails, among other things, agrarian reform. By the turn of the century, British industry had fallen behind international competitors. With the loss of export markets, unemployment became concentrated in the export trades. Employment opportunities outside the export trade areas could not, however, absorb the export unemployment because no special effort had been made to stimulate production for home consumption.[1] Increasing concentration of land ownership and the resulting inequalities in the distribution of wealth had impeded the efficient use of disposable resources, making it more desirable for English investors to export capital than to invest in the domestic economy. Thus, because it blocked the development of an internal market and a wider geographic and sectoral spread of economic growth, agrarian reform was the strategic issue in sustained growth and development.[2]

Agrarian reform was, in fact, the most important problem confronting Britain, Germany, France, Russia, and eastern and southern Europe in 1914. In Britain, a series of official inquiries undertaken during the 1870s and 1880s had revealed for the first time the extent of the territorial monopoly and collective wealth of landowners and had led to widespread demands for changes in the distribution and control of property and for much heavier taxation of unearned incomes. There was an unprecedented upsurge in agrarian agitation and protest in many parts of the country. Tenants turned against their landlords, frequently refused to pay their rents, and demanded an end to the system of great estates (Cannadine 1990: 36). The culmination of these events came when Lloyd George, in his "land campaign" of 1912–14, launched an attack on the rural and urban landowners. Consideration of agrarian reform was postponed, however, by the outbreak of war in 1914. In nearly all of Europe, serious agrarian reform did not take place until after World War II.

Elites preferred to develop investment opportunities abroad rather than damage their carefully erected monopolistic market positions at home through creation of additional productive capacity. Lenin contended that the export of capital, which in his view had become the typical feature of capitalism, was a result of the superabundance of capital accumulated in the advanced countries.[3] But the main capital exporters did not have capital-saturated domestic economies. During the nineteenth century, Brit-

1. Rearmament began to absorb large numbers of unemployed industrial workers in the 1930s (Tipton and Aldrich 1987a: 172).
2. Morris and Adelman have found that "sustained and widespread economic growth is likely only with above-average equity in land distribution" (1989: 1425).
3. Other theorists, as well, have traced the impetus for foreign economic expansion to the need for an outlet for surplus capital generated in advanced capitalist states (e.g., Baran and Sweezy 1966; Hobson 1965; Baran 1957; Sweezy 1942; Lenin 1948).

ain and France, the two largest foreign investors, suffered from inadequate investment at home. The monopolization of economic resources, both in land and industry, blocked the development of human resources, the application of new techniques, and the rational distribution of resources. Though Europe had raised its GNP per capita during the nineteenth century, by the start of World War I its lagging agricultural sector and the maldistribution of taxes and income had led to ever recurring bottlenecks and to a process of development so distorted from a welfare point of view that it eventually produced stagnation, social polarization, and crisis. The social polarization and conflict endemic throughout Europe during the early years of this century led, by 1914, to the first of two massively destructive regional wars.

Models of European and Third World Development

The data and evidence summarized in preceding chapters shows that, when World War I began, the dominant social, economic, and political system of Europe paralleled that which existed at the time in other regions, and which still exists in many areas of the Third World. Though preceding chapters have documented this similarity, its conclusions have not been drawn. The pattern of Third World development is analogous to that of Europe before World War II, and the categories and concepts used to analyze Third World development are applicable to European development as well. Theories need to be revised to take account of this. The best revision would seem to be one that takes into account the points of agreement and disagreement between the arguments and evidence summarized in preceding chapters on the one hand, and existing theoretical approaches to the study of development and underdevelopment on the other. In Table 7, the points of agreement are shown in boldface.

The neo-Marxist/dependency model is boldfaced, but is not followed by any boldfaced terms. This indicates that though dependency theories offer a model of development which is accurate at the level of description, they are in several respects inconsistent with the evidence I have presented in previous chapters: their application is wrongly restricted to the Third World, they focus their analysis on the state as the developing unit, and they assume that change is externally driven, with international forces as the agents. Liberal, modernization, neoclassical, world systems, and classical Marxist theories have all contributed to a model of western European development that is substantially inaccurate; some theories however, assume correctly that the process of capitalist development everywhere is internally driven and more or less the same everywhere. The European

Table 7. Points of agreement (in boldface) and disagreement between the arguments and evidence presented in this study and existing theoretical approaches to the study of development

Model of development	Applicability of model	Unit of analysis	Locus of change	Agent of change
Neoclassical	**Universal**	States	**Internal**[a]	Individuals/ the state
Modernization	**Universal**	States	**Internal**	Individuals
Liberal	Regionally/ temporally restricted	States	**Internal**	Groups
World systems	Temporally restricted	World system	External	World-market forces
Neo-Marxist	Regionally/ temporally restricted	States	External	Transnational or international forces
Classical Marxism	**Universal**	Modes of production/ **Social formations**	**Internal**	**Classes**

[a]See p. 5 n. 11 on the locus of change in neoclassical theory. Most neoclassical writers emphasize the role of endogenous institutional transformations in creating the conditions for the expansion of trade.

model that all these theories accept assumes that capitalism emerged in Europe far earlier and more completely than it actually did, that it was led by a strong, independent industrial capitalist bourgeoisie,[4] and that it was more or less even and internally focused. This is *not* an accurate model of European development. As I have shown in preceding chapters, models of Third World dependent development provide a far more accurate description of capitalist development in Europe before the world wars than is provided by liberal or classical Marxist theories.

Until fairly recently, liberal, modernization, neoclassical, and Marxist theorists assumed that Third World countries would replicate the path followed by Europe in the nineteenth century. Today, the general consensus among these scholars, as well as among world systems and dependency theorists, is that the Third World is developing in a radically different way. Liberal theorists offer a model of economic advance that in their view describes England's transformation from feudalism to capital-

4. In world systems theory, this class is found only in those western European countries that are part of the core of the world system. Individual Marxists criticized the bourgeoisies of specific European countries for their "weakness," and their compromises with or dependence on traditional elites; see Luxemburg on Poland (1976: 176), Gramsci on Italy (1949: 77–83), and Engels on Germany (1969: 17) and Italy (1895: 23–24).

ism through the development of trade, the division of labor, and the diffusion of capital and technology from advanced to backward sectors of the economy. Modernization theories center on a description of the transition from traditional society to modern society, understood as an evolution from a once universal original state to a universal end state. However, the processes of transition described by liberal and modernization theories bear no resemblance to processes of change in the contemporary developing world.[5] Neoclassical models of growth describe a process of endogenous institutional transformations making possible the expansion of trade (which then acts as an engine of growth), the spread of industrialization, substantial manufacturing exports, and generalized improvements in agriculture. This model has proved to be irrelevant to the experience of the contemporary Third World. In fact, Cynthia Morris and Irma Adelman (1988) have shown that, except for Great Britain, France, Belgium, and Switzerland, the model is irrelevant to European historical development as well. In preceding chapters I have questioned its applicability even to those few cases.

Liberal, modernization, and classical Marxist theories all assign the central role in European capitalist development to a new urban industrial bourgeoisie. But the bourgeoisie in Europe did not actually play the role assigned to them.[6] Despite the development of new productive forces, it was in fact the traditional elite that played the prominent role in capitalist development in Europe. Relations of production were not wholly transformed by the expansion of capitalism until after the world wars; neither was the class nature of this elite altered. All these models are irrelevant both to today's less developed countries and to the historical development of today's advanced industrial states. The models are based, not on the historical record, but on rhetoric derived from three sources: the revolutionary events of 1789, the claims of European superiority in the age of European imperialism, and the capitalist triumphalism common after 1917.

Dependency and world systems theories, while challenging many key tenets of social science theory, never challenge the West's image of its own development. Scholars working to develop these perspectives need to incorporate more accurate models of western historical development into their theories. In doing this, they must ultimately reject those aspects of their own theories that limit the application of models of dependent development to the Third World, and must reformulate their theories to

5. Recent events in eastern Europe have brought about a resurgence of modernization theory. See, for instance, Müller 1992, 1994.
6. The proposition remains true, however, for the United States, New Zealand, Canada, Australia, and perhaps South Africa.

account for dependent development in the core before World War II. One major conclusion of the present study—that development is similar across regions in important ways—argues against the tendency of world systems theory to emphasize the differences between regions. The principle underlying Wallerstein's advice to his critics (1988: 881) would, if applied to his own inquiry, undermine world systems theory:

> We can always pinpoint differences. It is the easiest of scholarly tasks, since everything is always different in some ways from everything else across time and space. What is harder and takes priority is to discover similarities. Only when we have exhausted our statements of the similarities is it prudent to analyze the residual differences. And this is all the more true if one's moral concern is with social transformation. One wants to make sure that a difference matters, that it truly suggests transformation.

Systematic variation in development experience may exist between countries, past and present, and may occur between developed and less developed countries of the world system *today,* but it did not exist between nineteenth century European countries and those which today form the Third World. The differences between Europe and the Third World, featured so prominently in the analysis of contemporary development, did not arise until after World War II. The dependency model is a universally applicable model of industrial capitalist development. This development is not a unitary process; there are regional and local variations. However, while there is a variety of developmental experience, that variety is found within states and within regions, not between regions.[7]

In liberal, modernization, and neoclassical[8] theories, states are the basic unit of analysis for studying processes of development. Dependency theory gives greater weight to social forces and to continuities between local and international relations, but it ultimately gives greatest weight to the functionally specific ways that *states* act as a result of their location in the international system.[9] State boundaries do not, however, define the unit that actually develops. The phrase "dual development" suggests, in fact,

7. In their examination of economic and institutional change in twenty-three countries during the nineteenth and early twentieth centuries, Morris and Adelman found that "variations within national boundaries often exceed 'average' differences among countries" (1988: 4).
8. In neoclassical theory, the agent of change is either an individual calculus of profit maximization (e.g., the independent creative entrepreneur, as in Schumpeter 1939), or the state, which changes institutions to maximize the revenues of rulers (e.g., North 1981; North and Thomas 1973, 1970; Olson 1982; Davis and North 1971).
9. In contrast to classical Marxism, dependency theory is concerned, not with class dependency, but with national dependency. Classical Marxism views national and class dependency as at least partly independent. See Packenham's discussion of dependency ideas as an effort to wed Marxism and nationalism (1992; chap. 1).

that economic development is essentially a subnational and transnational phenomenon: within states, some sectors develop and others do not. The units that develop and change, and that act or are acted upon in the process of development, are subnational and transnational.

Much is made in the liberal and dependency literature of the growing income gap between developed and underdeveloped countries. But this emphasis obscures the theoretically and empirically significant fact that elites in the Third World enjoy the same level of income and standard of living as elites in the developed countries (Sunkel 1973: 150). In fact, the more significant gap is the one between rich and poor within Third World countries. Development and underdevelopment do not correspond to a vertical division among nations or among regions, but to a transnational and horizontal one among classes. This remains true, despite the fact that wars and invasion have at times changed the balance of power among classes, broadening the distribution of wealth sufficiently to make some countries or regions more prosperous than others—as happened in this century with Europe, the United States, and Japan.

World systems and dependency theories claim that underdevelopment in Latin America is the result of the region's incorporation into the world capitalist economy as a raw materials producing area. But countries in the core were also incorporated into the system as raw materials producers (e.g., Denmark, Sweden, the United States, Canada, Australia). Moreover, core development and peripheral development before the world wars were generally more similar than dissimilar. These essential similarities call into question the notion that developmental outcomes are set by a global division of labor and by a process of synchronous regional differentiation.

If the history of today's developed and underdeveloped countries is any guide, capturing a larger share of global product does not necessarily mean that a country distributes the gains more equitably or uses them more productively within its borders. Whether or not states collaborate with foreign capital, or to what degree, seems to have made no significant difference either. Moreover, though state governments play an important role in development, they were not autonomous actors in the processes of economic and political development and change that took place in Europe during the nineteenth and early twentieth centuries, nor in those taking place in many areas of the Third World today. It is local dominant classes that are decisive in bringing about external reliance, in translating it into structural distortions, and in determining how the benefits of collaboration with foreign capital are distributed and used.[10] It is the local elite that

10. Warren (1980) has criticized dependency theory for blurring the distinction between imperialist and capitalist exploitation.

dictate the form, substance, timing, and pace of change, and determine if and how economic development and its benefits will spread across sectors and regions.[11]

Some Marxist scholars recognize the similarity of European and Third World development, but they attribute this similarity to concomitant or intrinsic and mainly economic qualities and effects of the capitalist mode of production.[12] A delineation of the laws of motion proper to the capitalist mode of production cannot, however, explain why Europe grew prosperous after the world wars and the Third World remained underdeveloped. Development and underdevelopment recur throughout history, often in the same regions, and their causation is essentially the same in any mode of production. The inhibition of development is generated by processes of class formation and of class and intraclass struggle which tend to occur with the opening up of new sources of wealth and with advances in the means of production.

The advent of capitalism generated the same cycle of greed, monopoly, and impoverishment that recurs whenever new sources of wealth or new means of producing wealth emerge. It is, therefore, not capitalism per se with which we should be concerned—forms of capitalism have recurred throughout history—but industrialism and other processes of expansion, discovery, and change.

Dependent development arises from class relations and processes of class formation common to Europe and the contemporary Third World. Dualism, its most characteristic manifestation, is neither an unintended consequence nor an unavoidable outcome of social, political, or economic processes: it is actively and dynamically perpetuated and recreated. Dual structures were and are maintained wherever they exist as a result of internal class relations that develop as new sources or means of producing wealth become available. In nineteenth- and early-twentieth-century Europe, as in the Third World today, traditional elites used the wealth and

11. Packenham asks, "What were the powerful egalitarian elements in the Brazilian tradition that were being smothered by foreign pressures?" Elitism, tolerance for massive socioeconomic disparities, capitalism, and authoritarianism "are powerful and authentic national traditions" (1992: 147). In fact, as Portes notes, domestic owners, managers of multinational subsidiaries, and top administrators of public enterprises "are united by their common position relative to subordinate groups and their interest in preserving the status quo." They "have coalesced in supporting the rise of conservative governments and have joined forces in opposing the various forms of populism and socialism in the region" (Portes 1985: 10–11). Morris and Adelman conclude that "domestic dominance of government policy did not assure widely beneficial economic growth" (1988: 210).

12. See, for instance, Senghaas 1985; Lall 1981; Bernstein 1979; Cueva 1977, 1976. Lall has argued that instead of concentrating on the "mistaken argument" that capitalism "can never lead to a repetition of the experience of the developed capitalist countries," neo-Marxist analysts "should be drawing attention to the intrinsic costs of the capitalist system as such, and to its continuously evolving dynamics" (1981: 19).

privileges they had acquired in the past to ensure that processes of capitalist development would not adversely affect their interests. By preserving the political and economic bases of traditional groups and restricting growth within the constraints posed by the concentration of capital and land ownership, dualism generated the structural distortions associated with dependent development.

The primary unit that changes in development is not the world system or the state, but the "social formation"—the "actual and specific" social entity "with given resources and given forms of economic and political organization and cultural features" (Alavi 1982: 178). In some regions of the world, where states were built up within once undivided fields of social interaction (e.g., Europe and the Middle East), the social formation that develops and changes is essentially transnational in nature and regional in scope. For instance, European states in the nineteenth century were rooted in a social formation that predated them and whose structures continued to overlap and intersect local class structures and processes of change throughout the course of state-building and industrial development. Europe's dominant classes were transnational. While bearing a kind of family resemblance to each other, they were often physically distinct from peasants within their own countries; often they were of a different nationality or religion, or spoke a different language. Even where they had the same nationality and religion, they had in all respects more in common with elites elsewhere in Europe than with the lower classes within their own countries.

Social formations can be global in scope, as is the case with a world capitalist system. In Marxist usage, social formations are concrete combinations of different modes of production organized under the dominance of one of them (Poulantzas 1973a: 10–12), a view that is consistent with world systems theories. But the causation and process of this global social formation would still be essentially social, driven primarily by processes of class formation and class struggle. Social forces mediate the influence of other structures and forces and limit the ability of states to act autonomously. Analytically, they should therefore be treated as prior to international forces and structures and to states, and more basic. Developmental change is driven not by the world system, states, individuals, or the logic of capitalist development, either at the local or global level, but by classes and class struggles within social formations.

All capitalist development has been dependent development, but the dependency is class dependency, not state dependency. It is a dependency internal to states, not between states. Its causation or process is local not global (in the geographical sense). Developmental change is driven by classes and class struggles. The driving and shaping of development by class struggle is not peculiar to the development of a region nor of an epoch: it is the universal within a multitude of specific variations in states and in regions. There is no truly universal model of capitalist development, in the sense that the specific historical conditions, forms, and mechanisms through which capitalism occurs (or fails to occur) are not important. But the notion that capitalist development in the contemporary Third World is "deficient" or "distorted," in contrast to some model of "normal" capitalist development realized by the now advanced countries of the west, is a fallacy.

The Great Divide: Europe and Latin America on the Eve of World War I

Latin America and Europe had achieved comparable levels of development and economic well-being by the beginning of World War I (see Statistical Appendix, Tables 1–6). The richest Latin American countries were as rich as the richest European countries, the poorest European countries were poorer than the poorest Latin American countries (see Statistical Appendix, Table 1). In Argentina, Chile, and Uruguay, average export levels in 1913 were above those of France, Germany, and Sweden (Banks 1971: 171–205). In Brazil, Colombia, Venezuela, and Cuba, agricultural exports grew just about as fast as industrial production in the leading industrial countries. In the countries that took advantage of this, output per head grew as rapidly as in western Europe before 1914.[13] In the decades before World War I, the annual rate of growth of exports from Argentina, Brazil, Ecuador, Peru, Colombia, Mexico, and Uruguay was greater than that of Belgium, France, and Great Britain (see Statistical Appendix, Tables 1, 7, 8a and b, 9, 10).

When World War I began, what disparities existed between Europe and Latin America resulted essentially from the earlier start on industrialization made by some countries of Europe and differences in natural resources.[14] The era of the world wars was the great watershed dividing the fortunes of Europe and the nonwestern world. Had Europe not experienced the world wars and the collapse of its traditional class structure,

13. Stover 1970: 62; Lewis 1978a: 223. Argentina, Chile, Brazil, Colombia, Cuba, Venezuela, and Mexico contain 66 percent of the region's population.
14. In 1913, three powers—Great Britain, Germany, and France—accounted for more than seven-tenths of Europe's manufacturing capacity. Their share of Europe's population was less than half. These three "held a secure lead in the development of European industry as a result of an early start at a time when proximity to coalfields was essential." Coal predominated as the source of energy for mechanical power, and the three powers controlled within their frontiers 93 percent of European coal output. The remaining quantity was mined in Belgium and the Austro-Hungarian Empire (Svennilson 1954: 16).

Europe and Latin America today would not look dissimilar to any signifi-cant degree.[15]

After the world wars a gap opened between Europe and the Third World, but *not* because Latin American growth slowed: it did not. In fact, its rate of growth increased. Between 1913 and 1950 the annual average GDP growth for Latin America as a whole was 3.5 percent, as against only 1.9 percent for the countries which today are the advanced capitalist coun-tries (Maddison 1991: 17). Latin America performed much better than the rest of the world in the 1930s and 1940s (Maddison 1991: 20). Manufactur-ing production almost doubled from 1937 to 1950 (Maizels 1970: 24). GNP increased at 4 percent per annum from 1935 to 1953, GNP per capita at 2 percent per annum. Between 1945 and 1955 total output rose at an annual rate of about 4.9 percent and output per capita by 2.4 percent (United Nations 1956: 3; see also Bairoch 1975: 184; Kuznets 1971: 30–31).

But while the average per capita income in the developing countries as a whole rose by 2.5 percent a year between 1950 and 1969, in the indus-trialized countries it rose by 3.3 percent. Exports from developing coun-tries rose at an average annual rate of 4.8 percent in those years, but in the industrialized countries they increased by 7.9 percent. Latin America's share of total world exports dropped from 12 to 6 percent between 1950 to 1969 (Lord and Boye 1991: 121). Though the rate of Latin American growth increased, it simply could not keep up with the phenomenal and unprece-dented surge of growth experienced by European countries following World War II.

Many of the factors regarded as the chief obstacles to economic develop-ment in Third World countries—lack of savings, shortage of entrepreneurs and skilled labor, inflation—do not explain this lag in Latin American development relative to European growth after 1945. There was an un-precedented flow of foreign investment into Latin America after 1955. Its rate of savings was not very much below that of the advanced western countries. Its entrepreneurs were sufficently numerous and talented to have increased its production of goods and services by 60 percent between 1945 and 1958. The labor force was sufficent to allow the manufacturing industry to expand its production by 90 percent during that period. Mone-tary instability was not an obstacle: inflation-ridden countries, such as

15. Practically all of Latin America avoided effective participation. Even the engagement of Brazil, an avowed legal participant in both world wars, was limited. "The differences in the intensity of participation, in the degree to which the actively engaged nation-states suffered invasion and the destructive effect of battles fought in their territories, and in the outcome of the war for them, meant, naturally, different impacts of war on their economies, with conse-quently different prospects for postwar economic growth" (Kuznets 1964: 69).

Brazil, developed at a rapid rate, while fairly stable ones, such as Cuba, progressed slowly (Ahumada 1963: 115).

But though Latin American countries were just as capable of developing an industrial complex of skills, institutions, and ideas, they did not. The growth of exports offered Latin American countries the opportunity to strengthen their infrastructure, increase productivity in food, and move towards industrialization for home and export markets, but they did not. The best use of the money gained from exporting would have been to spend as much of it as possible on creating physical, social, and human infrastructure: railways, roads, harbors, administrative networks, courts, markets, banks, hospitals, schools, water supplies; to cultivate a professional and trading middle class; to improve economic, legal, and political institutions; and to establish new ones in the process. But in Latin America, power was concentrated in the hands of landed classes, who benefited from cheap imports and saw no reason to develop an internal market, widen the geographic and sectoral spread of economic growth, or support the emergence of new classes (Lewis 1978b: 11).

Argentina provides a perfect case in which to view the relative significance of factors considered important in development and underdevelopment. In 1914, Argentina was one of the richest countries in the world, and was poised to join the ranks of the world's most advanced countries. Between 1880 and 1910, the value of its exports had increased sixfold, total production grew at an annual average of 5 percent per year, population by 3.4 percent, the crop area by 8.3 percent, and the railway system by 15.4 percent (Rock 1975: 1). By 1944, the net value of manufacturing output surpassed the net value of agricultural and livestock production, and more people were employed in industry than in agriculture.

Argentina had a temperate climate, an integrated national territory, vast stretches of fertile soil, large deposits of petroleum, easy access to the sea, a literate and fairly homogeneous population, adequate access to foreign technical knowledge, entrepreneurs with the technical competence needed for industrial growth; an adaptable, skillful work force; average wages comparable with many parts of western Europe, and relatively better opportunities for social mobility (Rock 1975: 67). With the exception of the Perón era, foreign capital filled the gap left by a periodically insufficient but usually adequate rate of domestic capital formation (United Nations 1959: pt. 1, 27–36). United States investment in Argentina nearly tripled in less than a decade, rising from $427 million in 1960 to nearly $1.2 billion in 1968. More than 90 percent of all United States investments (and a similar proportion from other sources) in Argentina during these years went into the most rapidly expanding sectors of the manufacturing industry— chemicals and petrochemicals, transportation, metallurgy, machinery, electrical equipment, and petroleum (Smith 1989: 34). Argentina's debt burden before World War II was less than that of Australia, Canada, and New Zealand.[16] It is often claimed that Argentina's post-colonial development was distorted by the policies of Great Britain, the foreign power which had the greatest influence there. But the British had less influence in Argentina than they did in Australia and Canada. By 1930, those latter countries led the world's exports in grain, and attracted massive European investment and hardworking European immigrants.

Between 1916 and 1930 Argentina had a democratic political system, with universal, secret, and compulsory suffrage for males at eighteen years of age. There were no qualifications in terms of income, property, or literacy. Between 1916 and 1930 voter turnout leaped from approximately 20 percent to more than 65 percent, and thereafter oscillated between 50 and 80 percent. Elections for the House of Representatives were direct. In 1916 presidential power passed smoothly from the long-entrenched Conservatives to the leader of the largely middle-class Radical Party. The Radical Party won presidential elections in 1922 and 1928.[17]

A comparison of Argentina with Australia is particularly instructive because the timing of their development was the same, as were their production and export structures. Argentina and Australia began to grow rapidly in the 1850s by selling the same commodities—cereals, wool, and meat. In 1913 their incomes per head were among the world's top ten. But while Australia industrialized rapidly thereafter, Argentina did not. Australia had no landed aristocracy. Its politics were dominated by its urban communities, who used their power to protect industrial profits and wages (Lewis 1978b: 25). In Argentina, on the other hand,

> millions of hectares of the best pampean land were appropriated by a tiny sector of the population. . . . The resources from which Argentine prosperity derived were monopolized by the very few. . . . This privileged stra-

16. Net interest owed abroad for Argentina in 1928 (−17.4) was less than for Australia (−27.5), Canada (−22.3), and New Zealand (−27.6) (League of Nations 1931a: 36).
17. Brazil also had a functioning representative democracy. Nationwide elections began in Brazil in 1821. The 1824 constitution extended the vote to "the mass of active citizens," and by its terms took in more people than was the practice of most European countries. Many more participated in elections than in most countries of Europe at that time. "Foreign observers were unanimous in praising a political system that seemed so like the bourgeois regimes of Europe. The main focus of their enthusiasm lay in the regularity of elections and in the alteration of parties in power. The government scrupulously observed the constitution, individual rights seemed protected, and no military leader or other dictator overthrew the elected government . . . . Cabinets had to receive the approval of the Legislature in order to govern, even if the Emperor could dismiss one Cabinet and summon another; when a Cabinet failed to gain the confidence of the Chamber of Deputies, it asked the Emperor to dissolve it and call new elections" (Graham 1990: 71).

tum consisted, by and large, of less-than-efficient entrepreneurs who showed very little interest in industrial activities. These factors combined to restrict what would otherwise have been an unusual opportunity for building a solid economy and a more open society. (Lewis 1978b: 144)

Capitalist development reinforced the social domination of large landowners everywhere. Large landlords initially captured much of the profits from market expansion by increasing their share of the export crop and investing little in food for the domestic market. As in Europe, large estates in Latin America became the main form of agricultural organization. When Latin American countries achieved independence at the beginning of the nineteenth century, land institutions remained substantially the same. The traditional landholding elite expanded as wealthy urban elements bought up large amounts of land from impoverished smallholders or from expropriated church properties. Typical of the distribution of landholdings was Mexico, where in 1910 1 percent of the population owned 97 percent of the total land, while 96 percent of the population owned only 1 percent of the land (Stavenhagen 1970: 227). Land-tenure institutions continue to be primary obstacles to economic and social development in Latin America.

Agrarian reform involves a massive and drastic redistribution of rights over land, a reordering of property relationships, and a consequent redistribution of power. Thus "land reforms, if they are at all meaningful in scope and intensity, are, by their very nature, revolutionary changes" (Carroll 1970: 103). Since success in exporting creates a vested interest, those who live by primary production tend to oppose measures for industrialization. The outcome of exporting primary products therefore depends on the balance of power between industrial and agricultural interests (Lewis 1978: 41a).

In Europe, agrarian reform was ultimately achieved not gradually, but within a short period of time and as a result of much violence and destruction—by means of revolution in Russia and the massively destructive world wars. In Australia, Canada, and New Zealand the landowning classes were circumscribed from the start, and so revenues were not used solely to enrich a traditional landowning class and their allies, as they were in Europe and in Latin America.[18] In the United States, where a strong landowning class developed in the south, a struggle between landowners and industrialists culminated in the Civil War and the victory of the industrial capitalist bourgeoisie. As a result smallholder patterns of land ownership evolved there. In Japan, a massive and spectacularly successful land

18. In these countries, there was no preexisting landed elite, and the colonists displaced, overwhelmed, or destroyed prior inhabitants.

reform, imposed by the Allied powers after World War II, led to the transformation of economy and society.[19] The Japanese reform transformed its
backward feudal economy, brought about a transfer of political power, and
increased the general productive capacity of the economy by the creation
of substantial effective demand in agriculture and by the increased supply
of domestic food and raw materials (Ladejinsky 1959). A very radical land
reform was also imposed under the auspices of the American occupying
forces in South Korea and Taiwan.

These countries were able to participate fully in the historically unprecedented boom of the 1950s and 1960s. As a result, today's advanced industrial countries are those which (1) never had an entrenched landed elite
(e.g. Canada and Australia); (2) saw a significant decline in the power of
landowners as a result of civil war (i.e., the United States); (3) experienced
a breakdown of their traditional social structures and massive land reforms as a result of devastating wars (e.g., most of Europe); or (4) had a
massive land reform imposed by external forces and experienced, as a
consequence, the breakdown of their traditional class structures (Japan,
Germany, South Korea, Taiwan).

Latin America did not experience any such breakdown of its traditional
social structure. Following the world wars, little change took place in land
institutions. It has been estimated that in the 1960s about 94 percent of the
total arable land in Latin America was owned by 7 percent of the landholders.[20] Land reforms introduced in Latin America in the 1950s and
1960s were brought to a halt by a continent wide anti-land-reform movement.[21] In 1980, with the exception of Cuba, the land tenure system of
Latin America was still characterized by the existence of large estates
(Theisenhusen 1980: 137). As in Europe, land institutions in Latin America
were an obstacle to the geographic and sectoral spread of economic
growth. And as in Europe, these institutions in Latin America "maintain
and legitimize the existing inequalities in the distribution of wealth,
power, and social status, which in turn impede the efficient use of disposable resources, depress the rate of investment in industry as well as agriculture and prevent the achievement of minimum social and political sta-

19. Before the reform, 54 percent of the cultivated land was owner-operated; after the reform
92 percent was owned by farmers. Between 1947 and 1949 the government bought and resold
5.8 million acres of land. Three years after the beginning of the reform approximately 3 million
peasants had acquired land. On the Japanese land reform, see United Nations 1950: 188–89;
U.S. Department of Agriculture 1951: 187–89.

20. In Brazil, half of the farmland was held by 1.6 percent of the owners. In Chile, 75 percent of
the cultivated area was controlled by 2.2 percent of the owners. In Guatemala, approximately
40 percent of the cropland was held by 500 landholders (Theisenhusen 1980: 136; Johnson
1964: 11).

21. See Feder 1970; Seligson 1984; Ruhl 1984; Wise 1983; Hough et al. 1982.

bility" (Barraclough and Domike 1970: 71). In the 1980s there were probably more poor and illiterate people in Latin America than in 1950. Because the real power structure in most countries in the region has changed little since World War II, Latin America has failed to achieve sustained and more equitable development and has remained in the Third World.

The key requirements of economic development are a continuous rise in per capita output and a balanced distribution of the steadily rising national income among all sectors of the population. Redistribution of income in favor of lower-income groups requires that the production of goods and services for which there is a demand among those groups, especially foodstuffs, expand more rapidly than production of nonessential goods; this is unlikely to happen, however, in the absence of land reform. Improving agricultural productivity and widening access to land depends on the reorganization of agriculture and the revamping of class relationships, as many scholars have emphasized (e.g., Moore 1966: 419–22, 490–91, 429–30, 438, 442). But agricultural elites tend to resist such measures. Economic development also requires a change in the structure of employment: workers must be assured of an increasing share in the productivity increments of each sector. The mechanisms that would insure this—of which trade unionism is the most effective—are weak in Third World countries. In Europe, the radical alteration of the traditional class structure as a consequence of the world wars strengthened the working class and weakened the upper classes.[22] New trade unions were organized and unions, which before the war had been hindered by police repression, were reorganized. For the first time parties representing labor became legitimate participants in the political process.

Latin America did not experience the massive slaughter and destruction that Europe suffered as a result of the two world wars. Crises arose there during the Great Depression and the era of the world wars, but these led only to a retrenchment of traditional structures. Corporative arrangements were introduced that perpetuated the traditional order on a renewed basis and turned urban laborers into industrial serfs. As a result, the developmental trajectories of the two regions began rapidly to diverge. After World War II, development in Europe has involved sustained growth rather than short-lived windfalls; it is associated with a more equitable distribution of income and is largely the outcome of the society's own performance, instead of deriving from foreign islands of capital. It is, in other words, no longer dependent development. After 1945, development in Latin America continued as before to be "in general limited to geo-

22. One indicator of the change in class power was the swell in labor organization after World War I from an average prewar level of 9 percent of the labor force to a postwar peak of 30 percent (Rueschemeyer et al. 1992: 91–92).

graphic areas tied to the main export sectors, while primitive productive and social conditions and colonial institutions continued to prevail in extensive areas and sectors in the remainder of the countries" (Sunkel 1993: 26). By the end of the 1970s only a few countries in Latin America had entered a stage of development in which capital accumulation and diversified industrialization of a more than superficial sort were bringing about the transformation of economic and social structures (Cardoso and Faletto 1979).

As Jorge Ahumada notes, "There is nothing inherent in the structure and dynamic of the Latin American economy . . . that can be expected to lead spontaneously . . . to a narrowing of . . . the glaring discrepancies in the distribution of private income" (1963: 116). But steady economic development cannot take place without progressive and radical social transformation. Because privileged classes do not voluntarily relinquish their privileges, radical social transformation rarely if ever takes place in the absence of war or natural disaster.

Europe after the World Wars

In Europe, World War I was widely considered a turning point in history, the ending of an era. By 1917 Rathenau, Czernin, and Stresemann all realized that what had begun as a war was turning into a revolution (Mayer 1969: 24, 31). German, Spanish, French, and English authors wrote of the decay of traditional European civilization. In Britain, the newspapers and a parliamentary commission investigated the "deterioration of the race" (Kennedy 1981: 114). "An age is over . . . the earth heaves . . . it is . . . the fearful convulsions of a dying civilization," wrote Keynes in 1920 (1988: 4). Throughout the 1920s, diagnoses of middle- and upper-class anguish testified to a great sense of transition.[23]

After World War I, European society became increasingly polarized along class lines.[24] Throughout the interwar period, the wealthy classes were continuously preoccupied with the rising tide of socialism at home and with the threat of Bolshevism from abroad. The policies pursued by European governments throughout the period were a reflection of this preoccupation. Rather than balancing German aggression with counter-

23. The world war, according to one commentator in 1918, "has so profoundly overturned the conditions of life for the French bourgeoisie that it is undergoing a crisis whose gravity just cannot be exaggerated" (Lichtenberger 1921: 388; in Maier 1975: 39). Numerous works of fiction marked the passing of traditional Europe most prominently the works of Proust, Ibsen, Chekhov, Mann, and Musil.
24. I document the polarization of European society during the first half of the twentieth century in a forthcoming book.

vailing power, the wealthy classes of Europe chose instead to gamble that Germany's drive for empire in Europe would stop short of destroying them and at the same time enable them to defeat communism at home and abroad. This gamble led eventually to World War II,[25] which leveled domestic economies, destroyed the industrial structure of the region, and changed the balance of class power throughout Europe. Following the war, the changes that had begun with World War I were institutionalized and became the basis for an era of peace and prosperity in Europe.

Radical changes in the class structures of both western and eastern Europe altered the whole basis of the economy of Europe. A new economic and political order was established throughout the region on the basis of interest groups, parties, unions, and other organizations linked to sectors of the economy that had been formerly excluded from power. Workers became a powerful organized force and in Western Europe, labor parties became fully legitimate participants in the political process.

The collapse of the region's traditional social structure enabled states in Europe to gain greater autonomy and thus to pursue policies of redistribution that put their economies on a fundamentally different footing.[26] After 1945, everywhere in Europe the state engaged in the redistribution of the national income by means of progressive taxation and the welfare state.[27] One consequence of this redistribution was the transformation of rural Europe. After World War II, rural ways of life and rural standards of living more closely approached those of cities than at any time in the past (Mendras 1970). The changes can be illustrated by two glimpses of the French village of Douelle: one immediately after World War II, when the old ways were still in force, and another in the mid-70s, by which time the life of the village had been utterly transformed. Douelle in 1946 was a village of 534 residents. Of its 279-member work force, there were 208 peasant farmers, 27 artisans, 12 shopkeepers, 19 salaried white-collar workers, and 2

25. Conflicts in Europe in the nineteenth and early twentieth centuries, and how and why they culminated in the world wars and the break-down of Europe's class structure, are the focus of a forthcoming work.

26. U.S. funds (i.e., the Marshall Plan), often thought to have been decisive here, would simply have reinforced the traditional social structure, rather than altering it, as they have in contemporary Third World regions.

27. The worst excesses of monopolies and restrictive practices were curbed by legislation: the German Law of 1957 against restraining competition and the Federal Control Office established under that law; the British Anti-Monopoly legislation of 1948, 1956, and 1964 and the actions taken by the Monopolies Commission; and corresponding laws and institutions in France, Sweden, and the Netherlands (Voigt 1962; Boswup and Schlichtkrull 1962; Edwards 1962; Guenalt and Jackson 1960). In addition, raising the level of employment was treated as a very high priority in the formulation of development strategies and plans and in the laying down of investment criteria (on the investment criteria debate of the 1950s, see Sen 1960; Dobb 1960; and Galenson and Leibenstein 1955).

workers in manufacturing not connected with agriculture. The 208 farmers worked on nonmechanized farm holdings averaging about five hectares each. Of the 4,000 children born since 1821, fifty had finished secondary school. Three-quarters of a resident's income was spent on food, and the staples were bread and soup. The peasants ate meat, and of an inferior quality, once a week. It took seven hours of labor to earn the money to buy a kilo of butter, eight hours for a chicken. Of the 163 houses, 150 used wood fires both for heating and cooking; 10 houses had coal stoves and 3 had gas or electric stoves. There were 50 radios in the village and 2 televisions.

Beginning in the 1950s, a program of land redistribution consolidated less productive small parcels into larger estates where new machinery was cost-effective. In addition, the government provided the rural population with the necessary resources for agricultural modernization. The average farm holding was 13 hectares. Artificial fertilizers were widely used and government agencies provided the seed for sowing. The resulting increase in agricultural productivity released labor, which flowed into industrial occupations.

Douelle in 1976 had 670 residents. Tertiary employment had largely replaced agriculture: of the 215 in the work force, 53 were farmers and 102 were office workers in the service sector, banks, and the government; 25 were artisans and 35 were employed as nonagricultural workers. Of the 212 houses, 197 had gas or electric stoves. It took 1.5 hours to earn the wages needed to buy a kilo of butter, 45 minutes to buy a chicken. There were 250 radios and 200 televisions. Most of the residents regularly went on holiday. All of the children were in school.[28]

One requisite of both economic development and democracy is that those who possess power and privilege be willing or compelled to relinquish both in some part. Historically, this has only occurred as the consequence of violent conflict and massive human and material destruction. This seems a grim and hopeless conclusion; it is grim, but not quite hopeless. The fact that Europe escaped its dependent development as a result of two devastating world wars need not be a prediction for Latin America and other regions of the Third World. But unless we reexamine history and find its relevance for the past, we may not be able to avoid repeating it.

In his essay "Strategy in Social Science," Barrington Moore (1958) contrasts current thinking in social science with that of prominent nineteenth-century thinkers. The major issue confronting contemporary theorists, Moore rightly notes, is the same one that Tocqueville, Mosca, Marx, Weber, and Durkheim faced: the feasibility of creating rational societies under the

---

28. From a study by the French economist Jean Fourastié; in Tipton and Aldrich 1987b: 166–67.

conditions of industrialism. Though the issue is essentially the same, current thinking lacks the critical and historical spirit that characterized sociological thinking in the nineteenth-century. Scholars concerned with the problems of development and social change today must recapture the spirit of those nineteenth century thinkers who grappled with the problems of society in transition. The past has greater relevance for the present than is generally thought. A more critical reading of it can help us to construct more accurate and reliable models of development and change.

Statistical Appendix

Table 1. Income per capita of the working population, expressed in international units, 1925–1934

Ranges	Europe	Latin America
1000–1100	U.K. Switzerland	Argentina
700–900	Netherlands Irish Free State	
600–700	France Denmark Sweden Germany Belgium	Uruguay
500–600	Norway Austria Spain	Chile
400–500	Czechoslovakia Iceland	Brazil
300–400[a]	Greece Yugoslavia Finland Poland Hungary Latvia Italy Estonia USSR Portugal	Mexico Rest of Latin America[b]
200–300	Bulgaria Romania Lithuania Albania	

Note: Listings within ranges are in descending order of average income. An international unit is defined as the amount of goods and services which one dollar would purchase in the United States averaged over the period 1925–34. See Clark 1940: 32–58 for a full discussion of calculations and sources used.

[a]Modal category for both Europe and Latin America.

[b]Clark has average indications for Argentina, Uruguay, Chile, Brazil, and Mexico only. On the basis of these indications, he places the rest of Latin America in this category.

Source: Colin Clark, *The Conditions of Economic Progress,* © 1940. Reprinted from page 54 by permission of Prentice Hall, Inc., Upper Saddle River, N.J.

Table 2. A comparison of basic social indicators for Europe (1910) and Latin America (1950)

	Life expectancy (years)[a]	Mortality rate (per 1000)	Infant mortality (per 1000)[b]	Adult literacy (%)[c]	University enrollment (per 1,000)[d]
Europe					
Austria	41	22	180	83	14
Belgium	47	15	137	87	4
Czechoslovakia	—	—	—	95	14
Bulgaria	—	—	—	61	1
Denmark	55	13	105	95	2
Finland	44	18	114	75	3
France	48	19	129	88	41
Greece	—	—	—	37	3
Ireland	—	—	—	32	3
Italy	46	21	153	60	22
Netherlands	53	14	111	90	4
Norway	55	14	70	95	2
Poland	—	—	—	72	32
Portugal	21	—	150	31	3
Romania	—	—	—	52	4
Russia (European)	—	30	250	45	—
Spain	41	31	159	48	16
Sweden	55	19	77	98	4
Switzerland	50	23	107	98	7
U.K.[e]	51	22	115	93	22
Yugoslavia	—	—	—	52	14
Median	48	19	122	75	4
Range	21–55	13–30	70–250	31–98	2–41
Latin America					
Argentina	59	9	72	87	79
Bolivia	44	—	170	32	5
Brazil	52	12	106	49	44
Chile	53	14	128	79	11
Colombia	45	—	124	57	9
Costa Rica	55	13	105	79	0
Ecuador	52	—	132	56	0
El Salvador	46	20	152	39	0
Guatemala	40	22	172	29	2
Honduras	48	—	137	39	0
Mexico	48	15	108	57	45
Nicaragua	48	—	137	38	1
Panama	63	—	67	66	2
Paraguay	—	—	—	66	1
Peru	43	—	104	47	12
Uruguay	60	—	64	81	12
Venezuela	59	—	81	52	6
Median	50	14	116	52	5
Range	40–63	9–22	64–172	29–87	1–79

continued

Table 2. *Continued*
[a]Life expectancy data for Bolivia, Ecuador, Honduras, Nicaragua, Panama, and Venezuela are from 1960–65. Figures are for males only except for Colombia and Peru, which are for both males and females.
[b]Infant mortality for Ecuador, Honduras, Nicaragua, and Panama are from 1960–65.
[c]Literacy figures for Bulgaria, Czechoslovakia, Ireland, Poland, Romania, and Yugoslavia are for 1928.
[d]University enrollment data for Czechoslovakia, Poland, and Yugoslavia are for 1919.
[e]Data for the U.K. are for England and Wales only.
Sources: Goldstein 1983: 241; Todaro 1977: 40–49; Urrutia 1991: 34–39. Vanhanen 1977: 174–175; Maddison 1991: 10; Banks 1971: 207–254; Altimir 1981: table 5.

Table 3. A comparison of income distribution in pre–World War II Europe and post–World War II Latin America

	Percentage received by income group		
	Top 5%	Top 20%	Lowest 60%
Europe			
Denmark (1908)	24	51	27
France (1933)	34	—	—
Germany (1913)	31	50	26
Netherlands (1914)	42	53	33
Norway (1907)	30	—	—
Poland (1929)	—	55	—
Sweden (1930)	30	59	19
United Kingdom (1913)	43	59	—
Median	31	54	26.5
Range	24–43	50–59	19–33
Latin America			
Argentina (1953)	27	—	32
Brazil (1960)	28	55	18
Chile (1968)	31	52	25
Colombia (1956)	42	56	31
Costa Rica (1961)	33	54	24
Ecuador (1960)	42	—	—
El Salvador (1953)	35	52	32
Guatemala (1953)	34	55	29
Mexico (1950)	40	60	25
Peru (1961)	38	—	18
Uruguay (1967)	19	—	29
Venezuela (1977)	32	49	28
Median	32	54	28
Range	19–42	49–60	18–32

Sources: Clough 1952: 671, 673; Goldstein 1983: 240; Kuznets 1963: 13, 37, 60–61; ECLAC, *Serie distribucion del ingreso:* various years; ECLA, *Estudio sobre la distribucion del Ingreso en America Latina: 1967;* Theisenhusen 1980: 132, Urrutia 1991: 51.

Table 4. Percent of population in towns of 20,000+ in Europe and Latin America

Europe (1910)		Latin America (1950)		Europe (1950)	
				U.K.	69
U.K.	62				
				Netherlands	56
		Uruguay	53		
Belgium	51				
		Argentina	50		
				Germany	46
				France	45
				Denmark	44
		Chile	43		
				Italy	41
				Austria	39
				Spain	39
Germany	35			Sweden	35
Netherlands	34			Hungary	34
		Venezuela	31		
				Norway	30
Italy	28			Greece	28
				Switzerland	27
France	26				
Belgium	25				
		Mexico	24		
		Colombia	23		
		Panama	22	Finland	22
Switzerland	20	Brazil	20		
		Bolivia	19		
Norway	18	Costa Rica	18		
		Ecuador	18		
		Peru	18		
Spain	17				
				Portugal	16
Sweden	15	Paraguay	15		
		Nicaragua	15		
Austria	14				
Greece	13	El Salvador	13		
Hungary	13				
Portugal	12				
Romania	11	Guatemala	11		
Russia[a]	10				
Finland	9				
		Honduras	7		
Bulgaria	6				
Serbia	4				
Median	16		19		39
Range	4–62		7–53		16–69

[a]Data are for European Russia only.
Sources: Goldstein 1983: 241; ECLAC, *Statistical Yearbook*, 1980; Hughes 1975: 173; Vanhanen 1977: 170.

Table 5. Sectoral distribution of labor force in Europe (pre–World War II) and Latin America (1950) (in percent)

	Agriculture	Industry
Europe[a]		
Yugoslavia	83	11
Bulgaria	82	10
Romania	80	11
Serbia	80	10
Russia (European only)	75	10
Finland	70	11
Greece	66	17
Spain	66	15
Poland	65	9
Hungary	63	17
Portugal	57	20
Italy	56	27
Austria	53	22
Sweden	51	32
Ireland	48	15
Norway	47	25
France	43	30
Denmark	40	22
Germany	38	43
Netherlands	28	33
Belgium	23	46
Switzerland	22	54
United Kingdom	8	54
Median	56	20
Range	8–83	9–54
Latin America		
Honduras	83	8
Guatemala	68	12
Nicaragua	68	11
Bolivia	65	8
Ecuador	65	10
El Salvador	61	12
Peru	60	19
Mexico	58	15
Paraguay	55	16
Brazil	54	14
Colombia	53	13
Costa Rica	52	11
Panama	47	9
Venezuela	42	11
Chile	31	31
Argentina	25	24
Median	56.5	12

continued

Table 5. *Continued*

[a]All European data are for 1910, except for Poland 1921, Ireland and United Kingdom 1936, European Russia (males only) 1897, Spain 1940, Yugoslavia 1920. Data for "Finland," an autonomous region of Russia in 1910, and for "Austria" and "Hungary," part of the Austro-Hungarian Empire in 1910, are for the territories of the post–World War II states.

Sources: Kuznets 1966: 106–7; 1963: 24, 70; Goldstein 1983: 24; Lampe and Jackson 1982: 336, 597; Spulber 1963: 367; Blum 1978: 419; Woytinsky and Woytinsky 1953: 464; Vanhanen 1977: 205; CEPAL 1979: 78.

Table 6. Sectoral distribution of gross national product in Europe (pre–World War II) and Latin America (1955) (in percent)

	Agriculture	Industry
Europe[a]		
Bulgaria	71	15
Romania	60	21
Italy	48	22
Hungary	44	24
Greece	41	20
Poland	41	38
France	35	37
Sweden	35	38
Denmark	30	33
Finland	30	26
Czechoslovakia	24	27
Norway	24	26
Germany	18	39
Netherlands	16	33
U.K.	6	46
Median	35	27
Range	6–71	15–46

continued

Table 6. *Continued*

Latin America[b]		
Guatemala	45	13
Paraguay	42	17
Honduras	41	16
El Salvador	39	17
Colombia	37	22
Bolivia	26	25
Costa Rica	26	20
Ecuador	25	19
Nicaragua	24	21
Peru	24	31
Brazil	21	31
Panama	21	13
Mexico	18	30
Uruguay	15	27
Argentina	14	38
Chile	14	37
Venezuela	8	47
Median	24	22

[a]All data for Europe are 1910, except for Finland 1940, Greece 1938, Hungary 1925; Netherlands and U.K. 1913, Romania 1926; Czechoslovakia 1920; Bulgaria and Yugoslavia 1926.
[b]Data for Bolivia, Costa Rica, and Nicaragua are for 1960; for Guatemala 1949. Data for Argentina, Chile, and Venezuela are for 1950 as percent of GDP.
Sources: Mitchell 1975: 426–35; Kuznets 1966: 88–93; Jörberg 1973: 390; Spulber 1963: 366; Lampe and Jackson 1982: 559; Woytinsky and Woytinsky 1953: 466; CEPAL 1979: 36; Banks 1971: 255–68; Reynolds 1985: 396–97.

Table 7. Average annual rate of growth of exports, 1883–1913

Europe		Latin America	
		Argentina	7.6
Germany	5.1	Ecuador	5.1
Netherlands	4.6		
		Brazil	4.5
		Mexico	4.3
		Colombia	4.1
Sweden	3.8		
		C. America	3.7
		Peru	3.7
		Uruguay	3.6
Belgium	3.5		
France	2.8		
United Kingdom	2.1	Chile	2.1
		Venezuela	1.3
Median	3.65		3.9

Sources: Maddison 1964: 166; Lewis 1978a: 196, 203; Banks 1971.

Table 8a. Per capita exports in Europe and in Latin America, 1913 (converted to US$ equivalents)

Europe		Latin America	
Switzerland	72		
Denmark	69		
Netherlands	67	Argentina	67
		Uruguay	62
U.K.	54		
Belgium	48		
Norway	42	Chile	42
Sweden	39		
Germany	36		
France	31		
		Costa Rica	25
Romania	23		
		Bolivia	18
Italy	14		
		Brazil	13
		Nicaragua	13
		Guatemala	12
Austria-Hungary	11	Venezuela	11
		Ecuador	10
		Peru	10
		Mexico	10
Spain	9	El Salvador	9
		Paraguay	8
		Colombia	7
Finland (1919)	6		
Portugal	6		
Greece	5	Honduras	5
Poland (1922)	5		
Russia	5		
Serbia	5		
Bulgaria	4		
		Panama	3
Median	18.5	Median	11
Range	4–72	Range	3–67

Sources: Banks 1971: 171–205; Maddison 1991: 2.

Table 8b. Per capita exports in Europe and in Latin America, 1950 (converted to US$ equivalents)

Europe		Latin America	
		Venezuela	230
Switzerland	192		
Belgium	191		
Sweden	157		
Denmark	156		
Netherlands	140		
U.K.	120		
Norway	119		
		Uruguay	105
Austria (1955)	100		
Finland	98		
		Argentina	79
France	72		
		Costa Rica	70
Czechoslovakia	63		
		Chile	47
Germany	41		
Hungary	36	El Salvador	36
		Colombia	35
		Panama	30
		Guatemala	28
Italy	26	Brazil	26
Poland	26		
		Bolivia	25
		Nicaragua	25
		Ecuador	23
		Paraguay	23
Portugal	22	Peru	22
Bulgaria	20	Mexico	20
Spain	14		
Romania	13		
Greece	12	Honduras	12
Russia	7		
Albania	6		
Median	52		28

Source: Banks 1971: 171–205.

Table 9. Per capita exports, Europe and Latin America, 1913, 1950, 1966 (converted to US$ equivalents)

	1913	1950	1966
Europe			
Albania	—	6	59
Austria[a]	—	100	231
Austria-Hungary	11	—	—
Belgium	48	191	717
Bulgaria	4	20	158
Czechoslovakia	—	63	193
Denmark	69	156	512
Finland[b]	6	98	325
France	31	72	220
Germany[c]	36	41	337
Greece	5	12	47
Hungary	—	36	156
Italy	14	26	155
Netherlands	67	140	542
Norway	42	119	416
Poland[d]	5	26	72
Portugal	6	22	66
Romania	23	13	62
Russia	5	7	38
Serbia	5	—	—
Spain	9	14	39
Sweden	39	157	546
Switzerland	72	192	546
U.K.	54	120	258
Median	18.5	52	206.5
Range	5–208	6–192	58–717
Latin America			
Argentina	67	79	70
Bolivia	18	25	34
Brazil	13	26	21
Chile	42	47	100
Colombia	7	35	27
Costa Rica	25	70	93
Ecuador	10	23	29
El Salvador	9	36	62
Guatemala	12	28	50
Honduras	5	12	61
Mexico	10	20	28
Nicaragua	13	25	80
Panama	3	30	71
Paraguay	8	23	23
Peru	10	22	64
Uruguay	62	105	68
Venezuela	11	230	304
Median	11	28	62
Range	3–60	13–230	21–309

continued

Table 9. *Continued*
[a]Austria: 1955, 1966.
[b]Finland: 1919, 1950, 1966.
[c]Postwar data are for the FRG.
[d]Poland: 1922, 1950, 1966.
Sources: Banks 1971: 171–205; Maddison 1991: 2.

Table 10. Average annual growth rates of per-capita GNP/GDP in Europe and Latin America

	GNP per capita
Europe	1830–1913
Denmark	1.7
Sweden	1.5
Switzerland	1.5
Germany (West)	1.4
Belgium	1.3
U.K.	1.2
France	1.2
Norway	1.2
Finland	1.2
Austria (1860–1913)	1.1
Netherlands	0.9
Russia	0.8
Italy	0.6
Greece (1840–1913)	0.6
Yugoslavia (1860–1913)	0.5
Bulgaria (1860–1913)	0.4
Portugal	–.2
Spain	–.4
Median	1.15
Range	–.4–1.7
	GDP per capita
Latin America	1870–1913
Peru	3.8
Colombia	3.7
Chile	3.3
Argentina	1.5
Brazil	1.2
Mexico	0.8
Median	2.4
Range	–.8–3.8

Note: GDP and GNP are both measures of national income. GDP (gross domestic product) is total domestic output; GNP (gross national product) is GDP plus income from property owned abroad. Country names refer to 1970 geographical boundaries.
Sources: Bairoch 1976: 309; Maddison 1983: 29; 1991: 17.

Table 11. Average annual growth rates of the volume of per capita GNP, Europe

	1830–1913[a]	1913–1950	1950–1973
Austria	1.1	0.2	4.9
Belgium	1.3	0.7	3.6
Bulgaria	0.4	1.3	6.4
Czechoslovakia	—	1.1	5.0
Denmark	1.7	1.1	3.3
Finland	1.2	1.9	4.5
France	1.2	1.3	4.4
Germany East	—	—	6.5
Germany West	1.4	0.5	5.0
Greece	0.6	0.9	6.2
Hungary	—	1.1	5.3
Ireland	—	0.5	3.0
Italy	0.6	0.8	4.7
Netherlands	0.9	0.8	3.7
Norway	1.2	2.2	3.3
Poland	—	—	5.4
Portugal	0.2	0.7	5.3
Romania	—	—	6.5
Spain	0.4	0	5.2
Sweden	1.5	2.5	3.0
Switzerland	1.5	1.0	3.0
U.K.	1.2	0.8	2.3
Russia	0.8	1.6	5.2
Yugoslavia	0.5	0.5	5.6
Median	1.15	.9	4.95
Range	.2–1.7	0–2.2	2.3–6.5

Note: At market prices; 1970 geographical boundaries.
[a]Data in this column for Austria, Bulgaria, and Yugoslavia are for 1860–1913; Greek data are for 1840–1913.
Source: Bairoch 1976: 309.

Table 12. Legislative selection and effectiveness in Europe (1913) and Latin America (1950)

	Legislative selection		Legislative effectiveness		
	Elective	Nonelective	Partial[a]	Insignificant[b]	Significant[c]
Europe					
Albania (1919)		x			x
Austria (1919)	x			x	
Belgium	x		x		
Bulgaria	x		x		
Czechoslovakia (1919)	x			x	
Denmark	x			x	
Finland (1919)	x			x	
France	x			x	
Germany	x		x		
Greece	x			x	
Hungary (1919)	x				x
Italy	x		x		
Latvia (1919)		x			x
Lithuania (1919)		x	x		
Netherlands	x			x	
Norway	x			x	
Poland (1919)	x		x		
Portugal	x			x	
Rumani	x		x		
Russia	x				x
Spain	x				x
Sweden	x			x	
Switzerland	x			x	
U.K.	x			x	
Yugoslavia (1919)	x				x
Latin America					
Argentina	x		x		
Bolivia	x		x		
Brazil	x			x	
Chile	x			x	
Colombia	x		x		
Costa Rica	x			x	
Ecuador	x		x		
El Salvador	x		x		
Guatemala	x		x		
Honduras	x		x		
Mexico	x		x		
Nicaragua	x				
Paraguay				x	
Panama	x		x		
Peru	x				
Uruguay	x			x	

[a]Executive power substantially outweighs but does not completely dominate legislative.
[b]Significant governmental autonomy, including, typically, substantial authority with regard to taxation and disbursement, and the power to override executive vetoes of legislation.
[c]Legislative activity is of a "rubber stamp" nature; or domestic turmoil makes implementation impossible; or the executive impedes the legislature.
Source: Banks 1971: 4–53.

Political Appendix

This appendix lists the entities that constitute "Europe" in this book and the boundary and name changes during the period of the study. "Europe" includes, in addition to all the territories on the continent of Europe, Great Britain, the provinces of the Ottoman Empire on the European continent, and Russia. Between 1815 and 1945 the following boundary and name changes were effected:

Albania: Part of the Turkish Empire until 1913. Occupied by Italy, and then Germany, 1939–1944.

Austria: Part of the Hapsburg Monarchy until 1918. The Republic of Austria was established in 1918. From 1938 to 1945, the Republic was absorbed in Greater Germany.

Belgium: Incorporated in France, 1795–1815. Part of the Netherlands, 1815–1830. Established as a separate, independent state of Belgium in 1830.

Bulgaria: Part of the Turkish Empire until 1878. Established as a separate country in 1878. United with "East Rumelia" in 1885. Acquired, lost and reacquired Southern Dobrudja in 1913, 1916, 1918; but permanently reacquired it in 1940.

Czechoslovakia: Established in 1918/1919 from the three Czech provinces of Cisleithania (Bohemia, Moravia, and Silesia) and the Slovak and Ruthene territories of the Hungarian Crown. From 1938 to 1945 the Sudetenlands were incorporated into Greater Germany; Teschen was seized by Poland; Slovakia was made a separate, independent state; the rest of Czechoslovakia was made a protectorate of Germany. The Slovak and Ruthene territories were ceded to the USSR in 1945.

Denmark: The Duchies of Schleswig, Holstein, and Lauenberg were ceded to Prussia in 1864. In 1920 the northern part of the old Duchy of Schleswig was returned to Denmark.

Finland: Part of the Swedish Kingdom until 1809. Ceded to Russia in 1809 as a Grand Duchy with a separate administration. An independent state of Finland was established in 1918. Some frontier areas, including some parts of the Viipuri province were ceded to the USSR in 1945.

France: In 1860 Savoy and Nice were acquired from Piedmont. From 1871 to 1918 Alsace and Lorraine were ceded to Germany, and from 1940 to 1944 they were temporarily lost to Germany again.

Germany: The German Empire was established in 1870. In 1918 most of Alsace and Lorraine were ceded to France. Danzig, Memel, northern Schleswig, and Eupen were ceded in 1920. Upper Silesia was taken by Poland in 1922. The Saarland was administered by France from 1920 to 1935. In 1945 large parts of the pre-1939 eastern territories were ceded to Poland and the USSR.

Greece: Part of the Turkish Empire until 1829. Established as an independent country in 1829, comprising the Morea, Euboea, the Cyclades Islands, and the mainland south of Arta and Thessaly. Thessaly and Arta were acquired from Turkey in 1881. Epiros, Macedonia, western Thrace, Crete, and most of the Aegean Islands except the Dodacanese were acquired in 1913. Eastern Thrace was acquired in 1919. The Dodcanese Islands were acquired from Italy in 1947.

Hungary: Up to 1918, included the lands of Transleithania: Transylvania, the Banat, Backa, and the semi-autonomous Croatia-Slavonia. However, from 1849 to 1868, the Banat and Backa constituted the autonomous Voivodina, and Croatia-Slavonia was attached to Austria. In 1868 the Voivodina was incoporated into Hungary, and Croatia-Slavonia was returned to Hungarian domination. In 1980, Fiume was directly attached to Hungary. In the independent state of Hungary established in 1919, the Slovak and Ruthene territories were lost to Czechoslovakia; Translyvania, several counties of Hungary proper, and part of the Banat was lost to Romania; the rest of the Banat, Backa, and parts of Hungary proper went to Yugoslavia.

Ireland: The twenty-six counties of southern Ireland became independent in 1921.

Italy: The state of Italy was established in 1860. Venetia was added in 1866, and the Papal States in 1870. In 1919 South Tyrol was added; Fiume was added in 1922. In 1945, South Tyrol, Fiume, Istria, and part of Venezia-Giulia were ceded to Yugoslavia.

Netherlands: In 1815 the Austrian Netherlands and Liège were added to its territories. These became the independent state of Belgium in 1830. The Grand Duchy of Luxembourg and part of Limburg were reacquired in 1839. The Grand Duchy of Luxembourg became independent in 1890.

Norway: Part of the lands of the Danish Crown until 1814 and of the Swedish Crown from 1814 to 1905, when it became independent.

Poland: Poland lost its independence when it was partitioned among Russia, Prussia, and Austria in 1772. It regained its independence during the Napoleonic Wars, but was repartitioned in 1793 and, for the last time, in 1795. In 1919, it was reestablished as an independent country and consisted of the former German territories of Posen, West Prussia, and part of Pomerania; the former Austrian territory of Galicia; and the former Polish provinces of Russia as well as parts of Russia proper. Upper Silesia was added in 1922; Teschen was taken from Czechoslovakia in 1938, but returned in 1945. From 1939 to 1945 Poland was again dismembered. In 1945, the eastern one-third of the prewar lands were ceded to the USSR, and most of East Prussia and the territory of the Oder and Neisse Rivers were acquired from Germany.

Romania: The principalities of Wallachia and Moldavia, under Turkish suzerainty, were united in 1859. Romania acquired independence after fighting a war of independence against the Ottoman Empire (1877–1878). In 1878, Southern Bessarabia was ceded to Russia, and all except the southern part of Dubrodja was acquired from Turkey. In 1913 this southern part was acquired from Bulgaria. In 1918, Bessarabia was acquired from Russia. In 1920, Bukovina, part of the Banat, and Transylvania were acquired. In 1940 Southern Dubrodja was ceded to Bulgaria, and Bessarabia and northern Bukovina were ceded to the USSR. Northern Transylvania was lost to Hungary from 1940 to 1944.

Russia: Russia received Polish territory in the partitions of 1793 and 1795. It acquired Turkish territory in the southern Ukraine, the Crimea, the Kuban, and Caucasia in 1791. Georgia was acquired in 1801, Ossetia in 1806, Finland in 1809, Imeretia and Abkhazia in 1810, Bessarabia from Turkey in 1812, Daghestan in 1819, Guria in 1829, Mingelia in 1857, Svanetia in 1858, and Abkhazia in 1864. Most of the Azerbaijan was acquired in 1813. Yerevan and Nakhichevan were acquired in 1828, Bokhara and Baluchistan in 1876 and the Kars region in 1878. Tashkent was acquired in 1865, Samarkand and

Bukhara in 1868, Khiva in 1873, and Askahabad in 1881. After the 1917 Revolution, Finland, Estonia, Latvia, and Lithuania became independent; Bessarabia was ceded to Romania, and the Polish provinces became part of independent Poland. All these were reacquired in 1939–1940, except for central Poland and Finland. Northern Bukovina was taken from Romania in 1940. Sub-Carpathian Russia (Ruthenia) and the northeastern part of East Prussia were added to the USSR in 1945.

Serbia: Established as an autonomous principality under Turkish suzerainty in 1817. Became formally independent in 1878. In 1913 it acquired part of the Sanjak of Novi Bazar and much of Macedonia. In 1919 it became part of the new state of Yugoslavia.

Sweden: Acquired Norway from 1814 to 1905. Lost Finland to Russia in 1809.

Switzerland: The independent cantons of Geneva, Valais, and Neuchatel were added in 1815.

United Kingdom: Incorporated Ireland in 1901. In 1921 the twenty-six counties of southern Ireland became independent.

Yugoslavia: Constituted in 1919 by adding to the previously independent Montenegro and Serbia, Croatia-Slavonia; part of the Banat, Backa, and parts of Hungary proper; and the former Austrian provinces of Carniola and Dalmatia, together with parts of Carinthia and Styria.

References

Adelman, Irma, and Sherman Robinson. 1978. *Income Distribution Policy in Developing Countries: A Case Study of Korea.* New York: Oxford University Press.

Ahumada, Jorge. 1963. Economic Development and Problems of Social Change in Latin America. In Egbert de Vries and José Medina Echevarria, eds., *Social Aspects of Economic Development in Latin America.* Vol. 1. Paris: UNESCO.

Alapuro, Risto. 1979. Internal Colonialism and the Regional Party System in Eastern Finland. *Racial and Ethnic Studies* 2, no. 3 (July): 341–59.

Alavi, Hamza. 1982. The Structure of Peripheral Capitalism. In Hamza Alavi and Teodor Shanin, eds., *Introduction to the Sociology of Developing Societies.* New York: Monthly Review Press.

——. 1975. India and the Colonial Mode of Production. In Ralph Miliband and J. Seville, eds., *Socialist Register, 1975.* London: Merlin Press.

——. 1964. Imperialism Old and New. In Ralph Miliband and J. Seville, eds., *Socialist Register, 1964.* London: Merlin Press.

Alavi, Hamza, and Teodor Shanin. 1988. Introduction to *The Agrarian Question,* by Karl Kautsky. Trans. Pete Burgess. London: Zwan Publications.

Albrecht-Carrié, René. 1972. *A Diplomatic History of Europe Since the Congress of Vienna.* Rev. ed. New York: Harper & Row.

Alfieri, Vittorio. 1859. *Del principe e delle lettere.* 22 vols. Florence: Barbera, Bianchi.

Almond, Gabriel A., and James S. Coleman. 1960. *The Politics of the Developing Areas.* Princeton: Princeton University Press.

Altimir, O. 1981. Poverty in Latin America: A Review of Concepts and Data. *CEPAL Review* 13 (April): 67–96.

Amin, Galal. 1974. *The Modernization of Poverty: A Study in the Political Economy of Growth in Nine Arab Countries, 1945–1970.* Leiden: E. J. Brill.

Amin, Samir. 1982. *The Arab Economy Today.* London: Zed.

——. 1979. *The Maghreb in the Modern World.* Harmondsworth: Penguin.

——. 1977. *Unequal Exchange.* New York: Monthly Review Press.

——. 1976. *Unequal Development: An Essay on the Social Formation of Peripheral Capitalism*. Brighton, Sussex: Harvester.

——. 1974. *Accumulation on a World Scale*. New York: Monthly Review Press.

Anderson, Eugene N., and Pauline R. Anderson. 1967. *Political Institutions and Social Change in Continental Europe in the Nineteenth Century*. Berkeley: University of California Press.

Anderson, Frank M. 1904. *The Constitutions and Other Select Documents Illustrative of the History of France, 1789–1901*. Minneapolis: H. W. Wilson.

Anderson, Perry. 1979. *Lineages of the Absolutist State*. London: Verso.

——. 1978. *Passages from Antiquity to Feudalism*. London: Verso.

Anderson, Roy R., Robert F. Seibert, and Jon G. Wagner. 1993. *Politics and Change in the Middle East: Sources of Conflict and Accommodation*. 4th ed. Englewood Cliffs, N.J.: Prentice-Hall.

Apter, David E. 1965. *The Politics of Modernization*. Chicago: University of Chicago Press.

Arendt, Hannah. 1958. *The Origins of Totalitarianism*. New York: Meridian.

Armeson, Robert B. 1964. *Total Warfare and Compulsory Labour: A Study of the Military-Industrial Complex in Germany during World War I*. The Hague: M. Nijhoff.

Armstrong, John A. 1973. *The European Administrative Elite*. Princeton: Princeton University Press.

Arndt, H. W. 1987. *Economic Development: The History of an Idea*. Chicago: University of Chicago Press.

Ascher, William. 1984. *Scheming for the Poor: The Politics of Redistribution in Latin America*. Cambridge: Harvard University Press.

Augé-Laribé, Michel. 1912. *La révolution agricole*. Paris: Librairie Armond Collin.

Avineri, Shlomo. 1968. *Karl Marx on Colonialism and Modernization*. New York: Doubleday.

Bade, Klaus. 1985. German Immigration to the United States and Continental Immigration to Germany in the Late Nineteenth and Early Twentieth Centuries. In Dirk Hoerder, ed., *Labor Migration in the Atlantic Economies: The European and North American Working Classes during the Period of Industrialization*. Westport, Conn.: Greenwood Press.

Badie, Bertrand, and Pierre Birnbaum. 1982. *The Sociology of the State*. Chicago: University of Chicago Press.

Baer, Werner, Richard Newfarmer, and Thomas Trebat. 1976. On State Capitalism in Brazil: Some New Issues and Questions. *Inter-American Economic Affairs* 30, no. 3 (Winter): 69–91.

Bairoch, Paul. 1993. *Economics and World History: Myths and Paradoxes*. London: Harvester.

——. 1981. The Main Trends in National Income Disparities since the Industrial Revolution. In Paul Bairoch and M. Levy-Leboyer, eds., *Disparities in Economic Development since the Industrial Revolution*. London: Macmillan.

——. 1976. Europe's Gross National Product, 1800–1975. *Journal of European Economic History* 5, no. 2 (Fall); 273–340.

——. 1975. *The Economic Development of the Third World since 1900*. London: Methuen.

Baldy, Edmond. 1922. *Les banques d'affaires en France depuis 1900*. Paris: Librairie Générale de Droit et de Jurisprudence.

Baloyra, Enrique, ed. 1987. *Comparing New Democracies: Transition and Consolidation in Mediterannean Europe and the Southern Cone*. Boulder, Colo.: Westview.

Banac, Ivo. *The National Question in Yugoslavia: Origins, History, Politics*. Ithaca: Cornell, 1984.

Banac, Ivo, and Paul A. Bushkovitch. 1983. The Nobility in the History of Russia and Eastern Europe. In Banac and Bushkovitch, eds., *The Nobility in Russia and Eastern Europe*. New Haven: Yale University Press.

Banks, Arthur S. 1971. *Cross-Polity Time-Series data*. Cambridge: MIT Press.

Baran, Paul A. 1970. On the Political Economy of Backwardness. In Robert I. Rhodes, ed., *Imperialism and Underdevelopment*. New York: Monthly Review Press.

——. 1957. *The Political Economy of Growth*. New York: Monthly Review Press.

Baran, Paul A., and Paul M. Sweezy. 1966. *Monopoly Capital*. New York: Monthly Review Press.

Barnes, Donald G. 1965. *A History of the English Corn Laws from 1660 to 1846*. New York: A. M. Kelley.

Barraclough, Geoffrey. 1967. *An Introduction to Contemporary History*. Harmonsworth: Penguin.

Barraclough, Solon L., and Arthur L. Domike. 1970. Agrarian Structure in Seven Latin American Countries. In Rudolfo Stavenhagen, ed., *Agrarian Problems and Peasant Movements in Latin America*. Garden City, N.Y.: Doubleday.

Bartlett, Robin. 1993. *The Making of Europe: Conquest, Colonisation, and Cultural Change*. Harmondsworth: Penguin.

Barzun, Jacques. 1932. *The French Race: Theories of Its Origins and Their Social and Political Implications Prior to the Revolution*. Columbia University Studies in History, Economics, and Public Law 375. New York: Columbia University Press.

Bateman, John. 1971. *The Great Landowners of Great Britain and Ireland*. 1883. Reprint, Leicester: Leicester University Press.

Battisti, Cesare. 1915. "Il Trentino e l'irredentismo italiano." In *Scritti politici e sociali*, R. Monteleone, ed. Florence: Nuova Italia, 1966.

——. 1914. "Trento, Trieste e il dovere d'Italia." In *Scritti politici e sociali*, R. Monteleone, ed. Florence: Nuova Italia, 1966.

Bauer, Otto. 1907. *Die Nationalitätenfrage und die Sozialdemokratie*. Max Adler and Rudolf Hilferding, eds. Vienna: Volksbuch Handlung Ignaz Brand.

Bayley, David H. 1975. The Police and Political Development in Europe. In Charles Tilly, ed., *The Formation of National States in Western Europe*. Princeton: Princeton University Press.

Becker, David, Jeffrey Frieden, Sayre Schatz and Richard Sklar, eds. 1987. *Postimperialism—International Capitalism and Development in the Late Twentieth Century*. Boulder, Colo.: Lynne Rienner.

Beckett, J. V. 1986. *The Aristocracy in England, 1660–1914*. London: Basil Blackwell.

Beetham, David. 1974. *Max Weber and the Theory of Modern Politics*. London: Allen & Unwin.

Bendix, Reinhard. 1978. *Kings or People*. Berkeley: University of California Press.

——. 1977. *Nation-Building and Citizenship*. Berkeley: University of California Press.

Ben-Dor, Gabriel. 1983. *State and Conflict in the Middle East: Emergence of the Post-Colonial State*. New York: Praeger.

Benns, Lee. 1930. *Europe since 1914*. New York: F. S. Crofts.

Benson, John. 1989. *The Working Class in Britain, 1850–1839*. London: Longman.

Berdahl, Robert M. 1972. Conservative Politics and Aristocratic Landholders in Bismarckian Germany. *Journal of Modern History* 44, no. 1 (March): 1–20.

Berend, T. Iván, and György Ránki. 1982. *The European Periphery and Industrialization, 1780–1814*. London: Cambridge University Press.

——. 1974. *Economic Development in East-Central Europe in the Nineteenth and Twentieth Centuries*. New York: Columbia University Press.

Bergesen, Albert. 1984. The Critique of World System Theory: Class Relations or Division of Labor? *Sociological Theory* 2: 365–72.

Berghahn, V. R. 1988. Corporatism in Germany in Historical Perspective. In Andrew Cox and Noel O'Sullivan, eds., *The Corporate State: Corporatism and State Tradition in Western Europe*. Aldershot: Edward Elgar.

Bernstein, Henry. 1979. Sociology of Underdevelopment vs. Sociology of Development? In David Lehmann, ed., *Development Theory: Four Critical Studies*. London: Frank Cass.

Bezanson, Anna. 1921–22. The Early Use of the Term Industrial Revolution. *Quarterly Journal of Economics* 36: 343–49.

Bigo, Robert. 1947. *Les banques françaises au cours du XIXe siècle*. Paris: Recueil Sirey.

Binder, Leonard, et al. 1971. *Crises and Sequences in Political Development*. Princeton: Princeton University Press.

Black, C. E. 1966. *The Dynamics of Modernization*. New York: Harper & Row.

——. 1943. *The Establishment of Constitutional Government in Bulgaria*. Princeton: Princeton University Press.

Blackbourn, David, and Geoff Eley. 1984. *The Peculiarities of German History: Bourgeois Society and Politics in Nineteenth-Century Germany*. Oxford: Oxford University Press.

Bleaney, M. F. 1976. *Underconsumption Theories: A History and Critical Analysis*. London: Lawrence & Wishart.

Bleiber, Helmut. 1966. *Zwischen Reform und Revolution: Lage und Kämpfe der schlesischen Bauern und Landarbeiter im Vormärz, 1840–1847*. Berlin: Akadamie-Verlag.

Blewett, Neil. 1965. The Franchise in the United Kingdom, 1885–1918. *Past and Present* 32: 27–65.

Bloch, Fred. 1977. The Ruling Class Does Not Rule. *Socialist Revolution* 7: 6–28.

Bloom, S. F. 1941. *A World of Nations*. New York: Columbia University Press.

Blum, Jerome. 1978. *The End of the Old Order in Rural Europe*. Princeton: Princeton University Press.

——. 1977. Russia. In David Spring, ed., *European Landed Elites in the Nineteenth Century*. Baltimore: Johns Hopkins University Press.

——. 1957. Rise of Serfdom in Eastern Europe. *American Historical Review* 62, no. 4: 807–36.

Bodenheimer, Susanne J. 1971b. Dependency and Imperialism: the Roots of Latin American Underdevelopment. In K. T. Fann and Donald C. Hodges, eds., *Readings in U.S. Imperialism*. Boston: Porter Sargent.

Boeke, J. H. 1953. *Economics and Economic Policy of Dual Societies*. New York: Institute of Pacific Relations.

Boersner, Demetrio. 1957. *The Bolsheviks and the National and Colonial Question, 1917–1928*. Geneva and Paris: Librairie E. Droz and Librairie Minard.

Booth, David. 1985. Marxism and Development Sociology: Interpreting the Impasse. *World Development* 13, no. 7: 761–87.

Born, Karl Erich. 1976. Structural Changes in German Social and Economic Development at the End of the Nineteenth Century. In James J. Sheehan, ed., *Imperial Germany*. New York: New Viewpoints.

Bornschier, Volker, and Christopher Chase-Dunn. 1985. *Transnational Corporations and Underdevelopment*. Westport, Conn.: Praeger.

Bosc, L. 1907. *Zollalliancen und Zollunionen*. Berlin: E. S. Mittler.

Boswup, William, and Uffe Schlichtkrull. 1962. Alternative Approaches to the Control of Competition. In John Perry Miller, ed., *Competition, Cartels, and Their Regulation*. Amsterdam: North-Holland.

Botzaris, N. 1962. *Visions balkaniques dans la préparation de la révolution grecque, 1789–1821*. Geneva: Librairie E. Droz.

Boulger, Demetrius C. 1904. *Belgian Life in Town and Country*. New York: Putnam.

Bouvier, Jean. 1961. *Le Crédit Lyonnais de 1863 à 1882: Les Années de formation d'une banque de dépots*. Paris: SEVPEN.

Bowen, Ralph H. 1947. *German Theories of the Corporative State, with Special Reference to the Period 1870–1919*. New York: McGraw-Hill.

Braudel, Fernand. 1984. *The Perspective of the World*. Vol. 3 of *Civilization and Capitalism, 15th–18th Century*. New York: Harper & Row.

——. 1982. *The Wheels of Commerce*. Vol. 1 of *Civilization and Capitalism, 15th-18th Century*. New York: Harper & Row.

——. 1981. *The Structures of Everyday Life*. Vol. 1 of *Civilization and Capitalism, 15th–18th Century*. New York: Harper & Row.

——. 1972. *The Mediterranean and the Mediterranean World in the Age of Philip II*. New York: Collins.

Braun, Rudolf. 1975. Taxation, Sociopolitical Structure, and State-Building: Great Britain and Brandenburg-Prussia. In Charles Tilly, ed., *The Formation of National States in Western Europe*. Princeton: Princeton University Press.

Breitman, Richard. 1981. *German Socialism and Weimar Democracy*. Chapel Hill: University of North Carolina Press.

Brenner, Robert. 1982. The Agrarian Roots of European Capitalism. *Past and Present* 97: 16–113.

——. 1977. The Origins of Capitalist Development: A Critique of Neo-Smithian Marxism. *New Left Review* 10, no. 3 (July-August): 25–92.

Brentano, Lujo. 1885. Über die zukünftige Politik des Deutschen Reiches. *Schmollers Jahrbuch* 9: 1–29.

Breuilly, John. 1982. *Nationalism and the State*. Chicago: University of Chicago Press.

Brewer, Anthony. 1980. *Marxist Theories of Imperialism: A Critical Survey*. London: Routledge.

Brown, Carl L. 1984. *International Politics and the Middle East*. Princeton: Princeton University Press.

Busek, Vratislau, and Nicolas Spulber. 1957. *Czechoslovakia*. New York: Praeger.

Buthman, William. 1939. *The Rise of Integral Nationalism in France, with Special Reference to the Ideas and Activities of Charles Maurras*. New York: Columbia University Press.

Caerleon, Ronan. 1969. *La révolution bretonne permanente*. Paris: Editions de la Table Ronde.

Cairncross, A. K. 1953. *Home and Foreign Investment, 1870–1914.* Cambridge: Cambridge University Press.

Caldwell, M. 1977. *The Wealth of Some Nations.* London: Zed.

Cameron, Rondo E. 1985. A New View of European Industrialization. *Economic History Review* 38, no. 1 (February): 1–23.

———. 1981. The Industrial Revolution: A Misnomer. In Jürgen Schneider, ed., *Wirtschaftskrafte und Wirtschaftswege: Festschrift für Hermann Kellenbenz.* Vol. 5. Stuttgart: In Komission bei Klett-Cotta.

———. 1961. *France and the Economic Development of Europe, 1800–1914.* Princeton: Princeton University Press.

———, ed. 1972. *Banking and Economic Development: Some Lessons of History.* New York: Oxford University Press.

Cannadine, David. 1990. *The Decline and Fall of the British Aristocracy.* New York: Doubleday.

———. 1980. *Lords and Landlords: The Aristocracy and the Towns, 1774–1967.* Leicester: Leicester University Press.

Caporaso, James. 1980. Dependency Theory: Continuities and Discontinuities in Development Studies. *International Organization* 34, no. 4 (Autumn): 605–28.

———. 1978. Dependence, Dependency, and Power in the Global System. *International Organization* 32, no. 1: 13–50.

Cardella, G. Palumbo. 1928–29. Crispi e la Politica Mediterranean e Coloniale. *Politica* 29 (April 1928): 150–79; 30 (June–August 1928): 387–431; 31 (June–August 1929): 350–80.

Cardoso, Fernando Henrique. 1979. On the Characterization of Authoritarian Regimes in Latin America. In David Collier, ed., *The New Authoritarianism in Latin America.* Princeton: Princeton University Press.

———. 1977. The Consumption of Dependency Theory in the United States. *Latin American Research Review* 12, no. 3: 7–24.

———. 1973. Associated-Dependent Development: Theoretical and Practical Implications. In Alfred Stepan, ed., *Authoritarian Brazil: Origins, Policies, and Future.* New Haven: Yale University Press.

———. 1972. Dependency and Development in Latin America. *New Left Review* 74 (July–August): 3–95.

Cardoso, Fernando Henrique, and Enzo Faletto. 1979. *Dependency and Development in Latin America.* Berkeley: University of California Press.

———. 1970. *Dependencia e desenvolvimento na America Latina: Ensaio de interpretacao sociologica.* Rio de Janeiro: Editora Zahar.

———. 1969. *Dependencia y desarrollo en America Latina: Ensayo de interpretación sociológica.* Mexico: Siglo Veintiuno.

Carneiro, Robert L. 1978. Expansion as an Expression of Competitive Exclusion. In Ronald Cohen and Elmer Service, eds. *The Origins of the State.* Philadelphia: Institute for the Study of Human Issues.

Caron, François. 1979. *An Economic History of Modern France.* New York: Columbia University Press.

Carr, E. H. 1947. *The Soviet Impact on The Western World.* New York: Macmillan.

Carr, Raymond. 1966. *Spain, 1808–1939.* Oxford: Clarendon Press.

Carroll, Thomas F. 1970. Land Reform as an Explosive Force. In Rudolfo Stavenhagen, ed., *Agrarian Problems and Peasant Movements in Latin America.* Garden City, N.Y.: Doubleday.

Carstairs, Andrew McLaren. 1980. *A Short History of Electoral Systems in Western Europe.* London: Allen & Unwin.

Carsten, F. L. 1967. *The Rise of Fascism.* Berkeley: University of California Press.

——. 1954. *The Origins of Prussia.* Oxford: Oxford University Press.

Cavanaugh, Gerald J. 1972. The Present State of French Revolutionary Historiography: Alfred Cobban and Beyond. *French Historical Studies* 7, no. 4 (Fall): 587–606.

Caves, R. E., et al. 1968. *Britain's Economic Prospects.* London: Allen & Unwin.

Chalmers, Douglas A. 1969. Developing on the Periphery: External Factors in Latin American Politics. In James N. Rosenau, ed., *Linkage Politics: Essays on the Convergence of National and International Systems.* New York: Free Press.

Charques, R. 1965. *The Twilight of Imperial Russia.* London: Oxford University Press.

Chartier, Roger. 1978. The Two Frances: The History of a Geographical Idea. *Social Science Information* 17, no. 4/5: 527–54.

Chase-Dunn, Christopher. 1975. The Effects of International Economic Dependence on Development and Inequality. *American Sociological Review* 40: 720–39.

Chenery, Hollis. 1986. *Development and Growth.* New York: Cambridge.

Chester, Sir Norman. 1951. *Central and Local Government.* London: Macmillan.

Chirot, Daniel. 1977. *Social Change in the Twentieth Century.* New York: Harcourt Brace Jovanovich.

Chlepner, B. S. 1945. Economic Development of Belgium. In Jan-Albert Goris, ed., *Belgium.* Berkeley: University of California Press.

Cholvy, G. 1978. Religion et révolution: La déchristianization de l'an II. *Annales historique de la Révolution française,* 78: 451–64.

Clark, Colin. 1957. *The Conditions of Economic Progress.* 3d ed. London: Macmillan.

——. 1940. *The Conditions of Economic Progress.* London: Macmillan.

Clark, George Kitson. 1951. The Repeal of the Corn Laws and the Politics of the Forties. *Economic History Review,* 2d ser., 4: 1–13.

Clark, J. C. D. 1986. *Revolution and Rebellion: State and Society in England in the Seventeenth and Eighteenth Centuries.* New York: Cambridge University Press.

——. 1985. *English Society, 1688–1832.* New York: Columbia University Press.

Clough, Shepard Bancroft. 1952. *Economic History of Europe.* 3d ed. Boston: D. C. Heath.

——. 1930. *A History of the Flemish Movement in Belgium: A Study in Nationalism.* New York: Richard R. Smith.

Coates, B. E., R. J. Johnston, and P. L. Knox. 1977. *Geography and Inequality.* London: Oxford University Press.

Coatsworth, John H. 1993. Notes on the Comparative Economic History of Latin America and the United States. In Walther L. Bernecker and Hans Werner Tobler, eds., *Development and Underdevelopment in Latin America: Contrasts of Economic Growth in North and Latin America in Historical Perspective.* Berlin: Walter de Gruyter.

Cobban, Alfred. 1971. *The Social Interpretation of the French Revolution.* Cambridge: Cambridge University Press.

Cohen, Benjamin. 1973. *The Question of Imperialism: The Political Economy of Dominance and Dependence.* New York: Basic Books.

Cole, Alistair, and Peter Campbell. 1989. *French Electoral Systems and Elections since 1789.* Aldershot: Gower.

Cole, C. Woolsey. 1939. *Colbert and a Century of French Mercantilism*. London: Frank Cass.

Collas, Henry. 1908. *La Banque de Paris et des Pays-Bas*. Dijon: Barbier-Léon Marshal.

Collier, David, ed. 1979. *The New Authoritarianism in Latin America*. Princeton: Princeton University Press.

Collins, Randall. 1995. German-Bashing and the Theory of Democratic Modernization. *Zeitschrift für Soziologie* 24, no. 1 (February): 3–21.

Committee on Finance and Industry. 1931. *Macmillan Report*. London: H. M. Stationery Office.

Corbridge, S. 1990. Post-Marxism and Development Studies: Beyond the Impasse. *World Development* 18, no. 5: 623–39.

Corradini, Enrico. 1915. Per la guerra d'Italia. In *Discorsi Politici*. Florence.

Crafts, N. F. R. 1984. Patterns of Development in Nineteenth-Century Europe. *Oxford Economic Papers* 36 (November): 438–58.

——. 1983. British Economic Growth, 1700–1813: A Review of the Evidence. *Economic History Review*, 2d ser., 36, no. 2: 177–99.

Crouch, Colin. 1986. Sharing Public Space. In John A. Hall, ed., *States in History*. Oxford: Basil Blackwell.

Crowley, C. W. 1930. *The Question of Greek Independence: A Study of British Policy in the Near East*. Cambridge: Cambridge University Press.

Cueva, Agustin. 1982. *The Process of Political Domination in Ecuador*. Trans. Danielle Salti. New Brunswick, N.J.: Transaction.

——. 1977. *El Desarrollo del capitalismo en America Latina: ensayo de interpretación historica*. Mexico: Siglo Veintiuno.

——. 1976. *La teoria de la dependencia ha muerto?* Lima: Tarea.

Cullen, L. M. 1968. *Anglo-Irish Trade, 1660–1800*. Manchester: University of Manchester Press.

Curtis, Roy Emerson. 1931. *The Trusts and Economic Control*. New York: McGraw-Hill.

Dahl, Robert. 1971. *Polyarchy: Participation and Opposition*. New Haven: Yale University Press.

Dahrendorf, Ralf. 1967. *Society and Democracy in Germany*. Garden City, N.Y.: Anchor.

Dakin, Douglas. 1973. *The Greek Struggle for Independence, 1821–1833*. Berkeley: University of California Press.

Danilevski, Nikolai Iakovlevich. 1871. *Rossiia i Europa*. St. Petersburg: Obshchestvennaia pol'za.

D'Annunzio, Gabriele. 1919. *Italy or Death*. Trans. Henry Furst. Fiume, Italy: Printed by the Publishers of *La Vedetta d'Italia*.

Daphnas, Gregorios. 1955. *Greece between the Wars, 1923–1940*. Athens: Ikaros.

Davies, Horace B. 1967. *Nationalism and Socialism: Marxist and Labor Theories of Nationalism to 1917*. New York: Monthly Review Press.

Davin, Louis E. 1969. The Structural Crisis of a Regional Economy. A Case-Study: The Walloon Area. In E. A. G. Robinson, ed., *Backward Areas in Advanced Countries*. London: Macmillan.

Davis, H. W. C. 1915. *The Political Thought of Heinrich von Treitschke*. New York: Scribner.

Davis, Lance E., and Douglass North. 1971. *Institutional Change and American Economic Growth*. Cambridge: Cambridge University Press.

Dawisha, Adeed. 1990. Arab Regimes: Legitimacy and Foreign Policy. In Giacomo Luciani, ed., *The Arab State*. Berkeley: University of California Press.

Dawson, Philip. 1972. *Provincial Magistrates and Revolutionary Politics in France, 1789–1795*. Cambridge: Harvard University Press.

Dawson, William Harbutt. 1913. *Industrial Germany*. London: Collins.

Denemark, Robert A., and Kenneth P. Thomas. 1988. The Brenner-Wallerstein Debate. *International Studies Quarterly* 32: 47–65.

de Schweinitz, Karl. 1964. *Industrialization and Democracy: Economic Necessities and Political Possibilities*. New York: Free Press.

Deutsch, Julius. 1934. *The Civil War in Austria*. Trans. David P. Berenberg. Chicago: Socialist Party, National Headquarters.

De Vries, Johan. 1976. Benelux, 1920–1970. In Carlo C. Cipolla, ed., *The Fontana Economic History of Europe*. Vol. 1, *Contemporary Economies*. Glasgow: William Collins Sons.

Diamond, Larry. 1990. Introduction: Comparing Experiences with Democracy. In Larry Diamond et al., eds., *Politics in Developing Countries: Comparing Experiences with Democracy*. Boulder, Colo.: Lynne Rienner.

Diamond, Larry, et al., eds. 1990. *Politics in Developing Countries: Comparing Experiences with Democracy*. Boulder, Colo.: Lynne Rienner.

Diamond, Larry, Juan Linz, and Seymour Lipset, eds. 1988. *Democracy in Developing Nations*. Boulder, Colo.: Lynne Rienner.

Djordjevic, Dimitrije, and Stephen Fischer-Galati. 1981. *The Balkan Revolutionary Tradition*. New York: Columbia University Press.

Dobb, Maurice. 1960. *Economic Growth and Planning*. New York: Monthly Review Press.

———. 1947. *Studies in the Development of Capitalism*. New York: International Publishers.

Dornbusch, Rudiger, and Sebastian Edwards. 1989. *Macroeconomic Populism in Latin America*. Working Paper 2986. Cambridge, Mass. National Bureau of Economic Research.

Dos Santos, Teotonio. 1970. The Structure of Dependence. *American Economic Review* 60: 235–46.

Dostoevsky, Fyodor. 1923. *Letters and Reminiscences*. Trans. S. S. Koteliansky and J. Middleton Murry. New York: Knopf.

Downing, Brian M. 1992. *The Military Revolution and Political Change in Early Modern Europe*. Princeton: Princeton University Press.

Doyle, William. 1980. *Origins of the French Revolution*. Oxford: Oxford University Press.

Drake, Paul, and Eduardo Silva, eds. 1986. *Elections and Democratization in Latin America, 1980–1985*. La Jolla, Calif.: Institute of the Americas.

Drew, Edward. 1969. *Politics in the Altiplano: The Dynamics of Change in Rural Peru*. Austin: University of Texas Press.

Driault, Edouard, and Michel Lhéritier. 1925. *Histoire diplomatique de la Grèce de 1821 à nos jours*. Vol. 2. Paris: Les Presses Universitaires de France.

Duby, Georges. 1980. *The Three Orders: Feudal Society Imagined*. Chicago: University of Chicago Press.

Dunn, Ethel, and Stephen P. Dunn. 1964. Religion As an Instrument of Cultural Change. *Slavic Review* 23, no. 3: 459–78.

Dupin, C. 1827. *Forces productives et commerciales de la France*. Paris: Bachelier.

——. 1826. *Effets de l'enseignement populaire de la lecture, de l'écriture et de l'arithméti-que, de la géométrie et la mécanique appliquées aux arts, sur les prospérités de la France.* Address to the opening session of the Cours normal de géométries et de la mécanique appliquées aux arts, 30 November 1826, at the Conservatoire des Arts et Métiers. Paris: Bachelier.

Durkheim, Emile. 1975. L'état. In *Textes*, vol. 3. Paris: Éditions de Minuit.

Dvornik, F. 1962. *The Slavs in European History and Civilization.* New Brunswick, N.J.: Rutgers University Press.

Economic Commission for Latin America [ECLA]. 1970. *Economic Survey of Latin America.* New York: United Nations.

——. 1967. *Estudio Sobre la distribución del Ingreso en America Latina, 1967.* Santiago, Chile: ECLA.

——. 1950. *Economic Survey of Latin America, 1949.* New York: United Nations.

Economic Commission for Latin America and the Caribbean [ECLAC]. Various years. *Serie Distribución del Ingreso.* Santiago, Chile: ECLAC.

——. 1980. *Statistical Yearbook.* Santiago, Chile: ECLAC.

Edwards, Corwin D. 1962. Cartelization in Western Europe. Washington, D.C.: U.S. Bureau of Intelligence and Research, Department of State.

Eisenstadt, S. N. 1966. *Modernization: Protest and Change.* Englewood Cliffs, N.J.: Prentice-Hall.

——. 1964. Breakdown of Modernization. *Economic Development and Cultural Change* 12 (July): 345–67.

Eisenstadt, S. N., and Rene Lemarchand. 1981. *Political Clientelism, Patronage, and Development.* Beverly Hills, Calif.: Sage.

Elbow, Matthew H. 1953. *French Corporative Theory, 1789–1948.* New York: Columbia University Press.

Elder, Neil. 1988. Corporatism in Sweden. In Andrew Cox and Noel O'Sullivan, eds., *The Corporate State: Corporatism and State Tradition in Western Europe.* Aldershot: Edward Elgar.

Elias, H. J. 1969. *Vijfentwintig jaar Vlaamse Beweging 1914–1939.* Antwerp: De Nederlandsche Boekhandel.

Ellis, Geoffrey. 1978. Review Article: The Marxist Interpretation of the French Revolution. *English Historical Review* 93: 353–76.

Emerson, Rupert. 1960. *From Empire to Nation: The Rise of Self-Assertion of Asian and African Peoples.* Cambridge: Harvard University Press.

Emmanuel, Arghiri. 1972. *Unequal Exchange: A Study of the Imperialism of Trade.* New York: Monthly Review Press.

Engelbrecht, H. C. 1968. *Johann Gottlieb Fichte: A Study of His Political Writings with Special Reference to His Nationalism.* New York: AMS Press.

Engels, Friedrich. 1971. The Abdication of the Bourgeoisie. 1889. Reprinted in Karl Marx and Friedrich Engels, *Articles on Britain.* Moscow: Progress Publishers.

——. 1969. *Germany: Revolution and Counter-Revolution.* New York: International Publishers.

——. 1950. The Origin of the Family, Private Property, and the State. In Karl Marx and Friedrich Engels, *Selected Works*, vol 2. London: Lawrence and Wishart.

——. 1895. *Violenza ed economia formazione del nuovo impero tedesco.* Rome.

——. 1894. La futura rivoluzione italiana ed il partito socialista. *Critica Sociale* 4, no. 3 (1 February): 35–36.

Esman, Milton J. 1988. Ethnic Politics: How Unique Is the Middle East? In Milton J. Esman and Itamar Rabinovich, eds., *Ethnicity, Pluralism, and the State in the Middle East*. Ithaca: Cornell University Press.

Evangelinides, Mary. 1979. Core-Periphery Relations in the Greek Case. In Dudley Seers, Bernard Shaffer, and Marja-Liisa Kiljunen, eds., *Underdeveloped Europe: Studies in Core-Periphery Relations*. Brighton, Sussex: Harvester.

Evans, Ellen Lovell. 1981. *The German Center Party, 1870–1933*. Carbondale: Southern Illinois University Press.

Evans, Peter. 1979. *Dependent Development*. Princeton: Princeton University Press.

Evans, Peter, Dietrich Rueschemeyer, and Theda Skocpol. 1985. *Bringing the State Back In*. New York: Cambridge University Press.

Evans, Peter, and John D. Stephens. 1988. Development and the World Economy. In Neil J. Smelser, ed., *Handbook of Sociology*. Newbury Park, Calif.: Sage.

Fairlie, S. 1965. The Nineteenth-Century Corn Law Reconsidered. *Economic History Review*, 2d ser. 18: 563–75.

Fedeeyev, Rostislav. 1871. *Opinion on the Eastern Question*. London: E. Stanford.

Feder, Ernest. 1970. Counterreform. In Rudolfo Stavenhagen, ed., *Agrarian Problems and Peasant Movements in Latin America*. Garden City, N.Y.: Doubleday.

Fejtö, François. 1948. Europe on the Eve of Revolution. In François Fejtö, ed., *The Opening of an Era: 1848*. New York: Grosset & Dunlap.

Fichte, Johann Gottlieb. 1845. Grundlagen des Naturrechts. In *Fichtes Werke*, 8 vols. Ed. Immanuel Hermann Fichte. Berlin: Veit und Cie.

Finer, Samuel. 1975. State and Nation Building in Europe: The Role of the Military. In Charles Tilly, ed., *The Formation of National States in Western Europe*. Princeton: Princeton University Press.

Finlay, George. 1877. *A History of Greece*. Oxford: Clarendon Press.

Fischer, Wolfram. 1978. Die Rohstoffversorgung der europäischen Wirtschaft in historischer Perspektive. In Jürgen Schneider et al., *Wirtschaftskräfte und Wirtschaftswege*, vol. 4. Stuttgart: Übersee und allgemeine Wirtschaftsgeschichte.

Fores, Michael. 1981. The Myth of a British Industrial Revolution. *History* 66, no. 217 (June): 181–98.

Fox, Edward. 1971. *History in a Geographic Perspective: The Other France*. New York: Norton.

Frank, André Gunder. 1972a. The Development of Underdevelopment. In James D. Cockcroft et al., eds., *Dependence and Underdevelopment: Latin America's Political Economy*. New York: Anchor.

———. 1972b. *Lumpenbourgeoisie: Lumpenproletariat. Dependence, Class, and Politics in Latin America*. New York: Monthly Review Press.

———. 1970. The Development of Underdevelopment. In Robert I. Rhodes, ed., *Imperialism and Underdevelopment*. New York: Monthly Review Press.

———. 1969. *Latin America: Underdevelopment or Revolution*. New York: Monthly Review Press.

———. 1967. *Capitalism and Underdevelopment in Latin America*. New York: Monthly Review Press.

Frazee, Charles A. 1969. *The Orthodox Church and Independent Greece, 1821–1852*. London: Cambridge University Press.

Fuchs, R. 1918. *Die Kriegsgewinne der verschiedenen Wirtschaftszweige in den einzelnen Staaten, anhand statisticher Daten dargestellt*. Zurich: University of Zurich.

Furet, François. 1978. *Penser la Révolution française*. Paris: Gallimard.

——. 1971. Le catéchisme de la Révolution française. *Annales* 26: 255–89.

Furtado, Celso. 1970. *Economic Development in Latin America: From Colonial Times to the Cuban Revolution*. Cambridge: Cambridge University Press.

——. 1963. *The Economic Growth of Brazil: A Survey from Colonial to Modern Times*. Trans. Richard W. de Aguiar and Eric Charles Drysdale. Berkeley: University of California Press.

Gagliardo, John G. 1967. *Enlightened Despotism*. New York: Crowell.

Galenson, W., and H. Leibenstein. 1955. Investment Criteria and Economic Development. *Quarterly Journal of Economics* 69 (August): 343–70.

Geffre, Claude, and Jean-Pierre Jossua, eds. 1989. *1789: The French Revolution and the Church*. Edinburgh: T. & T. Clark.

Gehrlich, Peter. 1973. The Institutionalization of European Parliaments. In Allan Kornberg, ed., *Legislatures in Comparative Perspective*. New York: D. McKay.

Gellner, Ernest. 1983. *Nations and Nationalism*. Ithaca: Cornell University Press.

Gerschenkron, Alexander. 1965. Agrarian Policies and Industrialization: Russia 1861–1917. In *Cambridge Economic History of Europe*, vol. 6. Cambridge: Cambridge University Press.

——. 1962. *Economic Backwardness in Historical Perspective*. Cambridge: Harvard University Press.

——. 1943. *Bread and Democracy in Germany*. Ithaca: Cornell University Press.

Gerth, H. H., and C. Wright Mills. 1946. *From Max Weber: Essays in Sociology*. New York: Oxford University Press.

Gestrin, Ferdo. 1962. Economie et société en Slovénie au XVIe siècle. *Annales E.S.C.*, 17, no. 4 (July–August).

Gibson, Ralph, and Martin Blinkhorn, eds. 1991. *Landownership and Power in Modern Europe*. London: Harper Collins.

Gilbert, Alan D. 1980. *The Making of Post-Christian England: A History of the Secularization of Modern Society*. London: Longman.

Gilley, Sheridan. 1988. Christianity in Europe: Reformation to Today. In Stewart Sutherland et al., eds., *The World's Religions*. London: G. K. Hall.

Gillis, John R. 1977. *The Development of European Society, 1770–1870*. Boston: Houghton Mifflin.

Goeldel, Herbert. 1917. *Wohlstandsverhältnisse in Ostpreussen*. Jena: G. Fischer.

Goldstein, Robert Justin. 1983. *Political Repression in Nineteenth-Century Europe*. London: Croom Helm.

Gonzàles-Casanova, Pablo. 1965. Internal Colonialism and National Development. *Studies in Comparative International Development* 1, no. 4: 27–37.

Good, D. F. 1984. *The Economic Rise of the Hapsburg Empire, 1750–1914*. Berkeley: University of California Press.

Gordon, David M. 1980. Stages of Accumulation and Long Economic Cycles. In Terence K. Hopkins and Immanuel Wallerstein, eds., *Processes of the World System*. Beverly Hills, Calif.: Sage.

Gosnell, Harold F. 1930. *Why Europe Votes*. Chicago: University of Chicago Press.

Gouldner, Alvin W. 1977–78. Stalinism: A Study of Internal Colonialism. *Telos* 34 (Winter): 5–48.

Gourevitch, Peter. 1984. Breaking with Orthodoxy: The Politics of Economic Policy Responses to the Depression of the 1930s. *International Organization* 38: 95–129.

——. 1978. The Second Image Reversed: The International Sources of Domestic Politics. *International Organization* 32: 881–911.

Graf, A. 1911. *L'anglomania e l'influsso inglese in Italia nel secolo XVIII.* Turin: E. Loescher.

Graham, Richard. 1990. *Patronage and Politics in Nineteenth-Century Brazil.* Stanford: Stanford University Press.

Gramsci, Antonio. 1971. *Selections from the Prison Notebooks of Antonio Gramsci.* Ed. and trans. Quentin Hoare and Geoffrey Nowell Smith. New York: International Publishers.

——. 1957. *The Modern Prince and Other Writings.* London: Lawrence and Wishart.

——. 1949. *Il Risorgimento.* Turin: Einaudi.

Grantham, G. W. 1975. Scale and Organization in French Farming, 1840–1880. In William N. Parker and Eric L. Jones, eds., *European Peasants and Their Market: Essays in Agrarian Economic History.* Princeton: Princeton University Press.

Gravier, Jean-François. 1947. *Paris et le désert français.* Paris: Le Portulan.

Gray, Robert. 1981. *The Aristocracy of Labour in Nineteenth-Century Britain, 1850–1914.* London: Macmillan.

Great Britain, H. M. S. Stationery Office. 1916. *Recommendations of the Economic Conference of the Allies Held at Paris on June 14–17, 1916,* cd. 8271.

Greenfeld, Liah. 1992. *Nationalism: Five Roads to Modernity.* Cambridge: Harvard University Press.

Grew, Raymond. 1978a. The Crises and Their Sequences. In Grew, ed., *Crises of Political Development in Europe and the United States.* Princeton: Princeton University Press.

Grew, Raymond, ed. 1978b. *Crises of Political Development in Europe and the United States.* Princeton: Princeton University Press.

Griffith, J. A. G. 1966. *Central Departments and Local Authorities.* Toronto: University of Toronto Press.

Groh, Dieter. 1973. *Negative Integration und revolutionärer Attentismus: Die deutsche Sozialdemokratie am Vorabend des Ersten Weltkrieges.* Frankfurt am Main: Ullstein.

Grünberg, K. 1922. Agrarverfassung. *Grundriss der Sozialökonomik* 7: 131–67.

Guenalt, Paul H., and J. M. Jackson, 1960. *The Control of Monopoly in the United Kingdom.* London: Longman.

Guérin, Daniel. 1939. *Fascism and Big Business.* New York: Pioneer Publishers.

Gulick, Charles A. 1940. *Austria from Hapsburg to Hitler.* Vol. 2. Berkeley: University of California Press.

Gusfield, Joseph. 1967. Tradition and Modernity: Misplaced Polarities in the Study of Social Change. *American Journal of Sociology* 72: 351–62

Guttsman, W. L. 1969. *The English Ruling Class.* London: Weidenfeld and Nicolson.

——. 1954. Aristocracy and the Middle Classes in the British Political Elite, 1886–1916. *British Journal of Sociology* 5: 12–32.

Habbakuk, H. J. 1967. England. In Albert Goodwin, ed., *The European Nobility in the Eighteenth Century.* New York: Harper & Row.

Habermas, Jürgen. 1976. *Legitimation Crisis.* London: Heinemann.

Halperin, Sandra. 1993. Nationalism and the Autonomous State in Nineteenth-Century Europe. In Ronen Palan and Barry K. Gills, eds., *Transcending the State-Global Divide: The Neo-Structuralist Agenda in International Relations.* Boulder, Colo.: Lynne Rienner.

Hammond, Edwin. 1968. *An Analysis of Regional Economic and Social Statistics.* Durham: University of Durham, Rowntree Research Unit.

Hanham, H. J. 1970. *The Reformed Electoral System in Great Britain, 1832–1914.* London: Cambridge University Press.

Hardach, Gerd. 1977. *The First World War, 1914–1918.* Berkeley: University of California Press.

Harley, C. Knick. 1982. British Industrialization before 1841: Evidence of Slower Growth during the Industrial Revolution. *Journal of Economic History* 42, no. 2 (June): 267–90.

Hausrath, Adolf. 1914. *Treitschke: His Doctrine of German Destiny and of International Relations.* New York: Putnam.

Hechter, Michael. 1975. *Internal Colonialism: The Celtic Fringe in British National Development, 1536–1966.* Berkeley: University of California Press.

Heckscher, Eli F. 1964. *The Continental System.* Gloucester, Mass.: Peter Smith.

———. 1954. *An Economic History of Sweden.* Cambridge: Harvard University Press.

Henderson, William Otto. 1958. *The State and the Industrial Revolution in Prussia, 1740–1870.* Liverpool: Liverpool University Press.

Herbert, Ulrich. 1990. *A History of Foreign Labor in Germany, 1880–1980: Seasonal Workers, Forced Laborers, Guest Workers.* Trans. William Templer. Ann Arbor: University of Michigan Press.

Herr, Richard. 1977. Spain. In David Spring, ed., *European Landed Elites in the Nineteenth Century.* Baltimore: Johns Hopkins University Press.

Hertslet, Sir Edward. 1891. *The Map of Europe by Treaty.* London: Harrison and Sons.

Hertz, Frederick. 1947. War and National Character. *Contemporary Review* 171 (May): 274–81.

Hettne, B. 1990. *Development Theory and the Three Worlds.* Harlow: Longman.

Hexter, J. H. 1961. The Myth of the Middle Class in Tudor England. In *Reappraisals in History.* Chicago: University of Chicago Press.

Heyer, Friedrich. 1969. *The Catholic Church from 1648 to 1870.* London: Adam & Charles Black.

Higgs, David. 1987. *Nobles in Nineteenth-Century France.* Baltimore: Johns Hopkins University Press.

Hilferding, Rudolf. 1981. *Finance Capital: A Study of the Latest Phase of Capitalist Development.* Ed. Tom Bottomore. London: Routledge & Kegan Paul.

Hill, Christopher. 1981. A Bourgeois Revolution? In J. G. A. Pocock, ed., *Three British Revolutions: 1641, 1688, 1776.* Princeton: Princeton University Press.

———. 1967. *Reformation to Industrial Revolution: A Social and Economic History of Britain, 1530–1780.* London: Weidenfeld and Nicolson.

———. 1940. *The English Revolution of 1640.* London: Lawrence and Wishart.

Hilton, R. H. 1951. Y-eut-il une crise générale de la féodalité? *Annales E.S.C.* 6, no. 1 (January–March): 23–30.

Hintze, Otto. 1975. Military Organization and the Organization of the State. In Felix Gilbert, ed., *The Historical Essays of Otto Hintze.* New York: Oxford University Press.

Hirschman, Alberto. 1981. The Rise and Decline of Development Economics. In *Essays in Trespassing.* Cambridge: Cambridge University Press.

———. 1971. *A Bias for Hope: Essays on the Development of Latin America.* New Haven: Yale University Press.

Hobsbawm, Eric. 1990. *Nations and Nationalism since 1870.* Cambridge: Cambridge University Press.

———. 1979. *The Age of Capital, 1848–1875.* New York: Meridian.

———. 1962. *The Age of Revolution, 1789–1848.* New York: Mentor.

———. 1959. *Primitive Rebels.* New York: Norton.

Hobson, J. A. 1965. *Imperialism.* Ann Arbor: University of Michigan Press.

Holborn, Hajo. 1969. *A History of Modern Germany, 1840–1945.* New York: Knopf.

Holland, Stuart. 1979. Dependent Development: Portugal as Periphery. In Dudley Seers, Bernard Shaffer, and Marja-Liisa Kiljunen, eds., *Underdeveloped Europe: Studies in Core-Periphery Relations.* Brighton, Sussex: Harvester.

Hough, Richard, John Kelley, Stephen Miller, Russell Derossier, Fred L. Mann, and Mitchell A. Seligson. 1982. *Land and Labor in Guatemala: An Assessment.* Guatemala City: Ediciones Papiro.

Howard, Michael. 1979. War and the Nation-State. *Daedalus* 108, no. 4 (Fall): 101–10.

———. 1976. *War in European History.* New York: Oxford University Press.

Hroch, Miroslav. 1985. *Social Preconditions of National Revival in Europe: A Comparative Analysis of the Social Composition of Patriotic Groups among the Smaller European Nations.* Trans. Ben Fowkes. London: Cambridge University Press.

Hughes, Christopher. 1975. *Switzerland.* New York: Praeger.

Hunt, Lynn. 1984. *Politics, Culture, and Class in the French Revolution.* Berkeley: University of California Press.

Hunter, James. 1976. *The Making of the Crofting Community.* Edinburgh: Donald.

Huntington, Samuel P. 1968. *Political Order in Changing Societies.* New Haven: Yale University Press.

Interamerican Development Bank [IDB]. 1973. *Annual Report.* Washington, D.C.: IDB.

Issawi, Charles. 1982. *An Economic History of the Middle East and North Africa.* New York: Columbia University Press.

Jackson, Robert H. 1990. *Quasi-States: Sovereignty, International Relations, and the Third World.* New York: Cambridge University Press.

Jackson, Steven, Bruce Russett, Duncan Snidal, and David Sylvan. 1978. Conflict and Coercion in Dependent States. *Journal of Conflict Resolution* 22: 627–57.

Jásci, Oscar. 1929. *Dissolution of the Hapsburg Monarchy.* Chicago: University of Chicago.

Jelavich, Charles. 1958. *Tsarist Russia and Balkan Nationalism: Russian Influence on the Internal Affairs of Bulgaria and Serbia, 1879–1886.* Berkeley: University of California Press.

Joad, C. E. M. 1951. What I Still Believe. *New Statesman and Nation,* (19 May), 557–58.

Johnson, Arthur A. 1979. *The Disappearance of the Small Landowner.* Fairfield, N.Y.: A. M. Kelley.

Johnson, John J. 1964. Introduction. In Johnson, ed., *Contemporary Change in Latin America.* Stanford: Stanford University Press.

Jörberg, Lennart. 1973. The Industrial Revolution in the Nordic Countries. In Carlo M. Cipolla, ed., *The Fontana Economic History of Europe. Vol. 2, The Emergence of Industrial Societies.* Glasgow: William Collins Sons.

Joyce, Patrick. 1980. *Work, Society, and Politics: The Culture of the Factory in Later Victorian England.* New Brunswick, N.J.: Rutgers University Press.

Kaiser, David. 1990. *Politics and War: European Conflict from Phillip II to Hitler.* Cambridge: Harvard University Press.

Kantorowicz, Ernst Hartwig. 1957. *The King's Two Bodies.* Princeton: Princeton University Press.

Katzenstein, Peter. 1985. *Small States in World Markets: Industrial Policy in Europe.* Ithaca: Cornell University Press.

———. 1984. *Corporatism and Change.* Ithaca: Cornell University Press.

Kaughman, Robert R. 1972. *The Politics of Land Reform in Chile, 1950–1970.* Cambridge: Harvard University Press.

Kautsky, John H. 1980. *The Political Consequences of Modernization.* Huntington, N.Y.: Robert E. Krieger.

———. 1899. *Agrarfrage.* Stuttgart: Dietz Verlag.

Kay, Cristóbal. 1989. *Latin American Theories of Development and Underdevelopment.* London: Routledge.

Kay, Geoffrey. 1975. *Development and Underdevelopment: A Marxian Analysis.* London: Macmillan.

Kedourie, Elie. 1984. *The Crossman Confessions and Other Essays in Politics, History, and Religion.* London: Mansell.

———. 1960. *Nationalism.* London: Hutchinson University Library.

Keith-Lucas, Bryan, and Peter G. Richards. 1978. *A History of Local Government in the Twentieth Century.* London: Allen & Unwin.

Kennan, George. 1960. *Russia and the West under Lenin and Stalin.* New York: Mentor.

Kennedy, Paul. 1987. *The Rise and Fall of the Great Powers: Economic Change and Military Conflict from 1500 to 2000.* New York: Vintage.

———. 1981. *The Realities behind Diplomacy: Background Influences on British External Policy, 1865–1980.* Glasgow: William Collins Sons.

Kern, Robert, ed. 1973. *The Caciques: Oligarchical Politics and the System of Caciquismo in the Luso-Hispanic World.* Albuquerque: University of New Mexico Press.

Kerr, Malcolm H. 1981. Rich and Poor in the New Arab Order. *Journal of Arab Affairs* 1, no. 1 (October): 1–26.

Keynes, John Maynard. 1988. *The Economic Consequences of the Peace.* 1920. Reprint, Harmondsworth: Penguin.

Kieniewicz, Stephan. 1948–49. The Social Visage of Poland in 1848. *Slavonic and East European Review* 27: 91–105.

Kindleberger, Charles. 1984. *Financial History of Western Europe.* London: Allen & Unwin.

———. 1964. *Economic Growth in France and Britain, 1851–1950.* Cambridge: Harvard University Press.

King, Merle. 1968. Toward a Theory of Power and Political Instability in Latin America. In James Petras and Maurice Zeitlin, eds., *Latin America, Reform or Revolution?* Greenwich, Conn.: Fawcett.

Kleinwächter, Friedrich. 1883. *Die Kartelle.* Innsbruck: Wagner.

Klima, Arnost. 1949. Bohemia. In François Fejtö, ed., *The Opening of an Era: 1848.* New York: Grosset & Dunlap.

Knorr, Klaus. 1975. *The Power of Nations.* New York: Basic.

Kocka, Jürgen, 1988. German History before Hitler: The Debate about the German *Sonderweg. Journal of Contemporary History* 23, no. 1 (January): 1–16.

Koebner, Richard, and Helmut Dan Schmidt. 1965. *Imperialism: The Story and Significance of a Political Word, 1840–1960.* Cambridge: Cambridge University Press.

Koenig, Harry C., ed. 1943. *Principles for Peace.* Washington, D.C.: National Catholic Welfare Conference.

Kohn, Hans. 1961. *The Hapsburg Empire, 1804–1918.* Princeton: Van Nostrand.

———. 1955. *Nationalism: Its Meaning and History.* Princeton: Princeton University Press.

———. 1946. *Prophets and People.* London: Macmillan.

Kossmann, E. H. 1978. *The Low Countries, 1780–1940.* Oxford: Clarendon Press.

Kumar, Kishan. 1983. Pre-capitalist and Non-capitalist Factors in the Development of Capitalism: Fred Hirsch and Joseph Schumpeter. In Adrian Ellis and Kishan Kumar, eds., *Dilemmas of Liberal Democracies.* London: Tavistock.

Kuznets, Simon. 1971. *Economic Growth of Nations: Total Output and Production Statistics.* Cambridge: Harvard University Press.

———. 1966. *Modern Economic Growth.* New Haven: Yale University Press.

———. 1964. The Aftermath of World War II. In *Postwar Economic Growth: Four Lectures.* Cambridge: Belknap Press.

———. 1963. Quantitative Aspects of the Economic Growth of Nations: Distribution of Income in Size. *Economic Development and Cultural Change* 21, no. 2, pt. 2 (January): 1–80.

Laclau, Ernesto. 1971. Feudalism and Capitalism in Latin America. *New Left Review* 67 (May-June): 19–38.

Ladejinsky, Wolf. 1959. Agrarian Revolution in Japan. *Foreign Affairs* 38, no. 1 (October): 95–109.

Lal, Deepak. 1983. *The Poverty of Development Economics.* London: Institute of Economic Affairs.

Lall, Sanjaya. 1981. *Developing Countries in the International Economy.* London: Macmillan.

Lambert, A. 1984. *Unquiet Souls.* London: Macmillan.

Lampe, John R., and Marvin R. Jackson. 1982. *Balkan Economic History, 1550–1950.* Bloomington: Indiana University Press.

Landes, David S. 1969. *The Unbound Prometheus: Technological Change and Industrial Development in Western Europe from 1750 to the Present.* London: Cambridge University Press.

———. 1954. Social Attitudes, Entrepreneurship, and Economic Development: A Comment. *Explorations in Entrepreneurial History* 6, no. 4 (May).

Langer, William L. 1969. *Political and Social Upheaval, 1832–1852.* New York: Harper Torchbooks.

Larrain, J. 1989. *Theories of Development.* Cambridge: Polity Press.

League of Nations. 1931a. *General Report on the Economic Aspects of International Industrial Agreements of the Economic Committee.* Geneva.

———. 1931b. *The Course and Phases of the World Economic Depression.* Report presented to the Assembly of the League of Nations. Geneva: Secretariat of the League of Nations.

———. 1926. *Health Organization Handbook Series No. 6: Official Statistics of the Scandinavian Countries and the Baltic Republics.* Geneva.

Leca, Jean. 1990. Social Structure and Political Stability: Comparative Evidence from the Algerian, Syrian, and Iraqi Cases. In Giacomo Luciani, ed., *The Arab State.* Berkeley: University of California Press.

246   **References**

Leeson, P. F. 1988. Development Economics and the Study of Development. In P. F. Leeson and M. M. Minogue, eds., *Perspectives on Development: Cross-Disciplinary Themes in Development Studies.* Manchester: Manchester University Press.

Lefebvre, Georges. 1962–64. *The French Revolution.* 2 vols. New York: Columbia University Press.

———. 1947. *The Coming of the French Revolution.* Trans. R. R. Palmer. Princeton: Princeton University Press.

Lenin, V. I. 1956. *The Development of Capitalism in Russia.* Moscow: Foreign Language Publishing House.

———. 1948. *Imperialism: The Highest Stage of Capitalism.* London: Lawrence and Wishart.

———. 1932. *The State and Revolution.* New York: International Publishers.

———. 1899. *The Development of Capitalism in Russia.* In *Collected Works,* vol. 3. 4th Ed. Moscow: Progress Publishers, 1964.

———. n.d. On the Right of Nations to Self-Determination. In *Collected Works,* vol. 4. Moscow: Progress Publishers.

Lerner, Daniel. 1958. *The Passing of Traditional Society.* Glencoe: Free Press.

Leroy-Beaulieu, Paul. 1911. *L'état moderne et ses fonctions.* Paris: Guillaumin.

Leslie, R. F. 1963. *Reform and Insurrection in Russian Poland, 1856–1865.* London: Athlone Press.

Levandis, John Alexander. 1944. *The Greek Foreign Debt and the Great Powers, 1821–1898.* New York: Columbia University Press.

Levine, Daniel H. 1988. Paradigm Lost: Dependence to Democracy. *World Politics* 40, no. 3 (April): 377–94.

Levy, Hermann. 1927. *Monopolies, Cartels, and Trusts in British Industry.* London: St. Martin's Press.

Levy, Marion J., Jr. 1966. *Modernization and the Structure of Societies: A Setting for International Affairs.* Princeton: Princeton University Press.

Lévy, Maurice. 1951–52. *Histoire économique et sociale de la France depuis 1848.* Paris: Institut d'Études Politiques, Cours de Droit.

Lewis, W. Arthur. 1984. The State of Development Theory. *American Economic Review* 74, no. 1: 1–10.

———. 1978a. *Growth and Fluctuation, 1870–1913.* London: Allen & Unwin.

———. 1978b. *The Evolution of the International Economic Order.* Princeton: Princeton University Press.

———. 1972. The Historical Record of International Capital Movements to 1913. In J. H. Dunning, ed., *International Investment: Selected Readings.* Harmondsworth: Penguin.

———. 1949. *Economic Survey, 1919–1939.* London: Allen & Unwin.

Leys, Colin. 1996. The Crisis in "Development Theory." *New Political Economy* 1, no. 1: 41–58.

Lichtenberger, André. 1921. Le bourgeois. *Revue des Deux Mendes,* 15 November.

Liefmann, Robert. 1933. *Cartels, Concerns, and Trusts.* New York: Dutton.

———. 1897. *Die Unternehmerverbände (Konventionen, Kartelle): Ihr Wesen und ihre Bedeutung.* Freiburg: J. C. B. Mohr.

Lieven, Dominic. 1992. *The Aristocracy in Europe, 1815–1914.* New York: Macmillan.

———. 1983. *Russia and the Origins of the First World War.* London: Macmillan.

Linz, Juan. 1984. Interests and Politics in Spain. In Peter J. Williamson, ed., *Varieties of Corporatism*. New York: Cambridge University Press.

Linz, Juan, and Alfred Stepan, eds. 1978. *Breakdown of Democratic Regimes*. Baltimore: Johns Hopkins University Press.

Lipset, Seymour Martin. 1983. Radicalism or Reformism: The Sources of Working-Class Politics. *American Political Science Review* 77: 1–18.

———. 1959. Social Requisites of Democracy. *American Political Science Review* 53 (March): 69–105.

Lis, Catharina. 1989. *Social Change and the Labouring Poor: Antwerp, 1770–1860*. New Haven: Yale University Press.

———. 1979. *Poverty and Capitalism in Pre-Industrial Europe*. Atlantic Highlands, N.J.: Humanities Press.

List, Friedrich. 1885. *The National System of Political Economy: International Commerce, Commercial Policy, and the German Customs Union*. Trans. Sampson S. Lloyd. London: Longmans, Green.

Livingstone, I. 1981. The Development of Development Economics. *ODI Review* 2: 1–20.

Lord, Montague J., and Greta R. Boye. 1991. The Determinants of International Trade in Latin America's Commodity Exports. In Miguel Urrutia, ed., *Long-Term Trends in Latin American Economic Development*. Washington, D.C.: Inter-American Development Bank.

Loughlin, John. 1985. Regionalism and Ethnic Nationalism in France. In Yves Mény and Vincent Wright, eds., *Centre-Periphery Relations in Western Europe*. London: Allen & Unwin.

Love, Joseph L. 1980. Raúl Prebisch and the Origins of Unequal Exchange. *Latin America Research Review* 15: 45–72.

Löwy, Michael. 1976. Marxists and the National Question. *New Left Review* 96: 81–100.

Lucas, Colin. 1973. Nobles, Bourgeois, and the Origins of the French Revolution. *Past and Present* 60 (September): 84–126.

Luck, James Murray. 1985. *A History of Switzerland*. Palo Alto, Calif.: Society for the Promotion of Science & Scholarship.

Luebbert, Gregory. 1991. *Liberalism, Fascism, and Social Democracy: Social Classes and the Political Origins of Regimes in Interwar Europe*. New York: Oxford University Press.

Lustig, Nora. 1993. Equity and Development. In Osvaldo Sunkel, ed., *Development from Within: Toward a Neostructuralist Approach for Latin America*. Boulder, Colo.: Lynne Rienner.

Luxemburg, Rosa. 1977. *The Industrial Development of Poland*. New York: Campaigner.

———. 1976. *The National Question: Selected Writings of Rosa Luxemburg*. Ed. Horace B. Davis. New York: Monthly Review Press.

———. 1951. *The Accumulation of Capital*. Trans. Agnes Schwarzchild. New Haven: Yale University Press.

Macartney, C. A. 1968. *The Hapsburg Empire, 1790–1918*. London: Weidenfeld & Nicolson.

———. 1934. *National States and National Minorities*. London: Oxford University Press.

MacDonald, Mary. 1946. *The Republic of Austria, 1918–1934: A Study in the Failure of Democratic Government*. London: Oxford University Press.

Machay, J. P. 1970. *Pioneer for Profit: Entrepreneurs and Russian Industrialization.* Chicago: University of Chicago Press.

MacIver, Robert M. 1932. *The Modern State.* London: Oxford University Press.

Maddison, Angus. 1991. Economic and Social Conditions in Latin America, 1913–1950. In Miguel Urrutia, ed., *Long-Term Trends in Latin American Economic Development.* Washington D.C.: Inter-American Development Bank.

———. 1990. *The World Economy in the Twentieth Century.* Paris: Development Centre Studies.

———. 1989. Measuring European Growth: The Core and the Periphery. In E. Aerts and N. Valerio, eds., *Growth and Stagnation in the Mediterranean World in the Nineteenth and Twentieth Centuries.* Leuven: University of Leuven Press.

———. 1983. A Comparison of Levels of GDP per Capita in Developed and Developing Countries, 1700–1980. *Journal of Economic History* 43, no. 1 (March): 27–41.

———. 1964. *Economic Growth in the West.* New York: Twentieth Century Fund.

Maehl, William Henry, Jr., ed. 1967. *The Reform Bill of 1832.* New York: Holt, Rinehart & Winston.

Magraw, Roger. 1983. *France 1815–1914: The Bourgeois Century.* Oxford: Fontana.

Maier, Charles. 1975. *Recasting Bourgeois Europe: Stabilization in France, Germany, and Italy in the Decade after World War I.* Princeton: Princeton University Press.

Maizels, A. 1970. *Growth and Trade.* London: Cambridge University Press.

Mamatey, Victor S., and Radomir Luza. 1973. *A History of the Czechoslovak Republic, 1918–1948.* Princeton: Princeton University Press.

Mann, Michael. 1984. The Autonomous Power of the State: Its Origins, Mechanisms, and Results. *Archives européenes de sociologie* 25: 185–213.

Manzo, Kate. 1991. Modernist Discourse and the Crisis of Development Theory. *Studies in Comparative International Development* 26, no. 2 (Summer): 3–36.

Marczali, Henrik. 1910. *Hungary in the Eighteenth Century.* Cambridge: Cambridge University Press.

Marks, Gary. 1989. *Unions in Politics: Britain, Germany, and the United States in the Nineteenth and Early Twentieth Centuries.* Princeton: Princeton University Press.

Marx, Karl. 1970. *A Contribution to the Critique of Political Economy.* Moscow: Progress Publishers.

———. 1963. *The Eighteenth Brumaire of Louis Bonaparte.* New York: International Publishers.

———. 1909. *Capital.* Vol. 1. London: William Glaisher.

Marx, Karl, and Friedrich Engels. 1970. *The Communist Manifesto.* New York: Pathfinders Press.

Maschke, Erich. 1969. Outline of the History of German Cartels from 1873 to 1914. In F. Crouzet, W. H. Chaloner, and W. M. Stern, eds., *Essays in European Economic History, 1789–1914.* New York: St. Martin's Press.

Masterman, Charles F. G. 1923. *England after the War.* New York: Harcourt Brace.

Mathias, Peter. 1969. *The First Industrial Nation: An Economic History of Britain, 1700–1914.* London: Methuen.

Mattingly, Garrett. 1955. *Renaissance Diplomacy.* Baltimore: Penguin.

Maurice, C. Edmund. 1887. *The Revolutionary Movement of 1848–49 in Italy, Austria-Hungary, and Germany.* London: George Bell and Sons.

Mayer, Arno J. 1981. *The Persistence of the Ancien Régime: Europe to the Great War.* New York: Pantheon.

———. 1969. *The Political Origins of the New Diplomacy, 1917–1918.* New York: H. Fertig.

Mazour, Anatole G. 1951. *Russia Past and Present.* New York: Van Nostrand.

Mazzini, Giuseppe. 1890. *Life and Writings of Joseph Mazzini.* London: Smith, Elder.

———. 1877. Mazzini on the Eastern Question. *Fortnightly Review,* n.s., 21, no. 124 (April): 558–79.

McHenry, Dean E. 1940. *His Majesty's Opposition: Structure and Problems of the British Labour Party, 1931–1938.* Berkeley: University of California Press.

McLeod, Hugh. 1981. *Religion and the People of Western Europe, 1789–1970.* Oxford: Oxford University Press.

———. 1973. Class, Community, and Region: The Religious Geography of Nineteenth-Century England. In Michael Hall, ed., *A Sociological Yearbook of Religion in Britain.* London: SCM Press.

McNeill, William H. 1974. *The Shape of European History.* London: Oxford University Press.

Megaro, Gaudens. 1930. *Vittorio Alfieri, Forerunner of Italian Nationalism.* New York: Columbia University Press.

Meier, G. E., ed. 1970. *Leading Issues in Economic Development.* London: Oxford University Press.

Mendras, Henri. 1970. *The Vanishing Peasant.* Cambridge: Harvard University Press.

Meredith, H. O. 1904. *Protection in France.* London: P. S. King.

Meyer, Henry Cord. 1955. *"Mitteleuropa" in German Thought and Action, 1815–1945.* The Hague: M. Nijhoff.

Michels, Robert. 1914. *Probleme der Sozialphilosophie.* Leipzig: B. G. Teubner.

Migdal, Joel S. 1983. Studying the Politics of Development and Change: The State of the Art. In Ada W. Finifter, ed., *Political Science: The State of the Discipline.* Washington, D.C.: American Political Science Association.

Miliband, Ralph. 1973a. Marx and the State. In Tom Bottomore, ed., *Karl Marx.* Englewood Cliffs, N.J.: Prentice-Hall.

———. 1973b. Poulantzas and the Capitalist State. *New Left Review* 82 (November-December): 83–92.

Miliukov, Paul N. 1917. The Representative System in Russia. In J. D. Duff, ed., *Russian Realities and Problems.* Cambridge: Cambridge University Press.

Mitchell, B. R. 1975. *European Historical Statistics, 1750–1970.* Abridged edition. New York: Columbia University Press.

Mokyr, Joel. 1976. *Industrialization in the Low Countries, 1795–1850.* New Haven: Yale University Press.

Molinari, G. de. 1879. Union douanière de l'Europe centrale. *Journal des économistes,* 4th ser., 5: 309–18.

Mommsen, Wolfgang. 1989. *The Political and Social Theory of Max Weber: Collected Essays.* Chicago: University of Chicago Press.

———. 1984. *Max Weber and German Politics, 1890–1920.* Chicago: University of Chicago Press.

Montagu, Lord. 1970. *More Equal Than Others: The Changing Fortunes of the British and European Aristocracies.* London: Michael Joseph.

Moody, Joseph N., et al., eds. 1953. *Church and Society: Catholic Social and Political Thought and Movements, 1789–1950.* New York: Arts.

Moore, Barrington, Jr. 1966. *Social Origins of Dictatorship and Democracy: Lord and Peasant in the Making of the Modern World.* Boston: Beacon.

——. 1958. *Political Power and Social Theory*. New York: Harper & Row.

Mori, Giorgio. 1979. The Process of Industrialization in General and the Process of Industrialization in Italy. *Journal of European Economic History* 8, no. 1 (Spring): 61–82.

Morley, John. 1882. *The Life of Richard Cobden*. London: Chapman and Hall.

Morris, Cynthia Taft, and Irma Adelman. 1989. Nineteenth-Century Development Experience and Lessons for Today. *World Development* 17, no. 9: 1417–32.

——. 1988. *Comparative Patterns of Economic Development, 1850–1914*. Baltimore: Johns Hopkins University Press.

Morse, Edward L. 1976. *Modernization and the Transformation of International Relations*. New York: Free Press.

Mousnier, Roland, ed. 1964. *Lettres et mémoires addressés au Chancelier Séguier, 1633–1649*. Vol. 1. Paris: Presses Universitaires de France.

Mouzelis, Nicos. 1988. Sociology of Development: Reflections on the Present Crisis. *Sociology* 22, no. 1: 23–44.

Müller, Klaus. 1994. From Post-Communism to Post-Modernity? Economy and Society in the Eastern European Transformation. In Bruno Grancelli, ed., *Social Change and Modernization: Lessons from Eastern Europe*. New York: St. Martin's Press.

——. 1992. "Modernizing" Eastern Europe: Theoretical Problems and Political Dilemmas. *European Journal of Sociology* 33: 109–50.

Muncy, Lysbeth W. 1973. The Prussian Landräte in the Years of the Monarchy: A Case Study of Pomerania and the Rhineland in 1890–1918. *Central European History* 6, no. 4 (December): 299–338.

——. 1944. *The Junker in the Prussian Administration under William II, 1888–1914*. Providence, R.I.: Brown University Press.

Munting, Roger. 1982. *The Economic Development of the U.S.S.R.* London: Croom Helm.

Murdoch, William W. 1980. *The Poverty of Nations: The Political Economy of Hunger and Population*. Baltimore: Johns Hopkins University Press.

Nadal, Jordi. 1973. The Failure of the Industrial Revolution in Spain, 1830–1914. In Carlo M. Cipolla, ed., *The Fontana Economic History of Europe*. Vol. 2, *Emergence of Industrial Societies*. Glasgow: William Collins Sons.

Nash, Manning. 1984. *Unfinished Agenda: The Dynamics of Modernization in Developing Nations*. Boulder, Colo.: Westview Press.

Naumann, Friedrich. 1917. *Central Europe*. Translated by Christabel M. Meredith. London: P. S. King & Son.

——. 1916. *Mitteleuropa*. Berlin: G. Reimer.

Neale, R. S. 1975. "The Bourgeoisie, Historically, Has Played a Most Revolutionary Part." In Eugene Kamenka and R. S. Neale, eds., *Feudalism, Capitalism, and Beyond*. London: Edward Arnold.

Nef, John U. 1967. *Industry and Government in France and England, 1540–1640*. Ithaca: Cornell University Press.

Neumann, Franz. 1944. *Behemoth: The Structure and Practice of National Socialism, 1933–1944*. London: Oxford University Press.

Newsinger, J. 1979. Revolution and Catholicism in Ireland, 1848–1923. *European Studies Review* 9, no. 4 (October): 457–80.

Niceforo, Alfredo. 1901. *Italiane del Nord e Italiani del Sud*. Torino: Fratelli Boca.

——. 1890. *L'Italia barbara contemporanea*. Palermo: Sandron.

Nolde, B. F. 1928. *Russia in the Economic War*. New Haven: Yale University Press.

North, Douglass C. 1981. *Structure and Change in Economic History.* New York: Norton.

North, Douglass C., and Robert Paul Thomas. 1973. An Economic Theory of the Growth of the Western World. *Economic History Review*, 2d ser., 23 (April): 1–17.

———. 1970. *The Rise of the Western World.* Cambridge: Cambridge University Press.

Nove, Alec. 1982. *An Economic History of the U.S.S.R.* Harmondsworth: Penguin.

O'Connor, James. 1973. *The Fiscal Crisis of the State.* New York: St. Martin's Press.

O'Donnell, Guillermo. 1979. *Modernization and Bureaucratic-Authoritarianism.* Berkeley: Institute of International Studies, University of California.

———. 1978. Reflections on the Patterns of Change in a Bureaucratic Authoritarian State. *Latin American Research Review* 13: 3–38.

———. 1977. Corporatism and the Question of the State. In James M. Malloy, ed., *Authoritarianism and Corporatism in Latin America.* Pittsburgh: University of Pittsburgh Press.

O'Donnell, Guillermo, and Delfina Linck. 1973. *Dependencia y Autonomía: Formas de Dependencia y Estratégias de Liberación.* Buenos Aires: Amorrortu.

O'Donnell, Guillermo, Philippe C. Schmitter, and Laurence Whitehead. 1986. *Transitions from Authoritarian Rule.* Baltimore: Johns Hopkins University Press.

Offe, Claus. 1976. Political Authority and Class Structures. In P. Connerton, ed., *Critical Sociology.* London: Penguin.

———. 1975. The Theory of the Capitalist State and the Problem of Policy Formation. In Leon N. Lindberg, Robert Alford, Colin Crouch, and Claus Offe, eds., *Stress and Contradiction in Modern Capitalism.* Lexington, Mass.: D.C. Heath.

———. 1974. Structural Problems of the Capitalist State. *German Political Studies* 1: 31–56.

Offe, Claus, and Volker Ronge. 1975. Theses on the Theory of the State. *New German Critique* 6: 137–47.

Ogg, Frederic Austin. 1930. *Economic Development of Modern Europe.* New York: Macmillan.

———. 1914. *The Governments of Europe.* New York: Macmillan.

O'Leary, Cornelius. 1962. *The Elimination of Corrupt Practices in British Elections, 1868–1911.* Oxford: Clarendon Press.

Olson, Mancur. 1993. Dictatorship, Democracy, and Development. *American Political Science Review* 87, no. 3 (September): 567–76.

———. 1982. *The Rise and Decline of Nations.* New Haven: Yale University Press.

Orsagh, Thomas J. 1968. The Probable Geographic Distribution of German Income, 1882–1963. *Zeitschrift für die gesamte Staatswissenschaft* 124: 280–311.

Osterud, Oyvind. 1978. *Agrarian Structure and Peasant Politics in Scandinavia.* Oslo: Universitetsforlaget.

Owen, Robert. 1969. *Report to the County of Lanark: A New View of Society.* London: Penguin.

Owen, Roger, and Bob Sutcliffe, eds. 1972. *Studies in the Theory of Imperialism.* London: Longman.

Packenham, Robert A. 1992. *The Dependency Movement: Scholarship and Politics in Development Studies.* Cambridge: Harvard University Press.

Palmer, Robert R. 1944. The National Idea in France before the Revolution. *Journal of the History of Ideas* 1, no. 1 (January): 95–111.

Pareto, Vilfredo. 1917–19. *Traité de sociologie générale.* Paris: Payot.

Parker, Geoffrey. 1988. *The Military Revolution: Military Innovation and the Rise of the West, 1500–1800.* Cambridge: Cambridge University Press.

Parsons, Talcott. 1966. *Societies: Evolutionary and Comparative Perspectives.* Englewood Cliffs, N.J.: Prentice-Hall.

Passelecq, Fernand. 1928. *Déportation et travail forcé des ouvriers et la population civile de la Belgique occupée.* Paris: Presses Universitaires de France.

Pavlovsky, Georgii Alekseevich. 1930. *Agricultural Russia on the Eve of the Revolution.* London: Routledge.

Pearson, Raymond. 1983. *National Minorities in Eastern Europe, 1848–1945.* London: Macmillan.

Pech, S. Z. 1969. *The Czech Revolution of 1848.* Chapel Hill: University of North Carolina Press.

Petrie, Charles. 1944. *Diplomatic History.* London: Hollis and Carten.

Petropulos, Anthony. 1968. *Politics and Statecraft in the Kingdom of Greece.* Princeton: Princeton University Press.

Pieterse, Jan Nederveen. 1991. Dilemmas of Development Discourse: The Crisis of Developmentalism and the Comparative Method. *Development and Change* 22, no. 1 (January): 5–29.

Pirenne, Henri. 1900. *Histoire de Belgique.* Brussels: Lamertin.

Pius IX. 1864. Syllabus of Errors. In *Dogmatic Canons and Decrees.* New York: Devon-Adair, 1912.

Plotnikov, N. 1969. The Transformations of One of the Most Backward Regions of Central Asia into an Advanced Industrial Republic: The Case of the Uzbek Republic. In E. A. G. Robinson, ed., *Backward Areas in Advanced Countries.* London: Macmillan.

Plumb, J. H. 1950. *England in the Eighteenth Century.* Harmondsworth: Penguin.

Poggi, Gianfranco. 1978. *The Development of the Modern State: A Sociological Introduction.* Stanford: Stanford University Press.

Polanyi, Karl. 1944. *The Great Transformation: The Political and Economic Origins of Our Time.* New York: Farrar and Rinehart.

Pollard, Sidney. 1973. Industrialization and the European Economy. *Economic History Review* 26, no. 4 (November): 636–48.

Porchnev, Boris. 1963. *Les soulèvements populaires en France de 1623 à 1648.* Paris: SEVPEN.

Porter, Anthony, and R. F. Holland. 1988. *Theory and Practice in the History of European Expansion Overseas: Essays in Honour of Ronald Robinson.* London: Cass.

Portes, Alejandro. 1985. Latin American Class Structures: Their Composition and Change during the Last Decades. *Latin American Research Review* 20, no. 3: 7–40.

Poulantzas, Nicos. 1978. *State, Power, and Socialism.* London: New Left Books.

——. 1976. The Capitalist State: A Reply to Miliband and Laclau. *New Left Review* 95 (January–February): 65–83.

——. 1975. *Classes in Contemporary Capitalism.* London: New Left Books.

——. 1973a. *Political Power and Social Classes.* London: New Left Books.

——. 1973b. The Problem of the Capitalist State. In Robin Blackburn, ed., *Ideology in Social Science.* New York: Vintage.

Pounds, J. G. 1959. Economic Growth in Germany. In Hugh Aitken, ed., *The State and Economic Growth.* New York: Social Science Research Council.

Prebisch, Raúl. 1950a. *The Economic Development of Latin America and Its Principal Problems.* New York: United Nations.

——. 1950b. *Theoretical and Practical Problems of Economic Growth.* Mexico: United Nations.

Price, Roger. 1981. *An Economic History of Modern France, 1730–1914*. London: Macmillan.

Puhle, Hans Jürgen. 1986. Lords and Peasants in the Kaiserreich. In Robert G. Moeller, ed., *Peasants and Lords in Modern Germany*. Boston: Allen & Unwin.

Pundt, Alfred G. 1935. *Arndt and the German Nationalist Awakening in Germany*. New York: Columbia University Press.

Ranis, G., and T. P. Schultz, eds. 1988. *The State of Development Economics: Progress and Perspectives*. Oxford: Basil Blackwell.

Read, Donald. 1964. *The English Provinces, 1760–1960*. New York: St. Martin's Press.

Reddaway, William F., ed. 1941. *The Cambridge History of Poland*. Cambridge: Cambridge University Press.

Reddy, William M. 1987. *Money and Liberty in Modern Europe: A Critique of Historical Understanding*. Cambridge: Cambridge University Press.

Renner, Karl. 1902. *Der Kampf der österreichischen Nationen um den Staat*. Leipzig: Franz Deutke.

Reynolds, Lloyd G. 1985. *Economic Growth in the Third World, 1850–1980*. New Haven: Yale University Press.

Riggs, Fred. 1964. *Administration in Developing Countries*. Boston: Houghton Mifflin.

Roberts, Henry L. 1951. *Rumania: Political Problems of an Agrarian State*. New Haven: Yale University Press.

Robson, William A. 1931. *The Development of Local Government*. London: Allen & Unwin.

Rock, David. 1975. *Politics in Argentina, 1890–1930: The Rise and Fall of Radicalism*. London: Cambridge University Press.

Rodney, Walter. 1972. *How Europe Underdeveloped Africa*. London: Bogle-L'Ouverture.

Rodríguez, Octavio. 1980. *La Teoría del subdesarrollo de la CEPAL*. Mexico: Siglo Veintiuno.

Rokkan, Stein. 1970. *Citizens, Elections, Parties*. Oslo: Universitetsforlaget.

——. 1967. Geography, Religion, and Social Class: Cross-Cutting Cleavages in Norwegian Politics. In S. M. Lipset and Stein Rokkan, eds., *Party Systems and Voter Alignment: Cross-National Perspectives*. New York: Free Press.

Roller, Michael. 1948. Romania. In François Fejtö, ed., *The Opening of an Era: 1848*. New York: Grosset & Dunlap.

Romein, Jan. 1978. *The Watershed of Two Eras: Europe in 1900*. Middletown, Conn.: Wesleyan University Press.

Romero-Maura, Joaquin. 1977. Caciquismo as a Political System. In Ernest Gellner and John Waterbury, eds., *Patrons and Clients*. London: Duckworth.

Rosenberg, Hans. 1966. *Bureaucracy, Aristocracy, and Autocracy: The Prussian Experience, 1660–1815*. Cambridge: Harvard University Press.

Rostovtzeff, M. 1957. *The Social and Economic History of the Roman Empire*. 2d ed. Oxford: Clarendon Press.

Rostow, W. W. 1960. *The Stages of Economic Growth*. Cambridge: Cambridge University Press.

Rota, Ettore. 1948. *Genesi storica dell'idea italiana*. Milan: Vallardi.

Roth, Guenther. 1963. *The Social Democrats in Imperial Germany: A Study in Working-Class Isolation and Nation Integration*. Totowa, N.J.: Bedminster.

Roxborough, Ian. 1979. *Theories of Underdevelopment*. Atlantic Highlands, N.J.: Humanities Press.

Rubinstein, W. D. 1987. New Men of Wealth and the Purchase of Land in Nineteenth-Century Britain. In *Elites and the Wealthy in Modern British History*. New York: St. Martin's Press.

——. 1981. *Men of Property: The Very Wealthy in Britain since the Industrial Revolution*. New Brunswick, N.J.: Rutgers University Press.

——. 1977. Wealth, Elites, and the Class Structure of Modern Britain. *Past and Present* 76: 99–126.

Rudé, George. 1989. *The French Revolution*. London: Weidenfeld & Nicolson.

Rueschemeyer, Dietrich, Evelyne Huber Stephens, and John D. Stephens. 1992. *Capitalist Development and Democracy*. Chicago: University of Chicago Press.

Ruhl, J. Mark. 1984. Agrarian Structure and Political Stability in Honduras. *Journal of Interamerican Studies and World Affairs* 26 (February): 33–68.

Sachs, Jeffrey. 1989. *Social Conflict and Populist Policies in Latin America*. Working Paper 2897. Cambridge, Mass.: National Bureau of Economic Research.

Saint-Simon, Claude Henri Comte de. 1802. Lettres d'un habitant de Genève à ses contemporains vie de Saint-Simon par Lui-Même. In *Oeuvres de Claude-Henri de Saint-Simon*, vol. 1. Paris: Éditions Anthropos, 1966.

Salvemini, Gaetano. 1915. *Guerra o neutralità*. Milan: Di Viandante.

Samuelsson, Kurt. 1968. *From Great Power to Welfare State*. London: Allen & Unwin.

Sayigh, Yusif A. 1978. *The Determinants of Arab Economic Development*. London: Croom Helm.

Schama, Simon. 1989. *Citizens: A Chronicle of the French Revolution*. New York: Knopf.

Schissler, Hanna. 1986. The Junkers: Notes on the Social and Historical Significance of the Agrarian Elite in Prussia. In Robert G. Moeller, ed., *Peasants and Lords in Modern Germany*. Boston: Allen & Unwin.

Schmidt, C. T. 1939. *The Corporate State in Action*. London: Gollancz.

Schmitter, Phillippe C. 1971. Desarrollo retrasado, dependencia externa, y cambio político en America Latina. *Foro Internacional* 12 (October-December): 135–74.

Schmoller, Gustav. 1900. Die Wandlungen in der Handelspolitik des 19. Jahrhunderts. *Schmollers Jahrbuch* 24: 373–82.

Schneider, Jane, and Peter Schneider. 1976. *Culture and Political Economy in Western Sicily*. New York: Academic Press.

Schumpeter, Joseph A. 1947. *Capitalism, Socialism, and Democracy*. London: Harper and Brothers.

——. 1939. *Business Cycles: A Theoretical, Historical, and Statistical Analysis of the Capitalist Process*. New York: McGraw-Hill.

Schwartz, Benjamin I. 1975. The Limits of "Tradition versus Modernity" as Categories of Explanation. *Daedalus* 101: 71–88.

Sée, Henri. 1942. *Histoire économique de la France*. Vol. 2, *Les Temps Modernes, 1789–1914*. Paris: Colin.

Seers, David. 1979. The Birth, Life, and Death of Development Economics. *Development and Change* 10, no. 4: 707–19.

Seligson, Mitchell A. 1984. Implementing Land Reform: The Case of Costa Rica. *Managing International Development* 1 (March-April): 29–46.

Sen, Amartya. 1983. Development: Which Way Now? *Economic Journal* 93: 372, 745–62.

——. 1960. *Choice of Techniques: An Aspect of the Theory of Planned Economic Development*. Oxford: Basil Blackwell.

Senghaas, Dieter. 1985. *The European Experience: A Historical Critique of Development Theory*. Dover, N.H.: Berg.

Sereni, Emilio. 1968. *Il capitalismo nelle campagne, 1860–1900*. Turin: Einaudi.

Seton-Watson, Hugh. 1977. *Nations and States*. London: Methuen.

——. 1967. *The Russian Empire, 1801–1917*. Oxford: Clarendon Press.

——. 1945. *Eastern Europe between the Wars, 1918–1941*. Hamden, Conn.: Archon.

Seton-Watson, R. W. 1934. *A History of the Roumanians*. London: Cambridge University Press.

Shaheen, Samad. 1956. *The Communist (Bolshevik) Theory of National Determination*. The Hague: W. Van Hoeve.

Shanahan, William O. 1954. *German Protestants Face the Social Question, 1815–1871*. Notre Dame, Ind.: University of Notre Dame Press.

Sharp, Evelyn Adelaide, Baroness. 1969. *The Ministry of Housing and Local Government*. London: Allen & Unwin.

Shils, Edward. 1960. Political Development in the New States. *Comparative Studies in Society and History* 2: 265–92.

Shiner, L. E. 1975. Tradition/Modernity: An Ideal Type Gone Astray. *Comparative Studies in Society and History* 19: 245–352.

Sideri, Sandra. 1970. *Trade and Power: Informal Colonialism in Anglo-Portuguese Relations*. Rotterdam: Rotterdam University Press.

Siegenthaler, J. K. 1973. Sicilian Economic Change Since 1860. *Journal of European Economic History* 2, no. 2: 363–416.

Sièyes, Emmanuel Joseph, Comte. 1970. *Qu'est-ce que le Tiers État?* 1791. Reprint, Geneva: Droz.

Simas, L. 1971. Salazar: A Political Inquest. *Portuguese and Colonial Bulletin* 11.

Singer, Hans W. 1950. The Distribution of Gains between Investing and Borrowing Countries. *American Economic Review: Papers and Proceedings* 40, no. 2 (May): 473–85.

Singer, Hans W., and Javed Ansari. 1977. *Rich and Poor Countries*. Baltimore: Johns Hopkins University Press.

Sklair, L. 1988. Transcending the Impasse: Metatheory, Theory, and Empirical Research in the Sociology of Development and Underdevelopment. *World Development* 16, no. 6: 697–709.

Skocpol, Theda. 1985. Bringing the State Back In: Strategies of Analysis in Current Research. In Peter Evans, Dietrich Rueschemeyer, and Theda Skocpol, *Bringing the State Back In*. New York: Cambridge University Press.

——. 1979. *States and Social Revolutions: A Comparative Analysis of France, Russia, and China*. Cambridge: Cambridge University Press.

Slater, David. 1992. Theories of Development and Politics of the Post-Modern— Exploring a Border Zone. *Development and Change* 23, no. 3 (July): 283–319.

Smith, Anthony D. 1986. State-Making and Nation-Building. In John A. Hall, ed., *States in History*. London: Basil Blackwell.

Smith, Denis Mack. 1971. *Victor Emmanuel, Cavour, and the Risorgimento*. London: Oxford University Press.

——. 1969. *Italy: A Modern History*. Ann Arbor: University of Michigan Press.

Snyder, Louis L. 1964. *The Dynamics of Nationalism*. Princeton: Van Nostrand.

Soboul, Albert. 1962. *Précis de l'histoire de la Révolution française, 1789–1799*. Paris: Éditions Sociales.

Sontag, John P. 1968. Tsarist Debts and Tsarist Foreign Policy. *Slavic Review* 27, no. 4 (December): 529–41.

Sorokin, Pitirim. 1927. *Social Mobility*. London: Harper.

Soucy, Robert. 1972. *Fascism in France: The Case of Maurice Barrès*. Berkeley: University of California Press.

Spring, David. 1977. Landed Elites Compared. In David Spring, ed., *European Landed Elites in the Nineteenth Century*. Baltimore: Johns Hopkins University Press.

——. 1971. English Landowners and Nineteenth-Century Industrialists. In J. T. Ward and R. G. Wilson, eds., *Land and Industry: The Landed Estate and the Industrial Revolution*. New York: Barnes & Noble.

——. 1960. Some Reflections on Social History in the Nineteenth Century. *Victorian Studies* 4, no. 1: 55–64.

Spulber, Nicholas. 1963. Changes in the Economic Structure of the Balkans, 1860–1960. In Charles and Barbara Jelavich, eds., *The Balkans in Transition*. Berkeley: University of California Press.

Stalin, Joseph. 1942. *Marxism and the National Question: Selected Writings and Speeches*. New York: International Publishers.

Stanworld, Philip, and Anthony Giddens, eds. 1974. *Elites and Power in British Society*. London: Cambridge University Press.

Statistisches Reichsamt. 1932. *Das deutsche Volkseinkommen vor und nach dem Kriege*. Einzelschriften zur Statistik des deutschen Reiches 24. Berlin: Statistisches Reichsamt.

Stavenhagen, Rudolfo. 1970. Social Aspects of Agrarian Structure in Mexico. In Rudolfo Stavenhagen, ed., *Agrarian Problems and Peasant Movements in Latin America*. Garden City, N.Y.: Doubleday.

——. 1968. Seven Fallacies about Latin America. In James Petras and Maurice Zeitlin, eds., *Latin America, Reform or Revolution?* Greenwich, Conn.: Fawcett Publications.

Stavrianos, L. S. 1961. *The Balkans since 1453*. New York: Holt.

Stein, Stanley J., and Barbara H. Stein. 1970. *The Colonial Heritage of Latin America: Essays on Economic Dependence in Historical Perspective*. New York: Oxford University Press.

Stern, Fritz. 1977a. Prussia. In David Spring, ed., *European Landed Elites of the Nineteenth Century*. Baltimore: Johns Hopkins University Press.

Stern, Steve J. 1988. Feudalism, Capitalism, and the World-System in the Perspective of Latin America and the Caribbean; and Reply. *American Historical Review* 93, no. 4: 829–72, 886–97.

Stewart, F. 1974. Technology and Employment in LDCs. *World Development* 2 (March): 17–46.

Stone, Lawrence. 1981. The Results of the English Revolutions of the Seventeenth Century. In J. G. A. Pocock, ed., *Three British Revolutions: 1641, 1688, 1776*. Princeton: Princeton University Press.

——. 1972. *The Causes of the English Revolution, 1529–1642*. London: Routledge & Kegan Paul.

Stover, Charles C. 1970. Tropical Exports. In W. Arthur Lewis, ed., *Tropical Development, 1880–1913*. Evanston, Ill.: Northwestern University Press.

Strayer, Joseph R. 1970. *On the Medieval Origins of the Modern State*. Princeton: Princeton University Press.

Streeten, P. 1983. Development Dichotomies. *World Development* 11, no. 10: 875–89.

Strikwerda, Karl. 1993a. The Troubled Origins of European Economic Integration: International Iron and Steel Migration in the Era of World War I. *American Historical Review* 98, no. 4 (October): 1106–29.

———. 1993b. Response to "Economic Integration and the European International System in the Era of World War I." *American Historical Review* 98, no. 4 (October): 1138–42.

Sugar, Peter F., ed. 1971. *Native Fascism in the Successor States, 1918–1945.* Santa Barbara, Calif.: ABC-Clio.

Sunkel, Osvaldo. 1993. From Inward-Looking Development to Development from Within. In Sunkel, ed., *Development from Within: Toward a Neostructuralist Approach for Latin America.* Boulder, Colo.: Lynne Rienner.

———. 1973. Transnational Capitalism and National Disintegration in Latin America. *Social and Economic Studies* 22: 132–76.

Supple, Barry. 1973. The State and the Industrial Revolution: 1700–1914. In Carlo Cipolla, ed., *The Fontana Economic History of Europe.* Vol. 1, *The Emergence of Industrial Societies.* Glasgow: William Collins Sons.

Sutton, M. 1982. *Nationalism, Positivism, and Catholicism.* Cambridge: Cambridge University Press.

Svennilson, Ingvar. 1954. *Growth and Stagnation in the European Economy.* Geneva: United Nations.

Sweezy, Paul. 1982. Core, Periphery, and the Crisis of the System. In Hamza Alavi and Teodor Shanin, eds., *Introduction to the Sociology of Developing Societies.* New York: Monthly Review Press.

Sweezy, Paul M. 1942. *The Theory of Capitalist Development.* London: Oxford University Press.

———, ed. 1954. *The Transition from Feudalism to Capitalism.* New York: Arena.

Taine, Hippolyte Adolphe. 1962. *The Ancient Régime.* Trans. John Durand. 1872. Reprint, Gloucester, Mass.: Peter Smith.

Teichova, Alice. 1974. *An Economic Background to Munich: International Business and Czechoslovakia, 1918–1938.* London: Cambridge University Press.

Temperley, H. W. V., ed. 1920. *A History of the Peace Conference of Paris.* London: Henry Frowde, Hoddard Stoughton.

Theisenhusen, William C. 1980. Current Development Patterns and Agrarian Policy in Latin America. In Ivan Volgyes, Richard E. Lonsdale, and William P. Avery, eds., *The Process of Rural Transformation: Eastern Europe, Latin America, and Australia.* New York: Pergamon Press.

Therborn, Göran. 1978. *What Does the Ruling Class Do When It Rules?* London: New Left Books.

———. 1977. The Rule of Capital and the Rise of Democracy. *New Left Review* 103, no. 2 (May–June): 3–41.

Thomas, Clive Y. 1984. *The Rise of the Authoritarian State in Peripheral Societies.* New York: Monthly Review Press.

Thomas, John A. 1939. *The House of Commons, 1832–1901: A Study of Its Economic and Functional Character.* Cardiff: University of Wales Press.

Thompson, F. M. L. 1977. Britain. In David Spring, ed., *European Landed Elites in the Nineteenth Century.* Baltimore: Johns Hopkins University Press.

———. 1963. *English Landed Society in the Nineteenth Century.* London: Routledge & Kegan Paul.

Thompson, Kenneth. 1974. Church of England Bishops as an Elite. In Philip Stanworld and Anthony Giddens, eds., *Elites and Power in British Society.* London: Cambridge University Press.

Tihany, Leslie C. 1976. *A History of Middle Europe from the Earliest Times to the Age of the World Wars.* New Brunswick, N.J.: Rutgers University Press.

Tilly, Charles. 1990. *Coercion, Capital, and the European States,* A.D. 990–1990. Oxford: Basil Blackwell.

———. 1975a. Food Supply and Public Order in Modern Europe. In Tilly, ed., *The Formation of National States in Western Europe.* Princeton: Princeton University Press.

———, ed. 1975b. *The Formation of National States in Western Europe.* Princeton: Princeton University Press.

———. 1975c. Reflections on the History of European State-Making. In Tilly, ed., *The Formation of National States in Western Europe.* Princeton: Princeton University Press.

———. 1975d. Western State-Making and Theories of Political Transformation. In Tilly, ed., *The Formation of National States in Western Europe.* Princeton: Princeton University Press.

Tipps, Dean C. 1973. Modernization Theory and the Comparative Study of Societies. *Comparative Studies in Society and History* 15: 199–240.

Tipton, Frank B. 1976. *Regional Variations in the Economic Development of Germany during the Nineteenth Century.* Middletown, Conn.: Wesleyan University Press.

———. 1974. Farm Labor and Power Politics. *Journal of Economic History* 34, no. 4 (December): 951–79.

Tipton, Frank B., and Robert Aldrich. 1987a. *An Economic and Social History of Europe, 1890–1939.* Baltimore: Johns Hopkins University Press.

———. 1987b. *An Economic and Social History of Europe from 1939 to the Present.* Baltimore: Johns Hopkins University Press.

Tocqueville, Alexis de. 1978. *Souvenirs.* Paris: Gallimard.

———. 1955. *The Old Régime and the French Revolution.* Garden City, N.Y.: Doubleday.

———. 1866. *Oeuvres complètes.* Vol. 6. Paris: Gallimard.

Todaro, Michael P. 1977. *Economic Development in the Third World.* London: Longman.

Tönnies, Ferdinand. 1912. Deutscher Adel im 19. Jahrhundert. *Neue Rundschau* 2: 1041–63.

Toye, J. 1987. *Dilemmas of Development: Reflections on the Counter-Revolution in Development Theory and Policy.* Oxford: Basil Blackwell.

Toynbee, Arnold. 1925. *Lectures on the Industrial Revolution of the Eighteenth Century in England: Popular Addresses, Notes, and Other Fragments.* 1884. Reprint, London: Longmans, Green.

Trebilcock, Clive. 1981. *Industrialization of the Continental Powers, 1780–1914.* London: Longman.

Treitschke, Heinrich von. 1916. *Politics.* London: Constable.

Tremel, Fanch. 1968. Les Bretons aussi sont colonises. *L'Avenir* 28 (February).

Trimberger, Ellen Kay. 1978. *Revolution from Above: Military Bureaucrats and Development in Japan, Turkey, Egypt, and Peru.* New Brunswick, N.J.: Transaction.

Troeltsch, Ernst. 1960. *The Social Teaching of the Christian Churches*. Trans. Olive Wyon. New York: Harper.

Trotsky, Leon. 1937. *The History of the Russian Revolution*. 3 vols. Trans. Max Eastman. New York: Simon & Schuster.

Tucker, Robert C. 1970. The Political Theory of Classical Marxism. In *The Marxian Revolutionary Idea*. New York: Norton.

Turcan, Pavel. 1969. The Development of a Backward Area in Czechoslovakia. In E. A. G. Robinson, ed., *Backward Areas in Advanced Countries*. London: Macmillan.

United Nations. 1979. *América Latina en el umbral de los años 80*. Santiago: CEPAL.

——. 1959. *El desarrollo económico de la Argentina*. Mexico: CEPAL.

——. 1956. *Economic Survey of Latin America 1955*. New York: Department of Economic and Social Affairs.

——. 1950. *Economic Survey of Asia and the Far East*. New York: Economic Commission for Asia and the Far East.

Urrutia, Miguel. 1991. Twenty-Five Years of Growth and Social Progress, 1960–1985. In Urrutia, ed., *Long-Term Trends in Latin American Economic Development*. Washington, D.C.: Inter-American Development Bank.

U.S. Department of Agriculture. 1951. *Agricultural Geography of Europe and the Near East*. Washington D.C.: U.S. Department of Agriculture.

Vandergeest, P., and F. H. Buttel. 1988. Marx, Weber, and Development Sociology: Beyond the Impasse. *World Development* 16, no. 6: 683–95.

Vanhanen, Tatu. 1990. *The Process of Democratization: A Comparative Study of 147 States, 1980–1988*. New York: Crane Russak.

——. 1977. *Political and Social Structures: European Countries, 1850–1974*. Ann Arbor, Mich.: University Microfilms International.

Veblen, Thorstein. 1915. *Imperial Germany and the Industrial Revolution*. London: Macmillan.

Verney, Douglas V. 1957. *Parliamentary Reform in Sweden, 1866–1921*. Oxford: Clarendon Press.

Vignes, Maurice. 1913. Le bassin de Briey et la politique de ses enterprises sidérurgiques ou minières. *Revue d'économie politique* 27: 1–40.

Vito, Francesco. 1969. Problems of the Underdeveloped Regions of Italy. In E. A. G. Robinson, ed., *Backward Areas in Advanced Countries*. London: Macmillan.

Voigt, Fritz. 1962. German Experience with Cartels and Control during Pre-War and Post-War Periods. In John Perry Miller, ed., *Competition, Cartels, and Their Regulation*. Amsterdam: North-Holland.

Volgyes, Ivan. 1980. Economic Aspects of Rural Transformation in Eastern Europe. In Ivan Volgyes, Richard E. Lonsdale, and William P. Avery, eds., *The Process of Rural Transformation: Eastern Europe, Latin America, and Australia*. New York: Pergamon Press.

Volpe, Gioacchino. 1925. Italia e Savoia; Italia ed Europa. In *Momenti di storia italiana*. Florence: Vallechi Editore.

Wallerstein, Immanuel. 1988. AHR Forum: Comments on Stern's Critical Tests. *American Historical Review* 93, no. 4: 873–97.

——. 1986. The States in the Institutional Vortex of the Capitalist World-Economy. In Ali Kazancigil, ed., *The State in Global Perspective*. Aldershot: Gower.

——. 1980. *The Modern World System*. Vol. 2, *Mercantilism and the Consolidation of the European World Economy, 1600–1750*. New York: Academic Press.

———. 1974a. *The Modern World System.* Vol. 1, *Capitalist Agriculture and the Origins of the European World Economy in the Sixteenth Century.* New York: Academic Press.

———. 1974b. The Rise and Future Demise of the World Capitalist System: Concepts for Comparative Analysis. *Comparative Studies in Society and History* 16 (January): 387–415.

Warner, Marina. 1979. *The Crack in the Teacup.* New York: Houghton Mifflin.

Warren, Bill. 1980. *Imperialism: Pioneer of Capitalism.* London: New Left Books.

———. 1973. Imperialism and Capitalist Industrialization. *New Left Review* 81 (September-October): 3–44.

Waterbury, John. 1983. *The Egypt of Nasser and Sadat: The Political Economy of Two Régimes.* Princeton: Princeton University Press.

Weber, Eugen. 1976. *Peasants into Frenchmen: The Modernization of Rural France, 1870–1914.* Stanford: Stanford University Press.

———. 1965. Romania. In Hans Rogger and Eugen Weber, eds., *The European Right.* Berkeley: University of California Press.

Weber, Max. 1978. *Economy and Society.* 2 vols. Guenther Roth and Claus Wittich, eds. Berkeley: University of California Press.

———. 1958a. On the Conditions of Bourgeois Democracy in Russia. In *Gesammelte Politische Schriften.* Tübingen: J. C. B. Mohr; Paul Siebeck.

———. 1958b. Russia's Transition to Pseudo-Constitutionalism. In *Gesammelte Politische Schriften.* Tübingen: J. C. B. Mohr; Paul Siebeck.

Weiner, Martin J. 1981. *English Culture and the Decline of the Industrial Spirit, 1850–1980.* London: Cambridge University Press.

Weiss, John. 1977. *Conservatism in Europe, 1770–1945: Traditionalism, Reaction, and Counter-Revolution.* New York: Harcourt Brace Jovanovich.

Wertheimer, Mildred S. 1924. *The Pan-German League, 1890–1914.* New York: Columbia University Press.

Whitaker, C. S., Jr. 1967. A Dysrythmic Process of Political Change. *World Politics* 19: 190–217.

Whyte, A. J. 1975. *The Political Life and Letters of Cavour, 1848–1861.* 1930. Reprint, Westport, Conn.: Greenwood Press.

Wiarda, Howard J. 1977. *Corporatism and Development: The Portuguese Experiment.* Amherst: University of Massachusetts Press.

Williams, G. 1978. Imperialism and Development. *World Development* 6: 925–36.

Williamson, Jeffrey G. 1965. Regional Inequality and the Process of National Development: A Description of the Patterns. *Economic and Cultural Change* 13, no. 4: 3–44.

Williamson, Peter J. 1984. *Varieties of Corporatism.* New York: Cambridge University Press.

Wise, Michael. 1983. *Agrarian Reform in El Salvador: Process and Progresses.* San Salvador: U.S. Agency for International Development.

Wolf, Eric R. 1982. *Europe and the People without History.* Berkeley: University of California Press.

Woodburn, James. 1980. Hunters and Gatherers Today and Reconstruction of the Past. In Ernest Gellner, ed., *Soviet and Western Anthropology.* London: Oxford University Press.

Woodhouse, C. M. 1968. *Modern Greece: A Short History.* London: Faber.

———. 1952. *The Greek War of Independence: Its Historical Setting.* London: Russell.

Woolf, S. J., ed. 1969. *The Italian Risorgimento.* London: Longmans, Green.

Woytinsky, W. S., and E. S. Woytinsky. 1953. *World Population and Production*. New York: Twentieth Century Fund.

Wright, D. G. 1970. *Democracy and Reform, 1815–1885*. London: Longmans.

Wright, Erik Olin. 1976. Modes of Class Struggle and the Capitalist State. *Kapitalistate* 4/5 (Summer): 186–220.

Wright, Gordon. 1964. *Rural Revolution in France: The Peasantry in the Twentieth Century*. Stanford: Stanford University Press.

Youngson, A. J. 1976. Britain 1920–1970. In Carlo C. Cipolla, ed., *The Fontana Economic History of Europe*. Vol. 1, *Contemporary Economies*. Glasgow: William Collins Sons.

Zeitlin, Maurice. 1984. *The Civil Wars in Chile (or the Bourgeois Revolutions That Never Were)*. Princeton: Princeton University Press.

Zeldin, Theodore. 1973. *France, 1848–1945*. Oxford: Clarendon Press.

——. 1970. *Conflicts in French Society*. London: Allen & Unwin.

Zernatto, Guido. 1944. Nation: The History of a Word. *Review of Politics* 6: 351–66.

Zimmerman, L. J. 1962. The Distribution of World Income. In Egbert de Vries, ed., *Essays on Unbalanced Growth*. The Hague: Mouton.

Index